SOFTBALL
SKILLS & DRILLS

SECOND EDITION

JUDI GARMAN
MICHELLE GROMACKI

HUMAN KINETICS

Library of Congress Cataloging-in-Publication Data

Garman, Judi, 1944-
  Softball skills & drills / Judi Garman and Michelle Gromacki. -- 2nd ed.
    p. cm.
  ISBN-13: 978-0-7360-9074-2 (soft cover)
  ISBN-10: 0-7360-9074-6 (soft cover)
  1. Softball--Training. 2. Softball--Coaching. I. Gromacki, Michelle. II.
Title. III. Title: Softball skills and drills.
  GV881.4.T72G37 2011
  796.357'8--dc22

                              2010048654
ISBN-10: 0-7360-9074-6 (print)
ISBN-13: 978-0-7360-9074-2 (print)

Acquisitions Editor: Justin Klug; **Developmental Editor:** Carla Zych; **Assistant Editors:** Michael Bishop, Elizabeth Evans, and Tyler Wolpert; **Copyeditor:** Patrick Connolly; **Permission Manager:** Martha Gullo; **Graphic Designer:** Keri Evans; **Graphic Artist:** Kim McFarland; **Cover Designer:** Keith Blomberg; **Photographer (cover):** Neil Bernstein; **Photographers (interior):** Matt Brown, Mel Franks, and Neil Bernstein; all photos © Human Kinetics; **Photo Asset Manager:** Laura Fitch; **Visual Production Assistant:** Joyce Brumfield; **Photo Production Manager:** Jason Allen; **Art Manager:** Kelly Hendren; **Associate Art Manager:** Alan L. Wilborn; **Illustrator:** © Human Kinetics; **Printer:** United Graphics

We thank California State University at Fullerton in Fullerton, California, for assistance in providing the location of the photo shoot for this book.

Human Kinetics books are available at special discounts for bulk purchase. Special editions or book excerpts can also be created to specification. For details, contact the Special Sales Manager at Human Kinetics.

Printed in the United States of America   10   9   8   7   6   5   4   3   2   1

The paper in this book is certified under a sustainable forestry program.

Human Kinetics
Web site: www.HumanKinetics.com

United States: Human Kinetics
P.O. Box 5076
Champaign, IL 61825-5076
800-747-4457
e-mail: humank@hkusa.com

Canada: Human Kinetics
475 Devonshire Road Unit 100
Windsor, ON N8Y 2L5
800-465-7301 (in Canada only)
e-mail: info@hkcanada.com

Europe: Human Kinetics
107 Bradford Road
Stanningley
Leeds LS28 6AT, United Kingdom
+44 (0) 113 255 5665
e-mail: hk@hkeurope.com

Australia: Human Kinetics
57A Price Avenue
Lower Mitcham, South Australia 5062
08 8372 0999
e-mail: info@hkaustralia.com

New Zealand: Human Kinetics
P.O. Box 80
Torrens Park, South Australia 5062
0800 222 062
e-mail: info@hknewzealand.com

E5073

*This book is dedicated to all those who pick up a bat and ball and begin to dream—
have fun and may your dreams come true!*

CONTENTS

CONTENTS

PREFACE

Catch the ball and throw it to a target. Hit the ball. Run the bases and score runs. Championship teams and successful players execute these fundamentals consistently and accurately. How do they do it? They understand the fundamentals and the game, and they develop their skills through practice, practice, practice. Using relevant and specific drills, they efficiently develop the necessary skills to be a winner!

Here is a book to help you reach your potential. *Softball Skills & Drills* is a comprehensive treatment of the fundamentals of softball. Regardless of the level of play, the fundamentals are the same. This book provides the skills, drills, and strategies that players and teams need in order to be the best they can be. It provides valuable information for coaches, players, and players' parents.

Each chapter starts with the basics and then progresses to advanced skills. The fundamentals are broken down and explained simply but in depth. Skill summaries and coaching tips are highlighted as keys for learning and teaching. The drills presented emphasize and teach the various components of each skill. Progressions for learning are included, as well as additional drills that can be used to provide variety and opportunities to practice and refine each skill. Coaches can use the drill finder to help organize practices. Photos and diagrams help clarify and show the skills. This book can also be used as a textbook for classes on softball coaching theory.

This second updated edition adds current theories, new drills, and expanded details. Adding their expertise to Hall-of-Fame coach Judi Garman are Cal State Fullerton coaches Michelle Gromacki and Dee Dee Weiman-Kingsbury. New topics include equipment selection, new technology, pitch recognition, and reading the pitcher. A new chapter on team offense examines game situations and strategies for scoring runs. Because pitching is the key to the game, we have expanded that section, adding more pitches and strategies as well as addressing composure on the mound.

The book starts with *offense* because the goal of the game is to score runs! The first chapter focuses on hitting, which is one of the most difficult challenges in all of sport. Topics include bat selection, basic mechanics, and corrections for common hitting problems. We also examine the mental aspects of hitting, including the advanced skills of pitch recognition and reading the pitcher (picking pitches). Drills are included for both individual and team practice. Chapter 2 covers playing small ball with bunting and slap hitting. Chapter 3 covers baserunning and techniques for stealing and sliding. Improving speed and knowing when to run are keys. Chapter 4 is new and covers team offense: game situations and strategies along with drills for situational hitting.

From chapter 5 on, the focus is *defense*. Defense involves throwing and fielding ground balls and fly balls. Chapter 5 covers how to make strong and accurate throws. Different positions and situations call for quick releases and various types of throws. The information in this chapter helps players learn how to be accurate and consistent whether throwing overhand, underhand, sidearm, or with various flips.

Catching begins with the care and selection of the glove and how to use it to make routine and desperation catches. Chapter 6 covers fielding ground balls—from gathering to scooping to executing backhands and diving with the goal of catching every ball. Chapters 7 and 8 look closely at the responsibilities and tactics of infield and outfield players.

Softball is a team game, and all nine players must work together. Chapter 9 examines how players work together to form a successful defensive team. Specific team defensive plays are covered: bunt and slap defense, double plays, pickoffs, relays, cutoffs, rundowns, and the ever challenging first-and-third play. Defensive adjustments and strategies are reviewed.

The pitcher dominates in softball, and pitching is the name of the game in chapters 10 through 13. The basics of the delivery and how to throw with accuracy and speed are explained in detail. The specific pitches covered are the fastball, drop, rise, curve, screwball, and change up. Because the pitcher must learn not only how but when to throw each pitch, guidelines for game management are included. The difference between a pitcher and a thrower is what's upstairs. How much to practice, proper warm-up, mixing pitches, maintaining control, and composure on the mound are also addressed. A pitcher must also be able to field her position, and chapter 13 details how to do so. And of course, a good pitcher needs a good catcher; because this role is so important, the last chapter is devoted to skills and drills for developing the catcher.

Use this book to develop your skills and increase your understanding of the game of softball. Whether players are participating in a local league, playing in the College World Series, or pursuing a gold medal, the consistent, proper execution of the fundamentals is the key to success. Practice hard, play smart, and have fun. A wonderful world awaits you.

ACKNOWLEDGMENTS

Some may think of softball as just a bat and a ball and believe it's only a game, but those for whom this game has opened up another world know that it is much more. Growing up playing ball on the Saskatchewan prairies, I had no inkling of the doors that softball would open for me.

I want to express my sincere appreciation to those who helped make my dreams come true:

To my mother, **Ruth Garman,** who passed on her love of sport to her daughters. She taught me how to play and was always my biggest fan. Society and the times never allowed her the opportunity to have the athletic experiences we have had, but she made sure her daughters could experience the joy of competition. She proudly tells folks she has two daughters in their respective Sports Halls of Fame. (My sister Lorraine Klippel is in the LPGA Hall of Fame as a teaching pro.)

To the **Saskatoon Imperials Fastpitch Team** and manager **Gail Hopkins,** who gave me my start as a player. We twice were Canadian Champions and played in the 1970 World Championships in Japan.

To athletic directors **Fred Owens** (Golden West College) and **Leanne Grotke** (Cal State Fullerton), who hired me and gave me the opportunity to build two programs into national champions.

To all the **colleagues** who shared their knowledge so we could grow together and improve the game.

To the superb, talented **athletes and assistants,** who really made it happen.

And to **Michelle Gromacki,** my former player, assistant coach, replacement at Cal State Fullerton, and the co-author of this edition.

To **JoAnn Zwanziger,** whose support over the years has allowed me to pursue my dreams.

Just a bat and a ball? Never. My hope is that this book helps you find success. May your journey be as blessed as mine.

Judi Garman

Special thanks to . . .

Judi Garman, for believing in me. She gave me my first coaching opportunity and continues to support my career. Judi has had a huge impact on my life and my career. Thank you for supporting my every turn as a coach and caring about me and my family.

Deanna Weiman-Kingsbury, for making a strong commitment to our Titan Program and trusting in me. Dee Dee has empowered me to be the very best that I could be. She is a true gift in my life. Thank you for your pitching expertise in this book.

Ken Ravizza, for being my mentor for nearly 25 years. If it wasn't for the understanding of the mental game of softball he helped me to develop, I couldn't have played the game successfully for as long as I did. Thank you for continuing your work with us.

Coaches and players and all of my past and current assistant coaches, for keeping me on my toes and allowing me to grow under my own direction. Learning is continuous, therefore, many of you were at the mercy of my mistakes. Thank you all!

My family, who stuck by me during my playing years and supported me in every way when my future was uncertain. Thank you for the continued support in my coaching career. I love you all.

Michelle Gromacki

(F) — Fielder

(T) — Tosser

(H) — Hitter

(R) — Runner

(P) — Pitcher

(C) — Catcher

(1B) — First-base player

(2B) — Second-base player

(3B) — Third-base player

(SS) — Shortstop

(LF) — Left fielder

(CF) — Center fielder

(RF) — Right fielder

- - - - - - ▶ Path of hit ball

─────────▶ Path of player

· · · · · · · · · ▶ Path of throw

HITTING

itting has been described as the most difficult task in all of sport. When a softball pitcher releases the ball, she is only 30 to 40 feet from the batter. The best college pitchers can throw 65 to 68 miles per hour, which is equivalent to a 90-mile-per-hour pitch in baseball. At that speed, the ball reaches the plate in .39 seconds. Factor in the various pitches that can be thrown (drop, rise, curve, screwball, changeup, and variations of those pitches), and the difficulty of hitting becomes obvious. Players aspire to a batting average of .300, which means that they fail to hit safely 7 times out of 10. Hitters find it difficult to get enough hitting practice. One estimate is that the average high school player practices hitting only 3½ hours per season. Meanwhile, the pitcher is throwing over 200 pitches a day.

To be good, consistent hitters, players must find a way to work on their hitting skills every day. Players should strive to become relentless competitors who concede nothing, never give in, and have no wasted at-bats. Coaches and players should keep a new stat: a Q average. Quality at-bats and the ability to get the job done (by advancing runners and scoring runs) should be celebrated and rewarded.

BAT SELECTION

The right bat makes it easier to hit well. Each player should choose a bat that's the right weight, length, and size for her and that fits her budget. The bat is an extension of the arms; it must feel right. It must be of a size and weight that the player can swing hard and can easily control throughout the entire swing.

As a general rule, bigger, stronger players prefer a heavier bat for maximum power. Smaller players usually benefit from a lighter bat that allows greater bat speed. Batters often use a bat that is too heavy, which leads to mechanical problems and sometimes injury. To determine whether a bat is too heavy, the player should grip it with one hand at the knob and hold it straight out parallel to the ground at shoulder height. If the bat wavers, or if the player cannot hold that position for at least a minute, the bat is too heavy. As weight increases, bat control usually decreases. In terms of length, the shorter the bat, the more control a hitter will have, but she will sacrifice power. The longer the lever, the more power the hitter will have, though with less control. The bat must also be long enough to allow full plate coverage when the player swings. Can she hit a ball hard off a tee placed low on the outside corner?

Most bats are built with a specific ratio of length and weight. Youth bats range in weight from 16 to 22 ounces (453 to 624 g) and in length from 25 to 31 inches (63 to 79 cm). College players usually swing a bat that weighs 22 to 26 ounces (624 to 737 g) and 32 or 34 inches (81 or 86 cm) long. Manufacturers use negative numbers to show the weight-to-length ratio (e.g., −9, −10, and so on). The length subtracted by the negative number is the weight of the bat. This means, for example, that a 31-inch bat with a −9 ratio weighs 22 ounces. Selecting the correct weight really depends on two critical factors: strength and hitting style.

Because the player will be swinging the bat many times, it must feel comfortable in her hands. The size of the hands will determine the thickness of the handle that a hitter can grip and manipulate comfortably.

The barrel size and location and the size of the sweet spot are other attributes to consider. The sweet spot, or "center of percussion," is the place where contact with the ball gives the hitter a good feeling rather than a sting. It is also the place that sends the ball the farthest. The bigger the barrel, the larger the hitting surface and the larger the sweet spot. The smaller the hitting area, the more bat control required to be successful. A bottle bat provides a large hitting surface and is an excellent bat for bunting and for beginners.

The type of grip that bat manufacturers put on the handle of their bats also affects the way the bat feels when the ball is hit. Leather or synthetic leather gives a tackier feel for a surer grip. Rubber grips absorb more of the shock on impact, and cushioned grips decrease the shock even more.

The composition of the bat helps determine how far the ball goes when hit. New materials, with names that seem to change every year, allow manufacturers to make bats with very thin walls. But rules vary, so players must be sure that the bat is stamped "Approved" for use in their league. The two primary categories of materials are aluminum alloys and graphite or titanium lined. Aluminum bats come in a variety of alloys, each with a different weight, but generally aluminum alloys are thinner and more durable and have a larger sweet spot. They come in single-layer or double-layer construction. Double-layer bats offer more durability and power because the ball rebounds off the bat with more authority. Graphite and titanium are sometimes added to thinner-wall aluminum bats to decrease weight and therefore increase the batter's hitting speed. The addition of these materials also reduces vibration and the sting a batter may feel on contact with the ball.

The thinner the wall, the greater the trampoline effect. The bat gives at contact with the ball and propels it away faster. The greater the trampoline effect, the greater distance the ball can go. And a bat with thin walls dents more easily. College players often get a new bat each year. We recommend that players save a good bat for games and use an old bat for practice. Players should use softer balls for hitting practice, if possible, and should never use their good bat on the hard plastic balls at commercial batting cages.

HITTING MECHANICS

Many philosophies are used in teaching players how to hit. Hitting coaches have their own ways of saying things, and many batters have distinctive styles. Through computer and video analysis, we are able to break down the swing and study the basic elements that all successful hitters use.

Grip

When gripping the bat, the hitter should apply pressure with the fingers, not the palms. She grips the bat where the calluses are. The bottom hand (left hand for a right-handed batter) controls the bat, and the top hand supports the bat loosely. The bottom hand grips the bat as a person would grip a golf club (see figure 1.1). The top hand is placed against the bottom hand with the door-knocking knuckles (middle knuckles) of both hands in a straight line. The arms are not crossed. The bat is gripped loosely—no white knuckles—and the wrists have flexibility. Some hitters curl the index finger of the top hand so that it only lightly touches the bat. For better bat control, the player may choke up on the bat by moving both hands several inches up from the knob. Of course, a choke grip means a shorter bat and less power.

Figure 1.1 Hitting grip.

Hand Position

The hands start close to the body, about 3 to 4 inches (7.5 to 10 cm) in front of the chest and between the shoulders. Both elbows are down, and the shoulders are tension free. Some players prefer a little movement back and forth with the hands and shoulders to keep them loose. We call this position the power position, or power alley.

Stance

A strong and stable athletic stance is the foundation for power throughout the entire swing. Both feet are pointed straight ahead toward the plate. The body is upright, and the hips, head, and eyes are level. The shoulders are basically level; the front shoulder is aimed at the pitcher and slightly down. The batter then turns the front hip and shoulder back slightly (inward) toward the catcher as if the hands are being pulled back by a rubber band. Weight is transferred down and back into the back side of the body for power. The feet are about 4 inches (10 cm) greater than shoulder-width apart, positioned outside the hips so that most of the body weight is on the inside of the legs and the balls of the feet. The knees are inside the feet and slightly bent (see figure 1.2). The player can hold a volleyball between the knees to get a feel for the correct position. A proper stance allows the hitter to have good rhythm and to shift easily back toward the catcher and then forward to the pitcher. To feel the power from their legs, players can stand barefoot in a sand pit and swing.

Three types of stances describe the position of the feet (see figure 1.3). All other elements of the stance described earlier remain the same.

- **Square stance**—Both feet are the same distance from the plate. This stance permits the best plate coverage and does not give the pitcher a read on the hitter. This is also the most balanced athletic position.
- **Open stance**—The front foot is two to three inches farther from the plate than the back foot. This stance produces a shorter swing and poorer coverage of the outside corner, but both eyes can see the ball better, and the more compact swing may allow the batter to make better contact.
- **Closed stance**—The front foot is two to three inches closer to the plate than the back foot. The batter will have more difficulty getting around on an inside pitch but will be better able to drive an outside pitch to right field.

Figure 1.2 Hitting stance.

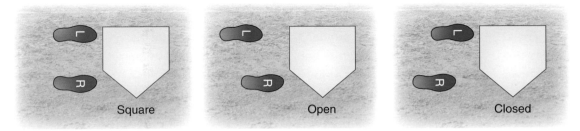

Figure 1.3 **Square, open, and closed stances.**

Position in the Box

The batter's position in the box depends on the skills of both the batter and the pitcher. The best position is the one that gives the hitter maximum plate coverage as she adjusts based on the type of hitter she is and the type of pitcher she is facing. The farther back the hitter is in the box, the more time she has to swing the bat. If the pitcher is very fast, the batter can move back in order to have more time to get the bat around. Against a slower pitcher, the batter should move up in the box if she is well ahead of the pitch with her swing. If the ball has a lot of movement, a hitter who stays back allows the ball to break even more, adding to the pitcher's advantage. The up position allows the batter to hit the pitch before it moves a lot and is particularly effective on drop balls. However, another strategy against a really strong drop-ball pitcher is to stay back in the box so the pitcher has to change her release point to bring the ball up to get a called strike. This may flatten out her drop ball. A team might try both to see what works best against that pitcher.

If the batter crowds the plate, she will have good outside coverage but will have to be very quick to get the bat out in front for an inside pitch. Standing too far from the plate will make the hitter vulnerable to outside pitches and curves. Against an effective pitcher who has great command of both sides of the plate, advanced players may stand in a position that takes away half of the plate. By crowding the plate, they can look for and hit the outside pitch while holding up on any inside pitch. Conversely, they can give up the outside pitch by standing back from the plate, thus going for pitches on the inside half of the plate. Batters can also set up to hit the ball where they want. If a pitcher is pitching you inside, back off the plate at the last moment and hit inside out to the right side.

Focus

The player must see the ball to hit it. Players should have their eyes checked to be sure they have the best vision possible. Both eyes are used when hitting. In the initial stance, the head drops slightly and turns enough so that the back eye can also see the pitch. Eyebrows should be level. Hitters can check if they are using the back eye by shutting the front eye and looking for the release point of the pitch with only the back eye.

The eyes can focus intently on an object for only a few seconds before the image becomes less clear. Using an eye shift helps the batter see the ball more clearly as the pitcher releases it. In the initial stance, the batter uses a soft focus with the eyes relaxed. She focuses on the pitcher's chest or shoulders with a soft, or general, focus. As the pitcher's hands separate, the batter shifts the eyes to the release point and goes from a soft focus to a hard focus while waiting to pick up the ball. The batter uses a look or glare that says she is going to attack the ball. She then tracks the ball all the way from the release to the contact point.

Stride

The stride is a step toward the pitcher with the front foot as the pitch is delivered (see figure 1.4). It serves as a timing mechanism for the swing and brings the body to a balanced foundation to hit from. During the stride, the batter must maintain balance. Therefore, the step is short—only 3 to 4 inches (7.5 to 10 cm)! The hitter does not want her center of gravity or head to move. The stride should be a glide or slide forward toward the pitcher. Key words for the stride are *stay centered, short, soft,* and *eyebrows level.* The front toe stays closed, with soft pressure on the inside ball of the foot, and the head moves little or not at all. During the stride, the hips are cocked slightly; the front shoulder, hip, and knee are turned slightly toward the catcher. The player can think of her belly button as the lens of a camera that is pointed at the catcher. Weight remains on the inside of the back foot. Have batters hold the bat on their belly button to check their turn back.

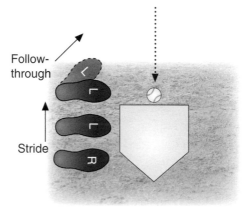

Follow-through

Stride

Figure 1.4　Hitting stride.

On the stride, the weight stays on the back leg. The knee is over the back foot and does not turn. The player can practice the correct form by placing a chair against the back side of the back knee. She strides while making sure that the back leg stays in contact with the chair. The batter must focus on the release point during the stride. The stride must be consistent and to the same spot on every pitch, regardless of pitch location, because the player starts the stride before she can identify what pitch is coming.

Timing determines when the batter steps. The step should be initiated early enough to be slow and deliberate, not jerky. As the pitcher goes forward (or the front knee goes up), the hitter lifts the front heel, the front knee turns in, and the weight and hands go back. The stepping foot should be down right before the pitch is released, allowing enough time for the batter to feel balanced and to complete the swing. The front heel must be down before the ball is within 10 feet (3 m) of the batter. The batter can still hit the ball if she steps too early, but she cannot hit it if she steps too late. Beginners often commit during the windup. As players practice and develop quicker hands, they learn to delay their commitment to the stride until they can clearly see the ball. Remember that once the batter strides forward and plants the front toe, the toe will start to open up on its own when the batter starts her swing. It is natural then for the hips, knees, and toe to follow each other. Coaches should videotape their players and show them the timing element and what it means to be late or early. The coach may ask a batter, "Where are you getting late?" and "How can you get on time?"

On the stride, the hands go back to the launch position so that the bat is behind the back leg (see figure 1.5). As when using a hammer, golf club, or tennis racket, the player must first go back in order to generate the stretch (referred to as loading) and power needed to go forward (think of winding a rubber band to create torque). The torso, hands, and arms go back as one unit. In softball, the hands go back only 3 to 4 inches (7.5 to 10 cm). The farther the hands go from center, the longer and slower the swing. The batter cannot hit a ball above the hands, so the hands stay at the top of the strike zone. (If hitters drop their hands, they can never hit a rise ball.) As the hands go back, they cock as if preparing to hammer a nail with the top hand. Cocking is *not* a hitch (i.e., a drop of the hands). The end of the bat will come close to the head, but the player must be careful not to wrap the bat around behind her. If the hitter takes the bat back too far, her body will twist, and her shoulders will come off line. The arms are bent in a 90-degree position with both elbows pointed down. The head does not move, and the shoulders remain level. The hands stay close to the body. The closer the hands are to the body (and the center of gravity), the faster the body can rotate, producing faster bat speed. Think of a figure skater making a fast, tight spin.

Some hitters perform better with the no-stride method of hitting. This method is simple, and it eliminates the problems created by poor striding mechanics. With this method, the batter begins in a balanced position with the feet about bat-length apart and the front toe closed. The batter rotates her torso slightly rearward (belly button to catcher) as she stretches the rubber band. As the batter brings her front knee inward, the front foot stays at the same angle and does not move from the starting position. This rotation will cause the front heel to rise up, putting the hitter in the same position as the batter who strides. The heel is then dropped to trigger the swing. (The batter should not just lift her foot up and put it down in one motion.) The rest of the swing is identical to the stride method. The no-stride method makes it easy for the hitter to maintain good balance, to keep the heels in line, and to achieve optimum stride length. Because there is little head movement and because good balance is maintained, hitters who use the no-stride method are not easily fooled by an off-speed pitch.

Hip Rotation and Pivot

The batter strides first and then rotates the hips. Dropping the front heel triggers the swing. These are two movements—a stride and then a pivot. The batter pushes hard against the inside of the back foot, then pivots hard on the ball of the back foot and drives (pops) the back hip into and against a rigid front side. As the front foot starts to receive the weight transfer, the front leg stiffens. This phase is a ballistic and aggressive rotational push forward with movement slightly up and out. The back heel comes up, the foot releases, and the weight goes forward off the back leg (see figure 1.6).

Figure 1.5   Hand position during the stride.

Figure 1.6   Hip rotation and pivot.

The lower the back heel is, the more weight stays back; coaches must emphasize getting the back heel up (while guarding against overrotation)! The back foot and back knee pivot toward the pitcher with the back leg in an L position. The hands do not move. The body rotates around an imaginary pole running through the middle of the body. The belly button rotates from looking at the catcher to looking directly at the contact spot and no farther. Contrary to what many a young player has been told, *the batter does not squish a bug* with the back foot; doing so does not allow the back foot to transfer the weight to the front foot.

The batter must stay connected and flow into the ball as she sequentially unlocks her body parts. The back hip moves into the firm front side, then the hands follow and the bat lags behind. Note that the hands do not come forward first to drive into the ball. The stronger leg muscles yank the smaller muscles (hands and arms) through the strike zone. The chest is on the ball. The goal is to go from slow loading to quick explosion. The hitter must be in a balanced position (50 percent of weight on each foot) to exert maximum force at contact. A straight line running down from the back ear to the pivot foot should pass through the shoulder, hip, and knee. If a hitter does not rotate around this stationary axis, she is lunging.

Swing

Now the hands take over. Good hitters have quick hands. The player must get the bat to the ball quickly. The bat should travel the fastest route—in a direct line to the ball with no wasted movement. An inside-outside swing takes the bat directly to the ball (see figure 1.7). Coming around the ball with a sweeping movement takes too much time. Sweeping occurs when the batter straightens the arms before swinging. To perform an inside-outside swing, the player imagines a straight line from the pitcher to the catcher and keeps the hands always inside that line. Alternatively, the hitter can use the concept that the hands always stay between her and the plate.

As the hips pivot, the knob of the bat starts to move forward. The first arm movement takes the knob of the bat to the ball. The batter leads with the elbow and then extends the back of the hand and the knob forward (see figure 1.8). The movement resembles a karate chop with the bottom hand. The batter should pull the knob to the front hip, keeping the bat on an even plane through the contact area as long as possible.

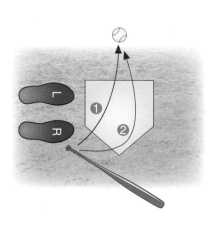

Figure 1.7 An inside-outside swing (1) versus a sweeping swing (2).

Figure 1.8 Bringing the knob of the bat forward.

Both elbows stay bent until the last moment, when the bat head is driven forward. The top end of the bat stays close to the batter's neck as long as possible. As the lead hand (knob) goes to the ball through the strike zone, the barrel of the bat lags behind. On the approach, the barrel always stays above the hands on a high pitch and stays below the hands on a low pitch. The batter swings the knob, not the bat head, then drives the bat barrel through the ball and whips the top hand through. The hitter should feel as if she is firing the bat at the ball.

The position of the wrists is critical to developing maximum power. The hands are at a 45-degree angle, and the wrist action is like the motion used to snap a flyswatter or towel. The batter does not roll the wrists or have the palm of the top hand up. Using either of these two methods to drive a nail with a hammer wouldn't work well, nor do these methods work well for batting. The batter wants quick hands and a whipping action to drive the ball. The swing must be tension free.

The player must not turn, or fly, the front shoulder open. She should keep the front shoulder down and pointed at the ball as long as possible. The hands can move without movement of the shoulders and head. The chin starts near the front shoulder and ends touching the back shoulder.

The batter should anticipate that each pitch will be a strike, preparing to attack the ball on every pitch. It is easier to hold up than it is to start late.

Contact

Hitters must know where to make contact with the different pitches they will see so that they can hit the ball hard in each location. We tell players to "hit the ball where it is pitched." The contact spot for a pitch down the middle is directly opposite the front hip. If the player were delivering a punch, she would want the recipient to be standing at this spot to receive the maximum blow. Contact for an inside pitch occurs sooner, in front of the body, and the hips must open earlier. On an inside pitch, the batter should drive the back elbow into the body to get the hands out sooner and to open the hips more quickly. Keep the hands well inside the base and near the body, on that straight line from the pitcher to the catcher. The bottom hand must get to the front hip, and the lead elbow must stay down. The batter needs to hit the back of the ball. Advanced hitters may actually slide the rear foot back (like a pitcher) to get the hips out of the way. For an outside pitch, the contact spot is between the center of the body and the back hip, so the batter must wait on the ball. The batter lets the ball get deep in the zone and hits inside the ball. The hips stay closed until contact, and then the back hip drives through. The hands are well ahead of the bat head on an outside pitch. The batter must be patient and wait for the ball to come to her. By using good rotation of the hips, the hitter can hit just as hard to the opposite field as she does when pulling a pitch. The batter should always look for an outside pitch, and if the ball is inside, then the batter should react and get faster.

To understand contact spots, players should imagine a clock: If the pitch is down the middle, hit it at 12 o'clock; if it's inside, hit it at 10 o'clock; and if it's outside, hit it at 2 o'clock (see figure 1.9). When hitting slow pitching, the speed of the swing remains the same; it is how long the hitter waits that

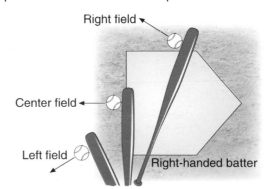

Figure 1.9 **Contact points for hitting the ball to left, center, and right field.**

determines success. To hit a slow pitcher, the hitter waits longer; she can think *hit to second base* if she is right-handed or *hit to short* if she is left-handed.

At contact, both arms are bent close to 90 degrees, and the bat is driven through the ball on a level plane (see figure 1.10). After the ball has left the bat, both arms are fully extended (see figure 1.11). Both arms are straight, and the hitter should be looking down both arms and the barrel of the bat. The thumb and forefinger of the top hand are on top of the bat, and the V between them points directly at the contact spot. As full extension of the arms is reached, deceleration occurs and the bat loses speed. The hitter moves her head down at contact and feels her chest go to the ball while maintaining a firm and rigid front side. The action is like that of a boxer driving the back hand and body into an opponent. Because of the pivot, the back foot and knee are pointing at the front leg. Most of the weight is transferred to the inside of the front foot and leg. The body is in a balanced position with the weight on the balls of the feet. The body flows into the ball.

Follow-Through

In the follow-through, weight transfers almost completely to the front leg but remains on the balls of the feet. The body is upright and well balanced. The hitter must not fall back on the heels. The head is down, and the back shoulder almost touches the chin (see figure 1.12). The front foot will open slightly after contact to about a 45-degree angle to the pitcher (see figure 1.4). This happens automatically; the hitter does not need to think about it. As momentum carries the bat behind the body, the wrists will

CRITICAL CUE:
Contrary to popular hitting myths, players should not

- squish a bug,
- roll the wrists at contact, or
- keep the back elbow up.

Figure 1.10 At contact, both arms are bent.

Figure 1.11 After contact, the arms are fully extended.

Figure 1.12 Follow-through position.

automatically roll over, well after contact. The hitter should not think about rolling the wrists. If she does, she will hit many ground balls and lose considerable power. She should keep both hands on the bat until the end of the swing. Some batters let go of the bat with their top hand after contact. A drawback of this habit is that the hitter may let go a little early and not fully use the upper hand to drive through the ball. If the batter is finishing high after a hard, aggressive swing, she will have no choice but to release the bat with the top hand, verifying that it is a good swing.

The hitter should not throw the bat after the swing because it might hit the catcher or another player. She should drop the bat straight down before she runs. If a player can't stop throwing the bat, she can carry it with her for a couple of steps until the habit is broken.

FRONT-FOOT HITTING

Some successful hitters are front-foot hitters, or linear hitters. In this style of hitting, the batter shifts her weight to the front foot during the swing. Little weight remains on the back foot, so the back toe is often pointed down or dragging forward. The contact spot is out in front of the front hip, almost a foot farther forward than it would be if the batter were pivoting. When practicing off tees or soft tosses, linear front-foot hitters must make sure to use a more forward contact spot. A front-foot hitter is susceptible to changeups. An advantage is that the hitter can more easily keep the shoulders level and the front shoulder closed. Another drawback is that the power comes from the upper body only. Linear and rotational hitters will have many similarities in their swing; the only real difference is in the weight transfer and contact spot.

LEARNING TO HIT

The purpose of practice sessions is for players to learn and gain confidence. Therefore, players must have opportunities for success. Hitters should start with the tee and progress to soft toss, front toss, the pitching machine, and live pitching using the drills at the end of this chapter. Hitters must practice as much as the pitchers, working every day on their hitting skills.

Practice sessions should include both quality and quantity. Hitting is a learned reaction. Only after many repetitions will the elements of the swing become automatic. To learn the fundamentals, players should break down the swing and isolate each element in practice. They should work on their problem spots but recognize that repetition for the sake of repetition is useless. More is not always better. Every practice swing should have a purpose.

Learning results from feedback and evaluation. Players should strive to learn something from every swing, whether a good swing or a poor one. They should note what they did right and what was not perfect. They should then establish a goal for the next swing or drill and repeat until the skill becomes ingrained and automatic. Perfect practice makes perfect. Once players learn and understand the fundamentals, they can analyze and self-correct regardless of their age.

Players can't think when they swing in a game. The skill must be automatic, and they can achieve that only through repetition. The goal is to be consistent: to see the ball, to hit the ball, and to avoid thinking too much.

HITTING MECHANICS CHECKLIST

HANDS

- Line up the middle knuckles.
- Use the power position. The hands are 3 to 4 inches (7.5 to 10 cm) in front of the chest and between the shoulders. The elbows are down with no tension in the shoulders.

STANCE

- Have your weight on the inside portion and the balls of your feet in a balanced position.
- Point your feet straight ahead.
- Position your knees between your feet and bend them slightly.
- Keep your hips level.
- Hold your head and eyes level.
- Position your front shoulder slightly down.
- Cock your front shoulder and hip slightly inward.
- Use soft focus on the pitcher's chest.

STRIDE

- Use a short, soft glide only 3 to 4 inches toward the pitcher.
- Ensure that the front toe and hip stay closed.
- Do not move your head.
- Cock the front shoulder, hip, and knee slightly toward the catcher. Keep your weight on the inside of the back foot.
- Move your hands back 3 to 4 inches to the launch position.
- Cock your wrists.
- Shift to hard focus on the release point.

HIP ROTATION AND PIVOT

- Pivot on the ball of the back foot.
- Point your back foot and back knee to the pitcher.

SWING

- Bend your arms 90 degrees and keep the elbows down.
- Take the knob of the bat to the ball.
- Keep your hands inside the plate.
- Make sure the barrel lags behind, above your hands on a high pitch, below your hands on a low one.
- Cock your wrists at a 45-degree angle.
- Keep both elbows bent.
- Keep the top of the bat close to your neck as long as possible.
- Keep the front shoulder down, closed, and pointed at the ball.

CONTACT

- Keep your head and eyes down.
- Make sure your arms are bent close to 90 degrees at contact. Drive the bat through the ball on a level plane.
- Drive the barrel head through the ball with the top hand.
- Keep your front side rigid and firm.

- Use a ballistic, aggressive, and rotational push forward.
- Transfer your weight to the inside of the front foot and leg.
- Make sure your belly button points to the contact spot.
- Point the back foot and toe at the front knee in an L position.
- Imagine a straight line passing from your back ear through the shoulder, hip, knee, and pivot foot.

FOLLOW-THROUGH

- Your back shoulder almost touches your chin.
- Your front toe opens to 45 degrees.
- The bat carries behind your body.
- Your wrists roll over.
- Maintain a balanced position.

COMMON MECHANICAL PROBLEMS

Check first for the following mechanical errors when a hitter is having problems. Although each hitter has her own unique style, batters who are struggling will often have one or more of these mechanical breakdowns. Suggested corrections and drills to fix each problem are also provided.

OVERSTRIDING

Result
- The hitter has poor balance, drops the back shoulder, or hits under the ball.
- Poor weight transfer to the front leg occurs so that the hitter lunges or weight stays on the back leg as the back side of the body collapses (the player forms a backward C facing the catcher).

Corrections
- Put more weight on the front foot.
- Use the no-stride method: Let the heel rise as the torso rotates and the knee turns inward, then drop the heel to trigger the swing (widen the stance to start).
- Start with your feet closer together so that the distance is not as great when you finish.
- Use a stride tutor or similar inhibitor (e.g., stand inside two 13-inch tires) as you do drills.
- Go from back side to front side without moving the head.
- Don't talk about getting out in front; instead, use the terms trigger, set.

STEPPING AWAY FROM THE PLATE

Result
- The hitter strides away from the plate, and the hips open too early.
- The arms do all the hitting because the body is not in position to drive the ball.

Corrections
- Keep your weight on the balls of the feet.
- Close your stance. Rotate the shoulders, front hip, and front toe slightly in toward catcher.
- Put more weight on your front foot in the initial stance so that less weight transfer occurs on the step.
- Shorten your stride.

(continued)

Common Mechanical Problems *(continued)*

Drills

- The hitter can practice striding in the bullpen when the pitcher is throwing.
- Place a two-by-four behind the heels of the batter, extending straight ahead in the direction her foot should go. The batter hits off a tee. The front foot should not step on or over the board.
- The batter hits outside pitches to right field off a tee. To do this, she must stay closed to the ball.

FLYING FRONT SHOULDER

Result

- The front shoulder pulls out too early, which results in sweeping the bat because the arms are forced to reach.
- The head turns with the shoulders, resulting in poor eye contact.
- The hips open prematurely as the hitter pulls off the pitch. Thus, the hitter cannot transfer weight into the ball.
- The hitter pulls the ball or misses it completely.

Corrections

- Aim your front shoulder at the ball.
- Exaggerate inward rotation in the initial stance to tuck your front shoulder in under the chin.
- Drive to the ball with your front shoulder.
- Keep your chin over the shoulder as long as possible.
- Focus on hitting from the back side, not the front leg. Keep weight on the back leg longer.

POOR HIP ROTATION, PIVOT, AND WEIGHT TRANSFER

Result

- The swing is slow and lacks power. The hitter becomes an arm swinger.

Corrections

- Concentrate on staying back and hitting with a quick, aggressive, and rotational move.
- Keep the weight on the back leg longer.
- Focus on standing tall and pivoting hard on the back foot.
- Keep a firm front side. Drive the back hip into the front hip.
- Maintain good balance at foot landing.
- Wait for the ball to come to you.

SWEEPING SWING

Result

- A long arc to the ball produces a slow bat.
- Power is lost because the hands leave the power alley by the chest.

Corrections

- Keep your hands close to your chest and keep the bat by your neck as long as possible.
- Lead with the front elbow and concentrate on keeping the arms bent until you swing.

Drills
- Resistance swing
- Front-elbow
- Fence swing
- Self-toss up the middle
- Back-hand self-toss: Hit with the front hand only.

UPPERCUTTING

Result
- The back shoulder and hands drop as the bat approaches the ball.
- The back side usually forms a backward C (toward the catcher).
- The player cannot shift weight to the front side.
- The hitter usually pops up or misses the ball completely (especially on rise balls).

Corrections
- Lower your front shoulder slightly in the initial stance.
- Emphasize a "straight" or "tall" back side.
- Don't hitch (drop the hands at the start of the swing). Make sure that your first hand movement is back and up, not down.
- When approaching the ball, keep the hands above the ball and keep the barrel above the hands.
- Start with the hands at chest height so that the only movement will be up (this is a drastic remedy).

Drills
- Two-tee drills: The player swings over a back tee.
- The player uses a high tee so that hand movement is directly to the ball.
- The player performs the back knee down tee drill.

SWINGING DOWN

Result
- The hitter swings down instead of level.
- Every ball is driven into the ground.

Corrections
- Level the swing at contact. Drive straight through the ball.
- Don't let the top hand do all the work or roll over the top of the bat at contact.
- Emphasize having the front arm leading the bat to the ball with the knob going to the ball.
- Stay balanced with good rotation.

SWINGING TOO LATE

Result
- The hitter does not get the bat head to the contact spot quickly enough.
- The ball is often popped up or hit weakly to the opposite field.

Corrections
- Make sure the hands go back more quickly, just as a tennis player would move the hands in preparing to return a hard serve.
- Start the hands forward earlier. Be on time.
- Get the legs into the swing more aggressively.
- Eliminate extra bat movement. Take the knob straight to the ball.
- Use a lighter bat or choke up.

(continued)

Common Mechanical Problems *(continued)*

SWINGING TOO EARLY

Result
- The batter pulls the ball or hits it off the end of the bat.
- The batter has trouble waiting on changeups and curves.
- The batter lunges and loses power (this occurs if the hitter transfers weight too early).

Corrections
- Understand contact spots. Have patience and wait for the pitch to arrive at the contact spot.
- Don't stride too early. React to the release of the pitch, not the pitcher's motion.
- Concentrate on driving the ball up the middle or to the opposite field.
- Close the stance and turn the front shoulder and hip slightly inward. Keep the front shoulder and hip in longer.
- Hit to the opposite field to force yourself to wait longer for the outside contact point.
- Have a tosser or pitcher fake toss or release to see whether your stride occurs on the arm motion or after seeing the pitch.

NOT DRIVING THROUGH THE BALL

Result
- The ball is pushed, not driven, and it does not explode off the bat. Power is limited.
- The hands get too far ahead of the bat, causing the barrel to lag too far behind.

Corrections
- Lead with the knob of the bat and swing the knob, not the bat head.
- Keep the barrel above the hands as long as possible with the wrists cocked. Whip the top hand through.
- Make sure your hands are at a 45-degree angle to permit a powerful whipping action. Fire the bat head at the ball.
- Use a quick, ballistic, and aggressive hip rotation.
- Stay connected. Flow into the ball as you sequentially unlock the body parts.

Drill
- Soccer ball tee drill.

NOT SEEING THE BALL

Result
- The hitter swings and misses or makes poor contact.

Corrections
- Have your vision checked.
- Make sure that your eyes are open during the swing.
- Turn your head so that you can use both eyes. Keep your head level so that your vision is not distorted. Shut your front eye to check whether your back eye is in a position to see.
- See the ball while getting ready to attack.
- Make sure your head does not move.
- Find out if the front shoulder is flying open and taking your head with it.

Drills

- The player bunts to the opposite side so that she must wait and can see the ball longer.
- Shadow: This drill can be used to make sure that the head is not moving on the stride or swing.
- Toss drills: The player calls the color of the ball or a colored spot on the ball as she hits it.
- When using tee drills, the player looks inside the tee after contact.

POOR BAT CONTROL

Result

- The hitter is unable to control the path of the bat or keep the barrel head above the hands.

Corrections

- Check your grip.
- Use a lighter bat or choke up.
- Don't overswing.
- Strengthen the arms, wrists, and hands.

Drill

- Strength zones—zone hitting

POOR BAT SPEED

Result

- The batter is late to the ball.
- The ball does not explode off the bat.

Corrections

- Be aggressive with the bottom half of the body.
- Check to be sure that the middle knuckles are aligned and that you hold the bat at the calluses of the hands.
- Use an inside-outside swing with the bat going directly to the ball.
- Use a tension-free swing with no "muscling up."

Drills

- Hum: The player hums constantly as she swings to see if she is tensing up. A variation is to hold a potato chip in the lips and stay loose enough that it doesn't break.
- Underload drills: The player swings a lighter bat to develop quick-twitch fibers and faster reactions.
- Fungo bat swings: The batter uses a fungo bat, baseball bat, or end-loaded bat to get the feel of whipping the end of the bat through the ball.
- High-tee drill: The player uses a high tee so that the hand movement is directly to the ball.

THE MENTAL GAME OF HITTING

Hitting is adjusting—adjusting to the pitch, the type of pitcher, the count, the umpire, and the situation. The mental game of hitting begins in practice. In a game, it begins on the bench, continues in the on-deck circle and on the approach to the plate, and reaches its greatest intensity when the batter steps into the batter's box. Batters must be in control of themselves before they can control their at-bat. Self-control leads to body and skill control.

Success requires discipline, concentration, and quickness. Hitters should focus on one pitch at a time and on the process of the at-bat—not the result. They learn from every swing as they obtain immediate feedback and make the adjustments necessary for success. Instead of making excuses on a missed opportunity, good hitters figure out what they learned from the situation (too late, too fast, under the ball, and so on) and make mental notes on how to use that knowledge to succeed the next time. They also take note of what they were doing well when successful.

Hitting is an attitude. It is confidence. Players should believe that they are always going to hit the ball solidly "on the money!" Focus on the number of "quality at-bats" and not the batting average (because a hitter may hit the ball well but at someone). Players should also understand that the difference between a .200 hitter and a .300 hitter is only 1 hit in 10 at-bats. Hitters must let the pitcher know that they are "the best" and that the pitcher has her hands full. Great hitters never let up. If they are 4 for 4, they strive to go 5 for 5. Successful hitters visualize success. They see themselves getting the winning hit. They live for the moment when the bases are loaded and they step to the plate with the game on the line. Good hitters have high standards, high expectations, and a high level of commitment.

Good hitters are aggressive, prepared to hit every pitch. The batter should stride to every pitch with the intention of hitting the ball. She should hold up on the swing only when she recognizes that the pitch location makes it a poor pitch to hit. The adjustment to hold up the swing should be made at the last moment. To do this, the player squeezes the bat and tenses up, stopping the swing before the bat goes through the strike zone. The approach to the pitch is "Yes, yes, yes, no" or "Yes, yes, yes, *yes*." If the batter does not prepare to swing at every pitch, she will not be able to pull the trigger when she really wants to swing. A checked swing is a pitcher's best friend. The batter should go hard to every ball; a swing and a miss is better than a checked swing.

Hitters should focus only on the ball, not its location over the plate. If the ball is around home plate and the hitter is confident that she can hit it, then she should go after it! Players should focus on their strengths and jump on any mistakes made by the pitcher. Hitters should know their best pitches to hit and their hitting zone. Good hitters consistently hit balls within their hitting zone (strength area), whereas weak hitters hit too many pitches in their weak area.

The batter must never be emotional and show her cards. The pitcher will read her reactions. If the hitter is emotional, the pitcher will think she owns the batter and will gain the upper hand. The batter must not react to the umpire because that will never work to her advantage. And she must always separate offense from defense. When at the plate, she should forget what happened on defense and stay mentally tough and positive.

The Count

Batters should try to think like a pitcher as they look for a pitch to hit. On the first pitch, the pitcher usually tries to get ahead in the count by throwing a strike. If she gets the strike, the next pitch will not be as good. The pitcher hopes the batter will chase the ball or that the umpire will call a strike if the pitch is close to the plate. The best pitch batters will likely see is that first pitch! Yet how many hitters take the first pitch with the justification that they want to see what the pitcher throws or that they want to get comfortable?

The hitter should not take a pitch to see what the pitcher is throwing. The next pitch will not be the same, and the hitter gets no feedback from taking a pitch. The batter has the opportunity to see the pitcher's delivery during the warm-up pitches.

Hitting sometimes seems as difficult as winning the lottery. The odds of hitting safely improve with three attempts, or chances, compared to with one or two, so batters should get their money's worth by using all three opportunities. If they swing and miss, at least they can gather information to make adjustments on the next swing (Was the swing too slow? Too early? Was I under the ball?). Hitters can learn nothing by taking a good pitch, and doing so only decreases the odds of success.

If the pitcher is behind on the count, the batter should expect to see the pitcher's best control pitch, usually a fastball, right over the plate. The batter should be ready to jump all over this pitch! With a runner on third and less than two outs, batters should look for a drop ball. The pitcher does not want to throw an "up" ball that can easily be hit in the air. The pitch selection charts in chapter 14 offer valuable information about what the pitcher and catcher are thinking and how they plan to set up the hitter. Pitchers generally establish a pattern during a game. By looking for this pattern, batters can know what pitch to expect. If they know what pitch is likely to be coming, they can more easily recognize and adjust to it. Table 1.1 offers some general guidelines for hitters based on the number of balls and strikes.

Table 1.1 The Count

0-0	Be selective and aggressive. Swing if the pitch is a strike when facing an overpowering pitcher. Get your money's worth; use all three chances to swing. In a sacrifice situation, bunt the first strike.
2-0	This is a hitter's pitch. The pitcher does not want to go 3-0.
3-0	This is usually a take, but the hitter should be ready if given the green light.
1-1, 2-1	Be selective but aggressive.
3-1	This is a hitter's pitch.
0-2, 3-2	With two strikes, choke up and enlarge the strike zone. Swing at anything close. Try to make contact and put the ball in play.

Two-Strike Adjustment

With two strikes, the goal should be to just make contact. Hitters should recognize that the pitcher will throw a marginal or waste pitch and that they have to make some adjustments. But they should not drastically alter their swing and stance. The goal is to avoid striking out and to put the ball in play so that the defense must make the out. Batters should expect no sympathy on taking a called third strike. Players can practice these two-strike adjustments in the batting cage:

- Move closer to the plate to protect the outside corner and to be able to reach outside pitches that can be driven to the opposite field.
- Enlarge the strike zone and swing at anything close to a strike. Don't let the umpire call you out.
- Focus on just meeting the ball and using a compact swing to put the ball in play. Don't swing for the fence.

Umpire's Strike Zone

The size and shape of the umpire's strike zone may require hitters to make adjustments for the pitcher they are facing. If the umpire has a wide strike zone, the hitters must move closer to the plate to hit the outside pitch with the sweet spot of the bat. Alternatively, they may choose to lay off that pitch completely. With two strikes and a high-pitch umpire, hitters must enlarge the top of the strike zone. A stubborn batter who refuses to adjust will strike out often and will not be successful.

Slump Busting

Everyone has slumps, and slumps are almost always temporary. When a player is struggling, she should fine-tune her mechanics, not perform a complete overhaul. Slumps often start in the head, beginning with a loss of confidence. A mechanical breakdown can also lead to bad days.

Here are some suggestions for breaking a slump:

- Ask the player this question: "What were you doing well when you were successful?"
- Encourage the player to try to see the ball better and longer. She should concentrate on hitting the ball up the middle or to the opposite field.
- Have the hitter open up her stance. An open stance shortens the swing, and the head position makes it easier to keep both eyes on the ball.
- Have the player choke up for better bat control.
- Advise the hitter to examine her mental approach. Remind her to focus on what she wants to happen and to avoid negative self-talk.
- Encourage the player to relax and avoid overswinging.
- Have the hitter work on her mechanics off a tee.
- Give the player a day off so she can get away from the pressure.
- Move the hitter down in the lineup, but make sure she understands why.

The Defense

Smart hitters survey the defensive setup and try to hit the ball where the defense is weakest. For example, if the outfield has shifted radically, expecting the batter to pull the ball, the batter should step back from the plate so that pitches are farther away from her body. More pitches are now outside, making it easier to take a pitch to the opposite-field gap created by the shift. If the outfield is playing so deep that the hitter cannot possibly hit the ball over their heads, the hitter can choke up on the bat and drop the ball in front of the outfield. When the infield moves in on top of the batter, the batter should look to drive the ball past them.

Preparation

When does the at-bat begin? It starts in the dugout as the batter puts on her helmet and batting gloves and gets her bat. She should have a set routine as she leaves the dugout, goes to the on-deck circle, walks to the box, and assumes her stance in the box. Each player should write a "script" on what she is going to do and then be consistent in following that scripted routine.

Three batters before her turn, the player should be ready to go with helmet and batting gloves on. While in the hole, she prepares her body by stretching and getting loose and thinking of nothing but hitting. She watches the pitcher and anticipates the game situation. While on deck, she takes good gamelike swings to time the pitcher and get into a rhythm; she is thinking about how and what the pitcher throws. She reinforces any pointers about her swing (e.g., keep the hands in). She visualizes the situation and a successful execution of the play. While walking to the plate, she is confident, uses positive self-talk, gets the sign, makes a commitment to it, and follows her routine. She tells herself, "I waited for this. I am ready for this." Then she takes a deep breath and steps into the box. She shuts off the thinking process. She picks up the pitcher's release point and aggressively attacks the ball. She tells herself to keep it simple: See the ball, hit the ball! Between pitches, she steps out of the box to regain focus (turning away from the plate for a second or two), analyze her reaction to the last pitch, and check the coach's sign. Then she takes a deep breath, follows her routine, and steps back confidently into the box. After the at-bat, she passes along any useful information to the next batter regarding the pitcher (dominant pitch, speed, and movement) or the umpire.

READING THE PITCHER

If it didn't help hitters to know what pitch is coming, the other team wouldn't hide the signals. Opinions vary regarding whether coaches should try to tell their batters which pitch is coming. If coaches are going to "pick the pitches," they must do it early—the coach must have enough time to relay the information to the batter, and the batter must have enough time to prepare for the pitch. The best situation is where the batter can "pick" the pitcher herself and know what pitch is coming. Some coaches will only call pitches that are not thrown very often (e.g., changeup) to take away the surprise. Batters must learn to hear only the coach's voice and must practice this in batting practice. To learn to pick the pitches, players must also practice good observational skills. During the games, have a contest to see what player can pick up pitches the fastest.

Most pitchers do have easily observed giveaways. Find out what they do differently on each pitch. On a changeup, you can sometimes see a stiff wrist as compared to a loose wrist. During warm-up pitches at the beginning of the game, the coach can time the pitcher (by counting 1 one thousand, 2 one thousand, and so on) to see how long it takes her to get a grip on the changeup. It will take longer than for other pitches. The coach can then call this pitch from the box. (Batters should be focusing on other things rather than counting before each release.) Videotape your pitchers to see if they have any giveaways and to practice picking pitches. Show a front view to teach your hitters. If you have an opponent's game film, study their pitcher too.

COACH PICKS FROM THE COACHING BOX

If the pitcher does not hide grips, the coach may pick up pitches very early and have time to tell the batter. Coaches must decide how they will relay that information. They may simply call "change" or may use phrases with hidden messages such as "looking good." Sometimes outfielders will give away the pitch by shifting position.

PITCHER GIVEAWAYS THAT THE BATTER CAN WATCH FOR

Facial expressions
- Tongue, mouth, sounds, eyes

Feet
- Placement of the feet on pitching rubber: side or center
- Distance of the spread between the feet
- Toe position: up or down, pointing at various angles

- Foot slide during the delivery (On a screwball, one of our Olympic pitchers made a dramatic slide of the right foot across the rubber.)
- Direction of the step (Pitchers will step off line to the glove side on a screwball to increase the angle.)

Grips

- Some pitchers will take their grip on the leg while taking the catcher's sign.
- Ball or grips seen through holes on the pitcher's glove
- Hand inserted into the glove palm up or down
- Amount of ball or "white" showing in the glove or when pulled out
- Finger placement on the seam, finger spread, or number of knuckles showing
- Change in position of an exposed finger in the finger hole
- Ball pressed or jammed into the hand to get a grip
- Space between the elbow and body as the pitcher gets a grip
- More time taken to get certain grips (can be timed by counting as previously explained)
- Amount of wrist showing during the presentation
- Palm up or down or in or out when taking a grip

Backswing

- Amount of white showing
- Grips showing
- Knuckles up during the circle; number of knuckles showing
- Finger spread
- Wrist angle and bend in the elbow
- Glove position on ball when overhead (A pitcher may place the glove on a different portion of the ball.)
- Speed of the backswing (This may vary, especially on the changeup.)

Release

- Turn of the trunk
- Length and direction of the stride

General tips

- If the ball is deep in the palm and the wrist is stiff, this means a slower pitch.
- If more than one knuckle is showing, the pitch will be a changeup.
- On the rise or curve, the pitcher will be working the side of the ball. The index finger may be on top of the ball. The batter will see more ball.
- On a drop ball, the whole hand usually shows; few varied grips are used, so this is usually consistent.

BATTING-TEE DRILLS

The most underrated piece of equipment is the batting tee. College teams use batting tees all the time, and most major leaguers go to the tee first before taking live batting practice. The tee makes it possible to break down the elements of hitting into the most fundamental form. If a player's mechanics are not correct, she can't hit the ball well off the tee. Coaches should do their teaching at the batting tee where they can closely watch all the elements of the swing and where the hitter can more easily correct any mistakes. Hitters can spend many hours alone working with a tee to develop and groove the swing. Start with high pitches first because the hands must go directly to the ball. Develop proper mechanics, and when they become automatic, move to lower pitches.

To make sure hitters keep their head still and on the ball, drop a coin at the base of the tee after each hit and have the batter call out the coin denomination.

Batting tees are available in a wide range of prices. ATEC has an excellent, durable tee that is available with a rise-ball extension. Plastic construction cones also work well. For high pitches, the cone or tee can be placed on a concrete block to make the ball high enough.

Here are some important rules for using the tee properly:

- Players should have a purpose for every swing.
- After the swing, players should review their mechanics and get feedback from the results of the hit.
- After contact, hitters should look inside the tee to make sure their head is on the ball and driving down.
- Players should use the tee at all contact locations and at all heights in the strike zone.
- A high tee is necessary to simulate a rise ball. Use tee extensions or simply put the tee up on a block.
- The tee should be placed so that the ball is at the correct point of contact. Players should ignore the home plate at the bottom of the tee when assuming their stance.
- To make hitting practice realistic, players should shift their eyes from an imaginary pitcher to the ball on the tee before swinging.

NO STRIDE

Purpose: To isolate and work on hip rotation and upper-body movement.

Procedure: The player steps to the spot where the front foot would be after the stride and starts in that position. She swings and concentrates on the pivot, hip rotation, and movement of the upper body. She drives the front shoulder to the outside corner of the plate. She keeps the head down and looks inside the tee after contact. The goal is to hit a hard line drive off the tee.

Variation: Put a target on a fence (a square of tape or a paper plate) for players to attempt to hit. They should avoid lifting their heads to watch the flight of the ball. They start out attempting to hit a target 10 feet (3 m) from the fence. As the players move farther back, it becomes more difficult for them to hit the target because the degree of error is magnified. It is like shooting a rocket at the moon; the trajectory may be off only a degree here on earth, but out in space it is miles off target.

TWO STRIDE

Purpose: To practice the stride and check for balance.

Procedure: The batter takes her stride with the hands going back to the launch position. She freezes and holds that position to review stride length, foot position, hand position, and balance. If all these are correct, she repeats the stride and this time swings to hit the ball off the tee. If she recognizes a problem, she repeats the stride and does not swing until all aspects are correct.

LONG TEE HITTING

Purpose: To allow players to see the outcome of their hits.

Procedure: Set up a tee at least 30 feet (9 m) from the net so that batters can see where the ball goes—ground ball, fly ball, pulled ball, and so forth. When a batter is close to the net, every hit looks good. The tee can also be set up at home plate so that players can see the results and work on the contact spot for opposite-field hitting.

SOCCER BALL

Purpose: To learn how to drive through the ball.

Procedure: Place a slightly deflated soccer ball on a tee. If the tee is an open tube, place a small bathroom plunger in the tee to hold the ball, or use a traffic cone and a plunger. The batter hits the soccer ball hard off the tee. If she does not drive through the soccer ball, it will not explode off the bat.

BACK KNEE DOWN

Purpose: To develop upper-body strength and quickness. The drill helps the player stop lunging by eliminating lower-body movement. The drill can reduce uppercutting. It emphasizes keeping the barrel above the hands and using correct timing.

Procedure: Use a low tee for this drill. The hitter kneels on a towel with the back knee bent down at a 90-degree angle, keeping the shoulders on a level plane. The drill can also be done off a soft toss. The player sees the bat hit the ball.

TOMAHAWK HITTING

Purpose: To develop proper wrist action at contact.

Procedure: The hitter kneels on her bent back knee. Set the tee for a high pitch. The player uses a bat and hits down on the top half of the ball using a tomahawk action. The player can perform the same action with one hand using a very small bat (a fisherman's club is the right size and shape).

BINGO

Purpose: To develop a level swing and proper mechanics by offering instant feedback.

Procedure: Position two tees at the same height with one directly behind the other. The batter drives the back ball into the front ball. The farther apart the tees, the more difficult it is to hit the front ball because errors are magnified. The path of the hit provides instant feedback on the mechanics of the swing. If the hitter misses to the left, she has an outside-inside swing. If the hitter misses by going above, she is dropping her back shoulder. When successful, the hitter should yell "Bingo."

IN-OUT TEE SWING

Purpose: To develop an inside-outside swing.

Procedure: Place one tee behind another with the back tee higher than the front one. The distance between the tees should be about 3 feet (1 m). The batter hits the ball off the front tee without making contact with the back tee. Using an inside-outside swing, the batter will miss hitting the back tee and receive instant feedback that she is swinging correctly. If the batter extends the arms and sweeps the bat, she will hit the back tee.

BAT CONTROL

Purpose: To develop bat control and to see the relationship of the bat to the ball.

Procedure: The batter hits off of a tee. If the coach or partner calls "above," the batter swings and misses above the ball. If the coach or partner calls "hit," the batter hits the ball.

TWO OR THREE TEES

Purpose: To increase power, teach location, and improve concentration. To practice using the same stride while adjusting to different contact spots.

Procedure: Set one tee at the contact spot for an inside pitch (front inside corner) and one for an outside pitch (back outside corner). As the hitter plants the front foot, a partner calls "in" or "out." The batter hits the ball called for by the partner.

Variations:

- For beginners, you can start by having them hit only the inside pitch and then go outside. Then alternate so that players can feel the difference between the two swings and develop muscle memory.
- The hitter performs the drill with the eyes shut.
- The pitcher stands behind a screen in front of the batter and fakes pitching an inside or outside pitch. The hitter recognizes the release point and hits the corresponding ball.
- Three tees can be used; the third tee is positioned down the middle. Set the inside tee about 3 inches (7.5 cm) higher than the middle tee, and set the middle tee 3 inches higher than the outside tee.
- The same drill can be done using a toss from the side. The batter hits the full length of the cage.

HORSE

Purpose: To practice hitting where the ball is pitched or to practice hitting to a certain field location.

Procedure: Set up a tee on home plate at any location. The hitter calls out a spot on the field and attempts to hit that target. If no field is available, make tape markers on a net or batting cage and hit into that. If the hitter is successful, she gets the first letter of horse and continues. If the hitter is not successful, the partner gets a turn. The first to spell horse is the winner.

TOSS DRILLS

These drills are useful because they do not require a lot of space or expensive equipment. Players can use rubber softballs, old softballs (tape the balls if the seams are coming apart), and Wiffle balls and can hit into a fence, carpet, curtain, or cage. Using different-size objects increases concentration: Try baseball- and golf-ball-size Wiffle balls, tennis balls, black-eyed peas, or popcorn kernels. Throw plastic coffee can lids or margarine lids underhand like Frisbees; they really go up. Start with a full-size bat but quickly move to using Thundersticks or small, thin bats made by cutting old broomsticks or dowels to bat size and taping the handles.

A good toss is essential for toss drills to be productive. The toss should be firm and level with moderate speed. To increase the accuracy of the tosses, place balls on the ground as targets to mark the contact spots. The target can also be at the batter's front hip.

Be safe! Make sure that the tosser is in a position where a ball or bat cannot hit her. Tosses are made from a kneeling or standing position, depending on the drill (see figure 1.13). Beginning players should toss from the side. More advanced players can toss from a 45-degree angle in front of the hitter. The tosser should use a backswing on the toss so that the hitter can key her timing off the arm. If the batters start to "cheat" on soft-toss drills, tossers should hold one ball in either hand, rotate the balls (like juggling), and then toss one up. This way batters do not know when the ball is coming.

Figure 1.13   Tossing technique.

BACK-HAND WIFFLE TOSS

Purpose: To emphasize the pivot and keeping the hands and back elbow close to the body.

Procedure: The tosser stands at a 45-degree angle in front of the hitter. She tosses Wiffle balls to the hitter's midsection. The hitter does not have a bat. From the stride position, the hitter pivots and catches (or hits) the ball with the back hand at a spot opposite the belly button.

LOCATION TOSS

Purpose: To learn to adjust to the contact spot for three pitches—inside, middle, and outside.

Procedure: The tosser is in a kneeling position and tosses balls to the three spots where the batter should make contact. The tosser calls the number of the spot where she will toss the ball as she tosses it (she calls "one" for inside, "two" for middle, and "three" for outside). The hitter makes contact at that location, saying "hit" on contact.

HIGH TOSS

Purpose: To learn to keep the barrel above the ball.

Procedure: The tosser throws from a standing position. The hitter hits tosses that are high inside and high outside.

BACK TOSS

Purpose: To practice keeping the hands inside the ball and driving the barrel through the ball.

Procedure: The tosser stands behind the batter. The batter turns her head slightly to track the ball. The toss should be on an inside-out path. The batter must wait on the ball, make contact out in front of the plate, and then drive hard through it.

TWO-BALL TOSS

Purpose: To adjust to hitting balls at different locations and to develop the skills needed for quick adjustment and vision tracking.

Procedure: While kneeling, the tosser throws two balls at the same time from one hand and calls which ball to hit. The tosser throws balls of different sizes or colors. She calls top or bottom, small or big, or a color.

FRONT BOUNCE

Purpose: To develop timing.

Procedure: The tosser stands about 15 feet (4.5 m) in front of the hitter. (The tosser can also be to the side: 6 feet [2 m] to the side and 3 feet [1 m] in front of the batter.) The tosser throws a tennis ball overhand, bouncing the ball up into the strike zone in front of the plate. The hitter uses the bounce as a trigger, or timing mechanism, to identify when she should take the hands back to launch position and begin the stride.

SELF-TOSS UP THE MIDDLE

Purpose: To develop proper mechanics to hit the ball up the middle. To force the elbows in and develop the proper flick of the wrist; to groove the correct swing and provide instant mechanical feedback on every hit.

Procedure: The hitter self-tosses and tries to take every ball up the middle. The hitter tosses the ball up with the bottom hand while resting the bat on the back shoulder. The toss should be to the contact spot and no more than a foot above it; using both hands to grip the bat, the player hits the ball as it descends. To avoid chasing balls, the hitter can stand 3 to 4 feet (1 to 1.5 m) from a fence and hit to it. Hit into a mat or use Wiffle balls to protect the fence. Alternatively, the player can stand at home plate and attempt to hit all balls over second base. She then repeats the drill, going from second base to home. (I [Judi] watched the famous Hall-of-Fame baseball star Ernie Banks do this drill at a clinic; he said he did it all the time as a player.)

FRONT SCREEN TOSS

Purpose: To practice reacting to live underhand pitching.

Procedure: A screen standing about 15 feet (4.5 m) in front of the hitter protects the tosser. The hitter takes a normal swing, hitting the ball where it is pitched. She should drive outside pitches to the opposite field and pull inside pitches. The tosser holds the release on some pitches to make sure the batter is reacting to the ball and not the arm motion.

ANGLE SCREEN TOSS

Purpose: To practice hitting the ball on the outside corner to the opposite field.

Procedure: The tosser sets up the same distance as for the front screen toss but at an angle (to the right of the right-handed batter), while the hitter sets up normally in the box. The pitch will come at the batter like an outside pitch, and the hitter needs to hit it back at the net, going back to the opposite field. This teaches the inside-outside swing.

QUICK HANDS

Purpose: To develop quick hands, the backswing, and a compact swing.

Procedure: The tosser stands in front of the batter and behind a screen about 15 feet (4.5 m) in front of the hitter. The batter starts with the bat pointing at the tosser and must quickly get the hands back and forward to hit the tossed ball.

SNAPBACKS

Purpose: To develop a small stride, compact swing, fast hands, and arm strength.

Procedure: The tosser stands on the side of the batter or stands in front of the batter behind the screen. The tosser tosses the ball to one contact spot in rapid succession, not allowing the bat to come to rest. The batter does not have time to adjust to different locations, so the tosses should be consistent. The tosser throws 6 to 10 balls in a row. The hitter hits each ball hard, using a full swing.

DOTTED BALLS

Purpose: To practice making an aggressive approach to every pitch while being able to hold up after receiving information that says, "Don't swing."

Procedure: Four circles, each the size of a quarter, are marked on several balls. Some balls have red circles, and some have green circles. The tosser hides the colors with her glove. The hitter strides aggressively, prepared to hit every toss. She hits the green dotted balls and holds up on the red ones by squeezing the bat and tensing up.

MACHINE DRILLS

Machines allow players to get many practice swings. Enough real pitching is never available. Machines can also be set up so that batters can work on particular pitches. As players progress, machines are most effective when they deliver the ball inconsistently, just as pitchers do. Batters must learn to adjust as they would in a game.

When using pitching machines, change the speed and location with every few pitches. Mix the balls (old and new) for more variety. Batters must not time the feeder's motions; the feeder should simply place the ball directly into the machine (hold the ball up first to make sure the batter is ready) so that the hitter picks up the pitch out of the chute (similar to seeing it off the pitcher's hip).

IN CLOSE

Purpose: To develop a small stride and quick reactions to the ball.

Procedure: The hitter stands about 30 feet (9 m) from the machine. Set the machine to throw at the regular speed used at the normal distance. The hitter must react quickly after seeing the ball and must use her normal swing, focusing on getting the bat out quickly.

EXECUTION

Purpose: To develop the ability to execute on the next pitch and to practice signals.

Procedure: The feeder signals a specific play to the batter, who is hitting off a machine. The batter then steps into the box and executes. This drill makes hitting practice gamelike and allows players to practice signals.

GOING FOR THE CONTACT RECORD

Purpose: To practice suicides and hit-and-runs; to encourage younger players to be aggressive and swing.

Procedure: Use a pitching machine or tosser. Challenge hitters to make contact with every pitch. If a hitter misses a pitch, the next batter is up. Tell players that the record is 100 in a row so they have something to shoot for, or pick a realistic or actual number for your level.

NO PULL

Purpose: To learn to wait for the outside pitch and drive it hard to the right side.

Procedure: The pitch is delivered outside, and the goal is to hit all balls to the right side of the cage or machine. The contact spot is over the outside back corner.

HITTING GAME

Purpose: To heighten competition and pressure in hitting practice.

Procedure: Players hit off a pitching machine in a cage. The batter scores no points for ground balls or for hitting the roof of the cage, three points for hitting the ball up the middle, and two points for hitting the side of the cage. The feeder and hitter compete against each other, getting 10 strikes each. Use a scorecard.

HITTING MECHANICS DRILLS

Hitting is a very complex skill. Coaches should use drills that break down the mechanics of the swing so the hitter can isolate specific components. These drills should be repeated until the action becomes automatic.

WALL STRIDE

Purpose: To learn to keep the front foot closed during the stride and to learn the contact spot.

Procedure: The player stands perpendicular to a wall. She strides against the wall, keeping the foot closed, and brings the bat slowly forward to the contact point. (The bat is parallel to the wall.) This is the contact spot for a ball down the middle.

SHADOW

Purpose: To learn to keep the head still during the stride.

Procedure: The sun must be behind the player so that she can see her shadow. She places a ball on the shadow of her head. She takes her step and makes sure that her head does not move off the ball.

STRIDE TO LAUNCH

Purpose: To take the stride and move the hands back repeatedly so that doing so becomes automatic.

Procedure: The player assumes a correct balanced stance. She strides and takes the hands back and up slightly to the launch position. The player does not swing. She repeats the stride many times.

FRONT ELBOW

Purpose: To learn the action of the front arm when hitting.

Procedure: The hitter assumes the batting position without a bat. A partner stands in front of the hitter and extends a flat hand for a target at elbow distance. The hitter drives her front elbow to the partner's hand and, after contact, straightens the arm and flips the wrist forward (palm down using a karate chop) as if hitting. Repeat the motion many times to develop muscle memory.

GLOVE IN ARMPIT

Purpose: To practice keeping the back elbow down and in and keeping the barrel up. The drill helps prevent sweeping the bat.

Procedure: The hitter places a glove under the lead arm and swings, keeping the glove there. The glove should not drop until the follow-through.

RESISTANCE SWING

Purpose: To feel the various elements of the swing and to develop muscle memory of the swing components.

Procedure: The drill requires a partner or a bat handle attached to a fence with surgical cord. The batter assumes the batting stance. The partner stands behind the batter, holding the top of the bat with both hands to offer resistance as the batter strides and swings half speed all the way through. The partner walks around the hitter, allowing the full range of motion and applying only the amount of resistance that permits a correct swing. The batter feels the importance of keeping the hands in close, using an inside-outside swing, rotating the hips, and transferring her weight to produce power.

BAT ON NECK

Purpose: To develop a compact swing by eliminating sweeping and dropping of the hands.

Procedure: The hitter starts with a bat on the shoulder and against the neck, and she keeps it there through her hip rotation. The bat leaves the neck only when the hitter throws it to the contact spot.

FENCE SWING

Purpose: To groove an inside-outside swing, get the hips turned, and take the knob to the ball, keeping the hands from dropping.

Procedure: The batter stands parallel to a fence slightly farther away than one bat length. She swings without contacting the fence and stays balanced with her weight on the balls of the feet. She must not cheat by leaning back. Using a net instead of a rigid fence is less intimidating. The player repeats the swing many times at moderate speed to groove the swing, then turns so she is perpendicular to the fence with her back foot 2 to 3 inches (5 to 7.5 cm) from the fence. She must swing without hitting the fence. If she drops her hands, she will hit the fence.

MIRROR SWING

Purpose: To understand, analyze, and evaluate the swing.

Procedure: The batter uses a full-length mirror to view her swing. Facing the mirror, she works on the first movement with or without a bat. The front shoulder is slightly down. She takes the lead elbow to the ball, then the knob. The hands start close to the chest for the inside-outside swing. The batter uses a side view to check the stride, with the hands going back to the launch position (no swing). She uses many repetitions to develop an automatic response. She swings and checks to see that she has a quiet head, correct shoulder angle, level hips, and the proper pivot. The batter can check alignment and balance using the plumb line from the shoulder to the foot. Require players to repeat this many times at home but without a bat in their hands.

ROPE HITTING

Purpose: To develop hand action, proper stride, and concentration.

Procedure: Use a 3-foot (1 m) piece of thick rope (taped at both ends to stop fraying). Place a Wiffle ball on a tee or cone. The batter takes a proper swing with the rope and hits the ball solidly. Batters should release the top hand on the follow-through to keep from hitting themselves in the back.

LINE-DRIVE CORD

Purpose: To learn to keep the hands up and stop looping.

Procedure: Wiffle balls are strung on a cord that is then attached to two fences or poles and tightened so that the line is taut. For ease in setting up the cord, use clips or hooks on the ends of the cord and a turnbuckle (available at hardware stores) so that you can tighten the cord after it is attached. The balls all start at one end. The batter hits the Wiffle balls to the other end, keeping the hands above the cord. This is an excellent training tool for slappers, who hit and then follow through down the cord.

POWER

Purpose: To learn to launch the ball and experience the fun of hitting with power.

Procedure: This drill is especially helpful and fun for younger players. Players move closer to the outfield fence to hit off soft toss, self-toss, or batting tees. Have younger players use tennis rackets and tennis balls. Have home-run contests. Players get to experience the power and excitement of swinging hard.

TRACKING

Purpose: To practice using a hard focus to see the pitch as it approaches the contact spot. The drill helps batters recognize strikes and the spin of pitches.

Procedure: The batter tracks the ball all the way from release to the contact spot, tracking off a machine or a pitcher in the bullpen. The batter identifies the location and makes a ball or strike call, saying "yes" or "no." If a pitcher is throwing, the batter calls out strikes and then pitch type as soon as she recognizes the spin. Using dots on the ball makes it easier for the batter to see spin.

UNDERLOAD SWINGS

Purpose: To develop quick hands and quick-twitch fibers by training at a faster speed.

Procedure: Hit Wiffle balls off a soft toss using an underload bat. Just as runners improve speed by running down hills, hitters can use the underload theory to increase swing speed by using a lighter bat or a hitting stick that allows faster swings. A hitting stick can be made from a broomstick or dowels. Foam pipe insulation is taped on the upper half to create the barrel. The hitting stick should be used to hit only Wiffle balls. Using a shorter bat and shortening the lever also increase quickness.

FIVE AT A TIME

Purpose: To learn the contact point and control the bat no matter where the pitch is.

Procedure: Using live pitching, the batter gets five pitches each at-bat. The batters go through three rounds, and they have a different goal for each round. For the first round, the goal is no pulls; for the second round, the goal is to hit up the middle; for the third round, the goal is to pull the ball. Keep score and make it a competition: Hitting to the correct field is a +1; hitting to the wrong field is a −1.

Here's a note regarding live batting practice: Everyone wants to bat off live pitching. Have them earn that right. Players must look good at the other stations (i.e., cage, soft toss, tees) before being permitted to join the live hitting group. During live hitting, players who are waiting their turn to face the pitcher can use tees or soft-toss stations that are set up near home plate. This helps to keep all hitters busy.

ALL BUT THE KITCHEN SINK

Purpose: To break a team batting slump and to have fun.

Procedure: The coach pitches all kinds of fruits and vegetables, and the batters take full cuts. Use watermelons, cantaloupes, grapes, tomatoes, eggs, cauliflower, and so on. If you want to give advance warning, have the players wear old clothes and be ready to clean up a mess. In the next game, you will be hearing them cheering their teammates to hit the watermelon, tomato, and so on.

STRENGTH SERIES

Purpose: To increase strength in the wrists and hands.

Procedure: The player uses a weighted or heavy bat and increases the weight as she becomes stronger. She does sets of 10.

1. *Zone hitting:* The hitter assumes the proper stance, pivots, and swings the bat in the strike zone. She breaks the wrist back and forth 10 times at each of nine contact locations—high pitches (inside, down the middle, and outside), waist-high pitches in the three locations, and then low pitches in the three locations. The total is 90 wrist swings.

2. *Windshield wiper:* With the arms extended in front of the chest, the hitter holds the bat head up. She rotates the wrists and bat back and forth like a windshield wiper. She keeps the hands at shoulder level.

3. *Pullovers (for the triceps):* Holding the bat with both hands, the hitter drops the bat directly back over her head. She then "throws" the bat forward with the bat head leading, keeping the elbows in during the throwing motion.

4. *Bat raises:* The hitter holds the bat at her side with the barrel pointed down. Keeping the arm at her side, she raises the bat head using only the wrist.

5. *Wrist circles:* With the arm and bat extended straight forward at shoulder level, the hitter makes wrist circles 10 times in each position and then repeats with the other hand.

CHAPTER 2

BUNTING AND SLAP HITTING

B unting plays an extremely important role in softball. Executing the short game is essential to a team's offensive strategy, and it adds excitement to the game. One of the most thrilling plays in the game is scoring a runner from third with a suicide squeeze. Bunting is not as difficult as hitting, and everyone on the team should be proficient at it. Too many games are lost because someone could not get a bunt down. A team that bunts well wins games.

The left-side running slap is designed to give the batter a running start before hitting the ball. Because the batter is taking a swing at the ball, the slap is considered a hit, not a bunt. This distinction is important because a foul on a third strike with a slap is not an out as it is with a bunt. This chapter discusses both the bunt and the slap hit because the starting position in the box is the same and because players should first learn to bunt before adding the slap. Because defenses are getting more sophisticated, a successful slapper must be able to drop a bunt when the defense is back and must be able to hit the ball through (slap) when the defense is in tight. The ability to also hit away keeps the outfield honest.

Although the short game is easier to teach and practice, it does require a good eye at the plate and bat control. The player must be able to put the ball on the ground. Short gamers are usually smaller and faster players who can get down the line quickly, creating pressure on the defenders to hurry the play. Lefties have an advantage because they are closer to first base. Having a short game can make a place for a player who does not hit well but has good speed and can simply put the ball in play. This chapter focuses on how to execute the various skills used in bunting and slap hitting. Information on when and why to use specific bunts and bunt plays is covered in chapter 4, Team Offense.

SACRIFICE BUNT

The purpose of the sacrifice bunt is to advance a runner or runners with the expectation that the batter will be out; hence, it is called a sacrifice. The batter gives up an out for the good of the team. The batter's concern is to bunt the next strike and put it down so that the only play is at first.

The sacrifice bunt requires the least body movement of any bunt. The basic position is at the front of the box so that any bunt directly down is in fair territory and will not bounce off the plate. Because the defense is anticipating most sacrifice bunts, the batter does not need to worry about turning early and giving it away. The bunter turns as the pitcher separates her hands so that as the bunter attempts the bunt, her shoulders are not moving. Turning early also gives the batter time to read the defensive positioning before directing the ball.

Stance

The batter must make sure that her feet are not outside the batter's box when pivoting and when making contact. The weight is on the balls of the feet. The knees are slightly bent, and there is a bend at the waist. Keeping the weight forward will also help the batter get out of the way of a wild pitch. She should maintain good balance. Batters use two types of stances when putting down the bunt.

- **Squared stance**—The batter steps with the front foot to the outside line of the box and then steps forward with the back foot so that both feet are in a side-stride position parallel to the front line of the box (see figure 2.1). The feet are shoulder-width apart. Beginners often use this stance because it is easier to get the timing correct and be stationary at contact. From this stance, the bunter will find it a bit more difficult to get out of the way of a wild pitch than from the pivot stance.

- **Pivot stance**—The batter pivots on the balls of both feet, turning the belly button toward the pitcher. The shoulders and hips are open to the pitcher. The feet stay in the basic hitting position (forward and back) with the back foot a couple of inches closer to the plate for better balance (see figure 2.2). The batter is in a better running position, has better outside plate coverage, and is in a better position for a slap and hit.

Figure 2.1 Squared stance with bat level.　　**Figure 2.2 Pivot stance with bat angled.**

Hand Position

As the bunter pivots, she has two options for holding the bat. Either technique can be paired with either of the two stances described earlier. Players should experiment to find which stance and hand positions are most comfortable. Beginners will usually start with the square stance and hands apart for better bat control. As players become more skilled, they should move their hands together and try the pivot stance. The most important thing is for players to be comfortable and to do what works best for them.

- **Hands apart**—In this technique, the bottom hand grips the bat with the knuckles up and the palm toward the ground. The top hand moves up the barrel to grip the bat above the tape as if shaking hands with the bat, while the bottom hand stays in the batter's usual location for hitting. The top hand grips the bat in the fingertips, away from the base of the fingers, leaving a V-shaped space between the thumb and forefinger. The bat deadens the impact by sliding back into the V as the ball hits the bat, and the hand acts as a cushion. By holding the hands apart, the bunter has better bat control.

- **Hands together**—In the second technique, the hands are together in the hitting position about a third of the way up the bat, with the top hand holding the bat loosely. Having the hands together makes it easier to slap and drive the ball if the batter decides to attack the defense.

Bat Angle

The bat can be held level or at an angle. Again, these two techniques can be combined with either the square or pivot stances and with the hands apart or together. More advanced players usually hold their bats with some degree of angle.

- **Level bat**—The bat is held horizontally at the top of the strike zone (see figure 2.1). The only movement of the bat is down; the bat is always kept level. A disadvantage is that a bunt on the ball's bottom half will often be a foul pop-up to the catcher. The advantage of this technique is that the batter can more easily judge the strike zone—anything above the bat is a ball, and the batter should never extend the arms upward to bunt the ball. The disadvantage is that it is easier to drop the bat head when attempting to bunt a low strike, which usually produces a foul ball.

- **Angled bat**—The bat head is aligned upward at about a 45-degree angle (see figure 2.2), and the bat head can be pointed slightly toward the pitcher. The batter can more easily slash or drive the ball down from this position. In addition, foul balls tend to kick more to the side, where the catcher cannot as easily make the out.

Contact Position

The bat is held in front of the chest and in front of home plate. The elbows are bent, pointed down, and slightly outside the body. The arms and shoulders are free of tension. The batter must be careful not to reach. Letting the ball get deep in the zone gives the batter better control of where she will bunt it. Her head faces the pitcher, and her eyes are level. At contact, the bunter catches the ball with the bat, allowing the bat and arms to give slightly to soften the impact. Making contact with the end of the bat, rather than the sweet spot, will help deaden the ball. The batter should bunt the top half of the ball.

To bunt a low pitch, the batter bends at the knees to lower the body while maintaining the same bat angle. She uses her legs as an elevator. As she lowers her hands and the bat, she must make sure that the bat head never drops below the hands.

The angle of the bat at contact determines the direction of the ball. If the bat is square to the pitcher, the ball will rebound directly back to her. The bottom hand is the control hand. By pulling it forward or backward, the batter can control where the ball will go. When a right-handed batter pulls the bottom hand back, the bunt will go toward third base; when the bottom hand is pushed forward, the ball will go to first. The adjustment of the bat angle is not drastic. The batter should practice with a partner to learn the required angle. The partner tosses a ball, and the batter bunts alternately to each side of the tosser.

Right-handed batters will find it much easier to bunt an outside pitch toward first and an inside pitch toward third. For the best chance of success, players should bunt the ball where it is pitched. Only exceptional bunters should try to do otherwise. Bunters should not aim for the lines. They must allow for a margin of error and for the spin on the ball. The target should be in the area 45 degrees from the front corners of the plate. There is nothing worse than a well-executed bunt that rolls foul just as the runner slides safely to the base.

A bunter's position in the box will also affect where the ball goes. If she wants the ball to go right down the foul lines, she stands a little deeper in the box. She stands in front of the plate if she wants the ball to drop well inside the foul lines and in fair territory.

COACHING POINTS FOR THE SACRIFICE BUNT

- Bunt the ball, then admire it! When you see that the bunt is down and that the ball is out of the running path, then run.

- Do not drop the bat on the ball. If necessary, carry it with you until you are well clear of the ball.

- If the first-base player fields the bunt and is waiting to make the tag, stop and force the defender to come to you to apply the tag, giving the base runner more time to advance. Do not back up! If you do, a dead ball, which is an automatic out, is called, and the runners have to return to their bases.

- Focus on running in the running lane to avoid an interference call.

PUSH BUNT

The push bunt is used to push the ball between the third-base player and the pitcher, or between the pitcher and the first-base player, hard enough so the shortstop or second-base player must charge the ball. The starting grip and body position are the same as those used for a sacrifice bunt. Players choose the stance, hand position, and bat angle that are most comfortable. There should be no visible difference between the setup for the sacrifice bunt and for the push bunt—hitters don't want to tip off the defense about their intentions. With a push bunt, the grip tightens and both arms extend forward together to push the bat to the ball (see figure 2.3). The push of the bat is slightly down and through the ball to avoid line drives or pop-ups. The bunter may choose to take a short step into the ball while pushing it. However, she must be careful not to step

Figure 2.3 Push bunt.

completely out of the box or on the plate during contact—that's an automatic out. She moves quickly out of the box after contact. The location of the pitch dictates which side to direct the ball to.

SLASH OR SLUG BUNT

The batter executes the slash, or slug bunt, by faking a bunt and then swinging away. The batter turns early, assuming a sacrifice-bunt position. The goal is to induce the corners to charge aggressively. The batter holds the sacrifice-bunt position long enough to get the corners to believe the bunt is on and to charge. At the last moment, when the ball is on its way, the batter rotates the shoulders and hips back slightly, being careful not to turn the rest of the body or head. The front shoulder comes to the chin. The backswing is about half of the distance used when hitting. If the hands are not already together on the rotation, the batter slides the lower hand up against the top hand to a hitting position. On the rotation, she cocks the wrists back to prepare for making a chopping motion. She hits the ball down at the feet of the charging corner or at the gap between the corner and the pitcher. The batter does not use a full swing but a compact chop or slash down to bounce the ball. The element of surprise and the sharp hit down are what lead to success. The batter must be careful not to rotate too far back trying to take a full swing. Doing so usually results in a late swing that produces a pop-up. An advantage of the squared bunt position is that it helps limit the backswing.

RIGHT-HANDED SNEAKY BUNT

The right-handed sneaky bunt is an extremely effective bunt, particularly for a power hitter when the third-base player is playing back at the bag. The batter's body screens the third-base player's vision until the last moment, giving the batter a great jump.

The bunt can be executed with one or two hands. The batter assumes a normal hitting stance but at the front of the box. The bunter maintains the batting stance until the last instant, taking a stride forward exactly as if hitting away. On the stride, the top hand slides about halfway up the bat (see figure 2.4a). Weight is transferred to the front foot. (Some batters may also prefer to step back slightly from the plate with the back foot.) The batter drops the bat straight down; the knob is located by the back hip, and the bat head is pointed toward first base (see figure 2.4b). The bat head is slightly higher than the knob. With weight on the front foot, the body leans forward toward the plate.

Figure 2.4 Right-handed sneaky bunt. *(a)* Position during the stride and *(b)* at contact.

The player keeps her head down to watch the ball meet the bat. Contact is made in one of two places—slightly behind the belt buckle or behind the back hip. Players must be sure to keep the bat angle facing fair territory (the bat is perpendicular or square to the pitcher)—even the slightest angle toward the first-base line will cause the ball to go foul. The batter does not swing at the ball; by using just the wrist of the top hand, she gently taps the ball forward several feet in front of home plate. The bunter then runs hard to first base. If contact is made behind the hip, the ball will sometimes go behind the batter as she leaves the box. If the ball hits the batter immediately, while she is still in the box, the bunt is a foul ball.

LEFT-HANDED DRAG BUNT

To execute the left-handed drag bunt, the batter must use a normal hitting position to avoid telegraphing her intentions. This bunt is used to surprise the defense or when the corners are playing deep. The running start and closer position to first give a speedy lefty a real advantage. She waits for a good pitch and drops the bunt.

The front foot steps back to start the hands and body in motion (see figure 2.5a). The hands move upward to shoulder height as the foot comes back. As the bat begins moving forward, the hands move up the bat to a bunting position. The back foot then crosses over, ideally landing on or near the lines marking the front corner of the box. Weight stays on the left foot after the crossover, and the head is on the ball. The hips and shoulders remain closed until contact is made. The batter must be careful not to

Figure 2.5 Left-handed drag bunt. *(a)* The step back with the front foot and *(b)* crossover step to contact position.

open up or pull off the plate before contact because she will be vulnerable to an outside pitch or a changeup. At contact, all momentum is toward the pitcher, not toward first base. The grip is firm, and the bat is extended with the bat head angled slightly forward (see figure 2.5b). Most bunters should use both hands; it takes a lot of strength and bat control to bunt with only one hand. Contact is well in front of the body and the plate. Weight is on the left foot as contact is made.

The bunter should learn to angle the bat so that she can drag down either foul line as well as drop the ball just in front of the plate. She looks for low pitches and goes with the pitch.

SQUEEZE BUNT

The two types of squeeze bunts are the suicide squeeze and the safety squeeze. The objective of both is to score the runner from third by surprising the defense. In the suicide squeeze, the runner is going on the pitch, whereas in the safety squeeze the runner goes home after seeing that the ball has been bunted successfully or after the throw has been made to first.

The suicide squeeze should be used when the count is in the batter's favor so she can expect to see a strike. The batter and all runners must know that the suicide squeeze is on. Miscommunication on this play can be disastrous, so the batter should give a return signal to confirm that she is aware that the squeeze is on. She then visualizes a successful squeeze before stepping into the box. She doesn't square to bunt until the last moment; then she pivots quickly into the bunting stance. This is much later than for the traditional sacrifice bunt. The batter must put the bat on the ball to protect the runner if the pitch is one that the catcher can catch—even if the pitch is a ball! If the batter can't bunt the ball, she should at least foul it off. The batter should imagine that her beloved child is sitting in a high chair directly behind home plate. The batter's job is to protect the child at all costs!

On the suicide squeeze, the runner anticipates the pitcher's release to get a good jump, leaving on the pitch as if stealing home. With a two-person umpire crew (where there is no umpire at third base), the runner can get a bigger jump at third. The batter must roll the ball away from the plate, preferably between the pitcher and the first-base player. She bunts the ball down, away from the foul lines, away from the catcher, and not too hard. A missed ball or a pop-up spells disaster. If the pitch is at the batter, the batter must rock back and still put the ball down. If the batter is a good slapper, she may be asked to slap instead of bunt. She needs only to hit the ball down, although a high bounce to short or second gives the runner extra time.

If the batter sees that the bunt has popped up, she must immediately step on the plate and hope to get a dead-ball ruling, keeping the runner safe. In this case, the batter will be out, but the runner is simply sent back to third. If the runner sees that the pitch is well out of the strike zone and that the batter has no chance of touching it, she should attempt to put on the brakes and get back.

A pitchout can hang a runner out to dry. The safety squeeze is used to protect against a pitchout and to take advantage of a defense that has weak arms. On the safety squeeze, the batter chooses the pitch to bunt. She has only one shot, however, because the element of surprise is gone after the first attempt. The runner goes on the result of the play. The batter feels less pressure because the runner is not going on the pitch. On a safety squeeze, bunting toward third base allows the runner at third to get a bigger lead because the third-base player must play the ball.

FAKE BUNT

In this play, the batter acts as if she is bunting but doesn't touch the ball. Because the batter wants the defense to react without thinking, she must not commit too early. After showing the bunt, she brings the bat back out of the strike zone to avoid being called for a strike attempt. If the runner is stealing, the batter leaves the end of the bat pointed where the catcher's eyes will be when she stands. The catcher will then have to adjust to see the runner.

LEFT-HANDED RUNNING SLAP

A left-handed batter can get a running start before hitting the ball by using the left-side running slap. The lefty is already several steps closer to first. Adding a running start puts tremendous pressure on the defense to make the play quickly. The play often moves the defense out of position as well. To be successful, the batter should have good speed and the ability to put the ball in play.

The batter stands in her standard hitting position so that she does not tip off the defense. The slapper must be in a position where the crossover step will put her on the lines of the front inside corner of the box. To execute the slap, the hitter runs first and hits second. She starts to move when the ball leaves the pitcher's hand. She must not anticipate the release. If she starts too soon, she will have to stop moving to slap the ball or will be way out of the box. The first step is a small jab step with the right foot, either forward or backward. The jab step acts as a timing mechanism. The left foot crosses aggressively over the right foot directly toward the pitcher (see figure 2.6a). The left foot should land on the front line of the box on the inside corner. The right foot then

Figure 2.6   **Left-handed running slap. *(a)* Crossover step and *(b)* contact and motion.**

opens slightly toward the pitcher. If the jab step is not used, the first step must include a pivot that opens the hips to the pitcher. The hips are square, but the front shoulder stays closed to permit total plate coverage.

The hands are held close to the body and high in the strike zone on the swing. The front side and front shoulder remain closed. The batter can use a choke grip for good bat control. The bat head is above the hands, which come forward with the crossover step. Both the bat head and the hands are above the ball, and the batter should try to hit the top half of the ball. The batter must be careful not to drop her hands at the start of the swing. She hits the ball as the left foot lands on the front line. The swing is an inside-outside swing. The knob is first, the head of the bat stays back, and the swing is down. The knob and hands stay inside the path of the ball. The hands are out in front. To hit to the left side, the batter should be late with the head of the bat. The batter contacts the ball behind her body and hits down to the ground to put the ball in play.

On the slap follow-through, the batter rolls through the box, being in motion as she hits the ball (see figure 2.6b). She does not need to be moving fast; the important thing is that she is in motion. The slapper continues running toward the pitcher after contact, being careful not to turn early to run to first. On the follow-through, the bat is an extension of the right arm. The batter follows through with the bat in the right hand.

Batters should take the following steps to learn the slap:

1. Stand at the plate and catch pitches with a glove on the left hand. This enables the player to become comfortable catching the ball and seeing it from the left side.

2. Add the crossover step to the exercise of catching pitches.

3. Add a bat and become proficient as a drag bunter.

4. Use the crossover step and hit off a tee. Draw a line to use as the inside line of the batter's box so that you can check alignment and make sure that the front shoulder stays closed. The hands should be even with the left foot and ahead of the bat, and the bat must have the proper angle at contact. Hit to the shortstop and the second-base player to learn the proper bat angle.

COACHING POINTS FOR THE SLAP

- Learn to bunt first.

- Avoid focusing too much on your footwork. Don't think *feet!* Think *contact!* Keep the feet under control.

- Don't drop the hands. If you have trouble correcting this problem, keep the bat on the shoulder and keep the hands below.

- Don't step away from the pitch or open your front side.

- Work all pitches—high, low, in, out.

- If you are not getting the ball down, separate your hands on the bat, or start with the bat at the one o'clock position.

- Work with both swing angles—swing down to bounce the ball as high as possible, and swing level to hit through or by infielders.

- Keep the statistic "reached on error," because that is the slapper's goal.

5. Run and hit off a tee.
6. Run and hit off a machine.
7. Slap off a pitcher. Begin with front tosses (with the tosser 10 to 15 feet [3.0 to 4.5 m] in front and behind a net) and progress to full pitching distance.

SLOW SLAP

Advanced slappers may also use a slow slap. With this technique, the slapper tries to punch the ball. She should drop the bat lower than for the regular slap, punch the ball, and then draw the bat back. The bat is on and off the top of the ball. The goal is to mis-hit the ball; the uglier the better. Because the ball is not hit sharply it will take the defense longer to get to the ball and make the play. The slow slap is most effective when the defense is playing back or doesn't charge well.

MENTAL PREPARATION FOR THE SHORT GAME

The fun of the short game is the element of surprise and keeping the defense guessing. Batters must not telegraph their intentions by changing their position in the box or by using a different hand or bat position. Bunters should execute on the first strike. If they turn to bunt or show a slap and don't execute, the element of surprise is lost.

As the batter approaches the on-deck circle, she should already know what the situation will likely call for. She can start preparing mentally for the job she will probably be asked to do. Before stepping in the box, she must know if she is bunting or slapping. If a signal is given, the batter should have no doubt about what her responsibilities are. If she has a question, she should not step into the box until it has been resolved. Time may be called if necessary, although doing so risks losing the element of surprise.

The batter should visualize executing the play successfully before stepping into the box. She must not think of being unsuccessful. When asked to bunt, players have a tendency to tell themselves not to pop up, and then the image of popping the ball up becomes the one they visualize. Coaches, too, must be sure to give only positive instructions.

The mental preparation for hitting described in chapter 1 is important for the short game. Bunters must understand the umpire's strike zone, must know what pitch to look for, and must understand the count.

BUNTING AND SLAP-HITTING DRILLS

Players should pair up so they can get many repetitions while working on bat control and ball placement. When partners are in close, the bunter should begin in a squared or pivot position, because there won't be time for her to turn her body to the correct position. For safety, use Wiffle balls when working on slug bunts and slaps. Always include drills in which players bunt and then run to first so that the players can work on proper timing; in games, bunters have a tendency to be in a hurry and to run while bunting.

AIR BUNT

Purpose: To evaluate and practice bunting technique.

Procedure: The coach calls a particular bunt, and the team acts as bunters assuming proper position in an imaginary batter's box. On the command "Ball," batters execute the basic movement. The emphasis is on proper bat angle and contact spot, good balance, and using the legs (think elevator) to lower the body for low pitches.

PARTNER FRONT SOFT TOSS

Purpose: To develop bat and ball control while bunting. This drill allows many repetitions in a small area and in a short time.

Procedure: Players practice all bunting skills using any type of ball. One player tosses underhand to the bunter. The players should be about 15 feet (4.5 m) apart. They use Wiffle balls when practicing chops, slashes, and slaps. The batter must begin in a bunting position because there is no time to pivot.

PEPPER

Purpose: To develop bat and ball control while bunting. This drill allows many repetitions in a small area and in a short time. Pepper is a good activity for keeping players warm while waiting for a game.

Procedure: Three or four players stand side by side and face a batter about 10 feet (3 m) away. Players field the ball and use an underhand toss to feed the batter, who executes all the short-game skills.

Variation: Play pepper with the hitter slapping the ball. All fielders are positioned to the pitcher's right, and the batter tries to slap all balls to that area. The batter can slap while standing still or with the run.

TARGET BUNTING

Purpose: To work on placing bunts in a target area under gamelike pressure.

Procedure: Use cones, rope, or chalk to mark the area in front of home plate where the bunt should be placed. Players bunt off of a machine and run to first so that the drill is gamelike. If the bunt is successful and in the targeted area, the batter runs to first and then returns to the end of the bunting line. If the bunt is unsuccessful, the batter runs around all four bases before returning to the bunting line.

FOUR-CORNER BUNTING

Purpose: To practice all types of bunts.

Procedure: Place a bunter at each corner of the infield, using each base as a home plate. A teammate or coach stands about 20 to 25 feet (6 to 7.5 m) directly in front of each batter and throws pitches to be bunted. Players attempt to place the bunts down the lines. Bunters rotate after five bunts each. The first two bunts go down the third-base line, the next two bunts go down the first-base line, and the last bunt is a squeeze.

SUICIDE SQUEEZE

Purpose: To practice fouling off bad pitches in order to protect the runner.

Procedure: The pitcher stands 10 to 15 feet (3 to 4.5 m) away from the batter and throws bad pitches. The batter must foul off all pitches.

INDOOR SUICIDE SQUEEZE

Purpose: To practice bunting all types of pitches.

Procedure: Two lines of players—throwers and bunters—face each other about 40 feet (12 m) apart. The throwers send short hops to the batters, who bunt all balls as if executing a suicide squeeze. The batters should line up in front of a wall, if possible, so that players don't have to chase missed balls.

BUNTING AND BASERUNNING

Purpose: To practice executing the sacrifice bunt and baserunning.

Procedure: Players form a bunting line at home, and running lines of three players are formed at first and third (see figure 2.7). On defense, use a pitcher and catcher or a machine and several fielders to retrieve the balls. The fielders are close to home; they field bunts and return the balls to the pitcher. The bunter must successfully bunt the first strike and then run to first in the running lane. Failure to bunt successfully or to stay in the running lane means that the player must continue running to right field as a penalty. If the bunter executes everything correctly, she joins the running line after touching first base. The runner on first goes when she sees that the bunt is angled down. On approaching second base, she looks to see if third is open, sees that it is and hits the inside of the base on her turn. She then joins the line at third. The runner at third takes a lead in foul territory and breaks for home when she is sure the bunt is down.

Variation: Batters slap the ball instead of bunting. Base runners go as soon as they see that the ball is hit down.

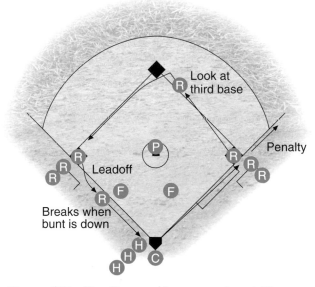

Figure 2.7   Bunting and baserunning drill.

SLAPPER'S FENCE SWING

Purpose: To train the slapper to use the inside-outside swing and to lead with the knob of the bat.

Procedure: The player stands facing a fence that is one bat's length away. She swings without making contact with the fence, leading with the knob and keeping the hands high. She does this with the eyes open and then with the eyes closed to groove the swing. The slapper adds footwork and continues running down the fence line after the swing, as she should on the follow-through.

SLAP AND RUN AROUND CONE

Purpose: To practice running toward the pitcher when slapping.

Procedure: The slapper hits off a pitcher or machine. Place a cone two steps in front of the batter's box, in line with the pitcher. The slapper must run around the cone before heading toward first base. The cone prevents the slapper from turning too early toward first.

ALTERNATE BUNTS AND SLAPS

Purpose: To eliminate telegraphing of the bunt or slap.

Procedure: A batter alternates executing drag bunts and slaps off a pitcher or machine. The emphasis is on keeping movements the same as long as possible. The pitcher or feeder calls "Bunt" or "Slap" when she recognizes what is coming.

TWO TEES

Purpose: To practice getting on the plane that the ball is on and staying there through contact. This drill forces the inside-outside swing.

Procedure: Place a tee at a location on the outside part of home plate. Place an additional tee 3 to 4 feet (1 to 1.5 m) in front of the original tee in the same location. Put a ball on both tees. The slapper tries to hit the first ball into the second ball. If the slapper doesn't stay on the plane that the ball is on through contact, she will be unsuccessful in hitting the second ball.

Variations: Move the tees to different locations. For the advanced slapper, increase the distance between the tees.

BASERUNNING, STEALING, AND SLIDING

T o score, players must reach four bases safely, and they only have three outs to do so. Therefore, unless they can depend on extra-base hits to get them home, they have to get something for nothing. They need to make things happen. Base runners with an aggressive reputation put pressure on the defenders, forcing them to "worry and hurry," which in turn leads to errors on routine plays. Aggressive running can get the team that extra base. Although speed is a great advantage, base runners also need good judgment to know when to go, proper technique to make the most of the speed they have, an aggressive attitude that allows them to take advantage of anything the opposing team offers, and the ability to execute under pressure. Baserunning is one of the few aspects of the game that players can control. Unfortunately, it is often the least practiced and most poorly performed aspect.

Beginners will usually be controlled by the coach and be told when to go and what to do. As players become more experienced, the coach usually gives them more freedom so that they can react on their own within the team's philosophy. The batter, the runner, and the trail runner all have a role to play. Each player must know what is expected of her. Coaches should do chalk talks and make sure to specify exactly what is meant by *halfway, a big leadoff,* and *staying tight.*

Players should practice baserunning whenever they have a chance. They can work on basic techniques on their own daily. Batting practice offers opportunities to develop reactions and work on game situations. Players should practice thinking for themselves. They must get over the fear of making outs and become intelligently reckless base runners who make things happen. Players must anticipate, not just react. They should challenge themselves to become known as dangerous and feared base runners!

IMPROVING SPEED

How important is speed? If a player can improve her speed to first base by one-tenth of a second, her batting average should improve by 50 points. The average defensive play on an infield ground ball takes three seconds at the high school and college level. The goal for the batter, then, is to be able to get to first in less than three seconds.

Everyone can get faster. Speed development should be a year-round conditioning activity. Players can study their running styles by looking at videotapes showing them running to first and around the bases. A track coach can analyze their technique and help them make corrections. By practicing every day, players can ensure that the improved technique becomes habit.

To improve speed, players need to learn proper running technique and concentrate on the following components:

- **Arm action**—The elbows are at a 90-degree angle and close to the body. The arms drive vigorously from the chest down past the hips. The player can think *lip to hip* or *cheek to cheek.* The thumb and forefinger touch lightly in a relaxed manner. The player drives the hands as if holding a hammer and pounding a nail just past her hips. The arms swing straight back and forth, not across the body. (Females tend to swing across the body.) The shoulders are tension free. The faster the arms go, the faster the legs go. To practice, the player should work only on arm action, starting slowly and increasing arm speed. Focus on keeping the shoulders relaxed and using proper arm swing.

- **Knees**—The knees are lifted high to form a 90-degree hip angle, with the toes in an upward position (full flexion at the ankle). Good flexibility in the hamstrings is required to get the legs up high. Stretches, especially toe touches with the knees slightly bent, will increase flexibility.
- **Foot placement**—The feet are straight ahead with the instep touching the outside of an imaginary line going to the target. Running on the balls of the feet produces better spring and keeps the eyes from bouncing so much.
- **Body lean**—The head is up, and the body is tall (erect). The lean is from the ankles, not the hips. Running is continuously losing balance and regaining it.

Being able to accelerate quickly is important in softball because of the short base-paths. To improve acceleration, players should do short sprints (about 5 yards or meters) as well as sprints starting from a prone position on the belly. Players must honestly evaluate the weight they are carrying. At the racetrack, a fast horse is sometimes handicapped by adding a five-pound weight to bring the horse's ability down to that of the other horses in the field. If five pounds can affect a strong racehorse, what does excess weight do to a base runner?

PAWING ACTION

Purpose: To learn to run explosively on the balls of the feet and to lift the knees.

Procedure: The player stands sideways to a fence, working the leg farthest from the fence. She does a butt kick, then lifts the knee high with a forward stretch of the foot. The toes are pointed up toward the sky. She paws the ground with the ball of the foot, just brushing the ground, and then immediately goes back up with a butt kick. The pawing action is repeated continually. The player then performs the exercise with the other leg. The longer the feet are on the ground, the slower the player will be.

ON THE BASES

Speed on the bases begins with an explosion out of the batter's box. Players should then work on the techniques that can improve speed around the bases. They should try to reduce the number of steps required to circle the bases. And they should always be looking for opportunities that get them to the next base and closer to the ultimate goal of scoring.

Out of the Box

To get a fast start, the player must be balanced and on the balls of her feet. She stays low, drives the elbows down, and explodes out of the box. The dominant arm and elbow drive back and outside the hip to initiate the running sequence. She uses a good follow-through on the swing and shifts her weight to the front foot. The bat is dropped with the bottom hand after the swing. The batter then pulls with the front foot instead of lifting it and replanting. Using this pull will improve quickness out of the box. The first step is then with the back foot, pushing hard with the back leg. The second and third steps are short and explosive. These first three steps and strong pumping of the arms propel the player out of the box.

Coaches should time how quickly players get to a line that marks halfway to first, keeping in mind that the times for lefties (under 1 second is the average time for high school and college players) will differ from the times for righties (the average time is 1.4 to 1.5 seconds).

To First Base

The player should develop the habit of running on or to the right side of the first-base line. A runner will be called out if she runs outside the running lane and, in the umpire's opinion, interferes physically or visually with the fielder taking the throw at first. About halfway to first, the runner takes a brief look to locate the ball and decide whether to run through the base or make the turn toward second (see figure 3.1). The runner turns only the head, not the shoulders. As the runner is running to first base, she should concentrate on pumping her arms while also listening and looking (after that halfway peek) for the first-base coach for additional information (hurry, make that turn, and so on).

On a close play, the runner concentrates on a spot 15 feet (4.5 m) beyond the base and runs through the base, being careful not to slow until after touching it. She touches the front of the base to reach it sooner. The runner doesn't lunge or leap at the base because doing so would slow her down and increase the chance of injury. A slide is used at first base only to avoid a tag, because sliding takes longer than running through the base. The runner leans forward as she touches first base and at the same time turns her head toward the coach to look for signals and listen for instructions. She should also look for an overthrow. Players should always run hard, even on routine outs, and they should always touch the base even if they think they are out. The defender may drop the ball or pull her foot off the bag. After touching the base, the runner stops quickly, as close to the base as possible (see figure 3.2). Many runners go far beyond first base when stopping, increasing the distance to second base. They lose valuable time and may eliminate any opportunity to advance. The runner should put on the brakes by straightening up and planting a heel to act as a brake. She then lowers the center of gravity slightly by lowering the hips, and she maintains good balance while taking short, chopping steps. The runner stops on or near the foul line, turns inward (toward the

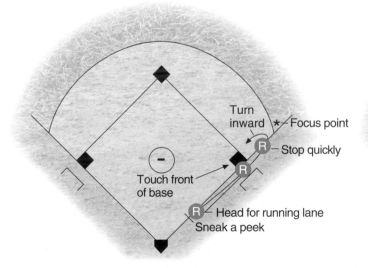

Figure 3.1 Key points on the run to first base.

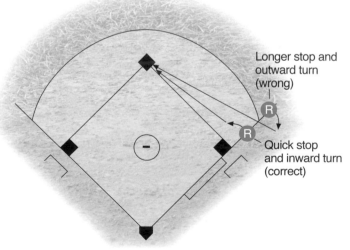

Figure 3.2 A quick stop and inward turn toward second put the runner in the best position to take second.

diamond), and locates the ball. The runner returns immediately to the base without making any movement toward second, but she should be ready to go to second on an overthrow or if the coach tells her to go. The runner should always follow the ball back into the pitcher's glove. Runners who turn away or fail to keep watching—or start a conversation with the coach—often do not see dropped balls or overthrows that could allow them to advance.

On a routine single, the runner makes an aggressive turn and maintains a balanced position (feet spread and hips down) while locating the ball. Only when she can't see the ball does the runner look to the coach for help on whether to run through the base or make the turn. On balls hit up the middle or to right field, the runner can see the ball and save time by making her own decision.

Every time the batter strikes out, she should run to first base, making it a habit even if the rules say she is not entitled to run (runner on first and less than two outs or catcher catches the ball). Running forces the catcher to react. By making it automatic, the runner never misses the opportunity to advance when the catcher drops the ball.

A runner going to first *cannot* back up to avoid a tag. Runners sometimes make this mistake when they bunt and the first-base player is waiting to apply a tag. If the runner backs up, the ball is then dead, the batter is out, and the base runners must return to the base they left.

Leadoffs

The purpose of a leadoff is to entice the defense to throw and make a mistake, to execute a delayed steal, to more easily advance on a passed ball or a ball in the dirt, or to get a good jump on a hit ball.

The runner should always use the same leadoff to avoid tipping off the defense about what she will be doing. The runner leads off aggressively on the release of every pitch to put pressure on the catcher and to be in position to take advantage of a dropped ball. A goal is to have the defense yell "Going" on every leadoff. A good jump is so essential for a successful steal that some coaches tell their players this: "You better be safe stealing or out for leaving early." Be aware that when there are three umpires a runner is more likely to be caught leaving early (if she does) than when there are only two umpires. Players should get a good jump and not be afraid of being called out once in a while. The two basic leadoffs are the rocker start and the stationary start. Players should find the technique that works best and should use it consistently at all bases. Coaches can time players to help them determine which method is fastest.

Rocker Start   The rocker start is the best leadoff because the body is already in motion as the ball is released. A further advantage is that this leadoff is more deceiving to the umpire because it is more difficult to judge exactly when the runner leaves the base. But an inexperienced umpire may react to the runner's movement and call an out, believing that the runner has left too soon even though the back foot is still in contact with the base. And although in theory the rocker start should be the fastest technique, timing it properly can be tricky, and some runners may leave more slowly when they use it. Practice is necessary to develop the proper timing, and runners must study each pitcher's windup to get the maximum advantage.

The left foot is placed at the front edge of the base (facing the next base and farthest from home plate). The right foot is one step behind and to the side of the base so that the runner won't trip (see figure 3.3 on page 54). Weight is over the front foot. Both elbows are bent in running position with the right arm forward. As the pitcher starts

her movement, the runner shifts her weight to the back foot and switches the position of the arms by bringing the right arm back. She begins the motion back as the heel of the pitcher's back leg lifts up. (An alternative timing mechanism is any movement by the pitcher.) As the pitcher starts a downward motion (or lifts the heel of the other leg off the rubber), the runner should be in motion forward, simultaneously pulling down with the left arm and taking a step forward with the right foot. At release, the runner pushes hard off the base with the left foot, using the base as a sprinter would use a starting block.

Figure 3.3 Rocker start.

Stationary Start   When starting from a stationary position, the runner cannot get a jump off the base that is equivalent to the other methods. And the umpire can more easily judge when the runner leaves the base, so she must be careful not to cheat by leaving early. However, the stationary start is easy to execute.

The runner is either in a forward-stride position with the arms in running position (see figure 3.4a) or in a sideways position with the arms hanging down a little lower, like those of a football lineman (see figure 3.4b). The rear foot is on the edge of the base closest to the base that the runner is advancing to. The runner assumes a well-balanced position, ready to react to the pitcher's movement. She pushes off the base when the pitcher's back heel lifts from the rubber. Doing this is quicker than waiting for the release, and the heel lift is easier to see.

Figure 3.4 Stationary start. *(a)* Forward-stride position and *(b)* sideways position.

Delayed, or Walking, Lead   A more advanced leadoff, the delayed lead has the runner in motion when the bat meets the ball. When the ball is bunted or hit, the base runner is better off being in motion than taking a leadoff, stopping, and restarting. The delayed lead can be used at first or third base in any situation except a straight steal or suicide squeeze. The runner tries to time the start so that she is leaving the base just before ball contact. She reacts to the ball as it approaches the hitter's contact spot. The goal is to be in full motion three steps off the base when the ball is bunted or hit. There is no need to bolt or panic; it is a walking lead. When the ball crosses the plate, the runner is under control and moving forward with catlike steps at the end. (She should never have to fill in dirt where she put on the brakes.) As the runner sees the bunt or hit angled down, she can continue to advance without losing a step or slowing down. If the ball is missed, the runner is no farther off the base than with a normal lead. And the runner will never be called out for leaving early! This is the easiest lead for players to use once they understand the concept. Note that the delayed lead should not be used at second base because the runner should leave on the pitcher's release to take advantage of the five-step lead she should take there.

Leadoff Distance   At first base, the leadoff should be one body length and one step (equal to three steps). This distance allows for a quick step and a dive back on a pickoff attempt. At second base, the lead should be five steps off the base because the runner is farther from the catcher. At third base, the lead is three steps and always in foul territory so that any batted ball that hits the runner is a foul ball and not an out.

At first base the runner leads off at the back of the base. This puts the runner farther from the first-base player if she is covering the base for a pickoff. If the second-base player is covering first for the pickoff, the leadoff should be outside the basepath to cut off the defender's path to the base and the thrown ball. At second base, if it is not a bunting situation, the runner leads off the base slightly to the outfield side to set up a better angle to cut the corner at third. She hits the inside corner with the right foot and goes home hard; this may be a half step slower to third, but it increases the chances for scoring.

After the ball is hit, the runner adjusts the length of the lead according to the location of the ball. When a ball is fielded or hit in the air, the closer the receiver is to the runner, the shorter the lead must be because the runner is more vulnerable to being put out. Conversely, when the ball is on the opposite side of the field, the runner can extend her lead. The runner should know how field conditions will affect footing and how far she can safely go. If the ground is soft or slippery, she should shorten her lead. The base runner does not head back to the base until the pitcher has the ball. She never assumes that the catch is made and always watches for an overthrow or a dropped ball.

The runner at second base must have the mentality that she is going to score on any base hit. If she thinks she will stop at third base, she will not be going as fast as she should be when she approaches third base. At that point, it is too late to accelerate when signaled to go home. She must think *home* and run accordingly.

Tagging Up

When a ball is hit in the air and caught with less than two outs, runners who have left a base must return and tag before they can legally advance. Runners who have remained on the base or who have tagged it may leave again as soon as the ball is touched.

When possible, a runner should watch the ball and the catch herself. She places her feet on the base in position for a good leadoff and turns her head to follow the ball. Making the decision herself eliminates the possibility for miscommunication and allows her to react more quickly. If she has to wait for the coach's command, a slight delay occurs as she registers and reacts to it.

Runners should tag on all foul balls. Runners can advance only on a caught foul ball, so they should always tag and be in position to go. If they can't tell if a ball is fair or foul, they should assume that it is fair. At third base, the runner should tag immediately on deep fly balls as soon as the ball is hit in the air. If the ball is very deep and it is obvious that the runner will advance easily, she should delay leaving a little to eliminate the chance of being called out for leaving early. If this ball is dropped or fumbled, the runner will still score easily. At first or second base, the runner tags only if the fly ball is deep enough that she can advance on the catch and resulting throw.

On shallow fly balls, runners (including a runner at third) *do not* tag because they have no hope of advancing if the ball is caught. From a normal leadoff position, the runner has a better chance of advancing should the ball drop because she is closer to the next base than she would be if she had tagged. The runner leads off as far as she can while still being able to return if the ball is caught.

The goal of all runners is to score. They should be aggressive, go for extra bases, and anticipate. If it appears that the ball will not be caught, runners should be as far away from the base as possible and should be going hard to the next base. They should not tag up! If a fielder makes a spectacular catch, runners can scramble back. This principle applies everywhere except at third.

When a caught fly ball is not deep enough to safely advance on, the base runner at third should still break hard toward home and try to draw a throw there. The goal is to get the defense to yell that she is going home so the defense will throw there. Once the throw is made, the runner from third should put on the brakes but maintain a balanced position (feet spread and hips down), ready to go either direction—back if the throw is on line to the catcher and forward to score if the ball is not caught by the catcher. The runner tracks the ball's flight all the way home, ready to react. She stops close enough to third to get safely back if necessary.

BETWEEN BASES

When a runner is between bases, she must always know where the ball is. She stays low, balanced, and ready to react forward or backward. She assumes a crouch position like a football lineman, with weight equally distributed, feet shoulder-width apart, and hips down. The runner doesn't lean or commit either way until the defense gives her a reason to go. The eyes are on the ball, and the arms hang loosely so she is ready to react either way. When she goes, she uses the same footwork that she uses when fielding a ground ball to that side (see chapter 6). The first step is a jab step, and a crossover step follows. The runner pushes off hard on the jab step and drives with the elbows to increase acceleration.

The base runner should stay in the path of the thrown ball. Whenever possible, she should interfere legally with the throw and make it more difficult for the defensive player to throw to the target. If the ball hits the runner, everyone should advance safely. But the runner should not sacrifice speed. A straight line is still the fastest route between two points, so she should not veer too far off line.

Whenever possible, runners should avoid being tagged out by a defensive player. A base runner is allowed to leave the basepath by 3 feet (1 m) to avoid a tag. With multiple base runners, a player who can't avoid a tag should stop and make the defense chase her, giving the other runners time to advance. Remember that a runner going to first base may never back up to avoid a tag. Runners must attempt to avoid contact with the defensive player fielding the ball because that also results in a dead ball.

When the base runners must return to a base, they should always hustle back. A careless return can result in an out on a quick throw or when a defensive player blocks the base. Runners should be prepared to dive back on any pickoff throw. Ideally, the runner dives to the back corner of the base farthest from the throw. But if the defensive player has blocked that corner, the runner must adjust to find an open corner. She starts the dive from a lowered body position using a swimmer's diving start. She takes a small jab step with the left foot toward the base, pivots to face it, and then lies out flat, reaching for the base with the closer hand. The arm and hand reach for the base just above the ground (see figure 3.5). The base runner should protect her fingers from injury by making a fist or half fist, and she should protect her face by turning away from the throw. After touching the base, she keeps the tagging hand on the base, holds her position, and listens for the coach's instruction or the umpire's call so that she knows what the next move is.

If the runner returns standing up, she tags the corner farthest from the throw and leans slightly away from the receiver, being careful not to lean too much and lose her balance as the tag is made. The defender covering the base may push with the tag, hoping the runner breaks contact with the base and the umpire calls her out.

Figure 3.5   **Diving back to the base.**

AROUND THE BASES

The shortest distance between two points is a straight line, and the goal is to take the shortest and quickest route possible. Each player's stride length is different, so players should count the number of steps they take to go from home to home; they should work to reduce that number throughout the season. For a tight, efficient turn, the runner angles 3 or 4 feet (1 m or so) to the right as she comes within 10 to 15 feet (3 to 4.5 m) of the base. This maneuver puts her in position to make the turn at the bag. She concentrates on the spot that she must run at to make the correct turn, and she runs to it in a straight line. The desired turn is as close to a right angle as possible. She tries to hit the inside corner of first base and second base with the left foot. To produce a sharp turn, the runner leans to the inside of the base and dips the left shoulder as the right leg swings over the planted left foot. She does not shuffle her feet or break stride. If the right foot will hit the inside corner, she tightens the turn by exaggerating the inside lean and throwing her head and shoulder toward the pitcher.

If the ball is not in front of her as she approaches second base, the runner picks up the third-base coach to get help. About 15 feet before the base, she turns only her head, not the shoulders, to see the coach. At third base, she uses the right foot on the inside corner to cut the distance going home.

How fast is fast? It is relative to the player's age level. The average college runner makes it to first base in about 3.1 seconds. Fast is 2.7. Coaches can time runners from bat–ball contact at home (anticipating contact while starting the watch) to the foot touching the base at first. They can also time runners from a standing start. The times in table 3.1 are from a standing start at home, not a swing. With a swing, times would be about .5 seconds slower.

Table 3.1 Standing Start Times for College Players

	Home to 1st (righty)	Home to 1st (lefty)	2nd to home	1st to 2nd	Home to home
Slow	Above 3.0 seconds	Above 3.0 seconds	Above 6 seconds	3.3 seconds	Above 12.5 seconds
Average	3.0 seconds	2.7-2.8 seconds	5.75 seconds		11.5-12.0 seconds
Good	2.8 seconds	2.5-2.6 seconds	5.3-5.5 seconds	2.99 seconds	11.0-11.3 seconds
Great	2.6 seconds	2.3-2.4 seconds	5.2 seconds or lower		10.8 seconds or lower

From Cindy Bristow at softballexcellence.com

WILD PITCHES

The aggressive, alert base runner watches the pitch all the way to the plate and antici-pates where it will go. For example, a low ball that is headed down has a good chance of being a wild pitch or a passed ball. The alert base runner is ready to react to that pitch and advance to the next base if the ball bounds a safe distance away from the catcher. The runner cannot wait for a coach to tell her to go; that is too late! She reacts imme-diately and slides hard into the next base. A runner who hesitates should stay. Some runners will have the green light to automatically go on any ball going down. Coaches can create a "Ball in the Dirt Club" that players join when they steal on a ball in the dirt.

RUNDOWNS

If caught in a rundown, the runner should keep moving. She must stay alive as long as possible, using quick changes of direction, head fakes, and changes of speed. She should stay as far from the throw as possible by changing direction as soon as the ball leaves the thrower's hand. The more throws the defense makes, the greater the chance they will make an error.

COACHING POINTS FOR BASERUNNING

- Read the ball off the bat, focusing on the contact spot.

- With no outs, be a little more conservative; with one out, be more aggressive.

- Study the defense before and throughout the game. Know each player's arm strength and accuracy. Know the position of each defensive player when the ball is hit. Always look for something to take advantage of. Is the fielder off balance? Is the defense asleep? Are they making lazy throws?

- Review the situation and how you should respond to every swing and hit—number of outs, game situation, and defensive alignment.

- Don't hesitate. When you have made up your mind, don't change it—go hard.

- Advance on balls hit behind you if the defense is back and you have a good possibility for success.

- When forced to run to the next base, go hard and slide hard to break up the double play.

- Know the rules. Understand infield fly, interference and obstruction, delayed calls, and the third-strike rule.

- Adjust your lead based on the throwing distance for the pickoff. The shorter the throwing distance, the more vulnerable you are to being picked off.

- Never leave a base until you are sure the umpire has called you out.

- Understand that on an attempted pickoff at third, the trailing runner has to go to second. Do not stand still and watch the play! If you are the trailing runner, always go hard to the next base.

Players can use the following strategies to get out of a rundown:

- **Try to trip a hard-charging defensive player.** Drop to the ground in front of her at the last second. Then get up quickly and run in the opposite direction.

- **Try to pick up a defensive obstruction call.** Look for a defensive player who has just thrown the ball and is still in the basepath. As soon as the ball is thrown, turn in the direction of the basepath and run into the player who has just thrown it. Then alert the umpire by calling "Obstruction." Continue the play until you are sure that the call is made in your favor.

- **Try to step into the ball.** Watch the thrower's eyes because they will indicate which way the ball is coming. Then step into it.

With two runners on base, the runner in the rundown tries to draw several throws to make time for the other runner to advance. If a runner is caught between third and home, the trailing runner should get to third base, and the lead runner should try to go home. The lead runner should not attempt to go back to third because the other runner should be safely there. If the defense is playing on the trailing runner, she should try to gain time for the lead runner to make it home.

If two runners end up on one base, one runner should hold tight on the base and be safe. The fastest runner should stay on the base; the slower runner should step off and get tagged out. The runners should not create an easy double play by both leaving the base. Let the defense chase or tag one runner and get only one out.

ON-DECK BATTER

The on-deck batter has more to do than prepare for her at-bat. With runners attempting to score, she takes a position behind home plate in a direct line with the runner but out of the way of the catcher and umpire. She assists runners by telling them whether to slide or stand up and by directing them to one side of the plate or the other. She uses hand signals to indicate up or down and left or right, and she should use verbal cues as well. With a runner on third base, she assumes an on-deck position closer to home plate than normal so that she can get to her position in time.

STEALS

Base runners have a greater chance of scoring if they can get to the next base without using up an out! The steal is an effective way to get into scoring position. A runner at first base with two outs must find a way to get to second. Not much can happen if she stays at first. Baserunning techniques for the steal are covered here. "When" and "why" to steal are covered under team offense in chapter 4.

The batter's job is to protect the runner on the steal. She moves deeper in the box to make the catcher's throw longer. If a runner is stealing third, a right-handed batter should also back away from the plate to hinder the catcher's view of third. The batter can further hinder the catcher's vision by beginning the swing and leaving the bat over the plate with the end of the barrel pointed at the catcher's eyes as she stands to throw. The batter can also create some confusion among the fielders by using fake slaps, fake bunts, and swinging and missing to freeze the defense and delay their base coverage. Even on a pitchout, the batter must do her best to legally interfere with the catcher's attempt to throw out the runner.

Straight Steal   The element of surprise is a big factor in a successful steal. The runner takes off for the next base when the pitcher releases the ball. The runner goes directly to the base and prepares to slide hard into the glove if she and the ball are arriving at the same time. The slide is away from the tag if the ball is already there. If the ball goes through, the runner must get up quickly and be ready to advance to the next base. The easiest base to steal is third base because you only have to beat one player: the shortstop.

Delayed Steal   The element of surprise is also the key to success with the delayed steal. The runner should have good game sense, good observation skills, quick reactions, and good sliding skills. She does not have to be the fastest player on the field—just the smartest! The runner takes a normal lead and then breaks for the next base as the ball is returned to the pitcher or thrown behind her. She can use the delayed steal on the battery, on the defense, or on a throw behind her.

- To execute the delayed steal on the battery, the runner looks for a lazy return to the pitcher or looks for a pitcher not looking her back. On the return to the pitcher, the runner goes as the ball leaves the catcher's hand.

- To use the delayed steal on the defense, the runner watches for the covering defensive player to vacate the base (walk away from the base) as the ball is returned to the pitcher. This often happens at second base, and an alert runner can easily reach the unattended base.
- To set up the delayed steal on a throw behind her, the runner can take a slightly longer lead to entice the catcher into making a pickoff throw. The runner breaks on the release of the ball to the base.

Double Steal   Two runners on base can use either a straight steal or a delayed steal. Signals should be used so that everyone knows what will happen. Both runners break on the pitch or throw, and they slide hard into the next base.

Slap-and-Steal   On the slap-and-steal, the runner goes on the pitch. The batter shows bunt and then slaps the ball. This play forces the middle infielders to worry about both covering the base and playing the ball. With a runner at first, a ball hit at the shortstop will keep her from covering second. Because the second-base player is moving to cover first base, second base is open. The runner turns just her head to make sure the ball is hit on a downward angle. If the ball is popped up, the runner puts on the brakes and hustles back.

Hit-and-Run   The runner goes on the pitch, and the hitter's job is to make contact. Ideally, the ball is hit on the ground and behind the runner. The runner must listen for contact, try to see if the ball is hit down or up, and listen for coaching help. She glances toward home on the third or fourth step to try to pick up the ball.

SLIDING

The ability to slide and the desire to do so are two important facets of aggressive baserunning. All players must be willing and able to slide in a variety of situations. Sliding should be mandatory unless it is obvious to the runner that the slide is unnecessary or she is given a signal to stand up. Good base runners know how to slide and which slide to use, and they practice sliding to become comfortable and proficient. Learning the proper techniques and practicing them give players confidence and help eliminate the fear of sliding.

Players should slide

- to go full speed to a base without overrunning it,
- to avoid a collision,
- to attempt to avoid a tag,
- to break up a double play,
- to knock the ball out of the fielder's glove, and
- on any close play!

After the slide, the runner must get quickly to her feet so that she is ready to advance to the next base. Fear of being hurt while sliding makes a base runner tentative and can cause injury rather than prevent it. A proper slide must be executed at full speed; if a player slows down, she is susceptible to injury. A player must not leap, jump, or tumble into a slide and must never slow down to prepare for one.

Sliding comes very naturally to most children, especially athletic ones. Coaches should teach players when they are young—before the fear factor is an issue. The progressions and drills at the end of this chapter will help players master the slide. As with many of the skills required in softball, players should experiment with all the techniques and use whichever slide works best for them and fits the situation.

Bent-Leg Slide

Players should first master the bent-leg slide, which is the most basic slide. It is the safest slide and the foundation for the pop-up slide. The base runner goes straight to the base without losing any speed. She starts the slide approximately 10 feet (two or three steps) from the bag. The distance will vary for each player, so players must practice to figure out what works. The slide should be started far enough away for the player to get under the tag, yet close enough for the player to reach the base quickly. The lead foot is extended, and the opposite leg is bent at a 45-degree angle and tucked under the forward leg. It doesn't matter which leg is bent under, though bending the left leg makes it easier to roll to the left and look to the next base. However, most players will favor one or the other, so work on this leg first.

Here is a method for determining the player's preferred leg: The player assumes a crab-walk position (the feet and hands on the ground, the belly up, and the back off the ground). When instructed to fall backward while tucking one leg under the other, the player will tuck the leg that feels most natural for her, and the legs will form a perfect figure four.

To perform the bent-leg slide (see figure 3.6), the runner leans back, extends the arms out like an airplane, and extends the striding foot (preferably the right foot) toward the bag as if kicking a soccer ball. The arms are high and out to the side for balance. The takeoff leg is bent and tucked under the knee of the forward leg. The runner goes straight to the bag because the goal is to touch it as quickly as possible. There is no leap or jump or loss of speed in the transition from the run to the takeoff.

The laces of the bottom foot face the base; the foot is slightly off the ground. The top leg is slightly bent with the kneecap facing up and with the foot about 6 inches (15 cm)

Figure 3.6 Bent-leg slide.

off the ground so the spikes don't catch. Keeping the knee slightly bent allows the leg to give at impact and prevents locked-knee injuries.

The runner falls on her butt and the upper part of the bottom leg. She does not slide on the side of the knees or legs. The body slides horizontally to the ground and is often turned slightly toward the bent-leg side. The buttocks and the upper portion of the tucked leg should absorb the impact.

The arms and hands are thrown over the head or across the chest to protect them, as well as to lessen the impact with the ground. The runner must be careful not to drag the hands on the ground. The chin is tucked to keep the head from hitting the ground, and the eyes are on the base. The back and shoulder blades are close to the ground, and the body stays low. The runner hits the base with the lead toe or heel.

Pop-Up Slide

To execute the pop-up slide, runners use the bent-leg slide, contact the base, and pop up to a standing position at the base, ready to advance to the next base. This slide is used when the runner realizes that no play is being made or that the throw is well off target. She should be able to read the situation just before she commits to this slide. For the pop-up slide, the player uses the same techniques as for the bent-leg slide, with these exceptions:

- The front leg is braced against the base at contact (the instep of the foot), and the shin of the bent leg is simultaneously pressed against the ground. The runner throws her head, shoulders, and chest forward and upward, keeping the arms across the chest or out in front of her (see figure 3.7).

- The slide is slightly later (to maintain speed going into the base), and the body is in a more upright or sitting position. Momentum will then throw the body upward and pop the slider to a sitting and then a standing position.

To learn the pop-up slide, players should practice standing up from a sitting position without using the hands. They can also lie flat in the bent-leg position and practice getting to a sitting position by bringing the arms to the chest while bending at the waist.

Figure 3.7 Pop-up slide.

Hook Slide

The hook slide is a technique in which the base runner slides to the side of the base instead of straight toward it. This puts greater distance between the base runner and the fielder, allowing the runner to avoid the tag. The defensive position of the receiver and the position of the throw determine which side runners will slide to. The throw is generally inside, so runners will usually be going outside, away from the defensive player.

The traditional hook slide involves bending the bag-side leg in a hurdle-stretch position and tagging the bag with the toes as the runner slides past the base. To hook slide to the right, the runner slides to a spot 2 to 3 feet (about 1 m) outside and beyond the base. She starts the slide late and extends the right foot past the bag so the left foot will hook the front corner of the bag's outfield side. The runner kicks the right foot forward and turns the ankle to the right so the outside of the foot slides along the ground. She leans to the right and drops the right shoulder. The outside of the right calf and the right hip absorb most of the impact. The body is flat with the head up. The eyes must stay on the inside corner of the base. The left leg is straight with a slight bend at the knee as the sliding player reaches toward the corner of the base. She touches the base with the shoelaces of the back foot. The toes of the left foot catch the corner of the base, causing the leg to bend (see figure 3.8). As the runner slides, she pushes the left shoulder and left hip down to the ground to keep the body from rolling to the right. For a slide to the left, the footwork is reversed.

Figure 3.8 Hook slide.

However, just as players are right- or left-legged in the bent-leg slide, they also have a good and bad leg in the hook slide. Most players have a difficult time hook sliding to their weak side, often getting their footwork mixed up or slowing down as they try to remember which leg goes where. This is where the bent-leg slide can be used. The runner slides to the side of the bag using the bent-leg technique and touches the bag with an extended hand instead of the foot.

Headfirst Slide

The headfirst slide is the fastest slide because it allows all the forward momentum of the run to continue. This slide is also the easiest to learn; it's just a glide and slide. But the headfirst slide has several drawbacks. This slide can't be used to break up a double play, and the runner can't recover quickly and continue to the next base. In addition, a headfirst slide is dangerous because contact is made with the hands, and the head and arms are in a vulnerable position. This slide should *never* be used at home, where the catcher can block the plate, because of the increased risk of injury.

To execute the headfirst slide, the player uses the same technique as when diving back to a base. She runs full speed to within 10 feet (3 m) of the bag, bends forward, and dives low to the base as if gliding on the top of the water. She bends the knees to get closer to the ground and uses a swimmer's diving start. (Note that players should

Figure 3.9 Headfirst slide.

never use a volleyball dive from a more upright position; if they do, they will stick on the ground and can easily hurt their back.) The force is horizontal as the player slides or glides along the ground. She swings both arms forward while keeping the head up to look for the base. The back is arched slightly as she slides on the lower belly and upper thighs. The feet, elbows, and hands are off the ground; the fingers are closed in fists for protection (see figure 3.9). The runner must keep the head slightly up as she slides so that she can see which side of the bag to go to depending on the location of the infielder and the ball. As the play is made, the slider protects her face by turning away from the action. From this position, she can easily spot the ball if it goes through and possibly advance to the next base.

Rollover Slide

Runners use the rollover slide to get around a defensive player who is blocking the plate. This slide can also be executed when the ball is already there and waiting. The player executes a bent-leg slide away from the base and reaches for the bag with the hand. If the infielder makes the mistake of reaching out to tag the hand, the runner pulls it away, rolls her body over, and touches the base with the other hand. This is a last-ditch effort when the play has the runner beaten, and it is sometimes called "going through the back door." The player does a bent-leg slide, but starts it late. She slides on her back to a spot 3 to 4 feet (1 to 1.5 m) outside and beyond the base. The left arm is extended out to the side. As she slides by the base, she pulls the left arm in sharply to the left side of the body and throws the right arm to the base, helping the body roll over to the belly (see figure 3.10a). After completing the roll, she reaches for the base with the right hand (see figure 3.10b).

Figure 3.10 Rollover slide. (a) Pull the left arm sharply to the left side and throw the right arm to the base. (b) Reach for the base with the right hand after completing the roll.

Slide Away

This is essentially the rollover slide without the barrel roll. The base runner slides past the base and grabs it with the inside hand and arm fully extended. She slides just past the base and reaches for it.

Learning to Slide

The methods, progression, and drills presented in this chapter can be employed with equal success indoors or outdoors. The younger the players are when they start to slide, the easier it is for them to learn. Younger players are usually fearless and eager to try. At no time should coaches use a sliding pit to teach sliding. The bed is too soft, and the player cannot slide into the base. As a result, the player learns to take off too close to the base and does not learn to land properly.

The best learning surface is a grassy area free of debris and sprinklers. In the beginning, players should not wear shoes. As the player becomes proficient, she can wear her shoes. Long pants, sliding pads, knee and elbow pads, and gardening gloves will help protect against abrasions. Players should wear helmets to protect the back of the head.

If a real base is used to teach sliding, it should be loose. Other safe objects can also be used. A large, heavy cardboard box (a refrigerator box from an appliance store or a large box from an auto body shop) can be flattened out to create a smooth sliding surface. Place it on the outfield grass and have your players, one by one, run 60 feet (18 m) and slide onto the box. For indoor sliding practice, place the flattened box on top of firm wrestling mats. Slip-and-slides or tarps are great fun outdoors and are a perfect way to end practice on a hot day. Just make sure the players have dry clothes for the ride home. With tarps, you can use swimming pool noodles to separate areas for different lines of sliders. The very best tool is the Slide Rite sliding mat from Schutt Manufacturing. It has a canvas sliding sheet over a cushioned mat. This can be used as a station for sliding and diving drills at practice every day. (I made my own using an old wrestling mat and a piece of canvas material secured at one end of the mat with duct tape.)

COACHING POINTS FOR THE SLIDE

- Always slide on a close play unless you hear a coach telling you to stand up!

- Never change your mind when sliding! Once you start to slide, finish it hard.

- Slide into the base, not through the base, except at home.

- When sliding into home plate, use the bent-leg slide: slide late and slide hard.

- Slide into first only when the throw is off line and the first-base player is trying to put a tag on you.

- Check the infield surface before the game so you can make necessary adjustments. Is it hard? Soft? Are the bases level? Is home plate raised? Are corners protruding?

Players can progress through the following sequence to become fearless, proficient sliders:

1. Players sit on the floor or grass and alternate placing one leg straight and the other in the bent-leg tucked position. Putting their hands behind their body while in the sitting position, they push themselves forward on the floor or grass. This step gets players used to the position and helps them figure out which side is more comfortable.

2. Players sit with legs crossed and extend the right foot (preferably). They lie down, grab their ears, and then extend their arms overhead as they lift the legs slightly and feel the correct body position.

3. From a standing position, players put the arms out like the wings of an airplane, then kick an imaginary soccer ball with the lead foot. Then they bend the opposite leg and sit down (landing on the buttocks) without their hands touching the ground. (If necessary, coaches on both sides of the player can support the arms to help bear the player's weight as she first sits down.)

4. Bat drill: Two coaches hold a bat horizontal and chest high, supporting the bat at both ends. The player runs under the bat, grabs it with both hands (palms forward), and kicks her foot forward. The coaches lower the bat, helping the player get into a sliding position.

5. Players bend and tuck the left leg under the extended right leg, throw the hands overhead (like a football referee signaling a touchdown), and lie down. They carry grass or small rocks in each hand so that they are not tempted to use their hands to break the fall.

6. From a half-speed run, players slide on a wet surface. Gradually, they increase speed and distance. Slip-and-slides, sheets of plastic, tarps, cardboard, or a Slide Rite can be used as a sliding surface, but players must work on proper technique and not goof off.

7. Players practice in the infield. Using a loose base will reduce the chance of a jammed ankle. The dirt in the sliding area should be loosened, and players should wear protective clothing.

BASERUNNING DRILLS

Base runners must learn to react to the ball off the bat, the position of the hit, and the fielder's play and must make many decisions on their own. Only through practice with gamelike situations can runners learn to react quickly and correctly. The following drills will help players develop baserunning skills. In addition, players should take every opportunity to run the bases during batting practice.

CATCH THE TENNIS BALL

Purpose: To develop quickness out of the box.

Procedure: The batter takes a normal swing and hits the top of a batting tee set at the front of the plate. She then breaks for first while attempting to catch a tennis ball dropped by the coach. The coach stands on the edge of the basepath and drops the tennis ball from eye level onto a flat board just as the bat hits the tee. The runner tries to catch the tennis ball before it bounces a second time. The coach starts close to home plate so the batter can easily catch the ball and then gradually increases the distance to challenge her.

Variation: This drill can also be done at first base, working on aggressive leads there: The coach drops the ball, starting close to the base, and the runner has to catch it before it hits the ground a second time. As the coach increases the distance from the base, the runner will need a more aggressive leadoff to get to the ball.

HOME TO FIRST

Purpose: To practice techniques for running to first, including developing quickness out of the batter's box.

Procedure: This drill requires a batter, a feeder or tosser, and five scattered defensive receivers. The remaining players rotate running to first. The first-base running lane needs to be drawn. The batter–runner hits a ball off a soft toss or a machine and focuses on getting quickly out of the box. She heads to the center of the running lane. Working with the first-base coach, she either makes a turn for second or runs straight through the base, pulling up short as soon as she hits the bag. The coach can use a chalk line or a cone at the side of the basepath as a reminder of when to look briefly at the play. The runner rotates to the first-base coaching box and watches to see if the next runner touches the front half of the base. She then rotates to the end of the line at home.

FOUL-LINE LEADOFFS

Purpose: To practice maintaining a balanced position after leading off.

Procedure: A pitcher uses second base as the mound (so that all players can see the pitch) and throws easily to a catcher near the pitcher's rubber. All runners are on the outfield foul line and use it as the base. They lead off on the pitcher's motion, take three steps, and assume a well-balanced position, ready to go in either direction. They then react to the coach's command of "Back" or "Go." On "Go," they run three or four steps and then return to the foul line to repeat the drill. Run the drill on both foul lines so that runners become accustomed to watching the pitcher's release from both sides.

TIMING THE JUMP

Purpose: To develop a quick reaction to the pitcher's release.

Procedure: The pitcher throws full speed to the catcher with runners at first base. Two coaches are at first with whistles. One blows a whistle when the ball is released, and the other blows a whistle when the runner's foot leaves the base. Players can measure their reaction time by how close the two whistles are. Alternatively, a video camera can be placed behind first base, and players can view the difference between the pitcher's release and the runner's leadoff.

HOW FAR FROM FIRST?

Purpose: To determine how far a player can lead off first base and still get back.

Procedure: Begin with several outfielders in left field with a bucket of balls and a first-base player in position. A runner is at first base, and extra runners are set up on the foul line so they can lead off and check their distance too. All the runners take leads as the first outfielder picks up a ball, holds it up in the air, and then throws to first as the runners attempt to get back. The next outfielder picks up a ball as the runners again take a lead. This drill can be done at other bases as well and from different field positions.

LEADOFFS WITH MULTIPLE RUNNERS

Purpose: To practice leadoffs at each base. The entire team can participate.

Procedure: With a pitcher throwing to a catcher, runners at each base work on getting a good jump; runners take three steps at first and third and five steps at second. Several runners work at each base. Each group completes three leadoffs at a base before rotating to the next base.

PICKOFFS

Purpose: To practice leadoffs and steals while working on defense as well.

Procedure: The defense assumes regular positioning. Runners start at first (wearing helmets). One runner at a time goes around all the bases. The pitcher throws a pitch, and the runner takes a lead at first. The catcher then attempts a pickoff with the runner diving back. On the second pitch, the runner steals second. On the third pitch, the runner steals third. The fourth pitch is a wild pitch or passed ball, and the runner goes home, giving the pitcher and catcher an opportunity to practice covering home.

Variation: Use a candy incentive. Place candy at the distance you would like the runners to be when leading off first. If they can grab the candy and get back safely, they can keep the candy.

WATCH AND TAKE ADVANTAGE

Purpose: To practice holding the leadoff until the pitcher has the ball.

Procedure: A pitcher with a bucket of balls on the mound throws to a catcher. Runners form a line behind first base and go one at a time (or several line up on the foul line, using it as their base, and go all at once). The runners work to get a good jump on the leadoff and then to maintain a balanced position until the ball is successfully returned to the pitcher. The catcher occasionally overthrows the pitcher, or the pitcher drops the ball. The runners look for errors and react by going to second.

FOOTBALL UP AND DOWN

Purpose: To develop the agility and quickness needed to escape a rundown.

Procedure: In staggered rows, players assume well-balanced positions as if between bases. The coach faces the players and gives hand signals to indicate the direction in which players should move (right, left, down, and up). Players shuffle to the side on right and left signals. On the down signal, they quickly hit the ground, absolutely flat. On the up signal, they get up quickly in order to be ready to go again. (In a rundown, players use the prone position to trip the defensive player.)

FIRST TO THIRD

Purpose: To practice picking up the coach's signal when running from first to third.

Procedure: The drill uses a right fielder, second-base player (for the relay), third-base player, and catcher. Runners line up behind first. The coach fungo hits to the right fielder. The runner assumes a three-step leadoff before the hit. On the hit, the runner approaches second and looks to the third-base coach for the signal to stop or continue to third. If stopped, the runner makes an aggressive turn and finds the ball. She returns to the end of the line, and the next runner goes. The right fielder throws to the second-base relay or the third-base player depending on the depth of the hit. The ball is then returned to the catcher at home for the next fungo.

SACRIFICE FLY WITH RUNNERS

Purpose: To practice tagging at third on sacrifice flies with outfielders throwing home.

Procedure: The drill requires outfielders, a catcher, and runners at third. Fungo fly balls are hit in front of the outfielders. A runner at third base assumes a leadoff, tags, and then goes home on the catch. The on-deck batter moves into position to help. The runner can slide or swing wide of the catcher to avoid contact. The drill offers an opportunity for outfielders to work on throws under gamelike conditions. The drill can also be performed off ground balls. The runner rotates to the on-deck circle and then returns to the base running line.

READ THE BALL IN THE DIRT

Purpose: To improve the base runner's reactions and reads and the catcher's blocking skills.

Procedure: A pitcher or coach takes the mound, and a catcher in full gear sets up behind the plate. A line of base runners is at each base. One runner at each base leads off on the pitch to the plate. The pitcher has three choices of pitches to throw: a fastball, a ball in the dirt, or a wild pitch. If it's a fastball, the runners must act as if they are about to get picked off—they should dive back to the bag, then get up quickly and sprint to the next base as if the throw was bad. If the pitch is a ball in the dirt, the runners read the angle down before the ball hits the dirt, and they go to the next base; players at third must determine if they can go home or not. If the pitch is a wild pitch, players at third must be ready to score or must read the quick bounce back off the wall.

SCORING FROM SECOND

Purpose: To practice coaching the runner going home.

Procedure: Outfielders and a catcher take their positions, and the remaining players form a line to run from second base (see figure 3.11). One runner is in the on-deck circle. The hitter fungo hits singles to the outfield. The runner is going all the way unless the third-base coach, who slides down the line to help, stops her. The on-deck batter moves into position at home to help the runner. The runner slides or swings wide (to avoid contact) as she approaches home. Runners rotate to the on-deck circle and then to the running line as the drill continues.

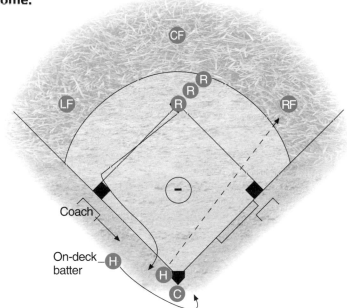

Figure 3.11 Scoring from second drill.

TEAM RACING

Purpose: To develop aggressive turns around the bases.

Procedure: Divide the team into two teams: One lines up at home, and the other at second base. On the coach's signal, the lead runner from each line runs the four bases. When a player gets back to where she started, she tags the next teammate in line, who continues the run. The team that finishes first wins. If this drill is played at the end of practice, have the losing team bring the bases in.

STRETCHING A SINGLE TO A DOUBLE

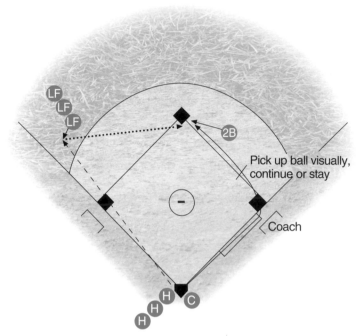

Figure 3.12 Stretching a single to a double drill.

Purpose: To practice making an aggressive turn at first.

Procedure: The drill requires three left fielders, a second-base player, a catcher, and a first-base coach. Batters form a line behind home plate (see figure 3.12). A batter fungo hits a single near the left-field line. The batter-runner takes an aggressive turn toward second. If the ball is not fielded cleanly or if the outfielder is not alert, the runner advances to second. The runner visually picks up the ball as soon as she rounds first; the first-base coach assists the runner.

BEAT THE BALL HOME

Purpose: To throw with speed around the four bases; to run fast enough to beat the ball home.

Procedure: Infielders are in their normal defensive positions. The batter-runner tosses a ball to herself and hits a ground ball. She then runs around the bases trying to beat the ball to home plate. The defense fields the ground ball and throws to first. The ball is then thrown around the horn (second to third to home) in a race to beat the runner. (The runner must wear a helmet for protection against errant throws.) Players cover the bases as they would in a game. With inexperienced teams, the race will be about even.

Variation: Advanced players must throw the ball back to first before advancing it to the next base.

LET HER RIP

Purpose: To allow players to have fun while working on baserunning and conditioning.

Procedure: Divide the squad into two teams: One team (the offense) will bat and is grouped at home plate, and the other team (the defense) will be chasing the ball. Half of the defensive group is at third base, and the other half is at first. The first batter hits off a soft toss or self-toss. She then gets a point for every base she touches before the two defensive players (coming from third and first) both touch the hit ball. Continue until all players on the offensive team have hit. Then the teams rotate. Play as many innings as time permits, keeping the overall score. This is a fun way to end practice!

BANG THE BATS

Purpose: To allow the coach to observe mechanics for every baserunning situation.

Procedure: Players form two lines of runners at home; the inside line is slightly ahead of the other line and to the inside of the basepath. The coach is at the pitcher's rubber holding two bats. When the coach bangs the bats together, the leader of each line runs to first. The runner in the inside line runs through first base, beating out an infield hit. The runner in the outside line makes the turn and goes to second. Now there are runners at first and second as well as lines at home. At the next bang of the bats, the first players in the lines at home follow their teammates to first and second. At the same time, the runner who was at second goes home, and the runner who was at first goes to third. Now every base is occupied. At the next bang, the runner at third tags and scores, while the others run the previous patterns. Two runners will now score with each bang of the bats. After scoring, runners go to the end of the opposite line to continue.

SLIDING DRILLS

Some players will find it difficult to slide in practice because there is no real pressure to get to the base. However, players must practice their technique in order to improve. Make sliding practice as gamelike as possible so that players are prepared to slide well when it counts.

COACH ASSIST

Purpose: To introduce basic sliding techniques and alleviate the fear of sliding.

Procedure: Two coaches stand on each side of a sliding mat. With their back hand, they take the slider's hand and assist the player through the slide. The coaches keep their knees bent and go with the player. Eventually, have the players only hit the coaches' hands as they make their slides.

Coaches can also run with the player, holding the player's hand as she kicks out and helping lower her gently to the ground.

CUSHIONED HEADFIRST SLIDES

Purpose: To introduce the headfirst sliding technique without high risk of injury.

Procedure: Use wrestling mats placed on a gym floor with a piece of cardboard on top or a grass outfield. Place a movable base 3 feet (1 m) from the end of the mat. Runners react as if stealing, and they begin their stretched-out slide about 10 feet (3 m) from the base.

EVERY BASE SLIDING

Purpose: To improve execution of various types of slides at each base.

Procedure: Three runners are at each base. At first base, the runner takes a lead and then dives back to the bag on a call of "Back" from the coach at first. When the coach says "Go," the first runner at each base runs to the next base and performs a certain slide—for example, a pop-up slide at second base, a hook slide at third base, and a rolloverslide at home. Runners then go to the end of the line to continue the drill and slide to the next base.

REACT TO THE BALL AND PLAY IN LEFT FIELD

Purpose: To practice picking up the ball and reacting to the play in a gamelike situation; to work on sliding technique at second and dive-back technique at first.

Procedure: A coach is in shallow left field with a bucket of balls. The first-base coach is in the first-base coaching box. Runners are in a line at home plate. The first runner runs to first base and makes the turn. The runner then picks up the ball and the left fielder (i.e., the coach holding the ball up high) in left field. If the coach drops the ball, the runner continues on to second and makes a bent-leg slide. If the coach fakes a throw, the runner dives back into first base with a head-first slide. The first-base coach checks for proper technique.

TIMED RUN

Purpose: To practice various slides in a competitive situation.

Procedure: The runner and coach begin at home with a stopwatch. The runner races to first and looks to right field to pick up an imaginary overthrow. She reacts by continuing to second and sliding into that base with a pop-up slide. She reacts to another overthrow and makes a headfirst slide into third. Another overthrow ends with a rollover slide at home. The coach times the runner's trip around the bases and compares it to others.

CHAPTER 4

TEAM OFFENSE

CRITICAL CUE:

Try to win one inning at a time. Players might not score runs each inning but may gain the upper hand in other ways. If no one scored, who applied more pressure? Who had the better at-bats? Who had more line-drive outs? Measuring success each inning by multiple standards keeps players motivated and involved. This translates to a more competitive ball club.

As the old saying goes, you can't win unless you score. And you have to score one more run than your opponent to win a ballgame. Run production, by any means available, should be the only goal of the offense.

The offense gets only three outs to make four bases. As a coach, you must develop a philosophy that makes run production a priority and then get players to buy into the philosophy. Players must be ready to hit, to make outs productive, and, whenever possible, to get something for nothing. The whole team must work together to put runners on base and to get the runners around the bases while making the fewest outs possible.

The players' abilities will largely determine which strategies are successful. For this reason, players must practice all the situations and skills that may be necessary to put their team on top. Every player must be able to execute the fundamental offensive skills called for in any given situation. Although a player may excel in certain areas, no player should be limited to a specific role. At various times, anyone on the team may be called on to execute a bunt or to run the bases.

An ideal winning offense is made up of a power game, a short game, and a running game. The short game and running game put pressure on the defense, and the power game puts pressure on the pitcher and catcher. Players must put the ball in play. The short game is easy to teach and practice (and working on the short game strengthens your own defense by providing the opportunity to practice defending against it). The more the ball is hit and the more aggressive the base runners are, the more defense the opposing team must play and the more likely it is that they will make a mistake. And hitting the ball over the fence or for extra bases can lead to a big inning and can be a big game changer.

The job of the coach is to have a solid understanding of game strategy and team personnel in order to put the team in the best position to win. That means combining a solid game plan with good game management. Every inning, the coach must review the details of the offensive situation, decide which strategies to use, and help players execute the plays that will help them win.

GAME STRATEGY

Coaches must prepare for games just as well as the players do. What a coach does can have as much bearing on the results as the players' skills.

Successful coaches use certain basic rules and strategies—combined with their own personal philosophies—to lead their teams. Coaches should consider these elements as they build their philosophy and game plan. However, nothing is absolute, and strategies may change from game to game depending on the opponent and the coach's own personnel. Players must also understand the basics of the game and their coach's philosophy; they too must become students of the game.

Know the Rules

The coach should strive to know the rules better than the opponent does. A knowledgeable coach can use the rules to the team's advantage and make sure that the team is not taken advantage of. The coach must also know how and when to apply the rules in a game—and how to properly approach and question the umpire. Know and understand the following rules and procedures:

- How to protest and appeal
- Designated player (DP) and flex player rules
- Rules for batting out of order, an unreported player, or an illegal player
- Correct penalties for rule violations
- Rules regarding fair and foul balls, being out of the batter's box, and a hit batter
- Rules for catch and carry, out of bounds, and legal catches
- Interference and obstruction rules
- Rules for illegal pitches or conferences

Study the Opponent

Coaches and players need to know their opponent. They should pay attention to the opponent's tendencies and chart the opposing batters' statistics with hitting charts. The team should also track the opposition's defensive statistics (and vulnerabilities) and should carefully observe the arms of the opposing players during warm-ups.

Get the Runner to Third

Build your baserunning and offensive strategy around this fact: The closer the runner is to home, the better her chance of scoring. Consider the number of ways to score from each base.

- Home plate: home run, errors
- First base: triple, home run, errors
- Second base: double, triple, home run, errors
- Third base: single, double, triple, home run, sacrifice fly, caught foul ball, squeeze, fielder's choice, steal, errors, wild pitch, passed ball, illegal pitch

Do everything you can to get the runner to third—bunting, stealing, being aggressive on the bases—and manufacture runs.

Consider the Number of Outs

The number of outs in an inning and in the game must always be considered. The third out is the most important; until the third out, anything is possible.

Early in the game, the team should try to avoid outs and try to get runners around the bases. Later in the game and when the score is close, the team may need to risk an out to get a runner in scoring position. When behind with few outs left in the game, you must be careful how you use them up! Save outs and go for a big hit. The conventional wisdom is as follows:

- When your team is behind and it's late in the game, be conservative.
- When your team is ahead, gamble and pour it on!
- When your team is behind by a lot, save outs and go for a big inning.

However, coaches must use their personnel as best they can! Using the bunt to try to get one run out of the weak part of the lineup may be the smartest move, even if conventional wisdom says not to bunt if you need more than one run. Going against the grain to maximize a player's ability to contribute may be the very thing that puts the team ahead—and it keeps the opponent from anticipating your every move.

Understand Statistics

As a coach, you must know and be able to interpret the statistics that your hitters put up. Slappers should have fewer strikeouts than power hitters. Coaches and players should keep track of how many times slappers get on base as a result of errors. This is what they are trying to do: beat the defense by putting the ball in play. RBIs are based in part on the achievement of others and being lucky enough to have runners on base when the player comes up. Hitting in the clutch is more significant. The batter's goal is to hit the ball hard. Keep track of the number of "stingers" players hit, including the balls that are caught because they are hit right at someone. Hitters should be measured by the degree of success they have in what they are trying to do to create runs. Coaches should evaluate their team's offensive statistics regularly throughout the season, but they should rate their players based on how many runs are scored—not on batting average. This is the statistic that matters most.

Fine-Tune the Batting Order

The best batters should have the most at-bats. Put these batters in the top three positions and they will get more chances. The first batter will come up to bat the most. The number four position comes to the plate with the most runners on base. But if all the good hitters are grouped together and all the weaker hitters are grouped together, the weaker hitters can't be used to advance the runners. Therefore, in most lineups, the hitters are spread out so that the weaker hitters may be called on to bunt, execute the hit-and-run, or put the ball in play.

Figure 4.1 Fine-tuning the batting order can maximize a team's hitting ability.

Other than determining the number of opportunities to hit, the effect that the batting order has on the game is debatable. Still, most coaches work to develop an order that increases the team's chance of scoring (see figure 4.1). Traditionalists say that the leadoff hitter should be a fast runner with a good on-base percentage. We like to put one of our best and most consistent hitters in the leadoff spot to set the table. And what a demoralizer it is for the opponent when she leads off with a home run! Putting the best bunter at number two means she will get more at-bats than players further down in the order. If the game is on the line and the last batter is up, should it be a bunter or a bigger hitter? The number three batter gets to bat in the first inning, preferably with runners on. Number three should be one of the best hitters. If she is a long-ball hitter, batting third in the first inning ensures that a deep fly ball will advance the runner with less than two out. If she bats in the fourth spot, there may be two outs, and the caught long ball is not productive.

The first inning is the only one in which the coach has control of the order. For each inning thereafter, the coach has no way of knowing who will lead off, bat second, and so on. But the responsibilities for batters in each inning are the same. The first batter's job is to get on base any way she can. The next batter's job is to move her into scoring position, and the batter after that must try to hit her in.

Don't put fast runners behind a slow runner who will slow them down on the bases. The weakest hitter should be placed at number eight. Number nine is someone who can get on base so that the top of the order has runners to bring home.

If you have a hitter who receives a lot of intentional walks, put your next best hitter behind her so that the opponent may think twice about walking her. This also sets up a good RBI situation. Or you could bat her first (pitchers hesitate to walk the leadoff player to start the game). When putting her in the fourth position, if the first three batters go down in order, she will lead off the next inning. But she may not get to bat as many times.

Coaches often move players up in the order when they are "hot." Just remember that when you make a change in your lineup, some players automatically have negative thoughts. Anticipate questions and provide an explanation, or your players will.

Choose Home or Visitor?

The advantage of being the home team is that you know what you must do. In a tiebreaker, if you are the visitor, you have to assume that the home team will get one run. At the 2002 World Championships, five of the eight teams always chose to be the visitor, thinking it is an advantage in close games and with the tiebreaker. As a coach, one of your goals is to develop your hitters throughout the season with live hitting practice. By choosing visitor, you are guaranteed at least five innings of batting practice each game. If your team is extremely nervous about a big game, you may want to choose visitor in order to give your players an opportunity to get their feet wet before going on defense. Also, if your team can score first, you put the pressure on the opponent because they must now score twice to beat you. And if you know you are really outclassed, choose visitor so that the opponent will only get to bat four times if leading by a lot. If playing in a tournament where the number of runs scored is important, choose visitor so you get all of your at-bats. If you think it might rain, choose home so you can get the game in without taking your last at-bat. And if you are far behind, you can delay and pray for rain so the game is not official.

DECISION MAKING

Managers tend to choose a strategy that is least likely to fail rather than one that might be the most efficient. As a coach, you must justify your strategy before you use it. Still, there is no guarantee that it will work. Don't second-guess yourself. All any coach can do is make the best decision possible with the information available at that moment.

If it is in your experience, it is in your head. Put your experience to work, but don't let it handicap you. Don't avoid using a particular strategy because of a single failure, and don't turn to a strategy only because it once worked very well. Evaluate and test your strategies. Practice as you intend to play. Adjust, regroup, and adapt when necessary. Don't be afraid to explain to your players why you make the decisions you do, and make sure the players understand their roles.

Consider Key Factors

To make good decisions regarding when to call a specific play, a coach must first address some key questions and considerations. Consider the ability of the pitcher, the speed of the runners, and the ability of the hitter, as well as the score, inning, and number of outs. Who are the next two batters? And who else is on the bench? Get in

CRITICAL CUE:
To succeed as a strategist, a coach must address the following questions before implementing a specific play:

What play should I call?

When in the count and with how many outs should I call the play?

Who will the batter and the base runner (or runners) be when I call the play?

How will we accomplish our goal?

Why should I call this particular play?

Where should the batter attempt to place the ball?

the habit of looking at your lineup card before the inning starts. Look ahead and be prepared. Will your hitter get a pitch that gives her a good chance of execution? For a suicide, you'd better expect a strike, so you should look for a count in your favor. If the pitcher is wild, can you really use a hit-and-run?

Additional points to consider include the weather, the distance to the backstop and fences, the playing conditions, the umpires, the score, and the opponent's strengths, weaknesses, and tendencies. Is the outfield grass long (slow) or short (fast) for ground balls? Is the infield hard or soft? If the infield is hard, bunts will get quickly to the defense, but slappers will have a great advantage if they can bounce the ball high. If the infield is slow, soft, or wet, a bunt is a good option because the defense will have a tougher time making the plays.

Monitor the Matchup

Early in the game, you (the coach) must get a feel for how well your pitcher is doing and also how well your batters are hitting the opposing pitcher. Will it be a high- or low-scoring game? If you suspect a low-scoring game, play for one or two runs by using bunts and hit-and-runs. If the opponent has better pitching and hitting, you need to do something else to give your team a chance. Try to create runs if your hits will be few—send players home, bunt, steal, use the hit-and-run. If your pitcher is strong and likely to give up only one run, take chances early. In a pitchers' duel, trade outs for runs. The closer the score, the more you play for one or two runs. When there is a big difference in score, outs become more important to the leading team, and runs become more important to the team that is behind. When your team is behind by a lot, chip away one run at a time. Focus on getting base runners and not home runs.

Analyze the Defense

Coaches must watch carefully to see what the defense will give up. Based on these observations, the coach must develop a plan, be decisive, and then pull the trigger. If the corners play deep, bunt! If the catcher is slow to her feet, steal! If the middle infielders break early, try some hit-and-runs. Coaching takes practice too, so take advantage of situations where you can learn to react and think under gamelike pressures (e.g., scrimmages, practice games, simulated games with specific game situations). To decide on the best choice of action, you must also anticipate your opponent's response. For example, if you move the runner on first successfully to second base and leave first base open, will the opponent walk the on-deck batter and take the bat out of her hand? Is this what you want? Maybe you do not want to bunt or steal in this situation.

Think a couple of pitches, batters, and innings ahead. Try to score early with hits and running, and save the bunts for later. Be aggressive early so you don't have to panic later. And don't be predictable.

BATTER UP

Hitters have a job to do in each at-bat. While in the hole, they should review what situations are likely to arise and prepare mentally for those possibilities. The situation, the position of the base runners, and the score will dictate the batter's goal. Although batters cannot control whether the batted ball is a hit or an error (unless it is a home run), good batters do have some control over where they hit the ball and what type of hit they make—that is, bunt, ground ball, fly ball. Some common situations are listed in table 4.1.

Table 4.1 Situational Hitting

Situation	Outs	Goal	Pitch to Look For
Leadoff batter	None	Get on base	Use a disciplined strike zone Look for a pitcher's mistake pitch May take one strike, looking for a walk
Runner at first	None	Avoid the double play, force-out, and line drive Usually use a sacrifice bunt	Ball low in the strike zone that the batter can bunt down
Runner at second	None	Advance the runner	Pitch batter can hit behind the runner: for a right-hander, an outside pitch; for a left-hander, an inside pitch
	Two	Score the runner	Ball to drive hard through the infield
Runner at third	Less than two	Score the runner with a ball through the infield or a deep fly ball	Expect a low pitch Ball to hit hard through the infield or an up pitch to hit for a deep fly ball
Runners at first and third	One	Avoid a double play and score the run If the runner is stealing second, hit at the shortstop	Ball that the batter can hit hard For a right-hander, an inside pitch; for a left-hander, an outside pitch
No runners on	Two	Extra-base hit	Ball in the hitting zone that the batter can drive hard
Runner stealing and batter taking the pitch	None, one, or two	Protect the runner	Move back in the box Point the end of the bat at the catcher's eyes
Hit-and-run	None, one, or two	Advance the runner with a possibility of reaching base	Any pitch that the batter can hit on the ground

Against a good pitcher, it may take one time through the order for the batters to figure out how to hit the pitcher. Don't panic. Give players some time and swings to get their bats going.

Of course, the batter must always consider the count as well. Table 4.2 on page 82 includes some guidelines for working the count. These are not absolutes, and sometimes the best strategy is taking the defense by surprise and doing the unpredictable. The coach may signal the batter instructions on what to do with each pitch, but if the batter is on her own, she should be thinking about how to use the count to her advantage. Batters should not get into a rut and become predictable; sometimes a good guess or a hunch can be the most effective response.

The coach may have the batter take a pitch when

- the pitcher is having control problems,
- the coach wants to call a certain play but not on the first pitch,
- the coach wants the pitcher to throw more pitches (e.g., when the pitcher has gotten the first two batters out on two pitches),
- the coach needs more time to assess the defense and decide what to call, or
- the relief pitcher needs more time to warm up.

The coach may signal for a swing and a miss to see how the defense reacts, to freeze the defense, or to help protect a base stealer, especially with an inexperienced catcher.

Table 4.2 Hitting by the Count

0-0	When facing an overpowering pitcher, the batter should swing at the first strike. Batters should not get in the habit of always taking the first pitch; the pitcher can take advantage by going right at the batter to get a first strike. In a sacrifice situation, the batter should bunt the first strike. This is a good count for executing the bunt-and-run, suicide squeeze, or hit-and-run.
1-0, 2-0	This is a hitter's pitch. The pitcher does not want to go 3-0. This is a good count for executing the bunt-and-run, suicide squeeze, or hit-and-run.
3-0	This is usually a take. However, if the team needs a big hit (and not another base runner) and has a power hitter at the plate, the coach might give her the green light to swing at the pitch if she likes it.
2-1	This is a good count to let the batter hit.
3-1	This is a hitter's pitch. Good hitters should have the green light; coaches should give the take sign only if they think the batter has a better chance of getting on with a walk instead of a hit.
0-2	The batter should make two-strike adjustments: choke up, enlarge the strike zone, and swing at anything close. The batter must try to make contact and put the ball in play. Be careful about stealing on this pitch because you don't want a double play on a strikeout. This count does not present many play options.
3-2	This count should be treated the same as 0-2. The batter must be ready to hit. On a full count with two outs, a runner at first is automatically going on the pitch. The runner should do the same on a 3-1 count with two outs. If the pitch is a ball, she safely gets second anyway, and if it is a strike, the play turns into a hit-and-run. With two outs, a runner staying at first has little chance of scoring.

CRITICAL CUE:

A coach should use a pinch runner when doing so will greatly improve the chance of scoring a run. In a close game, there may not be many opportunities to score, so the coach must not hesitate to pinch run early in the game. That may be the only time a slower runner gets on base. With two out, the coach may wait until the slower runner gets to second base (in scoring position) before substituting.

OFFENSIVE BASERUNNING PLAYS

Baserunning plays are designed to give fast runners the opportunity to steal, to help protect runners with average speed, and to put pressure on the defense. The batter is asked to protect the runner or bunt or hit the ball in certain areas to create defensive challenges. Signals are given so that offensive efforts are coordinated and no one is caught by surprise. The only surprises should be to the defense. The following sections cover steals, bunt plays, the hit-and-run, and other special plays.

Steals

Base runners have a greater chance of scoring if they can get to the next base without using up an out! The steal is an effective way to get into scoring position. A runner at first base with two outs must find a way to get to second. Not much can happen if she stays at first.

How aggressive the runners should be depends on the following considerations:

1. The score, inning, number of outs, and ability of the next batter. Runners must not take the bat out of the hands of a big hitter by being the third out of the inning or by vacating first base to set up an intentional walk.

2. The runners' capabilities—speed, quickness of reaction, and sliding ability. Runners should be realistic about their chance for success.

3. The condition of the basepaths. Slow basepaths (wet, soft) will slow the runners.

4. The ability of the defense, particularly the catcher, to stop the runners.

5. The coach's philosophy. Do the players make their own baserunning decisions?

On the steal, the batter's job is to protect the runner. The batter can also create some confusion among the fielders by using fake slaps, fake bunts, and swinging and missing to freeze the defense and delay their base coverage. Even on a pitchout, the batter must do her best to legally interfere with the catcher's attempts to throw out the runner.

Straight Steal

The steal is a good percentage play when the pitcher throws a lot of changeups, when the catcher has a weak arm, or when the shortstop is slow to cover the base (particularly third base). The element of surprise is also a big factor in a successful steal. When the coach calls for a steal, the batter is usually asked to take the pitch and protect the runner. A full swing and a miss may help freeze the shortstop and give the runner an advantage of several steps. However, a fake bunt will allow the defense to break early to the base.

The easiest base to steal is third base because there is only one player to beat: the shortstop. If the shortstop is a slow runner, is playing close to second, or is lazy on covering, then the steal attempt is simply a footrace. If the base runner has the speed and can get a good enough lead (the second-base player doesn't hold her tight after each pitch) to beat the shortstop to third, the runner should go for it! The batter can swing and miss to freeze the shortstop or can fake bunt to pull the third-base player in if she is covering third base.

As a coach, you should call for a steal with less than two outs if you hope to score on a fly ball. Use the steal when you believe there's a better chance of scoring on a botched steal attempt than on a hit. With two outs and the pitcher ahead in the count, have the runner steal if you want to have that same batter up again to lead off. Are you afraid to use the steal? Think about this: If the opposing catchers throw out 50 percent of your runners, this means that if you attempt 100 steals, you will be safe 50 times. Is this better than your team's batting average?

Delayed Steal

With the delayed steal, the element of surprise is the key to success. The runner breaks for the next base when the ball is thrown behind her (typically to the first-base player) or returned to the pitcher. Look for a lazy pitcher who doesn't pay attention to the runners, a pitcher who becomes upset easily by her performance or by the umpire, a catcher who pays little attention to the runners, or a catcher who is aggressive and makes many throws to the base. The delayed steal may be called along with a take signal to the batter (the play is then definitely on), or the batter may be uninvolved and free to react to the pitch. In softball, this play is rarely used at third. With younger players and weaker catchers, this play is often used on throws back to the pitcher.

- To execute the delayed steal on the battery, the runner looks for a lazy return to the pitcher or a pitcher not looking her back. On the return to the pitcher, the runner goes as the ball leaves the catcher's hand.

- To execute the delayed steal on the defense, the runner watches for the covering defensive player to vacate the base (walk away from the base) as the ball is returned to the pitcher. This often happens at second base, and an alert runner can easily reach the unattended base.

CRITICAL CUE:
Coaches often fail as strategists for the following reasons:

- They are overly conservative—their players never steal, squeeze, or get thrown out at the plate.

- They are too aggressive—their players run themselves out of an inning.

- They are too controlling.

- They give opponents too much respect.

- They have a poor game plan.

- They ask players to do things they are not capable of.

- They are too predictable.

- They are unable to calmly analyze the game—they get overwhelmed.

- To execute the delayed steal on a throw behind her, the runner looks for an aggressive catcher and sets up this play by taking a slightly longer lead, enticing the catcher into making a pickoff throw. The runner breaks on the release of the ball to the base. An aggressive catcher who throws often to first is a good candidate to use the delayed steal against.

Double Steal

Two runners on base can use either a straight steal or a delayed steal. Signals should be used so that everyone knows what will happen. The double steal works best with no outs and a good hitter up. Even if the lead runner is thrown out, one runner is still in scoring position. Consider having your players automatically execute the double steal whenever there is a dropped third strike with runners on first and second (figure 4.2). The batter is out, but runners can take advantage of the missed catch and also possibly force a hurried throw.

Figure 4.2 **Double steal on a dropped third strike with runners on first and second.**

Slap-and-Steal

On the slap-and-steal, the runner goes on the pitch. The batter shows bunt and then slaps the ball. This play forces the middle infielders to worry about both covering the base and playing the ball. With a runner at first, a ball hit at the shortstop will keep her from covering second. Because the second-base player is moving to cover first base, second base is open. The batter would not want to slap to the shortstop with a runner on second because the runner should not try to advance on a ball hit in front of her. When used with a runner on third, this play becomes a suicide squeeze with the slap replacing the bunt. The goal of the slapper in that case is just to put the ball in play. A variation is to attempt to freeze the shortstop with a fake slap. The batter uses a late swing and misses the ball as the runner steals second.

Bunt Plays

Bunting is an important part of the game of softball. The bunt can be used to add variety to your offense, to advance runners, to put pressure on the defense, and to take advantage of defensive weaknesses. Bunting can also help batters avoid double plays or break out of a slump. In addition, the bunt provides a tool to use against an overpowering pitcher. Bunt plays add an element of excitement to the game. Bunting is easy to teach and practice, and every player should be proficient at the bunting game. A team that bunts well wins games. Table 4.3 on page 87 presents an overview of when to use each type of bunt.

Sacrifice

This bunt is used often in softball with a runner at first and almost always with the tie-breaker. It is seldom called with two strikes or when you need a lot of runs to win. The purpose of this bunt is to advance the runner (or runners) with the expectation that the batter will be out; hence, it is called a sacrifice. Before you automatically call for the bunt, you need to consider several things: Are you bunting because it is the best thing to do to advance the runner or because it is "traditional softball?" Are you taking the bat out of a power hitter's hands? If you bunt the runner to second and open up first base, will the opponent walk your hitter? Can you afford the out at first? What are the chances of your next batter bringing the runner home? How strong is the defense and are they likely to get the lead runner? Do they turn a lot of double plays? Is the bunt your best chance to help your offense?

Bunt-and-Run

You can use the bunt-and-run play against a tight defense in order to get a runner with average speed to second. A fast runner may get two bases on the bunt. The batter should be a good bunter. The runner leaves on the pitch as if stealing, and the batter puts the ball in play by bunting the ball where it is pitched. An advantage for the bunter is that the placement is not important because the runner has a good jump; the batter must just get the bunt down. The runner goes hard, but she should try to see if the bunter has angled the ball down. She should also listen for the coach's help in case the ball is popped up. An alert, speedy runner can often get two bases on this play if the defense fails to cover third immediately. As the runner rounds second base, she looks for third base to see if she can beat the defense there. If the pitch cannot be bunted, the batter should take the pitch. The play then becomes a straight steal. The batter does not want to pop up a poor pitch for a double play and must focus on protecting the runner. If the pitch is above the hands, the batter should hold up (to avoid the pop-up). A 3-1 count is a great time to use this play.

Suicide Squeeze

One of the most exciting plays in softball, the suicide squeeze is used to score a runner from third (see figure 4.3 on page 86). On this play, two factors favor the offense: the element of surprise and the pressure put on the defense. The play is usually called with one out (with no outs, the offense should go for the big inning) and with the count in the batter's favor so she can expect a strike. When the count is 3-0 or 3-1, you know there will not be a pitchout. The pitcher should have good control, staying around the strike zone. Use the play with batters who have good bat control and against corners who are playing deep.

Figure 4.3 Suicide squeeze.

Safety Squeeze

Like the suicide squeeze, the safety squeeze is used to score a runner from third. The difference is that the runner does not go until she sees that the bunt is angled down toward the ground. The best place to bunt is to the third-base player. The defender at third cannot see what the runner is doing, which adds to the pressure of making the play. Because the runner waits to see where the ball is bunted, she is not likely to be put out on a popped-up bunt, a missed pitch, or a pitchout. The runner may be instructed not to go unless an error occurs on the play. A variation is for the runner to go after the defensive player fields the bunt and throws to first. This is a good call if the first-base player has a weak arm and the runner has good speed. The runner breaks when the ball leaves the fielder's hand, being careful not to be fooled by a fake throw by the third-base player. The safety squeeze puts less pressure on the batter because she can wait for a good pitch to bunt. Make sure the runner has clear instructions on whether she should respond to the bunt or to the throw. Use the safety squeeze to take the pressure off the bunter, to protect against a pitchout, when facing a wild pitcher, and when the defense has weak arms.

Push Bunt

With the push bunt, the objective is to get on base by pushing the ball between the third-base player and the pitcher or between the pitcher and the first-base player. Use this play when the corners are playing in tight or charging aggressively. The batter should push the ball between the defensive players. She should bunt the ball where it is pitched. A right-handed batter given an outside pitch should push the ball between the first-base player and the pitcher; the batter should push an inside pitch toward the shortstop. It is very difficult for even advanced players to bunt the ball in an opposite direction.

Slug Bunt

The slug bunt is a fake bunt and a swing away with an abbreviated backswing. Use this play against a charging defense. The batter should hit the ball right at the feet of the charging player or between the corner and the pitcher. When the defense is right on top of the hitter, the hitter can use a slug bunt to keep them honest the next time.

Fake Bunt

Use this play to read the defense and to set up plays. See how quickly the shortstop covers third with a runner at second. Use the fake bunt to rattle an inexperienced pitcher or to distract the catcher. Do not use a fake bunt with a runner stealing second or third because that allows the shortstop to break early to cover. A fake bunt can be used in combination with other plays to confuse the defense further. A fake bunt and a slap can be effective on a hit-and-run. A fake bunt–fake slap–bunt will have the fielders bouncing around like yo-yos. Another variation is a fake drag and hit: The batter acts as if she is going to drag bunt and at the last moment cocks the wrists back and hits hard through the ball.

Drag and Sneaky Bunts

The drag and sneaky bunts can be used to surprise the defense and get on base. These plays work best when the corners are playing back and the batter has good speed. They are also very effective when a power hitter surprises defenders who are playing deeper for her.

Table 4.3 Summary of Bunting Situations

Situation	Outs	Goal	Pitch to bunt
Sacrifice bunt	Less than two	Advance the runner	Bunt the next strike
Bunt-and-run	Less than two	Advance the runner	Bunt any strike and protect the runner if the pitch is a ball
Suicide squeeze	None, one, or two	Score the runner	Bunt or foul off the next pitch
Safety squeeze	Less than two	Score the runner	Bunt the next strike
Push bunt	Less than two	Reach base safely	Any strike
Slug bunt	None, one, or two	Drive ball past charging defense	Any strike
Fake bunt	None, one, or two	Rattle the pitcher Observe the defensive coverage	Any strike If the pitch is a ball, show bunt and then pull the bat back
Drag and sneaky bunts	Less than two	Reach base safely, surprise defense	Any strike

Hit-and-Run

The hit-and-run, which might more accurately be called the run-and-hit, is used with a runner on first or second. The runner leaves on the pitch, and the hitter's job is to make contact and hit the ball hard on the ground, ideally behind the runner. But the hitter should not fight the pitch; she should hit it where it is pitched. The runner must listen for contact, try to see if the ball is hit down or up, and listen for coaching help. She glances toward home on the third or fourth step to try to pick up the ball. The batter must go after any pitch that is hittable, not only strikes. If the batter cannot hit the ball, she should try to foul it off. If the batter cannot possibly reach the ball, she must do all she can to protect the runner and have the play become a straight steal. One strategy is to implement this rule: If the ball is above the batter's hands, she should swing and miss the ball, making the play a straight steal (versus a likely fly ball or pop-up). If this is your rule, the play could then be called a "run and optional hit." Some coaches don't want the batter to ever know that the hit-and-run is on: The runner just goes on the steal, and the batter is swinging when she wants. This accomplishes the same thing while taking pressure off the batter.

The hit-and-run should not be used when a pitcher has poor control or when the count is in the pitcher's favor and the batter is not likely to see a good pitch. The play is most useful when the runner has average speed and the batter is a good contact hitter. The play can also be called with a power hitter at bat because the runner will have time to return on a long fly. The hit-and-run helps avoid a double play, puts pressure on the defense, and opens holes in the infield if the defense breaks to cover the runner. This can also be a good call when batters are overswinging (especially against a slow pitcher) or when a batter has lost her aggressiveness and isn't swinging. It can also be used to force a batter to swing at the first pitch. Other times to consider this play are after a failed bunt attempt or after a defensive conference. The play can backfire if a double play results—but remember, any call is a roll of the dice.

Fake Swing

Use a fake swing to set the defense up for a future play, to read defensive coverage, to get defenders to back up (setting up a bunt play), or just to keep them guessing. The batter must sell the fake and must swing as if hitting the ball. To practice doing this convincingly, have the batter announce as she swings whether she is swinging over or under the ball. The batter's swing should be several inches above or below the ball.

Special Plays

Certain situations occur regularly in a game and offer unique opportunities to advance runners or to score. Coaches need to decide ahead of time how they want to respond, and the team needs to practice accordingly so players feel comfortable with the call when it is made during the game.

Second-and-Third Play (Ground Ball Go)

With runners at second and third, the runner at third goes home automatically on any ground ball regardless of the number of outs and no matter where the ball is hit (except when the ball stays just in front of home plate and is picked up by the catcher). This is an excellent play because it puts pressure on the infield. If the defense makes a mistake, the offense scores a run. Force the defense to try to make the tag on the runner sliding home, which is much more difficult than the routine defensive play of holding the runner and throwing to first. The play at home requires a quick throw, a tag on a hard-sliding runner, and an umpire's correct call on a close play. The element of surprise (the runner is going?) and the pressure on the infield to stop the run often lead to a bad throw. And if the hit ball goes to the pitcher, the runner has a chance to score because not all pitchers are good overhand throwers. This defensive play is certainly more difficult than the play to first, and it is not practiced nearly as much.

The runner must slide hard at home, creating a difficult tag play as well as tying up the catcher so that she cannot easily make a play on the batter–runner. (The catcher is often not even looking at second.) The batter's responsibility is to hit the ball on the ground, toss the bat away from home plate—knowing that the runner is coming home—and then try to get to second if the throw goes home. The runner automatically goes to second unless stopped by the first-base coach. The coach should hold the runner at first if the play at home happens so quickly that the batter has not reached first base and there is a good chance of her being doubled up if she attempts second base. The runner at second goes to third as soon as she sees the defense throw to home or first. The runner from second should not be in a hurry because the play will be made elsewhere; she must not run into a tag-out at short or third if the infielder is fielding the ball. The fielders' attention will be at home or at first, so the runner has plenty of time to take third base.

If the runner is out at home, your team is left with runners at second and third! Nothing lost and yet so much to be gained. If the defense makes a mistake or fumbles the ball, a run scores on what appears to be a routine ground ball. And if the runner is stopped at first, then the defense has the dreaded first-and-third play to contend with. On the next pitch, call for a steal of second base because 90 percent of the teams won't do anything to stop it. Conversely, how many times have teams missed opportunities to score when the runner stays at third and the ground ball is mishandled, takes a bad bounce, or is a slow roller? By having your runner automatically go on the ground ball, you can take advantage of any of these situations. All the decision making is taken out of the play. The runner is going home on all ground balls. She just reacts! Never again shake your head and wish your runner had gone home. Runs are difficult enough to come by; use this strategy to score on an infield ground ball, which is usually an out. I tried to keep count of how many runs we scored using this strategy over the years I coached, but we scored so many that I quit counting.

First-and-Third Options

The first-and-third play is one of the most difficult to defend, and it is challenging for the offense to run as well. The offense is often willing to trade an out for a run. With runners on first and third, the runner on first goes to second when the pitch is thrown. This runner's goal is to advance safely or draw a throw that may give the runner at third an opportunity to score.

A different offensive situation is set up when the batter walks and there is a runner at third. The batter who is walked runs to first but never stops at the base—she continues on to second. The rules state that the runner may proceed to second (even if the pitcher has the ball and is in the circle) as long as the runner does not stop and reverse direction while the pitcher has the ball in the circle. If the pitcher makes a motion to throw, the rule does not apply. What the defense does is determined by the reaction of the runners, and the runners try to react to the defensive sets. Because offense and defense are so entwined, they are discussed together in chapter 9 (see page 205).

Yet another option is to use a fake sacrifice bunt to open second base for the runner at first. The third-base player must cover a possible bunt, and the shortstop moves to cover third. The second-base player covers first base for the bunt, leaving second base open. If the center fielder covers the base, there is no backup, and any overthrow will clear the bases.

Fake Fall With Runners on First and Second

The batter fakes a bunt, and the runner at first takes a hard lead, turns, and falls down. The runner gets up and takes two steps toward first base, drawing the throw there, and then turns and runs hard to second base because no one is there. The shortstop is covering third and the second-base player is covering first for the bunt. The runner at second is slowly creeping toward third base and breaks to third on the throw to first base (the defense throws to first, thinking the runner is returning there).

Fake Sneaky Bunt With Runners on First and Second

This is a special play with runners on first and second. The coach must first determine that the third-base player is covering third on the steal. Call a double steal, and signal the batter to perform a fake sneaky. (This bunt is not shown as late as a sneaky bunt but not as early as a sacrifice bunt.) This will catch the third-base player off guard, and the goal is for the runner from second to beat the off-balance third-base player back to the bag. The catcher will see that the third-base player is not ready for the throw and will either delay her throw or make a bad throw, which might allow your base runner to score. Like all of the bunts, this one in particular needs to be practiced in order to be properly executed. This play is a great tool for scoring runs.

Washington Play

In college circles, this play is sometimes referred to as the University of Washington play. The batter–runner goes deep down the first-base line after having hit safely. She runs far down the line to give the play time to develop and to give the shortstop and second-base player time to vacate second base. The runner walks nonchalantly and very slowly back toward first base, keeping her eyes on the situation (see figure 4.4). The defensive players tend to vacate second base, going back to their positions and assuming that the play is over. Once the batter–runner decides that she can beat either defensive player to second, she breaks for second before stepping on first base. Once she breaks toward second, she must keep going to second unless the pitcher releases her by throwing or faking a throw. Because the batter–runner has not stepped on first (while returning to the bag), she is able to go to second. To signal the play to the runner, tell her to "go deep" as she approaches first.

Figure 4.4 **Setting up the Washington play.**

OFFENSIVE DRILLS

The best offensive practice is against the defense. Conditions should be as gamelike and realistic as possible. Competitions are a great way to create pressure. Everything that will be used in a game should be practiced in the same way it will be used in the game. Nothing should be left to chance or luck.

PITCHING MACHINE EXECUTION

Purpose: **To practice signals and execution.**

Procedure: **The person feeding the machine gives a signal, and the batter must execute successfully or go to the end of a short line. The signal giver should simply give the basic signal and not go through a series using a key as the coach does. This takes too much time, and players tend to get silly while doing it.**

HIT-AND-RUN

Purpose: **To improve the hitters' ability to execute the hit-and-run and to give runners practice responding at first base under gamelike conditions.**

Procedure: **With a full defense, use a pitching machine to increase the number of swings that batters get. Begin with a line of runners at first base and a line of batters at home. The batter hits any hittable ball and runs to first, then joins the line there. Runners take a normal lead and break to second on the pitch. After three or four steps, they look toward the plate area to try to find the ball and react accordingly. The defense plays the hit out.**

Variation: **Divide the team in half with a line of batters and a line of runners at first. A coach pitches; this coach has a bucket of balls and is protected by a pitching screen. Batters and runners execute the hit-and-run. They go to the end of the opposite line when their turn is completed.**

THE BUNTING GAME

Purpose: **To practice the short game both offensively and defensively; to learn where to place the bunt to be successful.**

Procedure: **Set up the defense with infielders only. Divide the rest of the players into teams that will compete to score the most runs. However, players can only bunt or slap. Depending on the age or ability of the players, you may or may not want to allow stealing. Players should also try to advance the runners from first and third on a bunt.**

EXECUTION OUT OF THE HAT

Purpose: **To execute offensive plays under gamelike conditions.**

Procedure: **The batter draws a piece of paper out of a hat and has to execute the play written on it. The base runner is also signaled or shown what play is on. Defensive players turn their heads so that they do not know what play is on.**

MOVE HER OVER AND SCORE THAT RUNNER!

Purpose: To practice using offensive tactics to advance and score the runner.

Procedure: The runner starts at first, and the batter has three outs to score her. The first attempt is to get her to second by any means (bunt, slap, hit to right, and so on). If the batter is unsuccessful in advancing the runner, the runner returns to first and there is now one out. The batter has three outs to score the runner. If the runner scores, she starts again at first base, and the drill continues until the batter has made three outs. Keep score and know the team record for the number of runs the batter produces.

OFFENSE VERSUS DEFENSE CHALLENGE

Purpose: The offense selects a play and tries to beat the defense.

Procedure: The offensive team is in the third-base dugout, and they select a play (e.g., runners at second and third, no outs). They announce it to the defense, and the defensive players huddle on the mound and review the defensive action they will take. Have coaches at first and third. The offense gets a point if they execute the play successfully, and they get a minus score if they fail. The defense gets a point if they are able to break up the play and get the out. They get a minus score if they make an error or are unsuccessful in stopping the offense.

SITUATIONAL HITTING PRACTICE

Purpose: To practice hitting, baserunning, and defense under gamelike conditions.

Procedure: Have pitchers pitch a prescribed number of innings all in a row. Clear the bases after every three outs, or start a base runner at a selected base each new inning.

Conduct the drill using one of these options:

1. Play nine outs. See who wins—defense or offense. Change the defense and hitters after nine outs and continue.

2. Modify the count to make batters more aggressive. Start with one or two strikes, or give the batters only one pitch (hit-and-run practice).

3. Give the batter one strike. If she gets a hit, she gets another strike. The batter stays up until she goes out.

4. Play "carry the team." Have teams of four players. Each team gets to hit until every batter is out once. Have a competition and keep track of the number of runs each foursome scores.

THROWING

uccessful players can catch the ball and throw accurately to a target. These skills are the foundations for success and are aspects of the game that coaches and players can control. Coaches must ensure that players use proper mechanics and that players practice. It takes a great deal of practice to develop catching and throwing skills to the point where they become automatic. Defensive practices should include time for players to warm up their arms and practice throws. Do not waste this time! Players must concentrate on the fundamentals during every catch and throw so that correct technique becomes habit.

The overhand throw, which outfielders use almost exclusively and infielders use most of the time, is the first throw players must master. With an overhand throw at close range, however, the ball is often out of sight of the receiver, making it difficult to track and catch. Therefore, when infielders are close to the receiver (for example, when the second-base player fields a ball in the gap and throws to first), a three-quarter or sidearm throw should be used so that the ball is always visible to the receiver. The situation, the thrower's body position, and the speed of the runner dictate the use of other throws. Therefore, the thrower may have to use an abbreviated windup, an underhand toss, a flip, or even a throw on the run. The situation may demand quickness, but accuracy is always the primary goal. The following sections describe the basics of each of these throwing skills.

GRIP

The grip, commonly referred to as a three-finger grip, is the same for all types of throws. A softball is so much bigger than a baseball that players can't use only three fingers (as they do in baseball) and have a secure grip. Therefore, they place all fingers on the ball. The player always grips across the seams using the fingerprint part of the fingers. The middle finger is placed in the middle of the ball on one seam, and the thumb is positioned underneath on the opposite seam. The index finger and the ring finger are equally spaced on each side of the middle finger and on the same seam (see figure 5.1). The little finger is curled in a relaxed position on the side of the ball. The thumb is under the middle finger as much as possible, and the player takes care not to lock the wrist. There should be space (or daylight) between the ball and palm and the webbing of the thumb.

The player obtains the proper grip by rotating the ball in the glove with the throwing-hand fingers until she finds the seams and can grip the ball correctly. The ball is pressed down into the glove to secure the grip and then lifted quickly from the glove with the ball pointed down and the back of the hand pointed up as the hands separate.

On a slow roller or a dead (stopped) ball, some players pick the ball up with only the bare hand. To get a firm, secure grip on the softball, players need to pick it up with both hands. By using the glove to catch the ball first, players also reduce the chance of not catching it. The player can

Figure 5.1 The three-finger grip.

then press the ball against the glove to secure the grip. Because of the large size of the softball, it is simply not possible to grip the ball firmly without using two hands. The more firmly the player grips the ball, the faster it can be thrown. Accuracy also depends on a sure grip. Are two hands slower than a one-hand pickup? Possibly, but the fielder will make up time by throwing the ball faster and more accurately.

FINDING THE GRIP

Purpose: To learn to find the proper grip on the ball quickly and automatically.

Procedure: The player takes the ball out of the glove with the throwing hand, developing a feel for the ball as she takes it out. This drill should be repeated until the process of gripping the ball is smooth, secure, and fast. Beginners may at first have to look at the ball as they get the proper finger placement. With practice, speed improves and the grip becomes automatic. This is a simple drill that players can do repeatedly even while watching television, but they must remember not to throw the ball!

TWO-HAND PICKUP

Purpose: To practice picking up the ball with two hands in order to get a secure grip.

Procedure: The player places the ball on the ground in front of her, picks it up with both hands, and throws it to a partner. The partner repeats the procedure on the return throw.

OVERHAND THROW

The basic components of the overhand throw are body position, arm action, release, and follow-through. Body position (basically upright) and arm action (with the throwing-arm elbow above the shoulder) define the overhand throw. Loading and transferring weight from back to front provide power. Proper body alignment keeps the ball on target. A strong release and follow-through contribute to speed and accuracy. For an accurate and strong throw, players must execute all four phases. Included later are drills that can be used to teach and develop each of these components.

Body Position

Before the throw is made, the player must turn the shoulders and hips sideways to the intended target and position her feet. A throw can't be made until the feet are in place. To check alignment, draw a line from between the player's feet to the target (see figure 5.2). The first step after catching the ball should be with the back foot (nonglove foot), which is turned outward at about a 45-degree angle and on this line. The inside of the ankle should be facing the target. The player's weight is on the ball of the foot of the back leg to load for power. She then

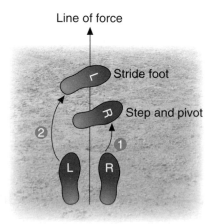

Figure 5.2 **Proper foot position for the overhand throw.**

steps toward the target with the glove-side foot, placing the arch of the stepping foot at a 45-degree angle on the drawn line. The player can step with the legs straight or bent according to personal preference, but the front knee should have some flex. The shoulders are level and sideways to the target. The front-foot touchdown is timed with the forward motion of the arm. When the front foot touches down, the upper half of the body should be in position to throw. The player pushes off with the back foot and shifts her weight forward. Power and speed are generated when the back side of the body is driven into and against a stable front side. The hips explode open with the navel pointing toward the target. When fielding ground balls, the right-handed player should follow this sequence: "Right, left, pick ball up, right, left, throw."

Arm Action

For consistent throwing, the hands must always start from a centered, balanced position. As the player begins the throwing motion after making the catch, she should bring both hands back to the middle of the chest about sternum high. The shoulders and trunk then rotate during the breakaway (separation of the hands). The thrower breaks away by firing the elbows to the side, creating a stretch across the chest with the throwing hand and glove lower than the elbows; as she executes this movement, the thrower forms a T with her body (see figure 5.3a). Note that outfielders break away at the waist to achieve greater arm motion and put more distance on the ball.

The stretch is similar to the one that a person might use when drawing back an arrow to shoot it. Both elbows are shoulder height. The glove is at midchest with the elbow still in line with the shoulder and slightly higher than the glove. The throwing arm is in a straight line to the side of the body (even with the shoulder) and has a bend at the elbow (see figure 5.3b). The ball moves in a circle to reach this raised position,

Figure 5.3 Arm action of the overhand throwing motion. *(a)* The thrower executes the breakaway, forming a T with her body; *(b)* points the glove to the target and lifts the ball behind the head so the back of the throwing hand is toward the body and both elbows are at shoulder height; and *(c)* starts the forward motion by simultaneously leading with the elbow and pulling the glove arm down.

moving from the glove to an extension backward and up to a point above the ear. The little finger leads the hand, and the elbow of the throwing arm points away from the body at shoulder height; the elbow is bent at about a 90-degree angle. If the elbow is not shoulder high, a sidearm throw results, which strains the elbow and produces a less accurate throw—that is, a curveball. At the top of the motion of the throwing arm, the wrist is cocked so that the thumb is pointing away from the body and the back of the hand is facing the body.

To start the forward motion of the throw, the player leads with the elbow of the throwing arm while simultaneously pulling the glove arm down (see figure 5.3c). The motion of the glove arm is important for maintaining correct alignment and developing force. The arms work in opposition as they do in swimming—the harder the glove pulls down, the faster the throwing arm goes forward. The player should move the throwing arm quickly, not dragging it. The rotation is such that one shoulder replaces the other.

Release

The wrist is flexible and loose. The player cocks the wrist back in preparation to throw as she lifts the ball above the shoulder with the back of the hand facing the target. She rolls the thumb under the ball, which forces the palm in the opposite direction. A coach walking behind the thrower should be able to high-five the ball. On release, the thrower snaps the wrist forward toward the target and down to provide velocity and accuracy.

This motion is similar to waving good-bye. The throw is slightly downhill because a ball in the dirt can be caught, whereas a ball that is 10 feet (3 m) over the receiver's head cannot be caught. The thumb is pointed to the ground, and the fingers are thrown (snapped) toward the target (see figure 5.4). The index finger goes at the right eye of the receiver, and the middle finger goes at the left eye; the V formed by these fingers should bridge the nose. The last thing the thrower should feel is the ball leaving the fingerprint area of the fingers. The thrower pulls the seams sharply down. The ball comes off the middle and index fingers last, creating a backward vertical spin toward the thrower, much like the backspin on a basketball jump shot. It is a 12 to 6 o'clock backward rotation. Placing a stripe on the ball will help players see the spin. Color a half-inch stripe or apply electrical tape across the four seams. To get the feel of the wrist snap and follow-through, players can practice by snapping a handkerchief.

When releasing the ball, the thrower must keep the shoulders level so that the ball goes in a straight line. When fielding a bunt, the player often does not have time to straighten up. Still, the fielder must always take time to level the shoulders, even in a crouched position. Overthrows occur when the back shoulder is lower than the front, an alignment that produces an upward angle for the path of the ball. Alignment and follow-through are critical. The ball goes where the player throws it.

Figure 5.4 **Release position for the overhand throw.**

COACHING POINTS FOR THE OVERHAND THROW

- Break away from a centered position.
- Don't push the ball. Stretch your throwing shoulder back and keep your elbow above the shoulder.
- Cock the wrist so the ball is facing away from the target.
- Turn sideways to the target—don't remain square. Use your whole body.
- Step with the glove-side foot. Turning sideways will help this feel natural.
- Don't palm the ball. Hold it with your fingertips and see daylight.
- If you have a sideways rotation of the ball, check to see if your thumb is rotating up at release instead of down toward the ground. Also, check that the elbow is shoulder high.

Figure 5.5 **Follow-through position for the overhand throw.**

Follow-Through

The player begins the follow-through by bending at the waist as the back side of the body releases. She throws the back (throwing) shoulder toward the target. She leads with the elbow to throw, and she drives her load (weight) into her front side for maximum power. She turns and tucks her glove into her front side as the throwing arm comes through. The back leg lifts slightly off the ground with the shoelaces pointed to the ground. The fingers point toward the target as the wrist snaps and the ball is released. The thrower must stay loose. She finishes with the chest over the front knee and the hand continuing down to lightly touch the outside of the glove-side leg (see figure 5.5).

The longer the throw, the more exaggerated the follow-through and the greater the bend at the waist. Infielders will generally touch their upper thighs, and outfielders will often touch their knees or lower. Players must be careful not to finish with the throwing arm across the body because this will pull the ball off line.

LONG THROWS

The faster the ball gets to the target, the better the chance of making an out. For long throws, players must use the overhand throw, which causes less strain on the arm. By coming over the ball, the overhand throw generates a vertical spin that produces a good, accurate bounce. The thrower can increase the strength of the throw by moving into the ball and transferring the body's momentum through the ball. Outfielders use the overhand throw almost exclusively, and infielders use it whenever they have time to set up properly. The ideal choice for any long throw should be the overhand throw.

Crow Hop

To get extra strength on their throws, outfielders should use the crow hop. After catching the ball, the player hops on the throwing-side foot and pushes hard as she drives her body and momentum forward. After releasing the ball, the outfielder pushes off the back leg and steps toward the target. In simple terms, the player replaces her feet. The fingers point to the ground at the finish. See chapter 8, page 165, for more details.

Long Bounce Throw

For long throws, outfielders should use the bounce throw. This is also a good throw for a shortstop who is moving away and is deep in the hole behind third base. Younger players who lack arm strength from third to first or from second to home should also use the long bounce. Rainbow throws take too long to reach the target and are not as accurate. The path of a ball that bounces to the target more closely approximates a straight line, which is the shortest distance between two points. The bounce throw is also helpful when the sun is in the eyes of the infielders. Keeping the ball low by using a bounce throw allows the ball to be tracked more easily. And a low trajectory permits the throw to be cut if necessary. Any long throw to a base should bounce approximately 15 feet (4.5 m) from the intended receiver.

Flattening the arc of the throw also increases accuracy. For accuracy, the thrower must have a consistent release point. The release point is slightly in front of the throwing shoulder and at a point where the player is still able to maintain a 90-degree angle at the elbow while keeping the hand pointed up. The wrist must be able to snap forward at a release point that allows the fingers to point to the target on the follow-through. This comes with practice, and practice produces consistency. Practicing the long bounce leads to more outs.

QUICK THROWS

If the ball is not hit directly to the fielder, she may not have time to get in position to make an overhand throw. If the runner is very quick, the fielder may not have time for a full windup. When close to the receiver, the fielder must show the ball so that the receiver can see it all the way to the glove. When the throwing distance is short, a player may have sufficient arm strength that a full overhand throw is not necessary.

Shortened Windup

Players may use a shortened windup when they need to be quick and can sacrifice strength and distance on the throw. A fielder charging a slow grounder will often need to use a shortened windup to beat the runner. Because of the speed of the play and the longer distance to first from third and short, players at those positions must often rush their throws. They often need to stay low and throw because there isn't time to stand up and make a big circle overhand throw. Strong catchers may also use the shortened windup for a quicker release. The catcher must have the arm strength to throw without having to transfer body weight to get the ball to the base. To execute the shortened windup, the thrower pulls the ball back quickly just above the ear. The main difference is that the first movement of the throwing arm is back, not down, shortening the arm circle. The action is similar to pulling an arrow back in archery. Footwork and body position are the same as those used for the overhand throw.

On the Run

When the thrower does not have time to assume a set position, she becomes a quarterback on the run. A good shortstop is able to throw on the run after fielding a slow rolling ball or a high bouncer hit by a slapper. A third-base player cutting off a bunt or slap in the hole will have a better chance of making the out by using this technique. This throw is sometimes the first throw in a rundown.

Using an abbreviated windup, the thrower releases the ball in one continuous motion while running toward the target. She should concentrate on the follow-through of the arm with the hand pointing directly to the target. Most throwing errors are high when throwing on the run. The ball sails high because the thrower does not use a firm wrist snap. The thrower must not lob the ball. The path of the ball should be a firm, straight line. The thrower must field the ball first, running through the ball without hesitation or stopping. Whenever possible, the chest should face directly to the target on release. After release, the fielder continues to run several steps toward the target.

Errors occur when the fielder rushes and tries to throw before securing the ball. When the runner has clearly beaten the play, the fielder should hold on to the ball. It's better to let the runner get one base than to take the chance of making an error that gives her additional bases.

Showing the Ball

The second-base player and other players who are close to the receiver should throw so that the ball always remains visible to the receiver and is thus easier to track, react to, and catch. This is what we call *showing the ball*, and it is done whether the throw is a wrist snap, sidearm throw, or underhand toss. When time permits, the body should be upright. To show the ball when close to the receiver, the fielder holds the ball up in her bare hand just above the shoulder and well away from the body, maintaining a bend in the elbow of about 90 degrees. Fingers are pointed up with the thumb underneath (see figure 5.6). By using a smaller arm circle, the thrower can keep the ball where it is always visible to the receiver. An overhand windup should not be used because the motion will cause the ball to disappear behind the body. In addition, because the player is throwing a shorter distance, a large arm circle is not necessary.

Figure 5.6 Proper technique for showing the ball.

Wrist Snap Toss

The wrist snap is used in rundowns and at other times when the thrower is very close to the receiver. The ball can be released very quickly with this method, and the receiver is able to see the ball the entire flight. Because it is simply a wrist snap, the position of the body and the footwork are not important. The player lifts the ball and throwing hand above the throwing shoulder without pulling the shoulder back. This saves time and helps keep the ball from going off line. The elbow is bent at 90 degrees. The player snaps the wrist so that the thumb points toward the ground, and she snaps the fingers at the target (see figure 5.7).

Sidearm Throw

Also called a three-quarter throw, the sidearm throw is used when players need quickness and can sacrifice strength and distance. Players should not throw sidearm over long distances. The weight of the softball and the increased stress on the elbow when throwing sidearm can lead to elbow injuries.

When a player is throwing sidearm, the elbow is below the shoulder throughout the entire arm motion and remains there when the ball is released (see figure 5.8). The sidearm throw places more emphasis on forearm and wrist movement than on the use

Figure 5.7 **Wrist snap toss.**

of the shoulder. Arm movement is more horizontal. Players must be sure that the thumb rotates down on release to produce proper spin. Allowing the thumb to rotate upward will produce a curveball and increase pressure on the elbow. The glove arm still works in opposition and should point to the target for proper alignment. The footwork is the same as that used for the overhand throw; the body remains sideways to the target on release.

Figure 5.8 **Sidearm throw.**

Many elbow injuries occur because athletes are taught improper sidearm mechanics. The shoulder positioning must be taught in relation to the elbow. The elbow should stay as close to a 90-degree angle with the shoulder as possible. To keep the proper angle of 90 degrees as the elbow drops below the shoulder, the player should increase the bend at the waist to allow the shoulders to follow downward and forward with the elbow. This allows for better control and longer follow-through toward the target.

Underhand Toss

The underhand toss is used when a quick release is required and the thrower is within 15 feet (4.5 m) of the target. A prime example is a throw to the catcher from the corners or pitcher on a suicide squeeze. Another use for the underhand toss is the short throw to a receiver covering a base for a force-out or double play. An outfielder may use the underhand toss to get the ball to a teammate if the outfielder is moving away from the target and the teammate is in a better position to make the throw. The underhand toss is a safe and accurate throw that pitchers often use for the throw to first base after fielding a ball to the first-base side. Pitchers who have difficulty making accurate overhand throws should use this throw for balls hit to their left when they have time to run the ball close enough to first base to make the play. Advanced infielders may also use this toss to get the ball to a teammate who is in better position to make a strong throw, such as when the second-base player backhands a ball behind second. With her momentum carrying her away from first base, she can toss to the shortstop, who can more easily make the throw to first.

The player should field the ball with two hands to ensure a secure grip. She then removes the glove to show the ball to the receiver. With a pendulum-like forward swing from the shoulder, the player throws the ball (like a pitcher) on a direct line with little arc, keeping the ball low. The elbow is locked, and the wrist is stiff. The ball is guided to the target with the palm up and the fingers extended to the receiver (see figure 5.9). The arm stops no higher than the shoulders. Backswing and body motion should be minimal. Locking the elbow and wrist helps eliminate overthrows that can occur when

Figure 5.9 **Underhand toss.**

adrenaline is flowing. The thrower keeps the body low, flexes at the hips, and strides toward the target. If time permits, the glove can be extended toward the target so that the arms can work in opposition. But the thrower must make sure that the arms go no higher than the shoulders. Using the glove arm will aid balance and improve alignment. When a fielder needs to release the ball quickly, she should shorten the extension of the arms and rely more on the wrist action of the throwing hand.

Glove Toss

The glove toss is a desperation throw used when the fielder has no chance of getting the throwing hand to the ball quickly. The fielder cocks the wrist of the glove hand back and then snaps forward, opening the glove to release the ball. The corners and the pitcher may use this toss on suicide plays. A player chasing a rolling ball and ending up close to the base might also use the glove toss. This toss is effective up to a distance of about 10 feet (3 m). Ideally, the fielder is running toward the target, and her momentum will help the toss get there. Because this is a desperation play, however, a player may use it from any angle as a last resort. Advanced players may use the glove toss when lying on the ground if they need to get the ball to a teammate to complete the play.

Backhand Flip

A backhand flip is sometimes necessary when the fielder doesn't have time to get her body around to face the target (the target is on the right side of a right-handed thrower). A typical example occurs when a second-base player is able to stay behind a ball hit to her right near second base. Without time to turn and face the receiver, she uses a backhand flip to the shortstop covering second. To make a backhand flip, after gripping the ball, the player points the elbow of the throwing arm toward the target and brings the back of the hand in toward the chest (see figure 5.10a). She stiffens the wrist and pushes the ball to the target while simultaneously taking a step in that direction. She steps with the foot nearer the receiver. The side of the foot moves toward the receiver with the toes pointed straight ahead. The body stays low, rising only slightly from the

Figure 5.10   Backhand flip.

fielding position. The shoulders remain square and level. Only the head turns toward the target. The fielder releases the ball as she extends her elbow (see figure 5.10b). The arm stops between waist and shoulder height with the fingers pointed toward the target. Arm action follows a horizontal path.

COACHING POINTS FOR WHEN TO USE LONG AND QUICK THROWS

THROW	WHEN TO USE IT
Overhand throw	For all long throws (outfielders will use it most of the time)
Long bounce throw	For throws from the outfield to home
	When the sun is in the receiver's eyes
	For throws by infielders deep in the hole
On the run	When the third-base player is cutting off a ball in the hole against a fast runner
	When an infielder is charging a slow roller against a fast runner
	For throws made when defending slaps
	For throws during rundowns
Shortened windup	When a quick release is needed
	When the thrower can sacrifice strength and distance
	For throws by the catcher to the bases; for throws from third or shortstop to first base
Wrist snap toss	For short throws when the thrower is close to the receiver
	For throws during rundowns
Sidearm throw	When the thrower can sacrifice strength and distance for quickness
	To show the ball to a nearby receiver, especially when a second-base player is throwing to a first-base player
	When fielding bunts
Underhand toss	On the suicide squeeze
	For forces and double plays when the thrower is within 15 feet of the base
	For throws by pitchers who have difficulty throwing overhand
Glove toss	When the thrower is 10 feet or less from the target
	When the thrower has no chance of getting the throwing hand to the ball in time
	On the suicide squeeze or on a diving stop
Backhand flip	When the target is to the right side of a right-handed thrower

WARMING UP THE ARM

Arm problems occur because of overuse, poor mechanics, or a lack of arm and shoulder strength. Players can build up their arms by performing weight training and gradually increasing the number of throws they make each day. They should constantly review and work on their throwing mechanics and take care not to overuse their arms. Many fielding drills can be done without throwing. Players can return the balls to a bucket to eliminate the need to throw. At any sign of soreness, players should apply ice for 20 minutes when they are finished practicing.

Before throwing all out in practice or in a game, players must warm up their arms to prepare for full-out throwing. A proper warm-up will help strengthen the arm as well as prevent injuries. The throwing progressions in tables 5.1 and 5.2 (pages 107 and 108) isolate and work the parts of the body used in throwing in succession so that players can build to a full motion that uses all the parts together at maximum intensity.

Players should always stretch their shoulder muscles (throwing arm only) before they warm up their arms. To perform the following three exercises, players flex the knees slightly and bend forward at the waist. They stretch slowly, doing a minimum of 20 repetitions of each exercise. If a player still feels tight in the shoulder, she should increase the number of repetitions until she feels her shoulder loosen.

1. With the throwing elbow bent at 90 degrees, the player slowly swings the arm forward, lifting the hand as high as possible while maintaining a 90-degree bend at the elbow. She then swings the arm slowly back, raising the elbow as high as flexibility permits (see figure 5.11).

2. With a 90-degree elbow bend, the player swings the arm across her body as far as possible to the glove side and then back, leading with the elbow and lifting it as high as possible on the throwing side (see figure 5.12).

3. The player stirs an imaginary pot with the fingers just above the ground. She uses big, slow circles 10 times in one direction and then 10 times in the other (see figure 5.13).

Players should warm up just before throwing. A common mistake is for players to warm up the arm at the beginning of practice and then do activities other than throwing, allowing the arm to cool off. If players are going to hit or the coach is going to talk a lot, the arm warm-up should be delayed until just before throwing activities. Players begin warming up at a distance that does not strain the arm, and they work up to the distance they

Figure 5.11 Arm swing forward and back.

Figure 5.12 Arm swing side to side.

Figure 5.13 Stirring the pot.

will need to throw. Throwing drills to warm up the arms should take 15 to 20 minutes, a valuable chunk of practice time that players must not waste.

Players should follow several specific rules to get the most out of the throwing drills:

- Players should not talk. Instead, they should concentrate on accuracy and on feeling the basics of the throw.

- Players who play similar positions should throw with each other because they make the same types of throws. In particular, outfielders should throw with outfielders, and catchers with catchers.

- Players should throw to a target on *every* throw in order to develop consistent control.

- Players should turn their body correctly on every throw, pretending that a camera is filming every throw for a demonstration tape.

- Players can critique each other's throws. Is the spin correct? Is the thrower balanced?

- Players should also work on catching techniques. They should move the feet and body to catch every ball with two hands in front of the throwing shoulder.

- Early in the season or any time that players are experiencing throwing problems, they should review the basics and work on drills that emphasize the basic elements of the throw.

- To develop arm strength, players can overload the throwing muscles by doing a little more each day. They can increase the length of time and the distance.

ELIMINATING SORE ARMS

Throwing distance should be adapted to the size and abilities of the players. College-age players will usually throw at a distance of about 30 feet (9 m) when warming up or doing basic throwing drills. Refer to tables 5.1 and 5.2 (page 108) for sample throwing progressions.

When players are doing a lot of throwing, care must be taken that injuries don't occur from overuse. Decreasing the throwing distance can reduce strain on the arms. When working on technique, players should not throw at maximum speed. Using smaller (lighter) balls allows more repetitions with less strain. Young players who lack the strength to throw a regulation softball will try to push the ball. Coaches can have their teams use smaller balls (baseball, tennis ball) so that young players can learn proper throwing mechanics. In the course of warming up, practicing defense, and playing games, players are throwing way too much. Coaches can reduce wear on players' arms when working on defense by eliminating the need to throw: Players simply place the balls in buckets. When practicing defense, players can throw every third or fourth ball and roll the ball to the side on other plays. In games, players must be sure that their arms stay warm and loose. Between innings, they should do warm-up throws as part of the routine. Infielders will throw to first base, returning balls that the first-base player rolls to them while outfielders do easy long tosses to each other. The center fielder takes a ball with her and throws to one of the other outfielders. To provide more throws, a player from the bench should go to the sideline and play catch with the third and closest outfielder.

Table 5.1 Practice Throwing Progression

This progression is meant to stretch and warm up the muscles used for throwing. Over time, it also builds strength in these muscles. The bulleted items are key points that players who are learning to throw should work on at each stage. Throws in steps 1 through 5 should be made with 50 to 75 percent effort. The number of throws can be adjusted to suit the age and ability of the players. As the distance increases, players should put an arc on the ball to reach the target.

The arm is not warm enough to throw at 100 percent effort until maximum distance is reached. Maximum distance means that the player can no longer reach her target on the fly. The player then starts decreasing the arc on the ball and shortening the distance to the target.

1. Working the wrist and elbow—20 throws at a distance of 10 feet (3 m)

- The throwing arm is in a straight line and is even with the shoulder.
- The player has a 90-degree bend at the elbow; the arm forms the letter L.
- The player focuses on the wrist snap and elbow follow-through.
- The wrist action is similar to when shooting a basketball.
- The player should try for as many rotations of the ball as possible.

2. Working the shoulder and upper half of the body—20 throws at a distance of 30 feet (9 m)

- The player squares up facing the target, with the feet wider than the shoulders in a comfortable athletic stance.
- The shoulders rotate, and the body forms a T at breakaway; the player should feel the stretch across the chest.
- The player does not step.
- The throwing arm is in a straight line and is even with the shoulder.
- The player has a 90-degree bend at the elbow; the palm faces away from the body.
- The player leads with the elbow while coming forward.
- The player must stay loose.
- The player should bend at the waist to follow through; the throwing arm lightly brushes the outside of the thigh.

3. Loading and using the legs—20 throws at a distance of 40 feet (12 m)

- The upper and lower halves of the body are partially isolated but beginning to work together.
- The shoulders rotate, and the body forms a T at breakaway; the player should feel the stretch across the chest.
- The player shifts weight to the back leg at breakaway in order to load for power.
- Infielders break away at the chest; outfielders break away at the waist.
- The player does not step.
- The player drives her weight into the front leg to throw.
- The feet turn 45 degrees with the throw.
- The back leg releases during the follow-through; the player bends at the waist, and the arm brushes the outside of the upper thigh.

(continued)

Table 5.1 (continued)

4. Stepping and throwing—15 throws at a distance of 60 feet (18 m)
• The upper half and lower half of the body are now fully connected.
• The player begins squared up and facing the target.
• The player steps forward with the throwing-side foot at a 90-degree angle to the target in order to load the weight.
• The glove-side foot follows but remains partially open.
• The upper body is in throwing position as the front foot drops.
• The player leads with the elbow and drives her weight to the front.
• The back leg releases during the follow-through.
5. Performing the long toss—15 throws at a distance of 80 to 185 feet (24 to 56 m)
• The distance is increased as the arm warms up.
• The arc is increased as the distance increases.
• Outfielders can use one-hop throws.
• The player stops increasing the distance when she can no longer reach the target on the fly.
6. Shortening the distance
• The player begins decreasing the distance.
• The arc is reduced as the distance is decreased.
• The distance is decreased until the arc is gone.
• Infielders finish with quick throws; outfielders finish with one-hop throws.

Table 5.2 Game-Day Throwing Progression

The game-day throwing progression is a modified version of the practice throwing progression. The mechanics are the same; however, there are fewer throws, and achieving maximum distance is not necessary. The number of repetitions for every step leading up to the maximum game-day distance is roughly half the number in the practice throwing progression. Once the player is ready to throw at 100 percent effort, becoming warmed up is now the goal. The number of throws will vary for each player, and throwing should be repeated at the given distance until the player is game ready.
1. Working the wrist and elbow—10 throws at a distance of 10 feet (3 m)
2. Working the shoulder and upper half of the body—10 throws at a distance of 30 feet (9 m)
3. Loading and using the legs—10 throws at a distance of 40 feet (12 m)
4. Stepping and throwing—8 to 10 throws at a distance of 60 feet (18 m)
5. Performing the long toss—5 to 8 throws at a distance of 80 to 120 feet (24 to 36 m)
6. Shortening the distance—as described for the practice progression (until warmed up)

OVERHAND THROWING DRILLS

Coaches must vary the throwing drills that players use each day to warm up their arms to continually reinforce different components of the throw. To get the most benefit from these drills, use the specific rules for throwing drills listed in the previous section. These drills can be used as part of a warm-up, or they can be used after the warm-up with players throwing at full strength. In the latter case, the emphasis should be on hard, strong throws and accuracy. When using a drill to emphasize a particular component, players should throw at a shorter distance to reduce the need to throw the ball hard and to better isolate that element. Throwing distance should also be adjusted based on the player's skill level and how warm the arm is.

SCARECROW

Purpose: To practice fielding and throwing techniques and to check mechanics.

Procedure: The player takes two steps forward to field an imaginary ground ball. She gathers the ball in and then quickly jump turns, breaking away to a throwing position with both elbows up. The player holds that position, checks alignment (sideways to the target, feet in proper position, and shoulders level), and maintains balance. The coach walks behind players and gives a high five to the ball in order to check for proper wrist cock.

RELEASE AND SPIN

Purpose: To develop proper release and spin.

Procedure: Partners face each other from about 6 feet (2 m) away. One player holds the ball in her throwing hand with a proper grip and puts the throwing-arm elbow in her glove at about chest height. Partners throw the ball back and forth at least 25 times. This exercise isolates the wrist action so that the players can feel this particular component. They should feel the wrist action, emphasize proper release, and check the vertical spin. The motion is "snap down and wave good-bye."

SEQUENCE THROWING

Purpose: To force concentration so that players can work on accuracy.

Procedure: Players use this sequence of targets when throwing to a partner. Because the numbers are not in a logical sequence, the thrower must concentrate on each throw.

1. **Left shoulder**
2. **Right hip**
3. **Right shoulder**
4. **Left hip**

SELF-TOSS AND THROW

Figure 5.14   Self-toss and throw drill.

Purpose: To practice moving into the ball when catching a fly ball.

Procedure: The player tosses a ball to herself, catches it, and throws it to a partner, who is at throwing distance. The player should not throw the ball too high on the self-toss, tossing it only slightly above the head and in front of the throwing shoulder (see figure 5.14). Players work on moving into the ball when catching. They also work on using both hands to catch the ball.

SIDEARM CORRECTION

Purpose: To help players know if their arm drops to a sidearm position.

Procedure: The player stands perpendicular to a tall fence with the throwing arm next to the fence. The fence must be taller than the player's extended arm. With the throwing arm held at a 90-degree position, the arm should miss touching the fence by several inches. The player marks this spot and uses it every time she throws. If the arm drops to sidearm when playing catch at this position, the hand will hit the fence, providing instant feedback. Players can do this drill daily until they eliminate the sidearm throw and the overhand throw becomes automatic.

TRIANGLE CATCH AND THROW

Purpose: To practice correct body position when catching and throwing, with emphasis on turning the feet and body to throw.

Procedure: Three players form a right triangle. The player at the right-angle corner assumes the proper receiving position and catches the ball from the thrower. After catching the ball, the player focuses on turning the feet and shoulders toward the third player (target), who is to her right, and throws the ball to that player (see figure 5.15). The receiver catches the ball and puts it in a bucket.

The thrower also has a bucket; she takes a ball from this bucket to repeat the drill. When the thrower's bucket is empty, players rotate to new positions. If the player fielding and throwing is left-handed, the receiver is to her left so that the player fielding and throwing has to turn her body.

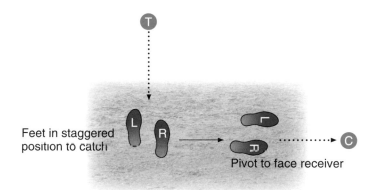

Figure 5.15 Triangle catch and throw drill.

SQUARE CATCH

Purpose: **To practice turning the feet in the direction of the throw and seeing the target.**

Procedure: **This is the best throwing drill I know! Four players stand in a square; they are positioned at throwing distance from one another. Players throw around the square 10 times in one direction, and then they reverse the ball. They catch the ball in proper receiving position and then turn their feet to proper throwing position.**

Variation: **To make sure the thrower is seeing the target before throwing the ball, have players in the square take turns dropping to one knee. The thrower throws around the square unless the next person is kneeling. The thrower must then move her feet and realign to proper position for a throw to another receiver. Players do not use a pattern for kneeling; they just randomly kneel to keep the thrower honest. If all players are kneeling, they all stand and restart the drill.**

QUICK RELEASE

Purpose: **To evaluate speed of release and throwing accuracy.**

Procedure: **Players pair up for a contest to see which pair can catch 20 balls first. The count begins with "one" on the first catch. On any overthrows, the partner must run the ball back to the line (for safety) before continuing. The pair sits when finished. Reward the winners. And to make sure all teams finish the drill, penalize the last two groups by having them run a lap. You can also count the number of completed catches in 20 seconds and keep team records.**

THROWING TO A TARGET

Purpose: **To emphasize and evaluate throwing accuracy.**

Procedure: **The catcher is sitting on a bucket on the third-base line in front of home plate. Fielders must make accurate throws home that don't require the catcher to move.**

Variation: **Use a catch screen or target at first. Set a stuffed animal on a stand and have players try to knock it off. If playing a big rival in your next game, get a stuffed animal that is their mascot.**

THROWS FOR RELEASE TIMES

Purpose: To measure the speed of the release and throw by timing the ball from glove to glove. This exercise demonstrates that a straight-line throw is much quicker than a rainbow throw.

Procedure: Players form a single-file line in left field. A player tosses the ball to herself, catches it, and throws to the catcher at home plate. Draw a throwing line that players must stay behind so that all are throwing the same distance. This drill is useful in tryouts.

Variations:

- Hit ground balls and fly balls to the throwers. Vary the field positions.
- Place balls on the line and have players do a dead-ball pickup and throw.
- Have players field bunts and throw to first. High school and college players need to be able to do this in 2.9 seconds or better.

THROWER IN THE BOX

Purpose: To locate a target and use proper body alignment for throwing.

Procedure: The thrower stands in the middle of a square or in the middle of the diamond. When using the diamond, receivers should use correct positions at the bases. The coach throws or rolls a ball to the thrower and calls out a position number where the throw is to be made, and the thrower sends it to that location. The receiver returns the throw quickly and accurately to the catcher so that the drill can continue. Go as fast as the players' skill will allow.

Variation: The catcher throws to the number called, and the coach continues to call out numbers for subsequent throws. This drill can be done with or without a player in the middle.

WET BALL

Purpose: To prepare for throwing in soggy conditions

Procedure: Players practice throwing with a wet ball so that they can adjust to the elements and prepare psychologically for difficult conditions. Many types of drills can be executed with a wet ball. Outfielders must often adjust to wet grass, so include numerous outfield ground-ball drills.

STAY LOW THROWS

Purpose: To practice staying low during and after release; to break a third-base player's habit of standing upright before throwing when charging a bunt.

Procedure: Place three to six balls near each other as if they were bunted. The player charges and throws to first base without first standing up. The player must stay low and throw all the balls continuously.

THROWING ON THE RUN

Purpose: To develop throwing accuracy when throwing on the run; to prepare for rundowns.

Procedure: Partners in two lines face each other 60 feet (18 m) apart. Make sure players are well spread apart so that an errant throw does not hit anyone. One partner does a self-toss and then runs hard at her partner for three to five steps and makes a chest-high throw. The thrower returns to her original position, and the partner repeats the drill going the opposite direction. To make the drill realistic, players should run at the speed they will use in a game.

SHOW THE BALL

Purpose: To practice showing the first-base player the ball.

Procedure: Fielders line up single file halfway between first base and second base. The coach or a player hits ground balls to one fielder at a time. The player fields the ball and shows it to the first-base player. The fielder cannot release the ball until the first base player says "yes," indicating that she has clearly seen it. The first-base player catches the ball and places it in a bucket.

Variation: Execute the drill at other infield positions requiring short throws to bases.

CIRCLE BACKHAND FLIPS

Purpose: To develop accuracy of backhand flips.

Procedure: Players in a tight circle pass the ball around the circle using flip tosses. This is a good drill to use while players are recovering from a conditioning exercise.

Variation: With a moving circle, players can practice leading receivers with backhand flips. The player tosses the ball using a backhand flip to the player in front of her. The tosser must lead a moving player. Have the circle go both clockwise and counterclockwise. Advance to running in both directions.

HIT-BALL LINE FLIPS

Purpose: To execute backhand flips off hit balls.

Procedure: Two lines of fielders stand about 10 feet (3 m) apart facing the hitter. A hitter hits a ball to the first player in the fielding line. The fielder flips the ball to a teammate at the front of the opposite line, who throws to a catcher near the hitter. The catcher feeds the hitter so that the drill can continue rapidly.

TARGET THROW

Purpose: To practice making quick and accurate throws in a high-pressure situation.

Procedure: Make a target on a wall, fence, or catch net. Record the number of throws that hit the target in 30 seconds. Balls are in a bucket, placed in a line, rolled, or tossed.

GOLF SOFTBALL

Purpose: To develop throwing accuracy with a fun practice game.

Procedure: Set up three to four cones about 50 feet (15 m) apart from one another. Divide the team into three or four groups. Each group throws toward its own cone. Each player's goal is to knock down the cone with the fewest throws possible (it can be on a bounce). The first person in each group throws the ball at the cone, and the ball is left where it lands. The second player in each group then throws at the cone. Players take turns throwing within their group. As in golf, each group keeps track of the number of throws it takes to knock over the cone. When each group is finished knocking over the cone at their location, the players rotate to the next cone (or hole). Coaches can make a little scorecard for each team and emphasize proper throwing techniques.

THREE-SECOND INFIELD

Purpose: To practice getting rid of the ball in a hurry.

Procedure: Infielders are in their proper defensive positions. Place a garbage can as a target at first base with a screen behind it. Make sure you have plenty of balls. The coach rolls or hits balls to players, who have three seconds to pick up the ball and throw it at the garbage can. The coach loudly counts off the seconds. This will initially fluster some younger players but will also help them learn to deal with game pressure and the speed of the game.

THROWING 3-2-1 GAME

Purpose: To practice making accurate throws under pressure in a fun team competition.

Procedure: Place three balls on the ground evenly spaced about three-fourths of the way from third to home. Divide players into two teams. The fielding team has a player at first and a group at second and third. The batting team lines up at home without bats but with helmets. When the coach yells "Go," the batter–runner runs as fast as she can to first base and on to second. The fielder at third runs to the first ball and makes a throw to a teammate at second, then goes to the second ball and makes a throw to the same fielder, then does the same thing with the third ball. The object is to make three good throws from the third-base line to second before the runner gets to second. If the runner gets there first, or if the fielders make a bad throw or catch, the batting team gets a point. If the fielder gets all three balls to second before the runner gets there, no points are awarded.

GET THE RUNNER

Purpose: To practice throwing to bases ahead of the base runner and backing up throws.

Procedure: At least three players line up behind all four bases. Players must follow two rules: (1) After throwing, the player always runs to the base in front of her (home to first to second to third to home); (2) The player must always throw to the base that the runner is going to.

The ball begins at home plate. The runner at first runs to second, so the throw goes from home to second. The thrower then runs to first, and the player who catches the ball at second throws to first. As soon as the second-base player throws the ball to first, she runs to third (rule 1). The next throw will then be from first to third. The first-base player runs to second, and the throw goes from third to second. The third-base player runs home (after throwing to second), and the throw goes from second to home. Play continues with the next throw going to third. Players just need to follow rule 1 regarding where the throw goes, and they always run to the next base after they throw. Meanwhile, the second player in line assumes the backup position, aligning with the direction of the throw. Each backup keeps adjusting because the throw is always coming from a different direction.

Runners swing wide as they approach the base, and they go to the end of the line at that base. They do not slide or get in the way of the throw. Receivers can still practice applying the tag at the base. Note: During the first few sequences, the players will be slow remembering the rules, but after a few times through, they should have the routine down.

CATCHING

f you can't catch, you can't play softball! Defense begins with catching the ball, whether it is a throw, a ground ball, or a pop fly. A good glove can make this task easier, but proper body position and technique lead to consistency and success. It is relatively easy for players to catch balls that come directly to them and when there is time for them to assume good body positioning. But errant throws and well-hit balls often don't permit this luxury. Add to this the game situation, the speed of the runners, and obstacles such as the wind, fences, and the sun, and the difficulty increases.

Catching is a psychological skill as well as a physical one. Players must believe they can catch everything. They need to go after every ball with all they have. Those who never give up on a ball will never have to ask or answer the question of whether they could have gotten the ball if only they had really tried. Those who make a total commitment to every ball will sometimes surprise themselves at the catches they make.

Players should strive to make catches look easy. Often the spectacular catch is the result of a player not getting a good jump on the ball and subsequently being in poor position to make the easy catch. This chapter describes the skills and techniques that will give players the best chance for success in making all types of catches. Later chapters include specific drills that can be used to develop these skills for position play.

THE GLOVE

The glove is a player's defensive weapon. The player must first find a glove that fits the hand comfortably. She must be able to squeeze the pocket shut around the ball so that it will not pop out. The size of the glove should fit the player's position. Infielders need a smaller glove (generally 10 1/2 to 11 1/2 inches) with a shallower pocket so that they can get the ball out quickly. Younger players should choose smaller gloves to maintain control. Youth sizes generally range from 9 inches (very small) to 11 inches. For growing players, avoid buying a glove to grow into because this will make it much more difficult for them to catch and control the ball. Because of the size of the softball, the pocket of the glove needs to be a little deeper than one for baseball.

To extend their reach, outfielders should use as large a glove as they can control. This is usually 12 to 13 inches for adults, 11 inches for children. A deeper pocket helps to keep the ball from popping out. When catching a fly ball, an open web allows the player to see the ball all the way into the glove.

Catchers and first-base players want a glove with a large pocket to protect their hands from being bruised by all the hard balls they will receive. A first-base glove is similar to a catcher's glove but has less padding and a more shallow pocket. It is longer to increase the reach. Only catchers and first-base players may use a mitt (a glove without fingers). A baseball catcher's glove does not have a pocket big enough to hold a softball, but a first-base player's baseball mitt can work well in softball.

Fortunately, manufacturers now make gloves specifically for softball and for a girl's smaller hand.

You get what you pay for in quality. Cheaper gloves can be very uncomfortable and impossible to break in. Leather offers the best comfort, durability, and control. Treated leather provides a faster break-in and increased durability, and it reduces the amount of care needed. Synthetic materials are lighter, less durable, and less expensive. They can be a good choice for younger players.

Comfort and workability are the keys. A player should choose a glove that will bend easily and soften while retaining its shape as it's broken in to fit the hand and form a pocket. To soften the leather, use a manufacturer's oil, a leather conditioner, petroleum jelly, or shaving cream. Apply a small amount of the product with a cloth to the pocket and back of the fingers, and let it absorb in overnight. Do not overoil; more is not better! You want a round, roomy pocket. To form the pocket, the player can play catch (or catch off a pitching machine) and throw a ball repeatedly into the glove.

The player's finger position will shape the pocket, which must be large enough to hold a softball. The player should never put the index finger in the glove's index finger slot because that is exactly where the softball will hit the hand and bruise it. Instead, find a comfortable position by putting the index finger outside the glove. Another option is to "double up" the fingers by putting three fingers in the last finger slot and the index finger alone in the next slot or by putting two fingers together in the last two slots.

Web design is a matter of personal preference. Web designs with spaces allow you to see the ball all the way into the glove. These designs are also a little lighter, and they allow dirt to fall through. Solid webs offer a better sun shield on pop-ups and fly balls. Pitchers should use a slightly larger glove and a closed web so they can hide their pitches.

A player must take care of her glove if it is to remain an effective tool. Always keep a ball in the pocket of the glove to maintain the pocket. Tie it shut with a rubber band or shoestring when not in use. Do not throw your glove around the field; keep it dry and wipe off built-up dirt with a dry cloth. When placing a glove on the ground, players should lay it carefully on the fingers with the pocket down.

When fielding balls *below the waist*, players should point the fingers of both hands down. For balls *above the waist*, they point the fingers up. If possible, players should catch waist-high line drives with the fingers pointed up by bending the legs lower and keeping the elbows bent.

POSITIONING THE GLOVE

Purpose: To practice adjusting the glove position depending on the location of the ball.

Procedure: The player starts with the glove above the head at 12 o'clock with the fingers pointed up. If the glove is on the left hand, the player makes a circle clockwise to 3 o'clock, then 6 o'clock, and continues around while keeping the pocket open as if to catch a ball. The player keeps the elbow bent and the glove close to the body in a catching position. For right-handers, at 3 o'clock, the fingers are still pointed up. As the hand drops below the waist, the fingers gradually rotate down until they point directly down at 5 o'clock. As the hand crosses the midline of the body at 6 o'clock, the hand rotates over to a backhand position (balls caught on the side of the body opposite the glove are caught backhanded). The player rotates the thumb down toward the ground, keeping the palm open to the ball. At 9 o'clock, the fingers have again rotated to an upward position. When the player is familiar with proper positioning, a partner tosses her balls to catch in various locations.

CATCHING THROWS

To catch a throw, the receiver should wait in a ready, balanced position, facing the thrower and ready to move quickly in any direction should the ball be thrown off line (see figure 6.1). The feet are slightly more than shoulder-width apart with the glove-side foot slightly forward. The knees are slightly flexed with weight on the balls of the feet. The arms extend toward the thrower with the elbows slightly flexed. The pocket is open toward the thrower to provide a chest-high target. The throwing hand is beside the pocket with the fingers of both hands pointed upward and the thumbs touching. The player should always catch with two hands to secure the ball and prepare for a quick release.

As the receiver catches the ball, she should move her feet so that she catches it just in front of the throwing shoulder. Because the throwing hand is already there to grip the ball, no effort is wasted in bringing the ball to the throwing position, thus reducing release time. As the thrower hurls the ball, the receiver should focus on the release point and then follow the ball all the way into the glove. The receiver should flex her arms as she catches the ball to lessen the impact. The goal is to have "soft hands," which will prevent the ball from popping out of the glove. The player should begin with nearly full extension of the arms so that a greater distance is available to absorb the impact. As the ball lands in the pocket of the glove, the throwing hand closes over the ball, and the fingers then grip the seams.

Figure 6.1 **The ready position for receiving a throw.**

BASIC FIELDING POSITION

Infielders and outfielders use a similar basic position for fielding, which is the athletic stance used in most sports. For every pitch, players should be balanced with weight on the balls of the feet so that they can react quickly in any direction. Fielders assume the *ready position* when the pitcher has the ball. The glove-side foot is slightly ahead of the other foot, and the feet are shoulder-width apart. The toes are turned inward (pigeon-toed) so that the weight is forward on the balls of the feet. Players should feel the two big toes and be balanced. The hands and elbows are loose and relaxed, and the hands can be on the knees. Outfielders may prefer to be more upright in the ready position. The focus is on the pitcher and the batter (general focus). At this time, fielders should review mentally the play they will make if the ball comes to them.

Fielders shift into the *set position* as the pitcher begins the windup, and they narrow their focus to the hitter's contact spot. (Focus has moved from general to specific, from wide to narrow.) The hands move to receiving position with the glove open toward the batter and the elbows outside the knees. We used to tell our players that the corners (first and third) should have their gloves closer to the ground than other

One Hand or Two?

A good glove with a good pocket makes one-hand catches fairly easy. When you have to react quickly, one hand is usually the best you can do. You can also reach farther with one hand. But when you have to make a throw, two-hand catches promote a quicker release. The throwing hand is already there to grip and release the ball quickly. Two hands also help secure the ball so it will not bounce out. With the bigger softball, this can easily happen. Therefore, whenever possible, players should catch with two hands.

fielders because of the shorter reaction time required at those positions. But because batters have become stronger and are able to hit the ball harder, safety has become a greater concern. Therefore, many players now put the glove in front of the face to protect against hard-hit balls at such a short distance. Middle infielders usually assume a position with hands about waist level or below in preparation for ground balls (see figure 6.2). Players should never put the glove on the ground because doing so limits their ability to move quickly forward or laterally. Having the hips too low will also inhibit movement, and players will often fall forward when making a play. Outfielders should hold their hands chest high with the palms toward the batter and pointed up (see figure 6.3). All players should assume a relaxed, balanced, and comfortable position.

As the pitch is released, the defensive player should step into what sport psychologist Ken Ravizza, co-author of *Heads-Up Baseball: Playing the Game One Pitch at a Time* (Ravizza and Hanson, New York: McGraw Hill, 1995), calls the "circle of focus," focusing all attention on the batter. The player should take a small step forward, step into that circle, and concentrate on the contact spot where the bat meets the ball. As the ball reaches the hitting zone, the player's feet should be quiet. By watching the angle and the speed at which the ball leaves the bat, the player can get a good jump on the ball.

Figure 6.2 **Middle infield set position.**

Figure 6.3 **Outfield set position.**

The player should not wait for the ball to reach her. She must react to the batted ball early so that there is time to get in proper position. If the batter does not hit the ball, the defensive player can step back out of the circle and relax a bit.

MOVING TO THE BALL

The goal in fielding is to get directly behind every ball so that the body can serve as a wall to stop the ball if necessary. Players should charge the ball and attack it, not letting the ball play them! A straight line to the ball is always the fastest route. Infielders should use direct angles and should avoid going around the ball. Outfielders, when they have time, may circle the ball and then move into it to gain momentum on their throws. The sooner players get to the ball, the quicker they can throw it.

The first step toward the ball is a jab step with the throwing-side foot. The jab step is a slight hop or push off the ground to begin the motion. The fielder then uses shuffle steps to square up to the ball for fielding. On a hard-hit ball, however, there may be time for only one step, which should be a step with the glove-side foot. The sooner fielders react to the ball off the bat, the easier it is for them to anticipate where the ball is going and to be there waiting for it.

COACHING POINTS FOR MOVING TO THE BALL

- Before charging, have your feet already in motion, much as a tennis player does while waiting for a serve. Have "twinkle toes" as you do a little tap dance with your feet. Doing this will help you overcome inertia and react faster.
- Make sure your line of vision extends well out in front of you. React to the ball on the first or second bounce. The sooner you pick up the ball and react, the better your chance of getting into proper position.
- Count the number of bounces as you field the ball. Doing this helps you focus on moving to the ball and fielding it as low to the ground as possible.
- Don't be lazy. The goal is to be square behind every ball. Consider a backhand or any other type of off-center catch a desperation play.
- Think of the approach as being like an airplane going in for a landing—not a helicopter!

CATCHING GROUND BALLS

Players use three basic techniques for catching ground balls hit at them. The speed of the ball, the bounce, the player's reaction time, and the speed of the batter determine which technique the fielder should use.

Gathering the Ball

Just before receiving the ball, the fielder stops, splits or spreads the legs (going from narrow to wide in a well-balanced position), and puts the glove on the ground (see figure 6.4a). The hips are down as if sitting on a chair, but weight is forward on the toes.

Figure 6.4 Gathering the ball. *(a)* The player receives the ball in a wide stance with the glove on the ground, and *(b)* uses soft hands to gather the ball to the abdomen.

Players must use their thigh muscles. Both hands extend forward, forming the large end of a triangle or funnel well in front of the feet. The fielder turns the elbow in to get the glove open to the ball. The angle of the glove should be approximately 45 degrees to the ground. The head is over the ball, and the glove foot is slightly ahead. The player guides the ball through the triangle to the point of the triangle attached to the belly button. The chin is tucked, and the eyes watch the ball all the way in. As the fielder gathers in the ball, the glove hand gives softly with the impact to cradle the ball (see figure 6.4*b*). The player uses the bare throwing hand to close over the ball and shifts her weight to the back foot as the ball is brought in toward the abdomen.

Scooping the Ball

Because of the short distances in softball, players don't always have time to charge and then stop to gather the ball. This is especially true on slow rollers, with fast runners, and on balls that bounce close to the fielder's feet (short hops). To scoop the ball, the player must keep the body low, hold the head down, and extend the hands. The ball is caught farther in front of the body than when gathering the ball. The glove action is a snap up instead of a gathering in. Ideally, the top hand is above the glove (see figure 6.5), and the hand and glove close together to trap the ball as jaws would (glove first and then bare hand). Beginners should keep the bare hand on the side of the glove; this will prevent injuries to the ends of the fingers if the player misjudges the ball. When a player gains confidence, she should place the throwing hand above the glove in position for a quicker release. The head is over the glove as the player snaps up the ball.

Figure 6.5 Scooping the ball.

Running Through the Ball

Players should always charge the ball, but with this method players run right through the ball as they make the catch. When there is no time to stop and catch the ball, the

COACHING POINTS FOR CATCHING GROUND BALLS

Gathering the Ball

- Pretend you are catching a raw egg. If you are correctly gathering the ball, you should hear no sound as you give with the ball.
- Always stay square on the ball so that you can use your body to block a bad bounce or a misplayed ball.
- Always pull the ball back to the belly button (center of the body). A common error is to gather the ball back to the throwing side, preparing to throw. If you misplay the ball, the body will not be in a position to block the ball.

Scooping the Ball

- Remember these key ideas: Catch farther out, snap the glove up, and scoop dirt.
- Keep in mind that balls will pop out of the glove more easily. Use your bare hand to secure the ball quickly. If the ball pops out, use both hands to catch it again.

Running Through the Ball

- Keep the head and body down until you are certain you have made the catch. Some players, thinking they must hurry, have a tendency to lift up to look at the target and runner.
- Go hard after every ball. There is no time to decide if you can or cannot get to the ball. That involves two decisions, and you don't have time to choose. Always think *I can* and go hard, running through the ball. When you go all out after every ball, your teammates cannot second-guess your efforts. There is no question that you tried your best!
- Stay square to the ball. Be in a position to use your body to block a bad bounce.

What Technique to Use?

- Hard-hit ball with no time to react—gather
- Hard-hit ball to your glove side and behind you—gather
- Hard-hit ball to your glove side but in front of you—scoop or gather depending on bounce
- Hard-hit ball to the throwing side—gather using backhand technique
- Short hop—scoop
- Slow roller—scoop or run through

body goes to the ball, rather than the ball going to the body. Infielders make the catch in front of and inside the glove-side foot and inside the body. Outfielders may find that they have better balance and are more comfortable scooping the ball outside the glove foot. They then field off the glove foot with one hand, throw off the opposite foot, and run through the throw for accuracy. With either technique, the player stays square to the ball until it is caught.

By running through the ball, players extend their reach to its maximum. When players stop and reach to catch a ball, their range is limited. Running through the ball also helps players maintain balance by allowing their momentum to continue forward. Players are then in position to throw on the run. When running full speed ahead, it is often impossible for a player to stop and reset the feet in time to make the play. A second-base player or shortstop charging a slow roller in front of her should focus on reaching and running through the ball to extend her range and should then make the play. Similarly, an outfielder should concentrate on charging a ground ball and should then use her momentum to throw the runner out at home (see figure 6.6).

Figure 6.6   Running through the ball.

MAKING DESPERATION CATCHES

When a player catches a ball that she could not get behind, it should be considered a desperation catch. Fielders should attempt to get behind every ball they field. Good anticipation and quick feet can make this happen. Failure to get behind the ball puts the fielder in poor throwing position and hinders the ability to block the ball when necessary. The best fielders make all plays look routine and effortless. Lazy players often make what appear to be spectacular catches because they fail to get quickly into proper position. These players cost their team games

Forehand Catches

Catches on a player's glove side are forehand catches. For the quickest reaction time, the fielder uses a jab step followed by a crossover step. Using a crossover step as the first step is slower and commits the player to a position that is more difficult to move from if she has to adjust to the line of the ball. To cross over, the player pivots on the foot closer to the ball and then steps across with the opposite foot. Keeping the body low, the fielder runs hard to the side, pumping both arms, and at the last moment extends the glove-side leg and the glove (with the pocket open) to the ball. The ball is fielded in front of the glove-side foot and just inside (see figure 6.7). (The glove is closer to home than the foot.) The fielder stays low with the weight on the front foot and her eyes on the ball.

Figure 6.7   The forehand catch.

Backhand Catches

Catches made on a player's throwing-arm side are backhand catches. The fielder often has time to turn and step but sometimes can only react with the glove.

- **Backhand with crossover step**—The first step is a jab step. The player then executes a crossover step just before reaching and catching (see figure 6.8). The player extends the glove-side leg to the ball, flexing the knee and dropping the hips. This is a one-hand catch. The glove catches the ball opposite or behind the forward foot. The elbow is at a 90-degree angle when possible. When the ball is on the ground, the movement of the glove is up, with the elbow leading and pointing to the sky. The fielder needs soft hands to keep the ball in the glove. The weight is on the forward foot, and the head is over the glove. The fielder must then take a short extra step with the throwing-side foot and push hard off that throwing foot to attain throwing position quickly.

- **No-step backhand**—Some balls come so quickly that the fielder has no time to move the feet. On these plays, the fielder should catch the ball beside the throwing foot and emphasize lifting the elbow (see figure 6.9).

Figure 6.8 Backhand catch with a crossover step.

Figure 6.9 No-step backhand catch.

Diving

Players should attempt to catch every ball. Sometimes the only way to reach the ball is to become airborne. By leaving the feet, players can extend their reach by at least one body length. Some coaches may not allow their pitchers to dive because of fear that they might injure their shoulders. But I have seen pitchers save a game by diving for and catching a popped-up bunt. Players should learn to dive and go all out to make the catch. The two basic types of dives are the headfirst dive and the bent-leg slide.

Headfirst Dive   To initiate a headfirst dive, the player keeps her body low and pushes off the balls of the feet. Both arms are extended toward the ball with the palm of the glove hand up and open to the ball. The fielder stays low and parallel to the ground like a swimmer doing a racing start. The player should dive as the ball approaches its lowest point and should land on the upper thighs and belly (see figure 6.10). Players should not use a volleyball dive with an arched back because they will not slide on the ground as they do on a gym floor. Back injury is a possible result. Players should extend the arms and use the throwing hand to trap the ball in the glove. They should not use one hand or the elbows to support themselves on the ground because wrist and arm injuries may result. A potential problem for players who keep some fingers outside their glove is that those fingers are unprotected and more susceptible to being jammed. When diving toward the glove side, the open pocket of the glove should face the infield, with the thumb up; when diving to the nonglove side, the thumb is down.

Figure 6.10   Headfirst dive.

Bent-Leg Slide   A bent-leg slide allows players to go all out while protecting themselves against an obstacle such as a fence or wall. To catch a ball using the bent-leg slide, the fielder should slide under the ball as if she were sliding into a base (see chapter 3, page 62). The catch should be made with the hands chest or waist high (see figure 6.11). It is also possible to use the body to trap the ball. If the player is near a fence, the bent-leg slide is preferred over the headfirst dive because the risk of injury is lower. The player should keep the extended knee bent so that it can give on contact with the fence.

Figure 6.11   Bent-leg slide.

CATCHING FLY BALLS AND POP-UPS

When moving toward a fly ball or pop-up, a player must always communicate that she plans to catch it. A simple "mine" will do. Calling loudly is a must to prevent collisions and injuries. Calling it early produces the best results. Before the ball is called, there is doubt about who is going to catch it, which means players are giving only about 80 percent effort. The earlier the ball is called, the earlier the commitment is made to make the play, and the more likely it is that the ball will be caught!

Figure 6.12 Catching a fly ball in front of the throwing shoulder when a quick throw is necessary.

Figure 6.13 Catching a short fly ball.

Surrounding teammates should confirm that they hear the call and are giving way by yelling a simple "take it!" A fielder should never call the ball for another player except in desperation. An example would be a fielder who is blinded by the sun and is able to get out of the way of another player, who then might be able to make a last-ditch effort.

Players should catch the ball at eye level, using both hands when possible. Letting the ball drop below the plane of the eyes allows it to be easily misjudged. The bare hand should be behind the pocket and ready to close the glove quickly so that the ball cannot bounce out. This method also keeps the throwing hand close for a quick release. The fielder should give with the ball by flexing the elbows and bringing the glove toward the body.

If a fielder must make a quick throw, she should catch the ball in front of the throwing shoulder with the body slightly sideways (see figure 6.12). She moves her feet to get her body behind the ball in this position. The fielder should also keep the ball well in front of her body so that she can move into the ball as she catches it, transferring this momentum into the throw. The fielder gives with the ball toward the throwing shoulder as she makes the catch and then grips the ball.

Short Fly Balls

When moving to a ball well in front of them, players must keep the body low, the head down, and the eyes on the ball as they run full speed toward it. The glove should not be extended until the last minute. When the fielder does extend the glove, she holds the palm up and the pocket open as she focuses on the ball (see figure 6.13). The elbow should be rotated in to open up the pocket. The fielder must not lift her eyes or body because doing so will tend to raise the glove. When the ball is in the pocket, the fielder should use the throwing hand to trap the ball. If the ball falls in front of her, the player should keep her chin and head down and short hop the ball. The fielder must not lift the head and body because this would allow the ball to get under the glove. The player should be in a position to use her body to block the ball and keep it from getting by her.

Long Fly Balls

On balls hit over their head, players must go back, of course, but a backpedal should not be used for more than three or four steps. Backpedaling sacrifices speed and balance. Fielders should backpedal only on balls hit directly to them that require little change in position.

On long fly balls, the player's first step should be a drop step. The side that the fielder thinks the ball is going toward determines which foot to step on. She lowers the hips, pushes them back hard, and then steps on the foot to the side that she thinks the ball will land (see figure 6.14a). The fielder pivots on that foot and pushes hard with the opposite foot (see figure 6.14b), then initiates a crossover step as she turns to run full speed on a straight angle to the place where she thinks the ball will descend. The fielder tries to keep her eyes on the ball to track its flight, running on the balls of the feet so that her eyes do not bounce excessively. The player should use good running form, pumping the arms. The glove is extended only during the last four or five steps, and the fielder always reaches and tries for the ball. When the fielder catches the ball, she quickly secures it with the other hand. If a throw needs to be made, the fielder braces against the front leg immediately after making the catch to stop her momentum. She regains her balance, pivots, and throws.

Figure 6.14 **Catching a long fly ball.** *(a)* **The outfielder drop steps on the foot to the side where the ball will land, then** *(b)* **pivots with that foot and pushes hard with the opposite foot to run full speed at the ball.**

Some players may find it difficult to read the direction quickly and drop step to the appropriate side. These players should drop step to the side that is most comfortable (usually the throwing-side foot) and should locate the ball as they take this step. If the ball is hit to the opposite side, they can use one of two techniques:

- **Inside (reverse) roll**—When using the inside roll, the outfielder can keep her eyes on the ball at all times. She pushes hard off the back leg to reverse direction and pivots inward, always keeping her nose on the ball (see figure 6.15 on page 130). This is a slower method than the outside roll because the player must stop and change direction. An advantage of this technique that is helpful for beginners is that the ball is always in sight. The inside roll should be used on fly balls that are easily within the fielder's range.

- **Outside roll**—When using the outside roll, the fielder loses sight of the ball for a moment while turning her back to it and circling around to pick it up on the other side.

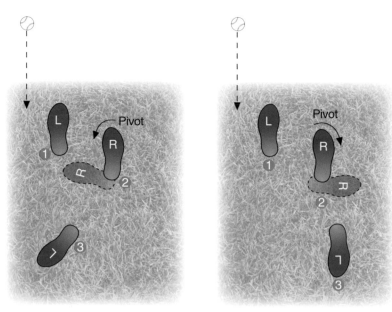

Figure 6.15 Inside, or reverse, roll.   **Figure 6.16** Outside roll.

The move begins with the drop step with the foot farthest from the ball. The fielder pivots hard on the back foot, crosses over with the opposite leg, and sprints back (see figure 6.16). Without breaking stride, the fielder picks up the ball on the opposite side. An outside roll allows the momentum of the body to continue to flow into the turn, so the fielder should use it on hard-hit balls that require a long sprint.

Which way should players turn when the ball is directly overhead? For very deep balls, turning to the glove side gives maximum extension. The glove can reach farther from that side. For balls that aren't as deep, turning to the throwing side allows fielders to get to the throwing position more easily with less movement.

COACHING POINTS FOR CATCHING FLY BALLS

- Work on developing good balance and quick feet. Then, even if you initially misjudge a ball, you can often recover in time to make the catch.

- Always catch with two hands.

- Always make sure that your first step is a drop step back. On long fly balls, a common error is to take several steps forward before judging the ball. This increases the distance that the player must go when the ball is over her head.

OVERCOMING OBSTACLES

Before players begin to field their positions in practice or in a game, they should familiarize themselves with all obstacles. They should count the number of steps from their position to any barriers. What materials are the barriers made of and how will the ball and the player rebound? Is there any give? Players can throw some balls at the fence or wall to check the rebound. Can the barrier be climbed? Players should check the sun, the lights, the wind, and the background. Sunglasses, hats, and eye black for glare can be helpful. Here are some tips for handling fences, the sun, and the wind:

Figure 6.17　**Blocking the sun.**

- **Fence play**—The fielder should move quickly toward the fence and should reach for and find the fence when time permits. Not knowing where the fence is often causes a player to stop out of fear. She should find it with the hips (which are padded) or the forearm and then come back for the ball. The fielder must not run to the fence with the arms or fingers extended because injury can easily occur. If time permits, the player may have a chance to locate the fence visually, but doing this requires her to take her eyes off the ball, and finding the ball again may be difficult. Using the bent-leg slide can provide protection when the fielder is running a long distance and doesn't have time to reach for and find the fence.

- **Sun play**—The fielder can use the glove to shield her eyes by placing it on the sun to block the glare (see figure 6.17). She sights the ball over or under the glove and removes the glove from the sun at the last second to make the catch. Another solution is to approach the ball at an angle to minimize the directness of the light. Fielders must communicate with their teammates. A player in a position less bothered by the sun may be able to make the play.

- **Wind**—Players should be aware of the direction and strength of the wind, and they should note any changes during the game. During warm-ups, players should observe how the wind affects the flight of the ball when hit and thrown. Depending on the strength of the wind, players may shift their positions to adjust for the effects. If the wind is blowing in toward home, they might move in four to six steps. Conversely, if the wind is behind the hitter, they might back up four to six steps, especially on "up" pitches. If the wind is blowing left or right, a normal shift is three or four steps in the direction of the wind. A strong wind can make communication difficult. Not only is it difficult to hear, but what appears to be a routine ball for one fielder may drift to another fielder's area. Players should call loudly and repeatedly so that everyone can hear. Once a fielder has committed to and called for the ball, she must stay with it no matter where it blows. A ball thrown into the wind will definitely slow down, and a crosswind will blow it off line. The higher the throw, the more the wind will affect it. Fielders should keep throws down and may need to increase the number of bounces.

GROUND-BALL DRILLS

Many repetitions are necessary to develop any skill, and players must practice fielding all types of ground balls every day to develop proper technique. To help players build confidence and proper skills, coaches should hit balls that players can field successfully while using correct technique. Hitting hard shots that put the fielders on their heels only reinforces poor technique and does nothing for confidence.

Players can practice glove work at short distances with partners rolling the ball back and forth. This technique not only saves time and the players' arms but also allows the coach to easily observe their technique. Fielding balls and putting them in a bucket allows many repetitions in a short amount of time while saving the strain on the throwing arm. Players should field hit balls at the correct distance for the position they play to simulate game conditions. Using a variety of drills helps eliminate boredom. Drills should not be so long that the players become too fatigued to practice good mechanics.

HIT, FIELD, AND TOSS TO BUCKET

Purpose: To practice fielding ground balls without making players wait or tiring their arms.

Procedure: Players are in groups of three: one fielder, one hitter, and one receiver with a bucket near her. After fielding the hit ground ball, the fielder tosses the ball to the receiver, who puts it in the bucket. Players rotate duties when the bucket is full. Players keep busy and don't waste their arms with needless throws!

SOFT HANDS

Purpose: To develop soft hands when gathering the ball.

Procedure: Partners stand 6 feet (2 m) apart and roll balls back and forth using an underhand toss. They field ground balls with their bare hands or by using flat gloves or wooden paddles. This forces players to give and gather the ball and to use two hands. The hips are down, and the arms create a triangle.

Variations: Instead of ground balls, players catch a ball or other object tossed in the air. For a fun drill that makes the point, use eggs or water balloons.

READY, SET, GO

Purpose: To practice fielding ground balls from basic "ready, set, go" positions.

Procedure: The coach faces the players, who are in a staggered position in three or four lines. On command, players assume "ready" then "set" positions. On the command "go," players take three steps forward to field and gather an imaginary ball. They catch and go to the throwing position with quick feet. Players don't retreat but take the ready position at that spot to continue the drill.

Variation: The coach can call for any type of catch following the command "go."

PARTNER SCOOPS

Purpose: To focus on the hand action for scooping ground balls.

Procedure: Partners take positions 6 feet apart and roll balls back and forth, keeping their feet still and fielding with a scooping action. Players reach for the ball sooner than when gathering. They should use the top hand as a jaw to trap the ball. Do this drill on grass to keep loose infield dirt from flipping into players' faces.

LINE SCOOPS

Purpose: To practice scooping balls while running.

Procedure: A fielding line faces a tosser at a distance of 30 to 40 feet (9 to 12 m). In turn, each fielder runs hard at the tosser, who rolls or tosses a ball that must be scooped by the fielder. The fielder tosses it back (underhand) to the tosser and goes to the end of the fielding line.

Variation: Rapid-fire toss is for advanced players. Players are in a line about 20 feet (6 m) from the tosser. The tosser throws balls quickly at the fielders' feet using an overhand throw. The tosser uses a harder throw and angles that are more difficult. The fielder moves toward the tosser, scoops the hard-thrown ball, returns it to the tosser, and goes to the end of the line.

EXPLODE THROUGH THE BALL

Purpose: To practice reaching and running through every ball.

Procedure: Fielders form a line about 10 feet (3 m) from the tosser. One at a time they run laterally as the tosser tosses the ball low and in front of them so that they have to reach. Each player focuses on exploding through the ball as she catches it. The fielder must not stop and reach because doing so would limit her range. Each player returns the ball with a toss, waits, and forms a line that reverses the direction.

CONE ROLLS

Purpose: To increase range while staying behind the ball.

Procedure: Place two cones about 12 feet (3.5 m) apart to serve as targets and boundaries (see figure 6.18). A tosser with a ball stands about 15 feet (4.5 m) in front of each cone. A fielder takes a position midway between the cones and several steps in front of them so that the cones will not interfere with her movement. The first tosser rolls a ball toward a cone. The fielder sidesteps to the ball, gathers it in, returns it underhand to the tosser, resets in the middle, and then goes the other way to field a ball rolled by the second tosser. The fielder must concentrate on footwork and staying square behind the ball.

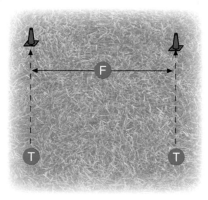

Figure 6.18 Cone rolls drill.

CHAMP OR CHUMP

Purpose: To field batted balls in a competitive situation.

Procedure: A hitter and a receiver face a line of three players about 20 feet (6 m) away. The first player fields the ball and returns it to the receiver. She continues until an error is made. Then the players rotate: The receiver becomes the hitter, the fielder becomes the receiver, and the hitter goes to the end of the line. The goal is to be at the front of the fielding line when the drill ends.

FENCE RANGE

Purpose: To emphasize running through the ball to increase range.

Procedure: Players form a single-file line a few feet away from the backstop and to one side of the tosser. The first fielder in line begins by throwing a ball to the tosser approximately 15 feet (4.5 m) away. The fielder then sprints full speed ahead to catch a return throw that the tosser throws to the opposite side well ahead of the fielder. The emphasis is on sprinting through the ball, not just reaching for it. The player retrieves the ball if she does not catch it and then starts a line ready to perform the drill in the reverse direction. Do this drill with fielders running along the backstop so that players can easily retrieve any balls they miss (see figure 6.19). You can use two groups and two tossers—one group on the first-base side and one group on the third-base side.

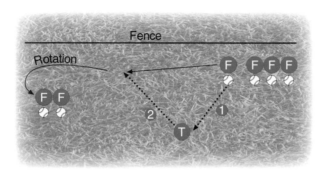

Figure 6.19 Fence range drill.

EVERYDAYS

Purpose: To practice all types of catches in a short amount of time. The drill is done "every day" at the beginning of infield practice.

Procedure: Partners stand about 10 feet apart (3 m) and throw ground balls to each other. The receiver stays low, keeps the glove on the ground, and uses little foot movement. The catching position is held until the ball is in the glove. The partner fields 10 balls for each of six types of catches before players rotate. (Any catching combination can be used.)

1. The partner throws balls directly to the receiver to gather.

2. Using an overhand throw, the partner throws short hops for the fielder to scoop.

3. The partner throws forehand balls to the receiver, who stands sideways. The receiver should not reach with the glove, but instead should let the ball come to her.

4. The partner throws backhand balls to the receiver, who is sideways in the crossover position.

5. The partner throws no-step backhands to the receiver, who is not sideways and has her glove already on the backhand side.

6. The partner makes quick throws to the receiver, who catches the ball without reaching and then simulates making a tag.

TWO-HITTER INFIELD

Purpose: To maximize the use of the infield and to keep players busy.

Procedure: Two hitters set up at home plate, one on the left side and the other on the right side. Each has a bucket of balls, and there is an empty bucket behind each base for balls to be returned to. Players are in normal infield position. Hitter 1 (on left side of home plate) hits to the first- and second-base players, who make all plays at first. Players cover as they would in a game; the first base player puts the ball in the bucket at first or returns it to a receiver to the left of hitter 1. Hitter 2 hits to the shortstop and third-base player, who make a play at third. Again, the player at third can use the bucket (which is faster and saves arms) or return the ball to a receiver to the right of hitter 2. On the next rotation, hitter 1 hits to the shortstop and second-base player, who make all plays at second, and hitter 2 works the corners, with throws to first and third.

INFIELD RANGE

Purpose: To develop greater range.

Procedure: Have a hitter at second, a hitter at home, and fielding lines at first and third, each with at least four players (see figure 6.20). The hitters hit at the same time, hitting ground balls in front of the fielders that force the fielders to reach for them. After fielding a ball, the player puts that ball in the other hitter's hand and runs to the end of the opposite fielding line. Have a bucket of balls behind the hitter. If a fielder misses the hit ball, she takes one out of the bucket to give to the hitter. Halfway through the drill, reverse direction so that players must reach to the other side.

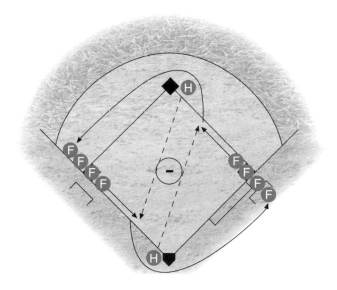

Figure 6.20 Infield range drill.

SOFTBALL SOCCER

Purpose: To teach aggressiveness when fielding ground balls.

Procedure: Players are divided into two teams. Set up a field like a very small soccer field with goalposts (or cones) or real goals (field hockey goals are perfect). Mark the field sidelines and mark a center line. The team on offense can run up to the center line and try to score by throwing the ball through the goal. The defense uses their gloves to stop the ball, and then they go on offense. Make the field dimensions appropriate for the age group and skill level. Use a soft safety ball or tennis ball for younger players. This can get quite competitive as players quickly change from offense to defense.

DIVING DRILLS

Coaches must work with fielders to practice diving for balls so that players can execute diving plays successfully in a game. For both of the following drills, players start near the ground and progress to a standing start. This helps the players overcome their fear of leaving their feet and hitting the ground. Using mats for a soft landing also helps players become comfortable diving and saves wear and tear on their bodies.

KNEE DIVES

Purpose: To learn to dive to catch the ball.

Procedure: The tosser is 6 feet (3 m) in front of the diver, who is on her knees. The thrower tosses soft safety balls to the side and just out of reach so that the fielder must dive to catch them. Players progress to starting in a squat position and then to a full standing start. When using a mat, have one tosser and never more than six fielders in a line; this way players don't waste too much time waiting for their turn but still have time to get ready for their next attempt. I recommend using the Slide Rite sliding mat from Schutt Manufacturing to develop players' confidence as they learn to dive and to save wear and tear on their bodies. When bad weather forces practice inside, this is an excellent drill if you have access to tumbling or wrestling mats.

ALL OUT

Purpose: To practice going all out on the dive.

Procedure: A fielder faces a tosser 20 to 30 feet (6 to 9 m) away. The first throw is over or to the side of the fielder's head. The fielder catches the ball and makes a good throw to the tosser. The fielder then runs hard toward the tosser, who flips a soft toss that the fielder must dive for to catch. The fielder then goes to the end of the line to wait for her next turn.

Variation: The player doesn't dive but plays a ground ball or short hop when she runs in.

FLY-BALL DRILLS

Proper footwork and body positioning are the foundation for catching fly balls successfully. Coaches should use the following basic footwork drills every day to help players develop good balance and proper reaction to the ball. The coach should throw balls to fielders instead of hitting them. This enables the coach to place the balls exactly where they need to be in order to isolate each technique. Players must also practice reacting to balls hit off the bat, but in these drills, hitting rather than throwing the ball takes a lot of time and creates difficulty placing the ball in the desired location.

DROP-STEP REACTION

Purpose: To learn to react and drop step to the appropriate side.

Procedure: The coach faces the players, who are in a staggered position in three or four lines. The coach points in a direction with a ball. Players react with a drop step in that direction. They then assume the ready position (exactly where they are) and repeat. When the drop step becomes automatic, players add the turn with inside and outside rolls.

ZIGZAG

Purpose: To execute proper footwork on the inside roll, good balance, and quick feet for fielding. This is a good warm-up drill.

Procedure: Players stand side by side in a line about 10 feet (3 m) apart from one another and face the coach. The coach points in either direction to begin the drill. Players run diagonally back using a drop step, run three steps, and then use an inside roll to change direction. They run three steps and again reverse direction. They continue zigzagging down the field.

BALL TOSS FOR INSIDE AND OUTSIDE ROLLS

Purpose: To practice proper footwork for catching fly balls.

Procedure: Each player has a ball and lines up behind the coach or a tosser. The first fielder takes a position facing the tosser about 20 feet (6 m) away. All the players in the line complete each step before they move to the next:

1. The tosser points in a direction for the initial drop step and diagonal movement and then tosses a ball to that side for the fielder to catch. The fielder catches the ball and goes to the end of the line.

2. Inside roll: The tosser points in a direction for the initial drop step and diagonal movement, then tosses the ball to the opposite side, forcing the fielder to use an inside roll to catch the ball. The fielder catches the ball and goes to the end of the line.

3. Outside roll: The fielder executes the previous step but with an outside roll, then goes to the end of the line.

4. Ball overhead: The fielder runs directly away from the tosser and turns her head to find and catch the ball; then she goes to the end of the line.

FOOTBALL

Purpose: To work on catching fly balls with good balance, glove work, and footwork.

Procedure: Each player has a softball. The player gives the ball to the coach and then starts running straight ahead with her back to the coach. The coach calls right or left and throws the ball in that direction. The fielder catches the ball and sprints to the end of the line behind the coach. A throw of 30 to 60 feet (6 to 18 m) is sufficient and allows for more practice than a very long throw.

CHAPTER 7

INFIELD

How important is the infield? Two-thirds of the total defense, or six of nine players, play in the infield. Much of your team's success is determined by how well the infielders perform, both individually and together. Infielders must work together as a unit. They need to understand their own responsibilities and coverage as well as those of their teammates. Each player must honestly evaluate her skills as well as those of the teammate beside her. What balls should she play and which ones should she leave for her teammate? Who has the stronger arm? Who is in the better position to make the play? Understanding and awareness are keys to successful team play.

Communication is vital. Infielders must talk about the batter's ability, the number of outs, defensive shifting, and the speed of the runners. They should remind each other who is covering the bag and taking the throw. By working together with understanding and communication, players form a cohesive and successful unit.

BASIC POSITIONING AND COVERAGE

Infielders normally follow general rules for defensive positioning and coverage responsibilities, making adjustments from these basic positions according to the game situation and the ability of the players. Other chapters explain how pitching, hitting, and team defensive strategies influence positioning and coverage. The following basic principles explain each position and its relationship to the other positions.

The first-base player and third-base player play in front of the bag and close enough to home plate to protect against the bunt. They play as far from the foul line as possible to help cover the holes in the infield and still get anything right on the line. They must protect the line because a hit on the foul line goes for extra bases.

The shortstop and second-base player play behind the baseline and as deep as they can and still make the play. The deeper they are, the more time they have to react and the better their range. The basic position, when there are no base runners and the defense is not making adjustments for the batter, is midway between the two respective bases. The middle infielders will make various adjustments according to the defensive play called, the pitch being thrown, the runners on base, and the batter's abilities.

Before the pitch is delivered, each player should review her next play if the ball is hit to her. *Where am I going with the ball?* When the pitch is delivered, each player has a job to do: field the ball, act as a relay, cover a base, or be a backup. Infielders must play the ball first. Then the rule is that the player closer to the base covers it, and the other backs up the base.

Steals:	Shortstop covers second with a runner on first.
	Shortstop covers third with a runner on second.
Bunts:	Second-base player covers first.
	Shortstop covers second with a runner on first.
	Shortstop covers third with a runner on second or third.
Relays:	Ball hit to left or center field—Second-base player covers second, and shortstop is the relay.
	Ball hit to right field—Shortstop covers second, and second-base player is the relay.

FIRST-BASE PLAYER

The first-base player will make more outs defensively than anyone on the team, so she must have a dependable glove and good agility. A first-base player who is able to catch all types of throws can make an average-throwing infield look great. Tall players have an obvious advantage because they can reach farther and offer a larger target. Many teams are hurt, however, when they put a tall player at first who cannot make the catch and the out. The first base player should be one of the best athletes on the field. Desired characteristics of the first-base player include the following:

- Agile, flexible, and mobile
- Quick hands and feet
- Tall and left-handed
- Accurate arm to other bases

The first-base player doesn't have to be left-handed, but a left-hander has advantages. When fielding bunts, the left-handed player does not have to take the time to pivot before making throws to second and third. A lefty can cover the hole between first and second base more easily because the glove is on the infield side. With the glove on the inside of the diamond, a lefty can also more easily give the target and make the catch.

The first-base player adjusts her position based on whether the batter is likely to hit, bunt, or slap hit. See figure 7.1 for the first-base player's positioning and coverage area.

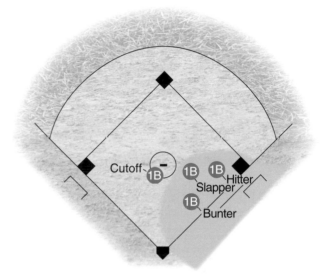

Figure 7.1 **First-base player's basic positioning and coverage area.**

- **Hitter**—The first-base player takes a position 3 to 4 feet (1 to 1.5 m) in front of the base and 2 to 3 feet (about 1 m) inside the line. One step gets her to the line.

- **Bunter**—The first-base player plays in as close as necessary to field the bunt while still having time to get back to cover the base on a hit. This distance will be from half to two-thirds the distance to home.

- **Slapper**—The first-base player plays halfway between the two previous positions while shading a little closer to the pitcher.

Some teams have the first-base player play three or four steps behind the baseline as in baseball. This eliminates the need for the first-base player to retreat to find the bag; everything is in front of her. This is a good idea if the player is slow getting to or finding the bag. Playing a few steps deeper also puts her in a stronger defensive position for hit balls. If the first-base player plays behind the base, the pitcher fields bunts down the first-base line.

Moving to the Base

The first-base player (playing in front of the base) must get back as soon as she recognizes that fielding the ball is not her responsibility. She should always turn to her right to face toward the infield. With a quick glance to locate the base, she sprints full speed to it. If she is not far from the bag, she can sidestep to it while watching the ball. If time permits, the first-base player can kick back and feel the base so she knows where it is while waiting for the ball. The base should be directly behind the feet and in the middle of the body.

Sometimes with a fast runner, the first-base player cannot get all the way to the base to make the play. Instead of running a footrace, an option is to establish a "short position." The first-base player stops short of the base, calls out "short," gives a target, and makes the tag there. The first-base player may also use this positioning with a fast runner at third. By setting up short, she cuts down the distance of the throw home and may prevent the runner from scoring easily on a play to first.

Receiving Throws

The set position to receive the throw is the basic athletic position with good balance. With weight on the balls of the feet and with the knees slightly flexed, the first-base player can be ready to move in any direction. Arms are extended toward the thrower. The first-base player should always use her glove as a target. She should help the thrower with verbal cues, calling "Hurry, hurry, hurry" on close plays or, on routine plays, calling the fielder's name to help her locate the target. The first-base player should catch with two hands whenever possible for a sure catch and a quick release. If a stretch is required, the catch should be made with one hand in order to extend the reach farther. The cardinal rule is to catch the ball first and then worry about tagging the bag.

After catching the throw, the first-base player touches the base, tagging the edge of the bag with the ball of the foot rather than the heel or toe. By using the ball of the foot, the first-base player can more easily keep the foot on the bag if she loses her balance or has to extend her reach. To prevent injuries, the player must tag the inside edge of the base, keeping the foot off the middle of the bag. Two basic footwork techniques are used for touching the base.

Catch and Touch   To use the catch-and-touch technique, the first-base player faces the throw with the heels about 6 inches (15 cm) from the edge of the base and with the feet facing the thrower (see figure 7.2a). The shoulders are square to the thrower.

Figure 7.2 **Catch-and-touch technique at first base.** *(a)* **The first-base player faces the thrower with heels about six inches from the edge of the base and the feet pointed toward the thrower.** *(b)* **After making the catch, she steps back and touches the base with the ball of the foot on the nonglove side.**

The first-base player steps toward the ball to catch it. After the catch, she steps back and touches the base with the ball of the foot on the nonglove side (see figure 7.2b). The sequence is step, catch, and kick back. As the player's skill level increases, this action will become almost one motion.

Which foot should the player step forward with? When the ball is straight to her, she should step with the glove-side leg. When the ball is to either side, she should step with the foot closer to the ball in order to get behind it. An advantage of this method is that the player can quickly get the foot off the base with less chance of the runner stepping on it. To help the first-base player get in the habit, during throwing warm-ups with her partner, have her kick back to an imaginary base using a smooth tagging motion.

Foot on the Bag   When using the foot-on-the-bag technique, the first-base player keeps one foot on the base as she steps toward the ball with the opposite foot (see figure 7.3). The foot on the bag is the foot opposite the glove. The ball of the foot is on the corner or the edge of the bag, depending on the position of the thrower. The first-base player wants to be as close to the thrower as possible, so the exact posi-

tion of the foot on the bag (corner or edge) is determined by where the thrower is. The front foot is slightly ahead so that the fielder can maintain good balance and be ready to move. The shoulders are square to the thrower. The player does not stretch and commit until she can judge the path of the ball, so she waits until the fielder throws it. The back-tagging foot turns sideways and pushes against the base with the ankle pointing down as the front foot strides toward the ball. After the tag, the player quickly removes the foot.

A disadvantage of this method is that on bad throws, players have a tendency to keep the foot on the bag and hope to reach the ball. Because catching the ball is the first priority, the first-base player should not hesitate to leave the base to make the catch. If the catch isn't made, the runner will probably advance another base.

Figure 7.3   **Foot-on-the-bag technique.**

Mis-Throws   Good first-base players must be able to catch all balls within their reach, whether the throws are high, low, to the side, or the most difficult type to catch—into the runner. Successful first-base players expect to make the catch and subsequent play on any throw that they can get the glove on.

- **Low throws**—The first-base player keeps her head down to watch the ball into the glove. Balls in the dirt at the feet will require her to gather in the ball with soft hands. If the player sees that the ball will bounce out in front, she stretches to reach it before it hits the ground. If that is not possible, she plays it as a short hop with a scooping motion. If the ball can't be caught, she blocks it.

- **High throws**—The player concentrates on catching the top of the ball. She stretches and maintains contact with the bag if possible. She may even stand on top of the bag to get higher. If the ball is too high, she jumps and catches it with one hand (glove) and then tries to land with one foot on the bag.

- **Throws to the side**—The primary goal is to catch the ball. It is better to give up the out than to have runners advance extra bases on an overthrow. If necessary, the first-base player leaves the base to make the catch and then kicks back to the bag. She does not keep her foot anchored to the base and hope that she can reach the ball.
- **Throws into the runner**—If the throw is well ahead of the runner, the player makes the catch, tags the base, and lets the momentum carry her into foul territory. If the runner and ball will arrive at the same time, the first-base player moves to the inside of the basepath to avoid the runner. She reaches up the line to make the catch and tags the runner as she goes by.

The first-base player should stretch only on close plays and when the ball can be reached while still keeping the foot on the bag. For the longest stretch, she reaches with the glove hand only. The instep of the throwing foot is against the bag, and the player steps forward with the glove-side foot after seeing the path of the ball. If the player goes into the splits, the glove must reach farther than the front foot. If she can't keep the foot on the bag, then the first-base player must go after the ball!

Special Plays

The first-base player must work well with several other fielders. To be successful, she must understand her responsibilities and her relationship with the second-base player, the right fielder, and the catcher. The second-base player covers first when the first-base player can't get back to the bag; the two players must have an understanding of who should field the ball when it is hit between them. The right fielder can sometimes throw out the runner if the ball gets by the first-base player. The catcher makes many types of throws to first, requiring the first-base player to receive the ball from different positions. Working together, these four players control the right side of the infield.

Fielding Bunts   The first-base player's ability to field the bunt is critical to team defense. Techniques and responsibilities are covered under "Bunt Defense" in chapter 9.

Working With the Second-Base Player   If the first-base player can field the ball and easily beat the runner to the base, she makes the play herself; however, she must tell the second-base player that she has the bag. This is the safe play because there is less chance of error. She tags the closest side and gives the runner the rest of the base. When the second-base player covers the base, the first-base player uses an underhand or sidearm throw, making sure the ball is visible to the receiver.

For balls in the hole between first and second base, the first-base player must know her range, the range of the second-base player, and the second-base player's position on each pitch. Usually, the first-base player should go no more than two or three steps into that area. In addition, the first-base player must avoid deflecting balls so that no one can make the play. Only hard-hit balls should get between the first- and second-base players. Players should call for the ball when possible and always communicate about who is covering the bag.

Any balls hit over the first-base player's head that require her to backpedal more than several steps should belong to the second-base player, who has the better angle coming across on a diagonal.

Working With the Right Fielder   On balls hit sharply to right field, the first-base player always covers the base so that the right fielder has the opportunity to throw out the runner. She assumes a position on the outfield side of the bag, ready to stretch if it's a close play. Because this will be a quick throw, the first-base player should assume that it won't be accurate. The catcher will be backing up the play.

Working With the Catcher   On dropped third strikes, passed balls, wild pitches, and pickoffs, the catcher often throws to first base. The first-base player must be at the bag and must be ready and in proper position to make the out.

- **Dropped third strike, balls behind the catcher**—The first base player takes an outside position at the base so that the catcher never has to throw across the basepath. If the catcher has trouble finding the ball, the first-base player can help by calling out the location. The first-base player gives an outside target with the glove and calls "outside" until the ball is on its way.
- **Bunts**—If the first-base player is back and taking the throw, she sets up on the inside of the diamond so the throw is inside the runner and the basepath. She calls "inside, inside" until the ball is released.
- **Pickoffs**—The first-base player sets up on the second-base side of first and at the back of the base. The outside of the left foot is against the base. She gives the target and turns to the left to apply the tag. See the full explanation in chapter 9, page 194.
- **Throwing home**—With runners at second or third, the first-base player should always expect the runner to be going home on a play to first. She makes the out and then pushes hard off the base, making sure to be well inside the basepath so that the batter–runner doesn't interfere. She quickly gets her feet in position for the throw home. With fast runners and an aggressive opponent, playing a "short first base" can help the player get the ball home more quickly.

Receiving Throws on the Back End of a Double Play   As soon as the ball is hit, the first-base player covers first in case the play goes there. When the play goes to second, she moves into position to receive the throw on the second-base side of first. The catching fundamentals are the same as those used on an infield ball. It will be a close play, so she must see the path of the ball and stretch to make the catch.

Playing Foul Balls   To play foul balls safely and successfully, the first-base player needs to know the distance to the fence and how balls will rebound. She should study the dugouts to be aware of openings and dead-ball areas. The first-base player should imagine a line going at a 45-degree angle from first base to the foul-line fence; she should play any balls that will land in front of the line (see figure 7.1). She leaves any balls behind this line for the second-base player, who has the better angle.

Other Responsibilities

Additional team defensive responsibilities of the first-base player are outlined in the following list. Although the first responsibility is always to play first base, when no play is occurring there, the first-base player should be ready to assist in other areas. The first-base player is more than just someone who stands at first base.

- Executing the cutoff. The first-base player is usually the cutoff on throws going home. She assumes a position near the pitching rubber (refer back to figure 7.1 for correct cutoff positioning). See full details of the cutoff play in chapter 9.

- Covering home on passed balls and wild pitches. Most coaches prefer that the first-base player cover home instead of the pitcher. The first-base player must react immediately to the ball, not wait to react to the runner going home.
- Covering home on intentional walks to a left-handed batter. The first-base player should take a position close to home plate (as if fielding a bunt) and in fair territory as the rules require. The third-base player is back in regular position in case the batter hits the outside pitch.
- Helping the catcher locate foul balls by calling the location and direction of the ball.
- Backing up the catcher on first-and-third plays if a runner is going and backing up second base on throws from left and center field. The first-base player takes a backup position about 15 feet (4.5 m) behind the intended receiver and in direct line with the throw. When backing up the catcher, the first-base player should be close to the fence so that she can quickly retrieve the ball off the fence.
- Using body position to block the base runner off the base after the runner makes a turn. The first-base player sets up between the runner and the base and tries for a pickoff.
- Watching for and participating in a rundown.

MOVING TO THE BASE

Purpose: To improve quickness and range in moving to first base.

Procedure: The first-base player takes a position halfway to home as if fielding a bunt. On the coach's command of "go," she sprints to the base (turning inward to the diamond), finds the base, takes the receiving position, catches an imaginary ball, and tags the base. The player repeats the drill, moving ever closer to home to increase the distance and push herself to improve quickness in getting to the base.

BAD HOPS AT FIRST

Purpose: To practice catching bad hops at first base.

Procedure: The first-base player is in receiving position at first base. Using an overhand throw, a thrower on the infield about 30 feet (9 m) from first throws bad hops to the first-base player. The thrower has a bucket full of balls. The first-base player catches the ball, makes the out, and puts the ball in a second bucket nearby. Do this drill every day to develop this important skill. The player gathers or short hops every ball and focuses on keeping her head down.

THREE THROWS FROM THE CATCHER

Purpose: To practice receiving three types of throws from the catcher and to work on the techniques involved in handling passed balls, bunts, and pickoffs.

Procedure: The first-base player catches the following throws and places the ball in a bucket by the base (see figure 7.4):

1. **The pitcher throws to the catcher, who intentionally lets the pitch get behind her. The catcher recovers the ball and throws to the outside of first base (1).**

2. **After catching the second pitch, the catcher tosses the ball out in front of the plate to simulate a bunt. She goes after the ball and throws it to the first-base player, who is calling "inside" and giving a target (2).**

3. **The catcher signals for a pitchout and after receiving the pitch, throws to the inside of the bag for a pickoff (3). For a complete explanation of pickoffs, see chapter 9.**

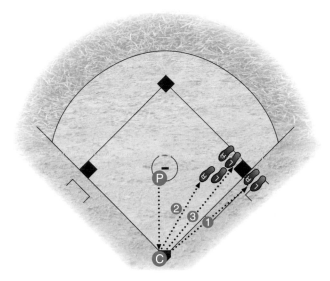

Figure 7.4   **Three throws from the catcher drill.**

COACHING POINTS FOR THE FIRST-BASE PLAYER

- On overthrows, tag the runner as soon as you get the ball if she is off the base. Chances are the runner has made some motion toward second base and is liable to be put out. Make this a habit and pick up some outs.

- Be careful not to deflect balls that should be left for the second-base player to field. When you commit to play the ground ball, the second-base player is on her way to first, and no one is there to play the deflection.

- Always hustle back to cover the base even when you think there is no play. The other infielders can't make one if you're not there. If a runner is at first, you can help hold her closer to the bag by returning quickly.

- When it is obvious that you have no play, quickly remove your tagging foot and take a step or two off the base to avoid contact and the possibility of injury or interference with the runner.

- Always assume that other runners are advancing on throws to first. Never be caught by surprise.

SECOND-BASE PLAYER

Second base is one of the most difficult positions to play because of its many defensive responsibilities. The second-base player must always have her head in the game. Although the natural reaction is to go to the ball, in some instances the second-base player must go the opposite way. In bunt situations, the second-base player must immediately break to cover first and then become a good first-base player.

Desired characteristics of the second-base player include the following:

- Right-handed thrower
- Quick feet and great range

- Ability to get a good jump
- Snap throw and quick release
- Good hands (plays a lot of first base)
- Game sense (smartest player on the team)
- Ability to react to the situation
- Quick release to turn double plays
- Ability to go back on pop flies

The many defensive responsibilities of the second-base player include the following:

- Covering first base on all bunts and on ground balls to the first-base player when she can't get back to first
- Backing up throws to the pitcher from the catcher
- Taking pickoffs at first and second
- Covering second base on steals when the shortstop has moved closer to third or for the element of surprise
- Taking relays from right field and from the right side of center field
- Catching pop flies and foul balls behind first base
- Performing the double-play pivot at second base on throws from the shortstop or third-base player
- Acting as the cutoff on first-and-third plays
- Working with the first-base player on grounders to the right side

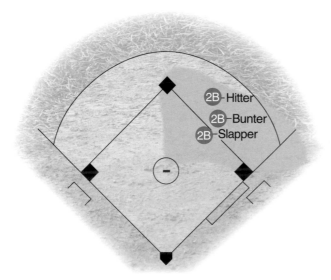

Figure 7.5 **Second-base player's basic positioning and coverage area.**

The regular fielding position of the second-base player is only about 6 feet (2 m) behind the line because she must be able to get to first to cover the base when necessary. The second-base player adjusts her position based on whether the batter is likely to hit, bunt, or slap hit. See figure 7.5 for the second-base player's positioning and coverage area.

- **Hitter**—The second-base player plays as far from home as her arm and quickness to first base will allow. Playing deeper increases the player's range by providing more time to get to balls hit up the middle and to the left.
- **Bunter**—The second-base player moves several steps closer to first in order to cut down the distance she must run to cover the base on the bunt. She goes to first base on every bunt attempt.
- **Slapper**—The second-base player moves in several steps and shades closer to first, just as she does when playing the bunt. This is the basic slap defense. Other options are covered in "Slap Defense" in chapter 9.

Special Plays

The second-base player is sometimes called the best first-base player on the team. She covers first base on bunts, slaps, and pickoffs when the first-base player can't get back. And because of her proximity to first, she can take the time to block some ground balls and still make the play.

Blocking Ground Balls   If the second-base player can't quite catch a ball, she should at least try to knock it down. Some players, because of the short throw to first, will take the time to block hard-hit balls. If a player is more comfortable blocking hard-hit balls, she can drop to one knee like an outfielder and use her leg to block the ball. The second-base player is close enough to first that she can take the time to smother and block the ball and make sure it doesn't get through. When playing on uneven ground that causes bad bounces, this may be the best option.

Covering First Base   The second-base player covers first base in all bunting situations and any time the first-base player cannot get back. This play is often a footrace with the runner because the second-base player must also run a fair distance. The throw must be on the inside of the diamond to avoid hitting the base runner. Therefore, the second-base player must often take an extreme inside position on the base (see figure 7.6). She places the left foot against the nearest side of the base, faces the thrower, gives the glove for a target, catches the ball, and immediately clears out of the area by moving toward the infield. If the ball is hit sharply (i.e., to the pitcher or to a pulled-in third-base player) and the batter–runner is not near first base, then the second-base player uses the standard first-base player's technique and footwork for tagging the base.

Figure 7.6   **Second-base player's receiving position when covering first.**

COACHING POINTS FOR THE SECOND-BASE PLAYER

- Go to first base in every bunting situation regardless of where the base runners are.

- Become a good first-base player. Practice fielding bad throws and stretching when necessary to make the out.

- When making overhand throws to first and second, use a three-quarter throw so that the ball is always visible to the receiver.

- Be comfortable and skilled using all types of throws because there will be situations that require varied throws from long and short distances as well as several kinds of double-play feeds.

- On a potential double play, look to tag the runner and then go to first.

- When fielding a ball on the basepath with the runner approaching, take a charge and don't be afraid to get an interference call.

- Use a fake pickoff (occasionally) to get the runner going the wrong way when the bunt goes down. See the section "Bunt Defense" in chapter 9.

SHORTSTOP

The shortstop is considered the key to a good defense. She is usually the team's best player and strongest arm because she handles a large percentage of the defensive plays. The shortstop plays as deep as her arm and ability permit because a deeper position provides a better angle to the ball and more time to react. The shortstop must have the ability to charge grounders and finish the play with a quick, strong throw to first. Generally a team leader, the shortstop is in a great location to communicate and direct the defense.

Desired characteristics of the shortstop include the following:

- Right-hander with the strongest arm
- Best fielder on the team
- Consistent fielder on all types of balls
- Exceptional fielding range in all directions
- Good speed to cover both second and third
- Leadership skills

The defensive responsibilities of the shortstop include the following:

- Covering second base and third base on steals. The shortstop is in the best position to get ahead of the runner and be in position to make the tag. A runner attempting to steal second interferes with the second-base player by being in front of her. A runner going to third is behind the third-base player and out of her line of vision.
- Covering second base on first-and-third plays.
- Taking pickoffs at second and third. The shortstop will cover the base the majority of the time. At times, the second- or third-base player may take the base if the shortstop is farther from the base than normal or to provide the element of surprise.
- Taking relays from left field and center field. With the strongest arm on the infield, the shortstop will take all relays from center field that she can easily get to. The second-base player will be the relay from the right side of center field.
- Executing the double-play pivot on balls thrown from the right side of the infield and from the pitcher.
- Catching foul balls and pop-ups behind third base.
- Backing up throws to the pitcher from the catcher if the second-base player is not there.
- Taking "charges" from base runners while fielding balls on the basepath.

The strength of the shortstop's arm will largely determine how deep she can play. The shortstop must be strong enough to field a routine ball and throw out the majority of runners from the depth she assumes. The best shortstops play at the edge of the infield dirt, or about 10 to 12 feet (3 to 3.5 m) behind the line. The shortstop adjusts her position according to the batter's expected type of hit. See figure 7.7 for the shortstop's positioning and coverage area.

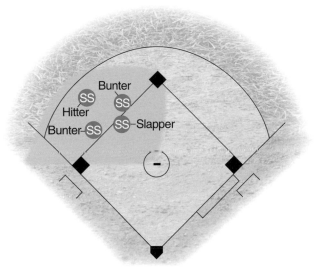

Figure 7.7 **Shortstop's basic positioning and coverage area.**

- **Hitter**—The shortstop plays behind the line as deep as her arm permits.
- **Bunter**—The shortstop moves several steps closer to the base that she will be covering so that she can get there faster, ahead of the runner.
- **Slapper**—The shortstop moves in front of the line so that she can get to the ball more quickly.

Special Plays

Balls in the hole to the shortstop's right require the longest infield throw to first. On shallow fly balls to the left side, the shortstop must work closely with the left and center fielders. Good communication is critical.

COACHING POINTS FOR THE SHORTSTOP

- Play the hit first and then the steal.
- React to the first bounce of a ground ball.
- Go to the ball and then, if you are not involved, cover the nearest base.
- When there isn't a play and there are runners on, make a play. Fake a throw and catch a runner off base.
- Learn to hold the ball (eat it) and not take a chance of making an error on a play when you are too late to make an out.
- When not fielding a ball, look for a place to go (backup position) and something to do.
- Communicate with your teammates on every play. Signal the number of outs and review who is covering the base. Don't leave anything to chance. The shortstop is usually the infield leader. Assume that leadership position.
- Work well with your pitcher. Return the ball sharply with a word of encouragement. Go to the mound when needed and appropriate.
- When shifting or adjusting your position, make sure you alert the third- and second-base players and adjacent outfielders so that they can adjust to help plug the holes.

Playing Balls in the Hole   When fielding a ball deep in the third base–shortstop hole (to the shortstop's right), the shortstop may not have enough time to plant the feet and get enough on the ball to make it all the way to first. The quickest path for a throw is a straight line, so a one- or two-bounce throw will get the ball there faster than the long rainbow throw.

Working With the Left and Center Fielders   Going after and catching the shallow fly balls—referred to as "Texas leaguers"—is difficult because of the natural fear of colliding with the outfielders who are also going for the ball. Communication is essential if those in position to go for the ball are to make a full-out effort. The shortstop must go back hard on all shallow fly balls with a resolve to catch the ball unless called off by an outfielder. Outfielders are in the best position to catch such balls because the ball is in front of them, so the shortstop must yield to any outfielder who calls for the ball. By working with the outfielders in practice catching many shallow fly balls or "tweeners," the shortstop can recognize the range of each player and work out who should catch which ball.

THIRD-BASE PLAYER

The third-base player should have the quickest hands on the team and must be fearless. When she is playing in to protect against the bunt, many hard shots will come her way. Add to this the many bunt options—including the slash, slap, push, and fake—and it is easy to see why third base is called the hot corner.

Desired characteristics of the third-base player include the following:

- Right-handed thrower
- Quick and agile
- Sure hands and quick reactions
- Height to help on high bouncers
- Strong and accurate throwing arm
- Ability to throw from set and off-balance positions
- Aggressive with the ability to charge
- Good range to the left to cut off balls to the shortstop
- Confident, cocky, and fearless

The defensive responsibilities of the third-base player include the following:

- Fielding bunts and slaps.
- Covering home when the catcher covers third on a bunt.
- Cutting off slowly hit balls between third base and the pitcher.
- Taking the relay from left field when the ball is near the foul line.
- Taking pickoffs at third base.
- Holding the runner at third.
- Covering home on intentional walks to right-handed batters. The third-base player should be in normal bunt position and in fair territory as the rules require. (The first-base player is back in a stronger defensive position in case the batter hits the outside pitch.)

The third-base player adjusts her position based on whether the batter is likely to hit, bunt, or slap hit. See figure 7.8 for positioning and coverage area.

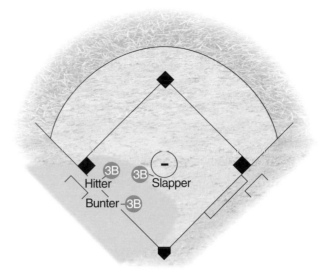

Figure 7.8 **Third-base player's basic positioning and coverage area.**

- **Hitter**—The third-base player takes a position 3 to 4 feet (1 to 1.5 m) in front of the base and 2 to 3 feet (about 1 m) inside the line so that one step gets her to the line. The deeper the third-base player can play, the more time she has to react to the ball; however, she cannot let the bunt beat her. With a strong right-handed pull hitter up and no chance of a bunt, the third-base player may play even with the bag or behind it. However, by playing behind the bag, she may be vulnerable by being too deep to make the play on slow balls or surprise bunts in front of her.

- **Bunter**—The third-base player plays as close as necessary to field the bunt and get the out. This will be somewhere between half and two-thirds the distance to home depending on the player's quickness, ability to charge the ball, arm strength, and quickness of release.

- **Slapper**—The third-base player is in several steps closer than the position used when expecting a hit. She must also move several steps toward the pitcher to help cut off slaps to the shortstop.

Special Plays

The third-base player is the first line of defense on the left side of the infield. She must be aggressive and on her toes. With a runner on third base, every effort must be made to keep the ball from going through and scoring a run. The third-base player must understand how to work with the shortstop to bolster the left-side defense.

Fielding Bunts   Because bunts are an important element of softball, the third-base player must be competent at fielding them. On bunts when the throw will go to second or first, the third-base player should be the most aggressive player because her body is in the best throwing alignment. For bunts when the throw will go to third, the third-base player should defer when possible to the first-base player, who is facing third. Because the third-base player will be fielding most of the bunts, she should work at developing quickness and fielding skills (which are fully described in chapter 9).

Working With the Shortstop   The third-base player should be a ball hog, taking any balls she can get her hands on while being able to maintain balance and make a play. She should cut in front of the shortstop to get any balls that she can field and throw, moving straight across the diamond and being careful not to angle back toward the shortstop. The third-base player *must* cut off any slow rollers in the third base–shortstop hole because the shortstop will not have time to make the play. The third-base player should not dive for ground balls in the hole because she will not be able to recover in time to throw. She can leave that ball for the shortstop to play. She should know both her range and that of the shortstop and should check her teammate's position on every pitch. She must know which balls are clearly hers and understand when she is in the best position to make the play. Any balls hit over the third-base player's head that require her to backpedal for more than four or five steps should belong to the shortstop, who has the better angle coming on a diagonal.

Fielding Foul Balls   To play foul balls safely and successfully, the third-base player should check the distance to the fence and should know how balls will rebound. She should be aware of dugout openings and dead-ball areas. With a runner on third base, it is critical to keep balls out of a dead-ball area because the runner automatically scores. When fielding foul balls, the third-base player should imagine a line going at a 45-degree angle from third base to the foul-line fence; she should play any balls that will land in front of that line (see figure 7.8). Balls behind that line should be left for the shortstop, who has the better angle.

Figure 7.9   Third-base player in position for the force play at third.

Force at Third   When the third-base player fields a ground ball near the base, tagging the base for the force at third and throwing to first should be a routine double play. For other force plays, the third-base player should clearly indicate to the shortstop that she has the bag. The position for receiving a throw from the infield is shown in figure 7.9. The player tags the base, then pushes hard off the base with the right foot to create momentum to turn the feet and shoulders fully to the throwing position.

Runner at Third   With a runner at third, the third-base player's first priority when fielding a ground ball is to keep the runner from scoring. The third-base player looks at the runner to see how far she is off the base. If the runner has strayed too far, the third-base player can go after her to get the out. The shortstop should be in position at third to make the tag. The third-base player should not be surprised by the runner going home. The runner may try to take advantage of the fact that the third-base player has her back to the runner. The third-base player then looks for the catcher's target and establishes a throwing lane to avoid hitting the runner with the ball.

Unless the runner is automatically going, the third-base player, because of her proximity, can stop the runner with just a look. The third-base player turns only the head to look, being careful not to pull the shoulders back from the throwing position (see figure 7.10). She quickly moves her feet to throw after she has decided where she will throw the ball. If the runner has stopped, the third-base player makes a hard, accurate throw to first so that if the runner goes on the throw, the first-base player will have a chance at doubling her off at home.

A fake throw can also be very effective at third base. The runner is anxious to go home and usually takes a big jump, making it easy for the third-base player to use a fake throw to pick her off. A full description appears on page 159.

Figure 7.10   Third-base player looking the runner back.

CHASE AND FAKE

Purpose: **To get the third-base player in the habit of faking the throw.**

Procedure: **Every time the third-base player makes a fielding error during practice, she must go after the ball and make a fake throw. Where there is no play, invent one!**

COACHING POINTS FOR THE THIRD-BASE PLAYER

- Knock down or block hard-hit balls on the line. The left fielder will not have a play anyway, so keep the ball from going through for possible extra bases.

- Assume that all bunts and shots on the line are fair. Play them out and let the umpire make the call.

- On bunts when you have no play, allow the ball to roll to see if it goes foul. Be quick to touch balls in foul territory that you want the umpire to rule foul.

- When fielding a bunt on which you must hurry your throw, make sure your shoulders are level. If you don't have time to stand upright, throw from a semicrouch (low position), but even up your shoulders to keep the ball level. Allowing your throwing shoulder to drop will produce a high throw.

- With runners on base, retreat quickly to cover your base when not fielding the ball. Because you are often drawn so far in, you cannot be lazy about getting back.

- On throws home, always establish a throwing lane to avoid hitting the runner. Look for the catcher's target and then move your body as necessary to keep your throw out of the runner's path.

BASIC INFIELD PLAYS

Although infielders require specific skills to play their positions successfully, many general infield skills are important for all infielders to understand and master. With good communication, the infield can make defensive adjustments that strengthen the defense and ensure that all bases are covered. The infield works together to turn double plays, create force-outs, and stop the offense from scoring. Here are some important elements for basic infield play. (Specific defensive plays such as bunt and slap defense, double plays, cutoffs, pickoffs, rundowns, and other defensive options are covered in chapter 9.)

Playing the Bases

Traditionalists recommend straddling the bag when waiting for the throw. However, this method of covering the bases has some real disadvantages:

- The fielder is in direct line with the base runner, and if the runner doesn't slide or she slides with cleats high, the fielder can easily be injured.

- The feet are planted parallel and in a poor position for fielding. The fielder has limited mobility for making a play on a wild throw.

- Throwing errors are usually to the runner's side of the bag. If the fielder covering the base must step to get the ball, the foot will be directly in the path of the oncoming runner.

- If the ball and runner arrive at the same time, it's difficult for the fielder to hang onto the ball. If the ball hits the runner, the defense is beaten.

We recommend a safer and more effective way to cover the base: The fielder stands on the side of the base that the throw is coming from but out of the basepath and takes a balanced fielding position with the foot that is closer to the bag slightly ahead of the other foot. Specific base-by-base applications of this principle are detailed in the following sections.

Figure 7.11 Third-base player's receiving position for throws from the catcher.

To Third Base On a throw from home, the third-base player should assume a position on the home plate side of the bag with the side of the left foot against the bag (see figure 7.11). She gives the target at the front edge of the bag. The third-base player is out of the path of the runner. If the throw is wide toward the middle of the diamond, she can use basic fielding skills to reach or block the ball. On a throw from the outfield, the third-base player places the side of her right foot against the bag.

To Second Base For a throw from the catcher, the shortstop takes a position on the inside of the diamond with the left foot slightly ahead of the right and against the front corner of the base (see figure 7.12a). The shortstop moves to the right-field side of the base when taking a throw from right field; the shortstop's right foot is touching the side of the base (see figure 7.12b). When taking a throw from left field, the second-base player stands on the left-field side of second with the left foot touching the base.

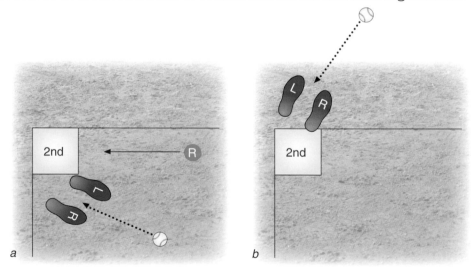

Figure 7.12 Shortstop's receiving position for (a) throws from the catcher and (b) throws from right field.

To First Base For a pickoff throw from the catcher, the first-base player or the second-base player takes a position on the second-base side of first; the player's left foot is on the side and toward the back of the base. This is the best position for blocking the runner off the base, and it forces the runner to take the longest route to tag the base.

Rules That Every Infielder Must Know

- Interference and obstruction
- Infield fly
- Two runners on a base
- Appeals for missing a base and leaving early on a tag-up
- Runner's lane on fielding plays and rundowns

Also, with this position, the second-base player does not have to run as far as she would if she straddled the base; therefore, she can get there more quickly. For throws from the outfield, the player covering first takes a position on the side of the base that the throw is coming from, placing the foot closest to the base against the side of the base.

Traditionalists argue that players who don't straddle the bag lose time applying the tag. If the throw is accurate, the tag time is the same. If the throw is poor, the proposed method may save a leg and allow the player to catch the ball.

Tag Plays

The tag play is used to get a runner out by tagging her with the ball before she reaches the base. This play is most commonly used to catch runners attempting to steal or when they have taken too big a leadoff. The first priority is to catch the ball and then to apply the tag.

Infielders should get to the base as quickly as they can. The goal is to be waiting at the base for the throw. As the infielder nears the base, she shortens her steps and lowers her center of gravity, keeping her body under control. The infielder goes in low because that is where the ball should be thrown. It is also easier to adjust upward than downward if the ball is off target. The fielder should turn the upper body to face the incoming throw.

To prevent knee injuries, the player bends the knees as she applies the tag. This helps absorb any impact with the runner. After the tag is made, the fielder clears out of the base area and looks for any additional plays.

Infielders should not chase after or reach for a runner who misses the base. The best method is to keep the glove at the edge of the base nearest the runner and wait for her to return to the base. On a hook slide, the infielder should keep the tag on the runner because the runner might overslide the base and lose contact.

Players should learn two methods for making the tag:

- **Two-handed tag**—The player catches the ball first. If the throw is on line, the player does not reach for the ball but instead lets it come to her. If time permits, the fielder uses both hands to hold the glove on the ground at the front of the bag. She looks for the foot or hand of the runner reaching for the base, and she waits for the runner to hit the glove and tag herself out. The fielder must be sure to protect the bare hand with the glove and to make the tag with the back of the glove so that the wrist can bend on impact (see figure 7.13). She should pull the glove back while making the tag, giving with the impact to absorb the shock and protect the ball. The two-handed tag is the

Figure 7.13 Two-handed tag position.

most secure tag, the one that is less likely to cause a fielder to lose control of the ball. If the throw is off line, the fielder should go get the ball and then dive back to make the tag.

- **Sweep tag**—On a late throw and a close play, the fielder is required to use a sweep tag. As the player catches the ball, she squeezes her fingers tightly to secure it. She bends her knees to get low to the ground and tags the runner with a rapid downward movement in front of the base. The fielder then gives with the impact and swings her arm back and up high in the air, showing the ball to the umpire.

Blocking the Base

The defensive player should take the base away from the runner whenever possible. If the ball arrives ahead of the runner, the fielder blocks the runner's path to the base with her body, either stopping the runner or causing her to take the long way around the block. The fielder catches the ball and drops to one knee, using the leg to block the base (see figure 7.14). If the player doesn't have time to drop the leg, she should at least lower the hips and become as big as possible. Obviously, when there is no chance for a play, the defensive player may not obstruct the runner. But in waiting for the play to develop, the defensive player should establish a position in the basepath between the runner and the base. Then, if no chance of a play develops, the fielder steps out of the basepath.

Figure 7.14   Blocking the base.

Force Plays

Force plays occur when a runner is forced to advance because the batter has become a base runner. To make the out, the defensive team can tag the runner or the base. A fielder should make the play herself if possible. The fewer throws a team makes, the less chance they have of making a mistake. A fielder making a play herself should wave off any teammate who may be moving to cover the base.

To receive a throw, the player gets to the base as quickly as possible. Throws coming from inside the basepath are taken on the inside of the bag. Throws coming from outside the basepath are taken on the outside of the bag. The receiver takes a position at the front of the base and places the side of the foot nearer the base against the front corner. She aligns her body so that her chest is facing the thrower and gives a target that recognizes the position of the runner so that the throw will not hit her. When the ball is accurately thrown, the receiver steps with the glove-side foot to the ball (see figure 7.15). The receiver must be careful not to reach too soon. She tags the base with the ball of the back foot, pushes off the inside edge of the base, and then steps in a straight line toward the next target. Whenever possible, the receiver catches with two hands and squeezes the ball in the glove. The receiver should anticipate a bad throw and be ready to stretch if necessary. If the throw is wide, the receiver moves to catch the ball first and then kicks back with the opposite leg. If the receiver can't catch the ball, she at least stops it.

If the receiver can't get to the base in time, she becomes a moving target for the thrower. Again, alignment is with the chest facing the thrower as the ball is thrown.

Ideally, the receiver catches the ball behind the base and then steps on the bag. Short steps and good balance will enable the player to react to balls that are off line. Timing and communication are the keys. The receiver should give a target, call the fielder's name, and request the location for the throw—inside or outside.

As soon as the force-out is made, the receiver vacates the base and looks for the next possible play. At second base, the shortstop covers all throws from the infield except hit balls that require her to be in a backup position. Other bases will be covered by the infielder closest to the bag and in the best position to make the out.

Figure 7.15   **Receiving the throw for a force play at second.**

Looking Runners Back

An important defensive goal is to prevent runners from advancing on ground balls, particularly on ground-ball outs. When fielding a ground ball with a runner at third, the first priority is always to keep the runner from scoring. Good communication from teammates will tell the fielder if the runners are automatically going. If they are, the fielder must look to see if she can get the lead runner. If the runners are not automatically going, then the fielder must "look the runner back" to keep the runner close to the base, to stop her forward momentum, and to keep her from easily advancing on a throw to first. The fielder looks at the lead runner to see how far she is off the base. If the runner has strayed too far, the fielder can go after her to get the out. The fielder must always check the lead runner even though that may not be the runner closest to her. Playing on a runner behind the lead runner will give the latter an opportunity to advance on the play.

All infielders except the third-base player look the runner back by turning the head and upper body toward the lead runner. (The third-base player turns only her head.) The infielder doesn't commit the feet to that throw, but she is ready to move the feet quickly into the proper throwing position for the throw that she chooses to make. When the runner is in the way, the thrower must establish a throwing lane.

Fake Throws

The shortstop, third-base player, and pitcher can try a fake throw to pull the runner off the base and create an out. The goal is to get the runner leaning the wrong way, thus delaying her return to the base and providing more time to make the out. With the ball gripped firmly in the throwing hand, the fielder uses a compact windup as she fakes the throw to first base, being careful that the ball does not slip out of her hand. She may totally ignore the runner in faking the throw or may first look the runner back and then attempt the fake. By totally ignoring the runner, the fielder is hoping to provide a false sense of security and encourage the runner to take a slightly bigger lead. The fielder then quickly brings the glove, the ball, and the throwing hand together to regrip for the actual throw. On sharply fielded balls, the fielder has time to attempt a fake, check the runner, and still make the play to first if the runner is not fooled. Getting the lead runner is certainly the preferred out.

INFIELD PRACTICE DRILLS

When practicing with all infielders in their defensive positions, the key is to keep everyone active. Combination drills with throws to various bases keep everyone in the game. Drills should be fast paced so there is little standing around. Using a catcher and a hitter on both sides of home plate will double the amount of balls hit, but it must be very clear which base the players should throw to.

When a coach or player is hitting to the infield, the catcher should place the next ball in the hitter's extended hand. This allows the coach or hitter to keep her eyes on the infield play, and it replaces the toss that too often ends up in the hitter's face. Competition makes the drills more gamelike, and using runners allows the defense to develop timing and game speed. A variety of ground-ball drills and specific game situations should be used to make sure all techniques are covered. Drills that improve conditioning should also be included. The following combination drills add variety to infield practice while accomplishing several goals.

ROTATING INFIELD

Purpose: To work on throws from the four basic infield positions and the first-base player's technique for tagging the base. (This is an excellent tryout drill. It is also an effective conditioning drill when using no more than five infielders.)

Procedure: Draw lines on the infield at the four positions where players are to field the ball (see figure 7.16). Five infielders line up behind line 1 at third base. A first-base player is in position. All five infielders field a ball at that spot, throw to first, and then run to wait their turn behind line 2 at the shortstop position. The hitter hits to all fielders in line before going to the next spot and the new line. At each line, fielders throw to first and run immediately to the next spot, where they can rest. Position 3 is near second base. Here, the emphasis is on showing the ball and using a three-quarter or sidearm throw so that the first-base player always sees the ball. Position 4 is a slow roller toward first base. The fielder charges, fields the ball well in front of the base, throws, and then runs behind the

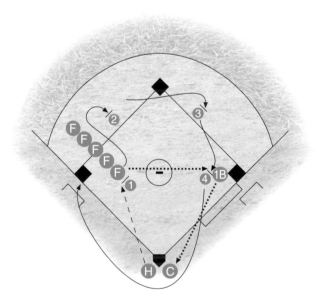

Figure 7.16 Rotating infield drill.

hitter to the third-base line to continue the drill. The first-base player does not field any balls; instead, she works on proper technique at the bag, always tagging the base for the out. She returns each ball to a catcher at home, who feeds the hitter. The first-base player should ignore all balls that she cannot catch so that she is ready for the next throw. The hitter hits the next ball as soon as she hears the previous ball smack the first-base player's glove. This drill should be done quickly.

Safety Reminders

- The first-base player ignores all throws that she cannot catch cleanly so that she can be ready for the next throw.
- Infielders must make sure that the first-base player is ready to receive the ball. This is good practice in looking to see the target before throwing, a routine that infielders should always follow in a game.
- Infielders must run to the next line so that they are not in the way of the hit or throw. From first base, they run behind the hitter.

MERRY-GO-ROUND

Purpose: To warm up or work on conditioning while fielding ground balls.

Procedure: Players form two fielding lines at opposite corners of the infield—one to the left of second base and one at home (see figure 7.17). Players in line at second must be careful not to trip over the base. Two hitters hit or throw from the area of the pitching circle, one to each line. Players field and then run to the end of the opposite line. Hitters hit ground balls, fly balls, range balls, line drives, and scoops. Players return the ball to their hitter or place it in a bucket at the line they are running to. Hitters should have a bucket of extra balls to replace balls that fielders miss so that the drill can be done at a steady pace.

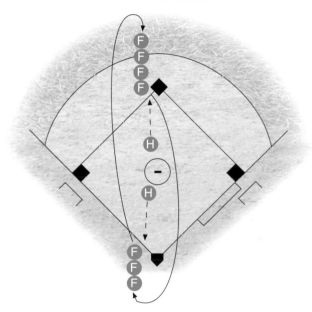

Figure 7.17   Merry-go-round drill.

4 × 4 GUT

Purpose: To practice fielding and throwing to all the bases in a pressure situation. Infielders practice covering the bases. The drill creates competition.

Procedure: Infielders take normal defensive positions with a hitter and catcher at home. The hitter hits four times to one player, who fields the balls and throws in order to home, first, second, and third. If an error occurs, she must start over. The cycle is repeated three more times.

FOUR CORNERS

Purpose: **To work on conditioning and on making accurate throws to first and third.**

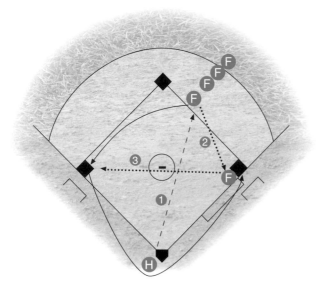

Figure 7.18 Four corners drill.

Procedure: **Infielders form a line at the second-base position. One fielder is at first base. A hitter hits to the first infielder in line. The fielder at second base fields the ball, throws to first, and sprints to third base to receive a return throw from the player at first (see figure 7.18). The fielder must be at third in proper receiving position (left foot against the home plate side of third), where she catches the ball and applies a tag. The fielder then sprints home to give the ball to the hitter and runs behind the hitter on the way to first; she must get to first base in time to catch the throw to first on the next hit ball. The fielder catches the ball at first base, throws back to the next fielder at third base, and goes to the end of the line at second base to wait for her next turn. Use no more than five players so that there is not a lot of standing around. Have an extra bucket of balls at home and first in case of errant throws.**

INFIELD LOOP

Purpose: **To work on conditioning and fielding ground balls.**

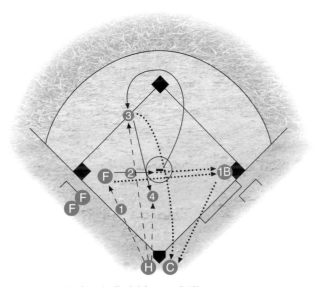

Figure 7.19 Infield loop drill.

Procedure: **Three fielders form a line at third, and a first-base player and catcher take their normal positions (see figure 7.19). A softball is placed on the mound. A hitter at home hits to the first fielder at the third-base defensive position *(1)*. The player fields the ball and throws to first. (Balls thrown to first are thrown immediately by the first-base player to the catcher at home.) She then runs to the ball on the mound and throws to first *(2)*. The fielder runs around behind second base, fields another ball hit to the shortstop position *(3)*, and throws that ball home. The hitter rolls a ball out to the same fielder, who is charging home *(4)*. The fielder fields that ball and places it on the mound. The drill continues with the next fielder. The catcher and first-base player should take a turn fielding the ball.**

OUTFIELD

When a ball gets through the infield, it is just a hit. When a ball gets by the outfield, it is usually a run and often means a win for the other team. The outfield is the last line of defense. Outfielders are not often noticed until they make a mistake. Good outfielders make catches look easy. They are smooth, not flashy. Outfielders should take pride in a job well done and should adopt the philosophy that no ball will ever drop in their area, that no hit will ever get by them, and that no runner will ever run on them.

Although some skills vary by position, all three outfielders should share the following characteristics:

- Good speed and agility
- Strong and accurate overhand throw
- Sure-handed
- Ability to anticipate and get a jump on the ball
- Good judgment under pressure
- A love of running—they must run, run, run and take charge of their territory.
- Ability to stay focused and alert

The center fielder should be the fastest of the outfielders because she has the most area to cover. She must get a good jump on the ball and be aggressive. The center fielder has priority on all balls. She should be a good diver because she can afford to gamble, knowing that a teammate will back her up on every attempt. The center fielder needs to be a vocal leader because she must communicate to the other outfielders and the middle infielders. The best outfielder on the team usually plays center field.

The right fielder has the longest throw to third base, so the most important consideration is the strength of her throws. A left-handed thrower is in the best position to make throws from the right-field line, but the player's throwing ability is a more important characteristic than which hand she throws with. A right fielder who can charge ground balls well and release the ball quickly is a real asset because she can turn what looks like a hit to right into an out at first.

The left fielder has the left-field line to cover. A right-hander has a slightly easier throw on balls hit down the line, but here too the important factor is throwing ability. The left fielder's longest throw is to home, so her arm can be the weakest of the three outfielders. The left fielder must be able to go back on balls effectively because most batters are right-handed and their hard-hit balls will be in that direction.

THROWING

Outfielders need to develop good velocity and accuracy on their throws. The long throw often required of outfielders demands particular attention to the mechanics of the overhand throw and the long bounce throw. For extra strength on a throw, outfielders may need to use the crow hop. Review the section on long throws and the drills in chapter 5 (pages 98-99 and 109-112). On the overhand throw, outfielders should think *over the top* and should exaggerate the follow-through by reaching forward and picking up grass. They should focus on a straight-line throw with good vertical backward spin to get the perfect bounce on the throw to the plate. The ball should come off the fingertips with the thumb pointing toward the ground. Outfielders should snap the wrist down and feel the fingers pulling on the seams.

Outfielders throw on a direct line in the air when close to the base or when throwing to an infielder for a relay. When the distance is too great for a quick, straight shot, the outfielder throws to the relay person or bounces the throw 10 to 15 feet (3 to 4.5 m) in front of the receiver. Throws to the relay person should be to the glove-side shoulder. Throws to the bases should be chest high for a force and knee high for a tag. Throws home from left field must be inside or outside the basepath to avoid hitting the runner. On throws home, the target is the plate no matter where the cutoff person is positioned. Ideally, the throw goes to the plate and through the chest of the cutoff. If the outfielder is going to miss the target, she should throw low to the cutoff and high to the relay.

When warming up, outfielders should include long-distance throwing to stretch and develop all the muscles involved in making longer throws. Players start about 30 feet (9 m) apart and gradually back up to a distance of about 100 feet (30 m). During games, outfielders should keep their arms warm between innings by throwing among themselves (left to center to right and back) or by using an extra player from the bench to warm up the nearest outfielder. They must throw sharply and accurately using correct technique.

Using the one-step throw allows outfielders to get rid of the ball quickly. By fielding with the throwing-side foot forward, the player needs to take just one step to throw. A right-handed thrower fields the ball with the right foot forward, then steps with the left and throws. The crow hop is added when the player needs more velocity on the ball or lacks arm strength. When using the crow hop, an outfielder may start with either foot forward, depending on the position of the feet when fielding the ball. A player will probably come to prefer either the left or right foot forward and will automatically adjust the feet to be in that position.

- **Crow hop starting on the left leg**—A right-handed thrower fields the ball with the weight on the forward left leg (see figure 8.1a). Then, when turning sideways to throw, she brings the right foot to the heel of the left foot (see figure 8.1b). The thrower hops on the right foot, steps forward with the left foot in the direction of

Figure 8.1 Crow hop starting on the left leg. *(a)* The player fields the ball with the left leg forward; *(b)* turns sideways to throw, bringing the right foot to the left heel; and *(c)* steps forward to throw.

the throw, and transfers the weight forward onto the left foot as she throws (see figure 8.1c). The outfielder should develop a rhythm or smoothness in executing the crow hop.

- **Crow hop starting on the right leg**—A right-handed thrower fields the ball with the weight on the forward right leg. After fielding the ball, she turns sideways while hopping on the right foot, steps with the left foot toward the target, and transfers the weight forward onto the left foot as she throws.

COACHING POINTS FOR THE OUTFIELDER'S THROW

- On short throws, use one step and throw.
- On medium to long throws, use the crow hop.
- Use an overhand throw. This is essential in order to avoid straining the arm and to create good vertical spin.
- Exaggerate the follow-through by reaching for the grass.
- Make straight-line throws—no rainbows.
- On throws to home, bounce the ball 15 feet (4.5 m) in front of the catcher. Two bounces are better than no bounce.

CATCHING FLY BALLS

The basic ready position for fielding is described in chapter 6. The key is to be in a balanced position, ready to move quickly to the ball. As noted, outfielders in their ready position generally hold their gloves a little higher than infielders do (see figure 6.3 on page 121). Players should use proper catching techniques whenever possible but must remember that the goal is to catch everything. *See the ball, catch the ball.* On routine fly balls, the catch should always be made with both hands slightly above the head and in front of the throwing shoulder. Players track the ball all the way into the glove.

Balls hit to left field will break toward the left-field foul line, and balls hit to right field will break toward the right-field foul line. The first hop will also usually break toward the foul lines. Fielders should position themselves accordingly. If a line drive is hit that will drop in front of a player, the player should try to get between the ball and the foul line. Right-field hits from a right-handed batter tend to have a lot of spin and will often curve.

Footwork

When the ball is hit, an outfielder's first movement is back—a short drop step of 2 or 3 inches (5 to 8 cm). This step back puts the body in motion and prevents the player from being caught back on her heels. The drop step is the key to having quick reactions. The player takes the drop step back and locates the ball. Then, after reading the ball, the fielder determines the angle she needs to take to catch the ball. *Drop step, locate, and go on an angle to the ball.*

For balls hit in front of her, after the drop step the outfielder pushes off the back foot and goes directly to the ball. For balls to the side, the fielder uses a jab step followed by a crossover step (see chapter 6, page 129). For balls diagonally back, she takes a quick pivot off the drop step to get in position and then does an inside or outside roll.

On balls diagonally back and over her head, after the first drop step the outfielder turns to the side that she perceives the ball is coming to. If the outfielder misjudges the ball or it drifts to the other side and is no longer in sight, she uses an inside or outside roll to turn to the opposite side (see chapter 6, pages 129-130).

As an outfielder is running with her back to home plate, going after a ball directly over her head, the ball will occasionally drift from one shoulder to the other. By simply turning her head to the opposite shoulder, the fielder can locate the ball for the catch.

Players should not think too much about footwork. Quick feet, balance, and good judgment are the keys to getting to the spot where the ball can be caught. Players should practice so that they are balanced and comfortable going after every type of ball.

The outfielder should run on the balls of the feet with a smooth stride to prevent jarring her eyes and blurring her vision. She should glide to the ball using good running technique, pumping the arms back and forth while keeping them close by her side. She should reach for the ball with the glove at the last second.

Angle to the Ball

To catch the ball, the outfielder must first reach the spot where it will come down. Great outfielders get there early and are waiting for the ball, making the catch look routine. If the ball is high enough and in front of her, the player can circle around it to get in the best catching and throwing position. However, on a hard-hit ball when the first concern is simply getting to it, the player must take a direct angle to the ball.

- **Circle around the ball**—On routine fly balls, the ideal technique is to circle around the ball, line up with the receiver, and be there waiting for the ball (see figure 8.2). This requires the outfielder to identify the direction of the hit and to be in the location where the ball will land in time to back off and gather momentum into the throw. She should sprint to a spot about 10 feet (3 m) beyond where the ball will land. The player never drifts to the ball; instead, she hurries and is there waiting. She moves her body around the ball to face the direction of the throw before making contact with it. The outfielder should track the ball from the hitter's contact spot to the glove. She times the approach so that when she touches the ball, all the momentum is moving forward and through the ball on line with the target. The circling technique is used for ground balls as well.

- **Direct angle to the ball**—A player often doesn't have the time to circle and be in position waiting for the ball. In this situation, quickness to the ball is the goal, and moving to the ball in a straight line on a direct angle is always the fastest way to cover any distance (see figure 8.2). The player sprints directly to the spot where she will field the ball and then turns her body abruptly to face the ball as she fields it.

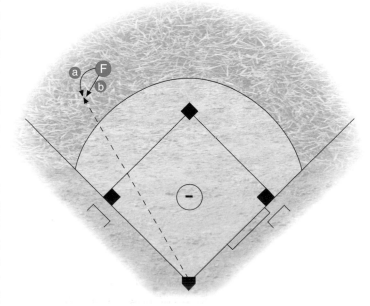

Figure 8.2 *(a)* Circling around the ball versus *(b)* taking a direct angle to the ball.

Short Fly Balls   When moving to a ball well in front of her, the fielder must keep her body low, her head down, and her eyes on the ball as she runs full speed toward it. The glove should not be extended until the last second. When the fielder does extend the glove, she holds the palm up and the pocket open as she focuses on the ball (as illustrated in figure 6.13 on page 128). The elbow should be rotated in to open up the pocket. The fielder must not lift her eyes or body because doing so will tend to raise the glove and let the ball get by. When the ball is in the pocket, the fielder should use the throwing hand to trap the ball. If the ball falls in front of her, the player should keep her chin and head down and short hop the ball. (Lifting the head and body would allow the ball to get under the glove.) The player should be in a position to use her body to block the ball and keep it from getting by her.

Long Fly Balls   On balls hit over her head, the fielder must go back, of course, but she should not backpedal more than three or four steps. Backpedaling sacrifices speed and balance. Fielders should backpedal only on balls hit directly to them that require little change in position.

On long fly balls, the player's first step should be a drop step. The side that the fielder thinks the ball is going toward determines which foot to step on. She lowers the hips, pushes them back hard, and then steps on the foot to the side that she thinks the ball will land (see figure 6.14a on page 129). The fielder pivots on that foot and pushes hard with the opposite foot (see figure 6.14b), then initiates a crossover step as she turns to run full speed on a straight angle to the place where she thinks the ball will descend. The fielder tries to keep her eyes on the ball to track its flight, running on the balls of the feet so that her eyes do not bounce excessively. The player should use good running form, pumping the arms. The glove arm is extended only during the last four or five steps, and the fielder always reaches and tries for the ball. When the fielder catches the ball, she quickly secures it with the other hand. If a throw needs to be made, the fielder braces against the front leg immediately after making the catch to stop her momentum. She regains her balance, pivots, and throws.

Some players may find it difficult to read the direction quickly and drop step to the appropriate side. These players should drop step to the side that is most comfortable (usually the throwing-side foot) and should locate the ball as they take this step. If the ball is hit to the opposite side, they can use one of the two techniques introduced in chapter 6 to get to the ball. Both of these rolls should be practiced regularly:

- **Inside (reverse) roll**—When using the inside roll, the outfielder must maintain an athletic stance: The knees and hips are bent so that the transition is smooth and the weight is transferred easily. She also needs to keep her eyes on the ball at all times. She pushes hard off the back leg to reverse direction and pivots inward, always keeping her nose on the ball (see figure 6.15 on page 130). This is a slower method than the outside roll because the player must stop and change direction, but it is safer for beginners because the ball is always in sight. The inside roll should be used on fly balls that are easily within the fielder's range.

- **Outside roll**—When using the outside roll, the fielder briefly turns her back to the ball while circling around to pick it up on the other side of the body. The fielder takes a drop step with the foot farthest from the ball, then pivots hard on the back foot, crosses over with the opposite leg, and sprints diagonally back (see figure 6.16 on page 130) to pick up the ball. This roll is a smooth chain of movements in which the momentum of the body flows into the turn, so it is effective on hard-hit balls that require a long sprint.

Which way should players turn when the ball is directly overhead? For very deep balls, turning to the glove side gives maximum extension. The glove can reach farther from that side. For balls that aren't as deep, turning to the throwing side allows fielders to get to throwing position more easily with less movement.

Diving for Balls

Outfielders can usually take the chance of diving for short fly balls in front of them. Because of the trajectory, the ball won't go far even if it is not catchable. On the other hand, it is risky for left or right fielders to dive for a line drive that is between them and the foul line because there is no backup. Outfielders can dive for balls that are falling between them if they are sure that the other outfielder can get to the backup position in case the ball gets through. See page 127 for a description of diving catches.

COACHING POINTS FOR CATCHING FLY BALLS

- Always catch with two hands. The ideal position is out front and above the head.
- Work on developing good balance and quick feet. Then, even if you initially misjudge a ball, you can often recover in time to make the catch.
- Make sure that your first movement is a short drop step back.
- Locate the ball and determine the best angle to take.
- When time permits, circle around to get behind the ball and take your momentum forward through the ball on line with the target.
- When you need to be quick, use a direct angle to the ball. Sprint to the spot for the catch and then turn toward the target to throw.
- Always attempt to keep your eyes on the ball.
- Be comfortable with both the inside and outside rolls. Use quick feet to maintain balance.
- Run on the balls of your feet using good running technique. Don't extend your glove until the last moment.

FIELDING GROUND BALLS

To field ground balls, the outfielder should keep the ball in front of the body. She positions the feet slightly closer together than an infielder would when fielding ground balls. Ground balls can be categorized as controllable (rolling smoothly and slowly) or uncontrollable (bouncing wildly). The game situation dictates how each should be played:

If there is no reason to take a chance of misplaying the ball	**Block it**
If there is an advantage in taking a slight chance that the ball will get through	**Scoop it**
If the play must be made or the team will go home a loser	**Do or die**

Blocking

When there is no possible play for a putout and no reason to take a chance, the outfielder blocks the ball. This technique should always be used on a sure hit with no runners on base, for uncontrollable balls, and on very rough ground when there is no backup should the ball get by the fielder. The goal is to make a wall behind the ball to eliminate the possibility that it will get by. The fielder runs directly to the ball, assumes a set position in line with the path of the ball, and waits for it to come the last 8 to 10 feet (2.5 to 3 m). She turns sideways to the ball in a stride position and drops on the back knee with the shin of the back leg lying parallel to the ground (see figure 8.3). The shoelaces of the back foot are flat on the ground so that the leg forms a barrier to the ball. The outfielder twists the upper body so that the chest remains facing the ball. She places the glove on the ground in front of her body to catch the ball.

Some players may feel comfortable using either leg, depending on the direction they are running. Players can choose to use the same leg on every play, however, because they have enough time to turn themselves in the proper position.

Figure 8.3 Blocking a ball in the outfield.

One-Hand Scoop

Outfielders use the one-hand scoop when a play to the infield is an option—for example, a throw to a base on a force play. This technique is safest on controllable balls or when a backup is in position. The outfielder charges hard at the ball and in the direction of the throw. To do this, she may have to come around the ball slightly. The outfielder keeps the ball in front of the body and is square to it when fielding. She stretches the glove in front of her body, keeping the glove low to the ground and concentrating on forward momentum. The fielder tracks the ball all the way to the glove. The glove action is a snap up or a light give to control the ball. If giving or gathering the ball, the player makes sure the glove is well out in front of the body so that even with the backward give, the glove remains in front of the body. Some players have a tendency to draw the glove too far back and run past the ball.

Should the play be made in front of the body or to the side? By fielding the ball in front of the body, the player can still block a ball that she can't handle. Fielding to the side is a little more advanced and is more comfortable for some, but it increases the odds that a ball will get by the player. Fielding in front of the body enables a quicker transition to throwing because the ball is closer to the throwing shoulder. Review the section on running through the ball in chapter 6. Because outfielders are scooping the ball to go after a runner, they should practice short throws to the bases after the scoop, throwing or flipping in one step.

Do or Die

Sometimes the game is over if the play is not made. So regardless of the type of ball (a hard shot, a ball taking uncontrollable bounces, a ball bouncing close to the feet, or a shot to the player's side), the outfielder must try to make the catch. She may have to short hop the ball or reach to the side without attempting to block it. She must charge directly to the ball, keeping her body under control. The fielder scoops up the ball using the technique described earlier for a one-hand scoop but without attention to fielding it safely.

COACHING POINTS
FOR CATCHING GROUND BALLS

- Remember that your goal is to always keep the ball in front of your body.
- Know the game situation. Can you afford to take a chance?
- Always block uncontrollable balls unless it is a do-or-die game situation.
- Scoop controllable balls when there is a possible infield play.
- Dive for short fly balls in front of you.
- Don't dive for hard-hit balls if there is no backup.
- Always be aware of your backup before you commit.

The main difference is the speed of the approach to the ball. Although the player is gambling with her glove work, she must maintain balance to have a chance at making the play. The player should estimate the time she has to make the play so that she does not commit an error by rushing more than necessary. On sinking line drives, the fielder will have to short hop the ball and hope to catch it.

BASIC POSITIONING AND ADJUSTMENTS

Outfielders must consider several factors when positioning themselves. (For additional information on adjusting to the game situation and the importance of communicating adjustments, see the section on defensive positioning in chapter 9.) The following factors influence where players should set up:

- *The players' own abilities.* How well does each outfielder go forward, back, or sideways? How strong are the outfielders' arms?
- *The speed, strengths, and weaknesses of adjacent players.* Outfielders should use the strengths of their teammates and should help with their weaknesses.
- *The ability of the infielders in front of them to go back.*
- *The type of pitcher, type of pitch, and pitch location.* The kind of pitch and the speed at which it is thrown affect the outcome. Outfielders should adjust in for a drop-ball pitcher, and they should adjust back for a predominately rise-ball pitcher. If the pitcher is slow, the outfield looks for the batter to pull the ball. When playing behind a pitcher with speed, the outfield expects late swings and more balls to the opposite field. Outfielders should know the count. If the pitcher is ahead, they pull in. If the pitcher is behind, they shade to the power alley and back up a few steps.
- *The type of hitter.* Outfielders should move back a few steps for the power hitters and should pull way in for the slappers. The outfielders should observe which way the batter is trying to hit the ball. An open stance indicates that the batter is trying to pull the ball, and a closed stance indicates that the batter is trying to hit to the opposite field. Shifts may be made according to the hitter's tendencies and the

pitcher's plan for pitching to the hitter. Outfielders must be careful not to leave significant gaps that can hurt the team if the pitcher misses her spot or hangs a pitch. Shifts should be only a few steps in the direction the batter is expected to hit the ball. The defense should play an unknown batter in regular position.

- *The number of outs, the inning, and the score.* The game situation determines whether outfielders play aggressively or play it safe. When the team is ahead late in the game, they play a few steps deeper to prevent extra-base hits, and they don't gamble on line drives or hard-hit ground balls. With the winning run on third base and less than two outs, they play in close enough that they can comfortably throw out the runner on a fly ball. A deep fly ball ends the game, so they don't have to worry about a ball over their heads.

- *The distance and height of the fence.* The outfield can use a high fence as an extra player and play in several steps. A deep fence or no fence means that they have to play back so that nothing gets by for extra bases.

Knowing the pitch to be thrown gives outfielders valuable information about what to expect. Having the infield signal when the pitcher is throwing a changeup can help the outfield adjust. Alerting outfielders that a pickoff will be called allows them to be prepared to back up the throw. By continuously talking and reviewing the game situation, the number of outs, and the speed of any runners, players will be less likely to make mental errors. Outfielders are in position to spot a steal attempt and should help alert the infield. Talking helps keep everyone's head in the game and results in a cohesive, coordinated team effort.

Playing the Fence

Outfielders must have no fear of playing the fence. Right and left fielders must also contend with a sideline fence. Outfielders must know how the ball rebounds off the fence and how the fence will absorb body contact. If it is a breakaway fence, they should practice going through it while making the catch. On high fly balls, the outfielder often has the luxury of first finding the fence and then focusing on the ball. Counting and remembering the number of running steps to the fence from the normal playing position can help the player know where the fence is when making a play. When a fielder is making a catch near the fence, the bent-leg slide is a safe option. On deep fly balls, the fielder must practice getting to the fence, finding it, and then coming back to the ball and making a catch. It won't always be easy, but the more the fielders practice, the less they will fear going back hard.

Dealing With the Elements

All players (including the infield) should check the sun, the lights, the wind, and the background. Players should use sunglasses, hats, and eye black for glare if they think these might help.

The sun is often a factor in the outfield. As described in chapter 6, the fielder can place the glove on the sun to block the glare (see figure 8.4), then remove it at the last second to make the catch. She can also block the sun by holding the bare hand close to the face or simply approach the ball at an angle to minimize the directness of the light. If she cannot see a ball hit to her area she should let her teammates know that and allow another fielder to make the play.

Because of the distance a ball hit to the outfield travels, the wind can have a strong impact on its destination. Outfielders must monitor the direction and strength of the wind during warm-ups and throughout the game. They may need to shift their positions a few steps to adjust for the effect of the wind on the flight of the ball as described in chapter 6 (page 131). If the wind is strong, fielders should call loudly and repeatedly so that their teammates can hear. When throwing the ball, outfielders must keep the throw down and may need to increase the number of bounces.

OUTFIELD RESPONSIBILITIES

Outfielders never just stand around—on every play there is something to do. From backing up infielders to covering bases or rundowns, outfielders have many responsibilities. Catching a fly ball may appear easy, but catching "tweeners" requires a lot of teamwork. With runners on base, the priority is getting the ball quickly to the infield and knowing where to throw. Outfielders also need to know the rules and how to use the rules to their advantage. They must understand their position well.

Figure 8.4 **Using the glove to block the sun.**

Runners on Base

Deciding where to throw the ball is the most difficult decision that outfielders must make. And they must often make this decision in a high-pressure situation. Before each pitch, the outfielders should review the situation and anticipate the play that they may have to make. How fast are the runners? What are the capabilities of the batter? Is the opposing coach aggressive or conservative? Knowing what to expect can help the outfield respond more quickly. Knowledge gives confidence, and confidence improves execution.

As soon as the outfielder catches the ball, she must get it to the infield. She cannot stand and hold the ball. The outfielder makes the play on the lead runner when possible. When she is unlikely to throw out a runner, she tries to keep the back runner from advancing.

When the runner is obviously not going, the outfielder can run the ball in or throw to the relay infielder. Closing the gap by running toward the infield helps eliminate errors on the throw. But the outfielder must first make sure that the runner is not going anywhere.

If there is no play, the outfielder can try to make one. When a ball is hit to the outfield with the bases loaded and two outs, all runners must get safely to the next base for the run to count. The slowest runner is usually the runner going to second because that runner has a tendency to slow down and watch the play at home. A quick throw to second can end the inning. In any bases-loaded situation, the outfielder should look for someone to throw out if she can't get the lead runner.

Tweeners

Balls hit between players must be caught. Fear of a collision, however, often causes a player to back off the play and leave it for a teammate. When both players back off, the ball drops safely. Players need to understand which fielder has priority, and they must communicate clearly about who will make the catch.

The outfielder has priority over an infielder because the outfielder is in a better position to make the play. The outfielders are moving in to make the play, so the ball and all possible plays are in front of them. Infielders should go back hard after the ball until an outfielder calls for it. The ball should be called for early so the infielder can get out of the outfielder's way. This means that the player must make the call *before* she is absolutely sure she can make the catch; calling it means that she will go for the ball and that other players are to give her the space to get it. If the infielder is to make the play, the outfielder acts as a backup. The outfielders must avoid coming so close that their footsteps or shadow scare the infielders off the ball.

The center fielder is usually the strongest outfielder and generally has priority over the other outfielders. The coach should clarify this after evaluating individual abilities. Players should understand and accept strengths and weaknesses, and they should practice giving way when appropriate. For example, when a ball is hit past two outfielders, the one with the stronger arm should make the throw. Position will also determine who can best make the play. On a ball hit between center and right, a right-handed right fielder is in the best position to throw to third.

Outfielders should not back off the ball too early. Each fielder should assume that she alone is making the play. Players must pursue the ball hard until one of them calls for it. On many fly balls, two outfielders could make the catch, so it is critical that the ball be called for early and decisively with an understanding of who has priority. Players should call for a fly ball when it is at its highest point. The other outfielder then backs up the play and, if possible, checks the runner and tells the fielder where to throw. The language should be "mine, mine, mine" and the response "take it, take it." A player should *never* call the ball for another player.

Backing Up

Errors will occur, and balls will get by fielders—but a good backup will limit the damage. Outfielders should hustle to back up every hit ball and throw. From the backup position, a player can also help direct the throw. Backup responsibilities do not end until all possibilities of further action are exhausted (see table 8.1 for a summary of the backup responsibilities of each outfielder).

Outfielders must hustle to back up the adjacent outfielder going for the ball. The backup player should be 10 to 12 feet (3 to 3.5 m) behind the fielder and in a position to react to a ball that gets through. Only then can the outfielder making the play try for the ball confidently and aggressively. Knowing that someone is behind her gives her the freedom to dive for balls.

On balls to the infield, the appropriate outfielder should move directly to the ball with the assumption that the ball will get by the infielder. All fielders should take several steps to the ball until it is clear which player is in the best position to be the primary backup. The outfielder should be set by the time the ball passes the infielder so that she can easily react to the ball.

If the ball is not hit in a particular outfielder's direction, she has the responsibility to back up a base. The outfielder lines up with the anticipated throw and takes a position about 20 to 25 feet (6 to 7.5 m) behind the base (see figure 8.5). The center fielder is the primary backup for second base. The left fielder covers third base and backs up second base on throws from the right side when the center fielder is not able to get there. The right fielder always backs up first on every throw from the infield. When the ball is hit toward the second-base player, the right fielder must first play the ball.

Table 8.1   Outfield Defensive Responsibilities for Backups, Base Coverage, and Rundowns

Left fielder
Backs up balls hit to the nonglove side of the shortstop, to the third-base player, and to center field; backs up throws to second base from the right side.
Covers third base any time the shortstop must go to second and when the third-base player cannot get back.
Lines up behind the third-base player on *rundowns*.
Center fielder
Backs up balls hit to the glove side of the shortstop, to the nonglove side of the second-base player, to the pitcher, and to left and right field; backs up throws to second, including pickoff plays from the catcher.
Covers second base when the second-base player and shortstop are committed elsewhere (for example, on a bunt with a runner at second).
Lines up behind the second-base player on *rundowns*.
May cover second on *pickoff plays* from the catcher.
Right fielder
Backs up balls hit to first base, to the glove side of the second-base player, and to center field; backs up all throws to first base and throws to second base from left field.
Covers first base when the first- and second-base players are committed elsewhere.
Lines up behind the first-base player on *rundowns*.

(The catcher will be moving into the backup position if no runners are on base.) If the infielder fields it, the right fielder still hustles to back up the throw. On all other infield ground balls, the right fielder must instantly sprint to backup position behind first base.

Outfielders must also be ready to adjust for secondary throws. A good example occurs when the center fielder is backing up second base on a sacrifice-bunt attempt. With a runner on first, the infielder fielding the bunt first looks to second to make the throw, and the center fielder must line up expecting that throw. If the infielder changes her mind and throws instead to first, the center fielder must quickly adjust her position toward left field to back up a possible pickoff attempt from first (see figure 8.6 on page 176). During defensive practice, players should occasionally overthrow bases to make sure backups are in correct position to make the catch.

Figure 8.5   Outfield backup position for a throw.

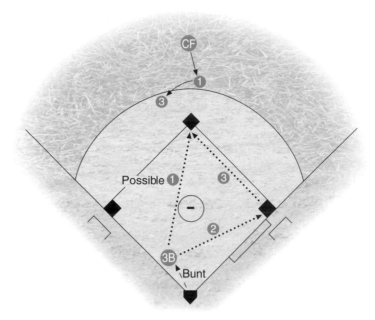

Figure 8.6 Center fielder's backup adjustments on a sacrifice-bunt attempt.

Covering Bases

In some instances, outfielders need to cover a base. They should know the proper foot-work to cover the base and how to apply a tag (see chapter 7, pages 155-158). On a bunt, the left fielder should be prepared to cover third base if the shortstop has gone to second and the third-base player is fielding the bunt. If the catcher is covering third, then the left fielder becomes her backup. On a bunt with a runner on second, the center fielder covers second because the shortstop is covering third. See table 8.1 for a sum-mary of the base-coverage responsibilities of each outfielder.

Rundowns

When runners are caught in a rundown, the outfielders are often part of the defensive rotation. Review the techniques involved (see chapter 9, page 199) and see table 8.1 for a summary of the rundown responsibilities of each outfielder.

KNOW THE RULES

Players must clearly understand the rules that govern dead-ball situations and the ef-fects of the catch-and-carry rule. With runners on base, outfielders should not catch and carry the ball out of bounds unless they can afford to give runners a free base. When there is not a fence around the field, lines placed at least 25 feet (7.5 m) beyond and parallel to the foul lines are used to indicate what is in bounds and what is out of bounds. A catch-and-carry means that a player catches the ball in bounds to get the batter out but then carries the ball into out-of-bounds (dead-ball) territory by stepping beyond the line. Play is stopped, and if the catch didn't make the third out of the inning, all runners automatically advance an extra base (so a runner on third would score). Catching a ball and falling over the fence produces an out as long as the fielder holds on to the ball, but catching the ball and then falling into dead-ball territory gives the run-ners a free base. Outfielders should not play a ball that is trapped (caught in a fence) unless doing so is to the team's advantage. Fielders should put up their hands to indicate the ball is trapped or has gone through a hole in the fence. Runners get the base they are going to and one more. If the fielder plays the ball and keeps it live, the runner may go for as many bases as she can. If the award of two bases keeps the runner from scoring, the fielders should not play a trapped ball and make it live; instead, they should take the umpire's ruling. Similarly, if the ball is headed out of bounds, fielders should choose to let it go and limit the runners' advance to two bases.

Outfielders must know when to catch foul balls. With a runner on third, they should not catch a deep foul ball unless the team can afford to give up a run when the runner tags up. (With a big lead, the out is sometimes more important than the run.) On foul balls close to the line, the base player can see the line better and should tell the outfielder whether to catch the ball or let it go. If in doubt as to whether the ball is fair or foul, players should assume it is fair.

OUTFIELD DRILLS

Outfielders must love to catch fly balls and should do so every day. Footwork and confidence can be developed using toss drills at a short distance. With a partner, players can roll grounders and toss fly balls to work on the basic skills. Machines can throw balls of all types (bloopers, line drives, deep fly balls, and grounders), so outfielders can work at regular distances on the skills needed. Players must also practice reacting to balls hit off the bat, but hitting takes a lot of time and does not always put the ball in the desired location. Batting practice provides the opportunity to practice playing balls off the bat. Outfielders should play their regular positions and use proper technique. No opportunity to improve should be wasted. Because 90 percent of all outfield balls are in front of the outfielders, practice should emphasize skills relevant to those balls. Coaches and players must be aware of the danger of overusing the arm. Outfielders can save their arms by returning balls to buckets instead of throwing long distance on every play. Four excellent catching drills—drop-step reaction, zigzag, ball toss for inside and outside rolls, and football—are included in chapter 6 and should be done regularly by outfielders (see pages 137)

AROUND THE BALL

Purpose: To practice circling around the ball when catching fly balls.

Procedure: Outfielders form a single-file line. A catcher sets up to the left of a hitter. The fungo hitter hits a high, soft fly ball to the left side of the first outfielder; the fly ball should be high enough to give the fielder time to get in position. The outfielder comes around the ball to line up for a throw to the catcher (see figure 8.7). Repeat the drill in the opposite direction with the catcher setting up to the right of the hitter.

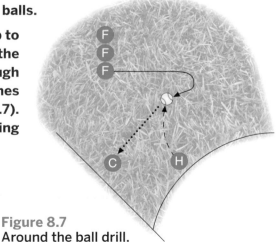

Figure 8.7
Around the ball drill.

CRITICAL CUE:
Here's a tactic that may be used by advanced players: With a runner at third who is going to score on a sacrifice fly, the fielder acts as if she is going to catch the ball above the head, but then she catches the ball at waist level. The goal is to catch the runner leaving early because she is anticipating that the catch will be made sooner—above the fielder's head.

FIELDING AT THE FENCE

Purpose: To learn to play the fence.

Procedure: This drill involves outfielders, a relay, and a catcher. The outfielders form a line in left, right, or center field. A tosser positioned about 15 feet (4.5 m) from the fence throws the ball so that it lands against the fence. From a fielding position about 20 feet (6 m) in front of the fence, an outfielder goes quickly to the fence, plants her foot against it, picks up the ball, listens for the relay's voice, and throws to her. Emphasize the bent front leg for the throw and hitting the relay.

Variation: To save the relay's arm, save time, and eliminate the need for a catcher, the relay can fake a throw home (still using proper technique) and put the ball in a bucket.

TENNIS RACKET FLY BALLS

Purpose: To practice communication on fly balls.

Procedure: Half of the outfielders line up in center field and the other half in right (or left) field. Using a tennis racket and tennis balls, the coach hits fly balls to the first outfielders in each line. The coach hits the tennis balls to places where the two outfielders will have to communicate in order to catch the ball. Balls should be hit over their shoulder and in front of them.

Variation: Add middle infield players. Work on communication between the outfielders and infielders on fly balls that are hit softly between the outfield and infield.

COMMUNICATE AND COVER

Purpose: To have adjacent outfielders practice communicating, taking an angle to the ball, and backing up each other.

Procedure: Two lines of outfielders about 40 feet (12 m) apart face a hitter with a catcher. Balls are hit between the two fielders. One outfielder calls for the ball and takes the direct (short) angle to the ball. The other outfielder takes a deep (long) angle and backs up her teammate, ready to field the ball. Players can put balls in buckets to save time and arms. Players rotate to the end of the opposite line.

BLOOPERS

Purpose: To communicate and establish coverage on balls hit between the infield and outfield.

Procedure: A catcher, middle infielders, and outfielders take their normal fielding positions. Use a ball machine or fungo bat to hit bloopers between the infielders and outfielders. Emphasize that the infielders need to go back hard until called off. If necessary, outfielders should dive for bloopers to make the catch. Players return the ball to the catcher at home, who feeds the hitter or machine.

DOWN THE LINE, UP THE ALLEY

Purpose: To practice fielding balls and taking angles for balls hit down the line and in the alleys.

Procedure: This drill requires four outfielders, receivers at second base and third base, a hitter, and a catcher (see figure 8.8). Because the center fielder is always involved on balls hit to the gap, it is best to use two center fielders—one in left center and one in right center. The left and right fielders are in normal position. The ball is fungoed alternately to the two pairs of outfielders in the alley and down the line. The first ball is hit down the left-field line, the second to the right-field line, the third to the left-field alley, and the fourth to the right-field alley. Outfielders work on short-angle and deep-angle coverage and on hitting the relay or bases. Each fielder should throw to both second and third base. Extra outfielders or pitchers cover the bases if the infielders are busy elsewhere. Players return balls to the catcher or use a bucket at each base.

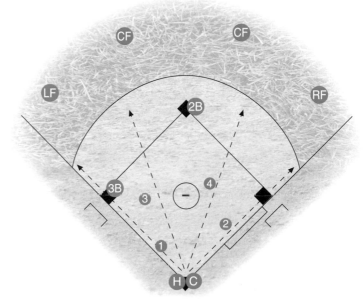

Figure 8.8 Down the line, up the alley drill.

DECISIONS

Purpose: To improve outfield decision making about whether to go for the lead runner or the batter.

Procedure: Use a full defense minus the pitcher, and have a line of runners at home and first going on the hit. The runner at home starts on the right side of the plate (out of the hitter's way) and goes on contact to make the play realistic. She touches first base and makes the turn for second. When the play is finished she joins the line at first base. The hitter hits various types of balls to the outfield. The fielder must decide whether to go for the lead runner or throw behind her and stop the second runner. Move runners to different starting positions and vary the types of balls played.

OUTFIELD AROUND

Purpose: To practice fielding all types of hits and throwing to bases from all outfield positions.

Procedure: Receiving players are positioned at first and third, and a hitter and catcher are at home. Use at least four outfielders because the drill requires a lot of running. (The same player makes three plays in a row.)

(continued)

Outfield Around (continued)

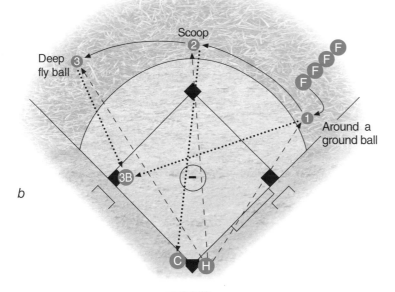

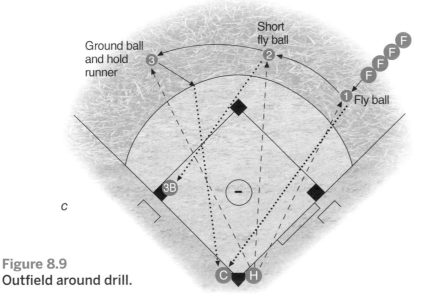

Figure 8.9
Outfield around drill.

Round 1

1. Players form a line in right field. Each player scoops a ground ball, throws to first, and then sprints to center field.

2. The player catches a deep fly ball in left center field and throws to third. She then sprints to left field.

3. The player catches a fly ball hit down the left-field line and throws home. She sprints back to right field, going behind home plate (see figure 8.9a).

Round 2

1. In right field, the outfielder comes around a ground ball and throws to third.

2. In center field, she scoops a ground ball and throws home.

3. She catches a fly ball to the deep left-field alley and throws to third (see figure 8.9b).

Round 3

1. The outfielder catches a fly ball to right field and throws home.

2. She catches a short fly to the right-field alley and throws to third.

3. In left field, she fields a ground ball, runs toward second to hold the batter–runner, and then sets and throws home (see figure 8.9c).

SECOND TO HOME AND HOME TO SECOND

Purpose: **To improve outfielders' decision making on whether to go for the lead runner or the batter–runner. The on-deck batter practices coaching the runner coming home, and the pitchers practice backing up home.**

Procedure: **Runners line up near home and second. Pitchers line up behind the first-base line. Defenders take positions in the outfield and at first, second, shortstop, and home. From home plate, the hitter hits balls to all parts of the outfield. The runner at second attempts to score, and the runner at home tries to reach second (see figure 8.10). The runner at home starts on the right side of the plate (out of the hitter's way) and goes on contact to make the play realistic. The runner at second assumes a leadoff position and then reacts to the hit. The outfielder must**

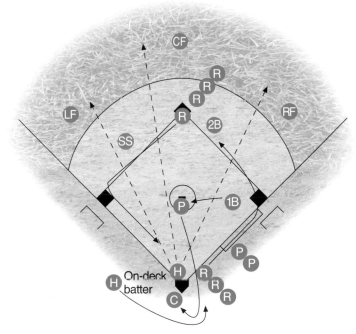

Figure 8.10   Second to home and home to second drill.

choose to throw home or to the second-base player or shortstop covering second. On the hit, the first-base player assumes the cutoff position, and the pitcher immediately takes proper backup position at home (see chapter 9). The on-deck batter moves into position behind home plate, facing the runner and giving hand signals to the runner to stand or slide to one side of the plate or the other. Runners can actually slide, or they can stay upright and swing wide to the right to avoid any contact. Players rotate. The runner going home moves to the on-deck batter circle (ready to coach the next runner at home) and then joins the runners at home. Pitchers rotate to the pitcher's mound on every hit.

HOLDING THE RUNNER TO A SINGLE

Purpose: **To improve the left fielder's ability to hold the batter–runner to a single.**

Procedure: **Several outfielders form a line in left field. A second-base player and catcher are at their normal positions. The outfielder assumes a normal defensive position. Runners are in a line at home and start on the right side of the plate out of the hitter's way. The runner goes on contact. The hitter fungo hits down the left-field line. The runner makes an aggressive turn toward second, putting pressure on the left fielder to field the ball cleanly and hold the runner at first.**

Variation: **Add right fielders to practice proper backup of second base.**

WEAVE

Purpose: To improve conditioning while working on catching fly balls.

Procedure: Four players start in a line in left field (see figure 8.11). Tossers are at the three bases, each with a bucket of balls. The tosser at third throws a ball to the first player, who fields and throws the ball back to the tosser and then runs toward center field to catch another ball thrown by the same person. The fielder returns that ball to another tosser at second base, who repeats the sequence as the fielder continues to run toward right field. A third thrower at first base repeats the sequence. Fielders wait in right field and then repeat the drill going the other way. This is a good drill for all players.

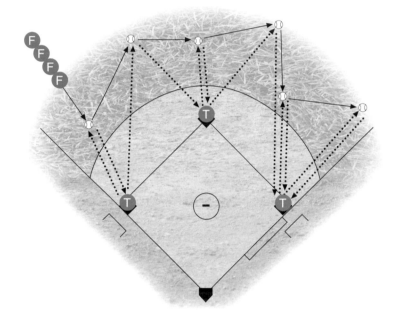

Figure 8.11   Weave drill.

FOUR IN ONE

Purpose: To work on scoops, short hops, bloopers, and relays. This drill teaches aggressiveness and is a good conditioning drill when the line is not too long.

Procedure: Players stand in a single-file line about 20 feet (6 m) from a tosser. They all complete each drill before moving to the next.

1. **The first player runs toward the tosser and scoops a rolling ground ball. The fielder tosses the ball back and returns on the run to the end of the line. All players in line complete drill 1 before the tosser starts drill 2.**

2. **For drill 2, each player fields a short hop, tosses the ball back, and returns to the end of the line.**

3. **In drill 3, each player fields a blooper, diving if necessary. The tosser simply pops (tosses) the ball up before the charging fielder. The fielder tosses the ball back and returns to the end of the line.**

4. In the last drill, players work on the relay throw. The first ball is a grounder that the fielder tosses back to the tosser. The fielder then turns to chase a ball thrown over her head. She gets the ball and hits the relay, who is the next person in line. The relay has moved out from the line and is waving her arms and calling for the ball. The relay makes the relay throw then turns and runs toward the tosser to field a ground ball and continue the drill.

TEAM DEFENSE

Softball is a team game. Together the team is stronger than the individual parts. All players have responsibilities on every pitch and every play. No one should be standing around; spectators belong in the stands. In other chapters, we look at the way the infield, outfield, and battery operate as separate units. This chapter covers situations in which everyone must work together to achieve success as a team.

DEFENSIVE POSITIONING

Chapters 7 and 8 describe basic positioning for the infield and outfield. From the basic defensive setup, individual adjustments (see table 9.1) are made for each pitch based on the coach's philosophy and factors such as the following:

- **Batter**—Power, speed, and tendencies.
- **Base runners**—Number, position, speed, and opponent's offensive philosophy.
- **Pitcher**—Speed, control, count, and pitch location.
- **Opposing pitcher and team**—The probability that a team will score more runs than their opponents. This will determine how aggressively they play each base runner.
- **Abilities of the defensive players**—Ability of each player and the players around her.
- **Game situation**—Score, number of outs, and inning. Does the opposing team play aggressively or safe?
- **Environment**—Field, outfield fence, wind, temperature, wet or dry conditions.

Players should go with the percentages. Statistics and scouting will tell players the positioning that offers the best chance of success. The game is a matter of inches and surprises, and players should play for the best odds.

An adjustment of one or two steps may be all that is needed for a player to be in the right place to make the play. But players must be careful not to leave significant gaps that can hurt the team if the pitcher misses her spot or hangs a pitch. Shifts should be only a few steps in the direction the batter is expected to hit the ball. The team should play an unknown batter in regular defensive position. Any changes and adjustments must be communicated to adjacent teammates to eliminate gaps and clarify the areas that each player is responsible for covering. Players can't work together if they don't know what their teammates are doing. They must constantly communicate. If the outfielders move back, they must warn the infielders that they need to cover more territory. Players should share information so that the wisest decision can be made; two (or more) minds are better than one.

- The center fielder adjusts the outfield because she is in the best position to communicate with the other two outfielders.
- The shortstop is usually the team leader on the infield and is usually the best infielder—her central position works to her advantage.
- The catcher has the entire defense in front of her, so she can most easily see the defensive setup and direct adjustments.

All players are involved in the specific plays covered in the rest of this chapter. Each player should understand her responsibilities and those of her teammates. She should work on the individual techniques involved and apply them to the teamwork required.

Table 9.1 Defensive Positioning Summary

Situation	Outfielders	Middle infielders	Corners
Batter			
Power hitter	Back 3 steps and 2 steps toward pull side	Back 2 steps	Back 2 steps
Bunter	In 5 steps	In 2 steps; second-base player 3 steps toward first base; shortstop 3 steps toward the base she covers	In as far as necessary to get the out
Slapper	All outfielders in 3 steps; left fielder 3 steps toward foul line	On baseline; second-base player in bunt position; shortstop shades toward third base	First-base player in 3 steps and shades toward pitcher; third-base player in 2 steps and 3 steps toward pitcher
Fast runner	Normal	In 2 steps	Normal unless looking for a bunt
Base runners			
Double play	Normal	Shade 2 or 3 steps toward second base	Normal
Runner on third and less than two outs	In 2 steps	On baseline	In 1 step
Winning run on third and less than two outs	In to a spot where player can throw out runner after catching a fly ball	In front of baseline	In 1 step
Team ahead by comfortable margin and fifth inning or later	Back 3 steps	Behind basepath	Normal
Runners on, close game	In 3 steps	On baseline	In 2 steps
Runners on first and third	In 2 steps	On baseline	In 2 steps in case of a bunt
Runner on first and two outs	Back 3 steps	Shortstop shades toward second base, expecting a steal	Normal
Pitcher			
Slow speed	Back 3 steps and 2 steps toward pull side	Behind baseline and 1 step toward pull side	Back 1 step
Fast speed and overpowering	Move 3 steps toward opposite field	Move 2 steps toward opposite field	Normal
Ahead in count	In 2 steps	Normal	Normal
Behind in count	Back 2 steps	Normal	Normal
Full count	Back 3 steps and 2 steps toward pull side	Back 1 step	Back 1 step
Drop ball	In 2 steps	Normal	Normal
Rise ball	Back 2 or 3 steps	Normal	Normal
Changeup	Back 3 steps and 2 steps toward pull side; right fielder stays in case of flare	Behind baseline and 1 step toward pull side	Back 1 step
Curveball	Back 2 steps and 2 steps toward batter's opposite field	Shade 1 step toward batter's opposite field	Normal
Screwball	Normal	Normal	Back 2 or 3 steps toward pull side
The elements			
No fence	Back 3 to 5 steps	Normal	Normal
High fence	In 3 steps	Normal	Normal
Wind blowing in	In 3 steps	In 1 step	Normal
Wind blowing out	Back 3 steps	Back 1 step	Normal
Hard infield	Normal	Back 2 steps	Back 1 or 2 steps
Soft infield	Normal	In 2 steps	In 2 steps

BACKING UP

Inexperienced players may think they have nothing to do on some plays. But the responsibility of backing up falls on everyone on every play. Any player not going after the ball or covering a base should move into a position to back up the hit or a throw. Players should always assume that a hit ball is going to be missed and will have to be fielded by the backup. The player moves to the ball first. If she is not making the play herself, she quickly goes 10 to 12 feet (3 to 3.5 m) directly behind the fielder making the play, being careful not to interfere with her or distract her in any way. If the first defender fields the ball successfully, the player adjusts to back up any possible throw. She should be in a direct line from the thrower to the intended receiver, about 20 feet (6 m) behind the receiver. For example, the pitcher should be close to the fence when backing up third or home so she can quickly retrieve the ball off the fence. On a hit ball, the backup player may move first to one position and then to another as the play develops, all the while hoping not to have to touch the ball.

Fielders have the following backup responsibilities:

Catcher:	Backs up first on an infield hit unless a runner is on second or third base.
Pitcher:	Backs up throws to third or home.
Right fielder:	Backs up balls hit to first base, to the glove side of the second-base player, and to center field; backs up all throws to first base and throws to second base from left field.
Center fielder:	Backs up balls hit to the glove side of the shortstop, to the nonglove side of the second-base player, to the pitcher, and to left and right field; backs up throws to second, including pickoff plays from the catcher.
Left fielder:	Backs up balls hit to the nonglove side of the shortstop, to the third-base player, and to center field; backs up throws to second base from the right side.
Shortstop or second-base player:	Backs up every return throw from the catcher when runners are on base.
First-base player:	Backs up the catcher on first-and-third plays if the runner is going; backs up the second-base player on throws from left and center field.

BUNT DEFENSE

The abilities of the defensive players must be the primary consideration of the coach in deciding how to defend the bunt and who will make the play. The speed of the bunter and base runners and their ability to execute the short game (with all its options) will also be a factor.

The third- and first-base players usually field most of the bunts. If the pitcher is a strong fielder, however, the coach may ask her to field many of the bunts, including those down the first-base line. The first-base player can then stay back to play first, and the second-base player can play in her regular position. The coach should select a plan that best uses the abilities of the players. The person in the best position to field and throw should call for the bunt. When deciding who has priority, consideration should also be given to who has the strongest and most accurate arm. Communication is the key. "I've got it" or "Mine" helps clear the area and eliminate confusion.

With a runner on first, in a typical bunt defense the first- and third-base players take positions close enough to the bunter that they can consistently get the out. This often means that the corners are at least halfway down the line. The pitcher's responsibility is to back up the corners should the bunt get past them. The pitcher fields only bunts hit directly to her. On all other bunts, she delays charging ahead and instead fans out to a backup position behind the player fielding the bunt.

When the third-base player fields the ball with a base runner on first, the catcher should follow her momentum to third base to cover the bag and prevent the runner from advancing from first to third. The third-base player calls "Mine," and the catcher follows with "I have third." The left fielder assumes a backup position.

The defensive assignments when anticipating a bunt with a runner on first base are as follows (see figure 9.1):

Second-base player:	Moves several steps toward first base. Covers first base.
Shortstop:	Covers second base.
Third-base player:	Covers the area between third base and the mound. If not involved in the play, retreats to cover third base.
First-base player:	Covers the area between first and the mound.
Pitcher:	Delays and fans out to a backup position, except on balls hit directly to her.
Catcher:	Fields all bunts close to the plate. Covers third base when the third-base player fields the bunt.
Left fielder:	Backs up third base. Covers third base if an infielder does not get there in time.
Center fielder:	Backs up second base for a throw from home. If the throw goes to first base, shifts her backup position to cover a possible second throw from first base.
Right fielder:	Backs up first base.

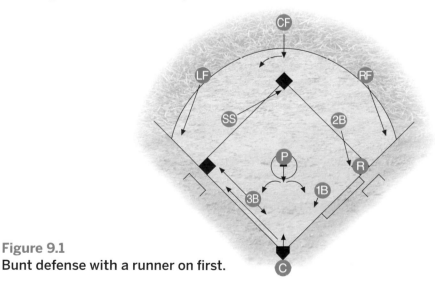

Figure 9.1
Bunt defense with a runner on first.

With a runner on second or third or with several runners on base, the shortstop must cover third. The second-base player still covers first. The first- and third-base players play up in their normal bunt positions. Second base is thus left open unless the first-base player is playing back. The center fielder covers this open base, and all defensive players must understand that they should never throw to second because there is no backup for a bad throw. Ideally, the center fielder just being there will bluff the runner into staying. With a runner at or running to third, players should not be throwing behind the runner anyway. The defensive assignments with a runner on second or third or with multiple runners on base are as follows (see figure 9.2):

Second-base player: Moves several steps toward first base to cut down the distance. Covers first base.

Shortstop: Moves several steps closer to third. Covers third base.

Third-base player: Covers the area between third and the mound.

First-base player: Covers the area between first and the mound.

Pitcher: Delays and fans out to a backup position, except on balls hit directly to her.

Catcher: Fields all bunts close to the plate. Does not leave home plate.

Left fielder: Backs up third base.

Center fielder: Covers second base.

Right fielder: Backs up first base.

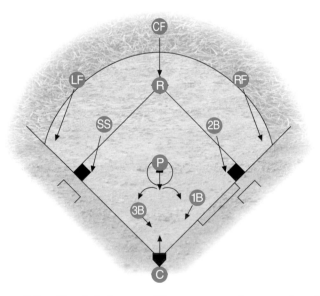

Figure 9.2 **Bunt defense with a runner at second or third.**

When anticipating a bunt, the corners must be in close enough to have a good chance of getting an out. With runners on base, the goal for advanced players is to get the lead runner. But if they can't get the lead runner, they must definitely get the batter. The goal is always to get an out on a sacrifice bunt. Whether it is wise to go after the lead runner will be determined by the speed of the runner, the speed and placement of the bunt, and how quickly the fielder gets to the ball. Even when these factors are in her favor, the defensive player must field the ball cleanly to get the lead runner. If she mishandles the ball even slightly and has any doubt about getting the lead runner, she must throw to first. Only advanced teams should go for the lead runner. For many teams, throwing to first base should be the only option.

Fielders should watch the batter for tips that she is bunting. They should key in on the top hand; as soon as it starts to slide up the bat, they yell "Bunt." The bunter's feet or position in the box may also give away her intentions. Watch the front knee for a little turn. The first-base player must be particularly observant with right-handed batters; likewise, the third-base player must watch closely with left-handed batters.

When the batter shows that she is bunting, the corners should begin to creep (move) in. As the bunt is put down, the fielders charge. They must be careful to charge the bunt, not the bunter. If they charge the batter, the ball may get by them.

Fielders should play all bunts as if they are fair and let the umpire make the call. If they cannot field the ball and get the out, they should let the bunt roll to see if it goes foul. The instant the ball reaches foul territory, a fielder should touch it with the glove or foot so that it is ruled a foul ball, not taking the chance that it will roll back into fair territory.

The player fields a bunt by positioning her body so that the feet are already in line to throw. An approach from the side, instead of straight on, allows the feet to be in throwing position. The fielder surrounds the ball and sets her feet toward the base that she wants to throw to (see figure 9.3). When possible, the ball should be fielded off the back foot so the fielder's weight is already back to make the throw. She fields with two hands to get a secure and firm grip. Advanced players should field with the feet aligned to throw to the lead base. If no play is possible there, the player still has time to adjust the feet for a throw to first base.

When the fielder must turn her body to make the throw, she always turns toward the glove to get the feet and shoulders in throwing position. This means that a right-handed first-base player fielding a bunt down the first-base line will turn her back to third when making a throw to second base. (The exception is when a right-handed first-base player throws to third base, as explained later in this section.)

The first-base player's footwork will be different from that used by the third-base player or pitcher. Footwork will also vary depending on whether she is a left-handed or right-handed thrower. A left-handed first-base player will field bunts with the left foot ahead and the weight on the throwing foot (see figure 9.4). The ball is fielded on the inside of the left foot. The first-base player then pushes off the left foot and steps directly to the target.

Figure 9.3 Third-base player fielding the bunt for a throw to second base.

Figure 9.4 Left-handed first-base player fielding the bunt for a throw to second base.

COACHING POINTS FOR BUNT DEFENSE

- Fielders should charge the ball, not the batter. They should watch the batter's top hand or front knee to pick up her intent. Then they should creep in accordingly.

- When fielding bunts in practice, players should play all bunts as fair. This saves time and helps players develop the habit of playing all balls out, as they should in a game.

- Players should field the ball with two hands to get a firm grip.

- Fielders should dive for any bunts that are popped up. This will be a big out!

- When hurrying a throw, a fielder may not have time to straighten all the way up, but she should be sure to level her shoulders to keep the ball on a straight line to the target. If the back shoulder is lower than the front shoulder, the throw will be high.

- With multiple runners, advanced players should approach each bunt with the feet in position to get the lead runner. If the player fields the ball cleanly, she looks to see if she can get the lead runner. If the player has any difficulty handling the ball, she should automatically go to first.

- When two players can field the ball, the player in the best throwing position should make the play. For example, for a play at third, the first-base player should field the bunt rather than the third-base player. For a play at second, the third-base player should make the play over a right-handed first-base player.

- On a wet or soft field, fielders should play in closer because the bunt will be slower.

The action is the same for throwing to any base. A right-handed first-base player throwing to first or second base fields the ball with the right foot ahead. She pushes off and pivots on the right foot as she turns and steps toward the base. Her back will be to the infield as she turns toward the glove. She must not spin and throw at the same time. A right-hander throwing to third base does not pivot around because it is too difficult to find third base quickly. She fields the ball with the left foot ahead and pivots on the back foot. The turn is toward the right shoulder with the eyes always toward third.

On bunts down the first-base line, the first-base player should tag the runner when possible. This play has less chance of error and puts the defense in a better position to make additional plays. If the first-base player can make the runner stop and back up, a dead ball results, which means that all runners must return to their bases. This is the ideal situation—the defense gets the out without making a throw, and the runners stay put.

SUICIDE SQUEEZE

A suicide squeeze is one of the most exciting plays in softball. With a runner on third, the batter hides the intent to bunt until the last moment and then bunts the ball. Meanwhile, the runner breaks for home on the pitch and is coming home regardless of where the pitch is or whether the bunt is down.

The defense should look for tips that the suicide is on. Often the opponent's dugout will become quiet, and more players will stand to watch the play. More signals may be given and more time taken, along with extra looks between the coach and the batter. The defensive team should also know the opposing coach's tendencies. They should look for the suicide squeeze any time a runner is on third with less than two outs. If the defense suspects a suicide squeeze, the catcher should call for a pitchout so that the batter cannot reach the ball and the runner is hung out to dry. The catcher will have the ball and can tag the runner or pick her off.

As soon as the squeeze is attempted, everyone should be yelling "Bunt." Seeing the runner break for home, all players should be calling "Four" or "Home." The corners charge the ball. The fielder making the play has her body low, fields with two hands, and uses the underhand toss to get the ball quickly to the catcher. The wrist stays stiff as she swings the arm and tosses the ball. The ball is released quickly on a fast but low trajectory, knee high and slightly up the line. This may be a desperation play. The fielder sometimes needs to catch the ball against the back side of the glove, not using the pocket, to save time.

SLAP DEFENSE

The fast slapper puts a lot of pressure on the defense to field the ball quickly and make the throw. The slapper tries to bounce the ball to the shortstop, who has the longest throw. To help reduce the time needed to complete the play, the shortstop moves in closer to the batter, assuming a position at least as close as the basepath and shaded toward the third-base line. The third-base player pulls off the line so she is in position to help the shortstop by cutting off slow hits and bouncing balls between them (see figure 9.5). The second-base player shades several steps toward first as she does for a bunt. The first-base player shades toward the second-base alley to cut off balls hit slowly toward the second-base player. The outfielders move in so they will be in position to field soft bloopers, and they shade several steps toward left field. The left fielder moves even closer to the left-field line in case the ball is slapped past the third-base player, who has opened up the line by moving in to help the shortstop.

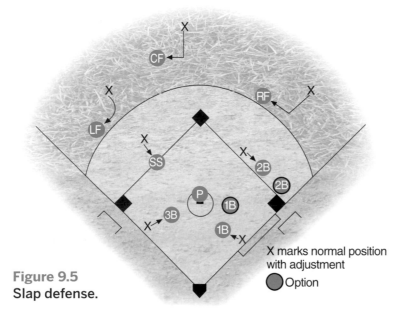

X marks normal position with adjustment

⬤ Option

Figure 9.5
Slap defense.

Another option is to have the first-base player take a position midway between the pitcher and first base to cut off the right-side alley. Using a taller first-base player in this manner helps cut off high bouncers in the right-side alley. The second-base player plays behind the line but near first base to eliminate the footrace with the runner to the base. This defense is vulnerable to a drag bunt.

PICKOFFS

When a runner takes a big lead, the defense can attempt to get her out using the pick-off. An alert catcher will always be looking for the opportunity to catch a runner off base. Not all picks are prearranged. Therefore, with runners on base, infielders must always cover their bases in position to take a throw for a possible out. When the defensive player goes to the base, the runner reacts, usually by going back to the base. When the runner is far enough off base and slow in returning, the catcher may attempt to pick her off. This is not a called pickoff but simply the reaction of an alert catcher. The play is set up by a defensive player who hustles back to cover the base and beats the runner there. When time permits, the base player should give a target with the glove.

To attempt a called pickoff, the catcher or coach will signal for a pitchout. The catcher must give the signal to the pitcher and the defensive player taking the throw. The player who will receive the throw must give a return signal to the catcher and must make sure that the backup knows the pickoff is on. It is critical that the backup be in proper position in case of a bad throw. The catcher may signal the defense even before she assumes the squat position, perhaps with a casual hand signal that is visible to everyone. The signal may also be given as one of the pitching signals, but this method requires all involved to be looking for the catcher's signals on every pitch.

The signals must be clear for the defense and not obvious to the offense. Here are some additional ideas for signaling the pickoff:

- The catcher may wipe the forehead, chest, or leg; pull on the mask; or throw some dirt. The signal can be given before assuming the squat position or while in the squat.
- The fielder who will receive the ball must give an acknowledgement with a return signal. Examples are a tap of the glove or body or picking up dirt.
- The backup must also receive a signal and give a return signal. Verbal signals are often the easiest. For example, players can communicate using last names: "Hey, Smith, nobody scores!"
- The catcher should not proceed with the play if she does not receive a return signal. She cannot assume that someone will be covering, and she should not waste the pitch.

The pitchout is used not only to see the opposition's intentions but also to get the out by picking off the runner.

- If the runner is attempting to steal, the pitchout will give the catcher more time and put her in better throwing position.
- If the hit-and-run is on, the defense might throw out the runner without giving the batter an opportunity to hit the ball.
- If the bunt is on, the runner will often take a bigger lead. The defense should attempt to get the runner for the out.
- If the suicide is on, a pitchout will prevent the runner from scoring.

A pitchout is not always called when trying for the pickoff. In that case, the pitch should be one that the catcher can handle easily—outside, preferably high, and not a drop ball. The battery must be wary of throwing changeups with aggressive runners on base.

Pickoff at First

To execute the pickoff at first, most often the second-base player will come in behind the runner, hoping to catch her by surprise. By moving back three or four steps into right field, the second-base player is out of the runner's line of vision. The second-base player must also cheat several steps closer to first if she has not already shaded that way anticipating a bunt. The second-base player breaks on the pitch and runs on a straight line to the inside of the base, placing the side of the left foot against the base. The right fielder moves with the second-base player so that both are in position in time for the play.

Because the second-base player will be taking the throw, the first-base player moves in as if covering a bunt and acts as a decoy, enticing the runner to take a bigger lead. The first-base player then ducks or moves to the side as the catcher makes the throw.

The first-base player may take the pickoff throw when she is playing back and when the pickoff is not prearranged. On called plays, the defense must be clear about who is taking the throw. The first-base player must indicate to the catcher and the second-base player that she is taking the throw. The right fielder is the backup for the play and should have already shaded slightly to the line because a bunt is expected when a runner is on first.

The player covering the base, either the second-base player or the first-base player, takes the base away from the runner by standing at the back of the base. When the defensive player takes this position, the runner must go a greater distance outside the basepath, making it more difficult for her to return to the base and touch the back corner. The defense thus has more time to make the play. The base player takes a position on the infield side of the base with the heels even with the back of the base and the body in the baseline (see figure 9.6). The player gives a target at the inside corner of the base about waist high. When she sees that the throw is on line, she drops down on the right knee to block the base as she catches the ball (see figure 7.14 on page 158). The runner will be diving back, not sliding.

If a right-handed player has not blocked the base runner off the base and the runner is going behind her, the player should turn counterclockwise to make the tag at the back of the base (see figure 9.7).

Figure 9.6 Position for receiving the pickoff throw at first base.

Figure 9.7 Right-handed player making the pickoff tag at the back of the base.

Although this means turning her back to the runner, she has more time and distance to apply the tag. It also provides easier coverage of the back corner, which is where the runner is going. If the runner breaks to second (delayed steal), teammates must loudly call "Going" because the player's back is to the runner. A left-handed player can more easily make a tag on the runner because the glove is on the same side as the runner. She can simply turn toward the runner to apply the tag. But when it is a close play and the runner is going behind her, she too should use the technique of turning to the base in order to have more time to apply the tag.

Fake Pickoff at First

Advanced teams might try a fake pickoff at first. The goal of the fake is to have the runner going back to the base as the bunt is executed. The runner loses many steps if she is going the wrong way when the bunt is put down. With a runner on first, on the pitcher's release, the second-base player runs two or three steps toward first as if setting up a pickoff. She then stops not far from her basic defensive position. To avoid being pulled too far out of the basic position by the extra steps, the second-base player can quietly shift two or three steps toward second base as the pitcher approaches the rubber. The defense can occasionally use this play to inhibit the runner. If the play is used too often, the runner will not believe a pickoff is really on.

Pickoff at Second

The shortstop, second-base player, or center fielder can take the pickoff throw to second. By using different players, the defense can catch the runner by surprise and make it difficult for her to know whom to watch. Another advantage of having several options is that one player may be closer to the bag and able to get there more quickly. For example, if the shortstop has pulled closer to third to protect against a steal of third or to be in better fielding position against a big pull hitter, the second-base player can more easily cover second. The catcher must know which player will be covering so that she can throw to a target. The infielders should signal to the catcher which player is covering the bag. Often the shortstop will act as a decoy by standing closer to third base, enticing the runner to take a bigger lead. Then the second-base player sneaks in behind the runner. If the shortstop will be making the play, she should back up several steps out of the runner's line of vision. Beginners may use only the second-base player because the runner and second-base player are on opposite sides of the bag, reducing the chance that one will interfere with the other. The center fielder must always back up the throw.

The center fielder can really surprise the runner by coming in from behind to make the pickoff. If this play is called, one of the other outfielders must shade toward center to get to a backup position behind second base. Should a wild throw occur, this outfielder is the only one who can stop the ball.

The receiving position for all receivers is between the runner and second base. The left foot is slightly ahead of the right and against the third-base side of second, the hips are down, and the body is well balanced (see figure 9.8). The player catches the ball (not reaching, but waiting for the ball) and drops to one knee, using the right leg to block the base. For a full description, see "Blocking the Base" in chapter 7, page 158.

Figure 9.8 **Position for receiving the pickoff throw at second base.**

Pickoff at Third

On the pickoff at third, the third-base player or shortstop takes the throw. This is often a called play initiated by the coach in order to get an aggressive runner. A misplay here means that a run scores, so some teams never attempt a pickoff at third, considering it too risky. When the third-base player is back near the base, she takes the throw. Of course, when the third-base player is at the base, the runner will usually not take a big lead, making a pickoff less likely to succeed.

The shortstop comes in behind the runner when the third-base player is pulled in. If the third-base player moves in as if to field a bunt, the runner will be drawn farther off the base. When assuming the ready defensive position, the shortstop should cheat a little toward third so that she can get there more quickly. She must be careful, however, that the shift does not give away the pickoff attempt. The shortstop should not play deeper because doing so would increase the distance to third, and she is not in the runner's line of vision anyway.

Communication is essential. Everyone must know who is covering the base. The left fielder backs up third for an overthrow. The receiver takes a position at the front corner of the bag and gives a knee-high target on the inside of the baseline to establish a throwing lane. Both feet are on the infield side of the base; the right foot is on the front corner of the base. Care must be taken to avoid hitting the runner with the throw because she will then usually score.

When the defense suspects a squeeze, the catcher should call for a pitchout and try to strand the runner. The third-base player must be well in front of the bag to encourage a good lead—but not so far in that the offense calls off the squeeze. A pitchout allows the shortstop to break early to cover third.

Pickoff Strategy

When should the defense use a pickoff? Although the coach sometimes calls the pickoff play, an alert catcher is always looking for the opportunity. When the play works, it is definitely a boost to the defense. A successful pickoff can demoralize the offense, often changing the momentum of the game. The element of surprise contributes to the chance of success. A team should not overuse the play.

The defense should consider several points in deciding whether to attempt the pickoff play:

- Does the defense, particularly the catcher, have the ability to make the out?
- Is the pitcher struggling so much that getting an out is a high priority?
- Is the runner off the base far enough to get the out?
- Would it be useful to set a pattern to keep aggressive base runners closer to the bag?
- Is the runner slow in returning to the base and not very alert?
- When the offense may be putting on a bunt, steal, or hit-and-run, does the base runner take an extra step?
- Is the field soft, providing poor footing?
- Is this the first pitch of a first-and-third play? If so, the defense can pitch out to see what the runners are doing and whether they can get the runner at third.

A team must always consider the game situation:

- The number of outs. With two outs, the defense should determine whether the runner is likely to score. If not, the defense should not risk the chance that an error will score her.
- The ability of the next batter. What are the chances of getting the batter out and ending the inning there? An error on a pickoff play can be costly.
- The count. With two strikes and two outs, the focus should be on the batter. The pickoff should be called when the pitcher is ahead on the count.
- The philosophy of the opposing coach. Does the coach like the team to run? How aggressive is the runner likely to be?
- How important the runner is. If the runner is not that important, the defense should go after the batter.

The pickoff throw should not be made when the catcher does not catch the ball cleanly, when the runner is not far enough off the base for the defense to have a chance of getting her, when no one is covering the base, or when there is no play. Any misplay on the pickoff attempt gives the runner an opportunity to advance, so the defense should not risk a throw unless they have a legitimate chance of being successful. A fake throw may hold the runner. The defense can also fake covering the base, driving the runner back by running behind her.

With multiple runners, the defense must be careful about throwing behind the runners and giving an alert lead runner the opportunity to advance. The defense must not use the pickoff too often because the chance for error increases and because the play slows the game.

COACHING POINTS FOR THE PICKOFF

- Make sure that the catcher and adjacent infielders know who is taking the throw.
- Don't waste the throw. Throw only if there is an opportunity to make an out.
- Use a look or a fake throw instead of throwing when doing so will hold the runner close.
- Make sure the receiver takes the base away from the runner when time permits.
- Use the element of surprise to pick off the runner. An out is not always the result of a quick release or the strongest arm.

STEALS

When a base runner goes to the next base on a pitch or throw, it is scored as an "attempted steal." Catching the runner stealing requires not only a quick, accurate throw from the catcher but also a total team effort. Good communication is necessary to alert the defense that the runner is going and to make sure everybody knows who is covering the base.

Straight Steal

When a runner attempts to steal second, the shortstop takes the throw because she can face the runner and the runner's position will not interfere with the throw. The runner would be in front of the second-base player trying to get to the bag. On an attempted steal of third, the shortstop must take the base if the third-base player is well up in front of the base. The third-base player would not be in a position to see the runner, and it would be difficult for her to retreat on a full run and make the play. The third-base player may take the throw when playing back close to the bag, but she must clearly indicate to the catcher and shortstop that she is covering the bag.

The shortstop will either break with the runner and go directly to the base or wait to see if the ball is hit and then play it if it comes her way. The coach will usually dictate the philosophy used. If the runner likes to steal, the shortstop will often go with the runner. If the batter is a good contact hitter and the hit-and-run play may be on, the shortstop will hold her ground and play the ball. The second-base player then covers second for a possible double play. A pitchout frees the shortstop to go to the base immediately and not worry about the ball being hit.

The receiver must get to the base quickly. Ideally, she should be waiting at the base for the throw. She then applies the tag and takes the base away from the runner. See chapter 7 for specific tagging techniques.

Delayed Steal

On a delayed steal, the runner steals on a throw. The runner takes her lead and steals on the throw back to the pitcher or a throw to another base. She might also take a slightly longer lead than normal to draw a pickoff attempt and then break on a throw behind her. When the runner breaks, the defense must yell loudly that she is going so that the player with the ball can react and make the throw to the base that the runner is advancing to. If the base runner is caught between bases, the defense uses the rundown techniques described next.

A delayed steal should never occur. The catcher must carefully watch all base runners and return the ball to the pitcher only after chasing the runners back to their bases. The catcher can do this by simply looking in their direction, by bringing the arm up as if to throw, or by taking a step in their direction. The catcher should never throw behind a runner who is far enough off the base to attempt a steal on the throw. Instead, she should throw ahead of the runner to keep her from advancing and to chase her back. With multiple runners, attention must always be on the lead runner. The catcher should throw to pick off a runner only if she has a real chance of success. A throw may provide the opportunity for another runner to steal on the play.

RUNDOWNS

The purpose of the rundown (sometimes called a pickle) is to make an out on a runner caught between bases. If the defense fails to get the out, they must at least make sure the runner does not advance a base. Three or fewer throws should be enough to get the runner. Using only a few throws cuts down the potential for error and gives other base runners less time to advance. If a team needs more than three throws, they have not run hard enough at the runner to make her commit in one direction. The perfect play retires the runner without a throw. Players should execute the rundown with confidence and a belief that it is the runner who is in trouble.

Figure 9.9 Dart throw for rundowns.

When a runner is caught between bases, the player with the ball should run hard (full speed) at her to make her commit to a full-speed move in one direction. The direction should not be to the advanced base; the defensive player should chase the runner back to where she was. Therefore, the first throw must be ahead of the runner. To throw, the player holds the ball up (visible to the receiver) as if throwing a dart (see figure 9.9). The arm should not go back past the ear. The thrower should not fake because she could lose her grip and might also fake out the receiver. She makes the throw at moderate speed.

The throwing path is *not* on the basepath where the ball might hit the runner and be difficult for the receiver to see. The throw should never go over the runner. Just before releasing the ball, the thrower steps left or right to create a throwing lane. The receiver moves to the same side as the thrower. Throws should be shoulder high and on the diamond side of the basepath because more backup is available. The throw is made with moderate speed when the receiver calls "Now." The receiver should give a target with the hands together slightly above the shoulders.

As the receiver catches the ball, she steps toward the runner to close the gap and get closer for the tag. If possible, the tag is made with two hands to secure the ball and to permit a quicker release if there is another runner. The receiver must be two or three steps in front of the base when catching the ball. She should take the base away from the runner so that the runner's dive won't allow her to reach the base before the tag. If the runner is running toward the defensive player, the tag is made with a bent arm using a bullfighter's motion, as if pulling a cape back on a charging bull. Using this motion protects the arm and the ball, and by avoiding a collision, the player can go quickly after other runners. She comes up ready to throw.

The fielders' rotation is to follow the throw and go to the end of the opposite line. The front player in each line steps up to throw or receive the ball. The fielder runs outside the basepath and never crosses it. She must not stay on the basepath where the runner can run into her and get an obstruction call. Two players should be in each line, preferably infielders because they are more experienced playing the base (see figure 9.10).

Figure 9.10 Rundown rotation and positioning.

On rundowns between first and second, the catcher, first-base player, second-base player, and shortstop are usually involved. But if the catcher has to stay at home because other runners are on base, then the pitcher, right fielder, or center fielder will join in. Between second and third, the first-base player, second-base player, shortstop, and pitcher or left fielder are usually in the play. Between third and home, the catcher, shortstop, first-base player, and third-base player usually make the play, although sometimes the pitcher or left fielder becomes involved.

COACHING POINTS FOR THE RUNDOWN

- Get the runner in three or fewer throws.
- Throw ahead of the runner first to chase her back.
- Throw with the motion of a dart thrower on the signal "Now." Keep the throw on the inside of the basepath.
- Tag with your arm bent like that of a bullfighter.
- Rotate by following the throw and going to the end of the opposite line.
- Stay out of the basepath and out of the runner's way unless you have the ball.
- After tagging the runner, come up ready to throw.

DOUBLE PLAYS

When trying for a double play, the first priority is to field the ball and then, if possible, get the lead runner. Because of the short basepaths, the defense has relatively little time to turn two, so this is a difficult task. The second-base player and shortstop must shade (cheat) by moving two or three steps closer to second base when they take their defensive positions. Several elements are required for success: The fielder must field the ball cleanly and quickly and make an accurate feed, and the pivot player must perform a quick release.

Feeder　The feeder must not rush when fielding the ball. The ball has to be caught first. If the ball is bobbled, the team may have to forfeit going for two. If in doubt, the feeder goes for one sure out and the safest play, which is usually the out at first. When close to the bag, the feeder shows the pivot player the ball and then throws shoulder high to the pivot player's throwing shoulder. A dartlike throw is the most accurate type of throw but also the one that requires the most time. Other throws that may be used are the underhand toss, the glove toss, and the backhand flip.

The fielder should tag the runner herself if she can get the out. If a double play is a real possibility, the fielder should not waste time chasing a runner who goes outside the basepath; she should make the throw instead.

Pivot Player   The second-base player makes the pivot on balls hit to short or third. The shortstop makes the pivot on balls hit to first, second, and the pitcher. An exception is a ball that pulls the pitcher to her extreme right, in which case the shortstop has to be the backup. Both the second-base player and the shortstop should use the following technique when making the pivot:

- The pivot player sprints to the base in line with the throw, showing her chest to the thrower.
- When time permits, the pivot player slows almost to a stop behind the bag and waits for the throw. The pivot player should expect a bad throw and should be ready to react in any direction to make the catch.
- The pivot player catches the ball first and then tags the base. When the player reaches with two hands, the feet will naturally fall into place.
- The pivot player does not cheat but makes a sure out! She touches the base when she has the ball, making sure the umpire can see the out.
- The pivot player must be quick in getting rid of the ball, so she should work on a quick release.
- The rule is to always get one out:

  Bad throw: The pivot player catches the ball first and touches the base with the foot that can more easily reach the base.

  Late throw: The pivot player steps toward the throw and stretches to complete the force play (similar to a first-base player).

  Unassisted double play: When fielding the ball within two or three steps of the base, the second-base player or shortstop makes the play herself, yelling "I've got it" to avoid a collision.

Footwork   To keep it simple, the pivot player needs to become comfortable with only two basic sets of footwork. The choice of footwork will be determined by the location of the fielded ball (infield side or outfield side of the baseline), how close the thrower is to the base, and how quickly the pivot player is able to get to the base. These factors also determine the type of throw that must be made.

The *push-off* is most commonly used when the ball is coming from the inside of the basepath. The push-off should put the body about 2 feet (.6 m) from the bag and out of the runner's path, opening a throwing lane. The pivot player steps directly toward first to shorten the throwing distance.

- **Shortstop's push-off**—The left foot is against the edge of the base facing third base (see figure 9.11*a*). The shortstop must push off hard after the catch and pivot on the back foot, turning to get the shoulders parallel to the baseline and in good throwing position (see figure 9.11*b*).
- **Second-base player's push-off**—The ball of the left foot contacts the edge of the base nearer right field (see figure 9.12*a*). After the catch, the second-base player pushes backward off the base, transferring the weight to the right foot (see figure 9.12*b*). She is now in a perfect position to step with the front (left) foot and throw.

Figure 9.11 Shortstop's push-off. The player *(a)* pushes off the left foot and *(b)* transfers her weight to the right foot to step and throw.

Figure 9.12 Second-base player's push-off. The player *(a)* pushes off the right-field edge of the base with the left foot and *(b)* transfers her weight to the right foot to step and throw.

The *drag* is used on long throws from outside the basepath when the pivot player has plenty of time to get to the base. The pivot player moves her body across the bag after catching the throw.

- **Shortstop's drag**—The shortstop approaches with her chest toward the thrower and receives the ball as she takes a small step on the right foot before the bag (see figure 9.13*a* on page 204). The shortstop then steps completely across the bag with the left foot in the direction of the throw and drags the toe of the right foot across the middle of the bag (see figure 9.13*b*). Using the middle of the bag allows for a margin of error in either direction and helps the umpire see contact. The shortstop then steps with the right foot behind the left foot (see figure 9.13c), turns the shoulders parallel to the baseline, steps with the left foot toward the target (see figure 9.13d), and throws. The sequence is step, drag, step, step, throw. The player must be sure to do all four steps before throwing.

- **Second-base player's drag**—The footwork is reversed for the second-base player. She takes a small step on the left foot before the bag (see figure 9.14a), steps with the right foot across the bag and drags with the left foot (see figure 9.14b), and then steps with the left foot toward first base and makes the throw (see figure 9.14c). This sequence requires only three steps before the throw: step, drag, step, throw.

Figure 9.13 Shortstop's drag. The player *(a)* takes a small *step* with the right foot; *(b)* crosses the bag with the left foot and *drag*s the toe of the right foot across the middle of the bag; *(c) step*s with the right foot behind the left; and *(d)* turns, *step*s with the left foot, and throws.

Figure 9.14 Second-base player's drag. The player *(a)* takes a small *step* with the left foot, *(b)* crosses the bag with the right foot and *drags* the left foot, then *(c) step*s with the left foot and throws.

The pivot player clears the basepath but stays close to the bag and keeps her body compact. When stepping across the base, the player keeps the heel of the stepping foot only about 2 to 3 inches (5 to 7.5 cm) from the base. The pivot player's step forward is directly toward first base for the shortest, quickest throw.

TIMED DP

Purpose: To practice quickly executing a double play.

Procedure: A coach hits a ball, and the infielders execute a double play. Keep time from when the ball touches the middle infielder's glove to when it arrives in the first-base player's glove. In this drill, players will try harder to execute correctly, and it is a good opportunity to evaluate their skill.

FIRST-AND-THIRD SITUATIONS

The first-and-third play is one of the most difficult plays to defend, and it is challenging to run offensively as well. What the defense does is determined by the reaction of the runners, and the runners try to react to the defensive sets. For this reason, the following sections describe both the offensive plays and the defensive options.

With runners on first and third, the goal of the offense is either to score the runner from third or to advance the runner from first to second so that two runners are in scoring position. The offense will often sacrifice the runner going from first to second, taking the out if the runner at third can score. The goal of the defense is to keep the runner at third from scoring and to hold the runner at first. If the runner attempts to go to second base, the defensive goal is to get her out without letting the run score.

The best plans of either the offense or defense can go awry. Because of the risk involved, the defense may decide not to give the opponent the chance to win or tie the game based on the fielders' ability to execute this play. Many coaches would rather have a hit decide the game, and they choose to ignore the play entirely or use a simple plan. Ninety percent of teams do nothing to defend against a first-and-third play. The key to success for either the defense or the offense is to be fundamentally sound. The team that capitalizes on this play is the team that can run it without making mistakes. Scout the opponent because few change their strategy from game to game. If your opponents tend to be cautious with runners on first and third, send the runner at first and take them out of their comfort zone.

Offensive Baserunning Options

The offense will use a first-and-third play in the following situations:

- Both base runners have speed and ability on the bases.
- The offense is struggling, and the team needs to make something happen.
- The defense is jittery.
- A weak hitter is at the plate.
- The team is facing a strong pitcher who is in control.
- It is late in the game with at least one out.

Two common setups can occur. With a runner at third, the runner at first executes a straight steal, or when the runner arrives at first by a walk, she simply continues to second. The defense must be prepared to react to both situations.

Batter Walks With a Runner at Third   After reaching first base, the batter continues to second with no hesitation, even if the pitcher has the ball. The runner runs full speed to first, and after making the turn to second, she slows to a trot. If it appears that no throw will be made to second, the base runner speeds up about 10 feet (3 m) from second and slides hard into the base to avoid being caught by a surprise throw and tag. If a throw is made, the runner puts on the brakes and reverses direction, attempting to become involved in a rundown. If the defense runs the runner back to first, she may take off again on the throw back to the pitcher. Likewise, if the defense immediately throws to first base after the walk, the runner takes off on the first-base player's return throw to the pitcher.

Runner at First Steals With a Runner at Third   In this offensive play, the batter takes a pitch, and the runner at first executes a straight steal. The runner stays alive and gets the defense to react so that she can take advantage of their defensive plan. Here are some of the options for the runner:

- The runner executes a straight steal on the first pitch. If the ball is cut or not thrown to second base, the runner goes to second. She takes advantage of the defensive team's inaction.
- The runner slowly advances to second; then, as the throw is made, she quickly speeds up and slides into the base.
- The runner sells a steal by running full speed toward second but slows down about 20 feet (6 m) from the base. If the ball gets to second base, the runner retreats and gets in a rundown. If the ball is not thrown or is cut off, the runner continues on to second base.
- The runner fakes a stumble and falls down halfway to second. This usually draws a throw to the second-base player, giving the runner at third a chance to score.

- The runner overslides and crawls back to second base, attempting to get the defense to give chase so that the runner at third has a better chance of scoring. A deep slide may get the infielder to turn her shoulders, giving the runner heading home more time to score.
- The runner tags on a pop foul and runs to second.
- The runner executes a delayed steal as the ball is returned to the pitcher.

Bunting Strategy for the First-and-Third Play A fake sacrifice bunt can open second base for the runner. The third-base player must cover a possible bunt, and the shortstop moves to cover third. The second-base player covers first base for the bunt, leaving second base open. If the center fielder covers the base, there is no backup, and an overthrow will clear the bases.

Options for the Runner at Third The coach at third can tell the third-base runner which option to use. The coach must make sure that the players are very familiar with her terminology and know exactly what is expected on each play she calls. On the leadoff, the runner goes as far as the third-base player lets her; the runner must never let the third-base player get behind her.

The runner at third also reacts to the plan of the defense:

- If the ball goes directly back to the pitcher, the runner on third returns to the base immediately. She must stay there until the ball leaves the circle or the pitcher makes a motion as if throwing.
- If the defense is throwing to second and using a player to cut off the throw, the runner at third may draw the cut to ensure that the runner at first advances safely to second. The runner at third does not take a normal lead; she waits on the base until the catcher makes the throw. She then leads off hard (fakes a break) so that the defense assumes that she is going, which forces the defense to execute a cut. The runner then immediately returns to the base because the player making the cut is looking for the opportunity to pick her off. If the runner on third takes a normal lead and then breaks a couple more steps, she will be so far off that the defense has a good chance of a pickoff.
- If the runner from first succeeds in becoming caught in a rundown, the runner at third reacts accordingly and goes for home when the opportunity arises. In this situation, the runner at third looks for the following:
  - The ball is in the fielder's glove, not in the throwing hand. The runner will gain a little time.
  - The infielder forgets about the runner.
  - The runner at first base is being chased back to first by a right-handed thrower. The thrower will have to turn the feet and shoulders to make the throw home (slower), and the runner at third can better see the throw coming. The closer the runner is pushed to first, the farther the lead runner can lead off. With a right-handed thrower chasing the runner to second, the lead runner must be careful not to get picked off third because she will not see the ball coming. If the runner at third becomes caught in a rundown, the other runner should attempt to get to third base.
- The runner may go home on the throw to second, making sure that the ball gets past the pitcher. The runner must have excellent speed and good reactions to

challenge the defense in this manner. This play is used most often when the defense does not use a cut.

- The runner may take a big jump to draw the throw from the catcher. An experienced runner knows how to get in the way of a ball thrown to third by the catcher. The runner stays between the catcher and the receiver—in the path of the flight of the ball—and hopes that the ball hits her. This works more effectively at lower skill levels.

Defensive Options

The goal of the defense is to keep runners from advancing and to get at least one out on the play. Primary attention must always be paid to the runner at third. Teammates must yell "Home" the instant the runner at third breaks. The defense gives up on the runner in the rundown to make sure that the runner at third does not score. If the runner on third gets too far off, the defender with the ball runs directly at her to get her to commit to a direction. Once one play has been made, fielders must be alert to a possible play on the other runner. These options can be used for walks and steals too.

Runner Caught in a Rundown   If the throw goes to second and the runner is caught in a rundown, the defense uses the regular rundown techniques to chase the runner back to first. The primary concern is still the runner at third, so players listen closely for their teammates to yell "Home" should the runner break. When that occurs, they direct all attention to the third-base runner. If the runner is hung out to dry between home and third, the player with the ball runs directly at her to make her commit to one direction. When in doubt, the defender should throw ahead of the runner to chase her back to third. On rundowns between first and second, the team should give up the rundown if the lead runner is threatening to score. In any rundown between first and second, the defense should tag out the runner quickly, being careful not to become tangled up in making the tag or be left in a poor position for a throw home.

Throw to the Pitcher   The defense runs this play after the batter has been walked. The catcher looks to third to see if the runner can be picked off. If there is no sure play, the catcher returns the ball quickly to the pitcher in the circle. With the ball in the circle, the runner at third must return to the base. She cannot leave again (unless another play is made), so the defense can now ignore her. The pitcher watches the batter–base runner approach first base. If she continues to second, the pitcher moves to the back of the circle to be closer to second base, being careful not to make any motion that releases the runner at third. When the runner is 10 to 15 feet (3 to 4.5 m) from second, the pitcher throws to the shortstop covering the base for the tag. The pitcher must throw early enough to allow for the runner's sudden acceleration into the base. The shortstop can help the pitcher's timing by calling "Now." The first-base player and third-base player remain at their bases in case a rundown follows. The pitcher then steps slightly off line to clear the throwing path home if the runner at third goes.

Throw to the Second-Base Player in Pickoff (Short) Position   This is a play option to use when the batter has walked with a runner on third. An advantage of throwing to a short second base is that the throw home is shorter and has more chance of getting the runner. The second-base player is in position for a quick tag that may surprise the runner, and her position on the basepath may even discourage some runners from trying to advance to second.

The second-base player takes a position on the basepath about 15 to 20 feet (3 to 6 m) from first base (see figure 9.15). If the runner is going fairly fast, the second-base player will stay closer to second. The catcher has the option of throwing to the second-base player as the runner rounds first. The second-base player can apply the tag to the runner or hold the runner at the base if the throw arrives early. If the runner at third breaks for home, the defense must shout "Home," and the second-base player must forget the runner at first and go after the lead runner. The goal is always to get the lead runner. The throw goes to the catcher if the runner on third breaks for the plate. If the runner stops, the second-base player chases her back to third by running at her and then making the play at third. The shortstop must immediately cover second in case the runner gets past the second-base player or in case there is a rundown.

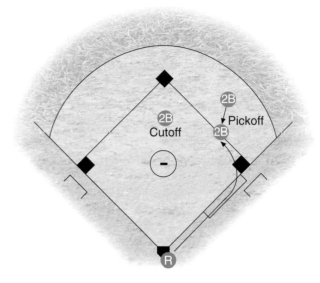

Figure 9.15 Pickoff and cutoff second-base positions.

Throw to the First-Base Player Near the Bag When the batter has walked, a throw from the catcher to the first-base player may keep the runner from continuing on to second. Many runners will then simply give up on trying to advance. The first-base player is close to the bag and on the baseline between first and second base. The shortstop covers second in case the runner gets by first.

Throw to the Shortstop at Second Base On this play, the catcher, after checking the lead runner, holds the ball to see if the batter continues to second. If the runner is advancing, the catcher throws to the shortstop covering second. The defense should use this play only if both players have strong, accurate arms and a slow runner is at third. The catcher does not throw down until the runner approaches second base. If the throw is too early, the runner will have time to stop and set up a rundown. This play is used most often with two outs.

Throw to the Second-Base Player in the Cutoff Position This difficult play requires many accurate throws. The defense must know what they are capable of. The second-base player takes a position in a direct line from home to second and about 15 to 20 feet (3 to 6 m) behind the pitcher's rubber (see figure 9.15). The player's body is sideways with the chest toward third base, which is the best position from which to make a throw home. The target is given to the catcher with the glove shoulder high. The catcher throws to the shortstop covering second base. The throw should be through the second-base player at a height where she can catch the ball easily. If the runner at third breaks for home, the second-base player cuts the ball and throws home. She must not watch the runner while making the catch. The second-base player focuses on catching the ball and relies on teammates to call for the cut by yelling "Home" or "Going." If the lead runner does not break on the throw, the second-base player fakes a catch and allows the ball to go directly through to the shortstop covering second to get the runner coming from first. A fake catch may stop the runner at third from going.

Response to a Straight Steal If the runner on first executes a straight steal, the catcher's first look is always to third to see if the runner can be picked off. If there is not a play at third, then the catcher throws to the shortstop at second base or to the second-base player in the short or cutoff position, depending on the team's strategy. The catcher may also choose not to make a play and may return the ball sharply to the pitcher.

The catcher has several options:

1. Pick off the runner at third.

2. Fake a throw to second and then attempt a pickoff at third, hoping to catch the lead runner leaning or breaking for home.

3. Throw to second base. The second-base player in the cutoff position cuts the throw if the base runner at third goes home. If the runner does not break for home, the throw goes through to the shortstop for a tag or a possible rundown back to first.

4. Throw to the second-base player in the basepath. The catcher keeps her body aligned as if she were throwing to second base but instead throws to the second-base player in the short position (as described earlier) to set up a shorter return throw to home if the runner at third goes.

Other Considerations   The defense must also be prepared for the possibility that the offense may bunt, slap, or run fake plays with runners at the corners. Scouting the opposition in order to know their tendencies will help, but the key is to be prepared for anything. Using a pitchout may help the defense set up the offense. If the offense chooses to play it safe and not steal, the defense should look for tactics such as fake breaks that the offense may use in hopes of drawing throws and creating errors.

COACHING POINTS FOR FIRST-AND-THIRD PLAY

- Coaches must know the capability of their defense.

- When considering a play, the coach should weigh the risks involved against the importance of the run at third and the value of keeping the other runner at first.

- Because young players find it difficult to decide quickly how to respond, the coach can call the play to be used before the pitch (with a runner already on first) or after the pitcher throws ball three (in case of a walk).

- If the first-base player holds the ball at first base, this may discourage the runner from taking off for second after a walk or putout. Sometimes the umpire will call time if all players are standing still, even though that is not the intent of the rules. The alert base runner may be planning to take off on the first-base player's throw back to the pitcher.

- If the offense attempts or fakes a bunt, the defense should not throw to second base because there is no backup there. The center fielder will have to cover the base (the middle infielders have moved to the corners to play the bunt), and there is no one behind her.

- Returning the ball quickly to the pitcher is the easiest defense because the runner at third must return immediately to the bag. The defense can ignore her and concentrate on the other base runner.

Sometimes the defense may be wise not to make a play, such as in any of the following instances: (a) when there are two outs, (b) when the batter is not a big threat, (c) when the pitcher is in control, or (d) when runs are not that important. The defensive team may choose to make the opponent win with the bat rather than let them create their offense with baserunning and possible defensive errors. If the defense chooses not to make the play, they can try to bluff the runners into staying put. The catcher can fake a throw, or the team can use verbal cues to indicate that they are going for the runner. The coach may call "Get the runner if she goes" while signaling that the team will make no throw. Players can also talk and bluff the runner and opposing coaches. Teams that vary both offensive and defensive strategies create an element of surprise that will often lead to success.

RELAYS

Relay throws are used when the ball is hit over or through the outfield and help is needed to get the ball to a base. Over a long distance, two throws are more efficient than one and are always faster than a rainbow throw or a throw that bounces several times.

The shortstop is the relay for throws from the left fielder and center fielder. The second-base player is the relay for throws from right field. The exception is for balls on or near the foul lines. For those balls, the third-base player or first-base player becomes the relay because these players can more easily get in line with the fielders. If two players are in position where either could assume the relay role and one has a significantly stronger arm, that player should make the relay.

Distance between the relay and the target base depends on the strength and accuracy of the arms involved. A general rule is that the outfielder throws about 60 percent of the distance. The player making the relay moves with the outfielder until the outfielder stops, moving as if joined by a rope. As the outfielder bends to get the ball, the relay player lines up sideways on a straight line to the intended target.

Communication is vital because the relay player must know where to throw the ball. Because the defensive team always wants to throw ahead of the runner or runners, the throw will likely be going to third or home. The catcher and third-base player are in the best position to view the situation, and they need to yell loudly the commands of "Three, three" for third base or "Four, four" for home plate. They must make the call early so that the relay player has time to line up properly. The player covering the base shouts "Right" or "Left" to help the relay player line up.

After the runner passes first base, an option for the defense is to have the first-base player back up any relay that the second-base player is taking. Another option is to have the first-base player cover second base so that the second-base player can back up the shortstop. With these options, the tradeoff is that the first-base player cannot act as a cutoff.

With a backup player in position, the relay player should let a low throw or a very high throw go and allow the backup player to make the play. The poor low throw should be a catchable one-bouncer, and the very high throw can more easily be played by the backup player.

As the outfielder picks up the ball, the relay player must wave her arms and yell so that the thrower can find her quickly. The relay player doesn't stop calling or waving until the ball is on its way. She then turns sideways toward the glove to catch the ball over the throwing shoulder while moving sideways toward the infield.

COACHING POINTS FOR THE RELAY

- The outfielder should throw 60 percent of the distance.
- The relay player moves with the outfielder as if joined by a rope.
- The catcher or third-base player calls for a throw to "Three" or "Four."
- The base player calls "Left" or "Right" to line up the relay player with the target.
- The relay player waves her arms and hollers until the outfielder releases the ball.
- The throw to the relay player should be shoulder height. The relay player turns sideways to catch the ball over the throwing shoulder while moving toward the infield.

Being in motion eliminates the extra step needed for a hard throw. The relay player moves toward the target, sees it, and throws.

CUTOFFS

A cutoff is used to intercept a throw to a base. The purpose of the cutoff is to assist on weak throws or throws that are off line. If the throw is too late and the runner has already scored, the cutoff is used to stop other runners from advancing. The cutoff is most commonly used on throws going home, and the first-base player is usually the cutoff. On balls hit near the left-field foul line, the third-base player may serve as the cutoff while still playing the base. On balls hit sharply to right field, the first-base player's first responsibility is to play first base.

The cutoff player takes a position about 30 feet (9 m) in front of the plate (near the pitcher's rubber) and directly in line with the thrower and the catcher (see figure 9.16).

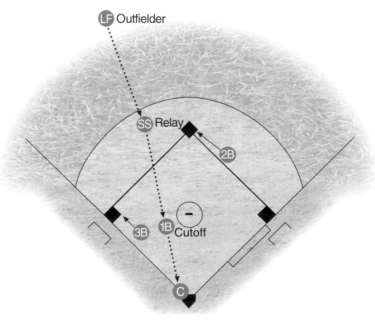

Figure 9.16 Cutoff position.

The catcher has the responsibility to position the cutoff by calling "Right," "Left," or "OK" until the cutoff player is properly aligned. The thrower's target is home plate no matter where the cutoff player is. The cutoff player should wave both arms so the thrower has a better target. The cutoff player should anticipate the upcoming play by noting the progress of the runners.

If the throw is off line, the catcher will call "Cut four" if the ball has a chance of getting the runner at home with the cutoff's help. If the catcher does not make the call but it is obvious that the ball needs help, the cutoff player should take the initiative and make the cut. The cutoff player should not make the cut if the throw is straight enough that the catcher can play it and get the out at home. Even if the throw appears slow or is bouncing, cutting it and making another throw takes more time. No call means that the cutoff player should let the ball go through and should pivot quickly away to allow the catcher to see it. The cutoff player should fake a cut to stop other runners from advancing.

If the throw is too late, the catcher calls for the ball to be cut using one- or two-word cues—such as "Cut two, two, two"—until the cut and throw are made. When "Cut" is called, the cutoff player should turn so that the front shoulder points at the target as the catch is made (as she would on a relay). The cutoff player catches the ball near the throwing shoulder for a quick release and looks for a play on the runner approaching the base called for by the catcher.

If the runner is not advancing home, the cut can be used to make sure that the ball doesn't get by the catcher. The call must be made well in advance so that the cutoff player has time to react. If the cutoff player has any doubt about whether to cut the throw, she should let the ball go through. The first effort must be to get any runner attempting to score.

Teams might consider not using a player to cut off a throw. If the runner is beating the throw and is going to be safe at home, the catcher may move up and short hop the ball. Because the ball from the outfielders should be coming home on a bounce anyway, this becomes an easy thing to do. The catcher can then go after any other base runners if she chooses to cut the ball. Advantages of this play are that you won't have players cutting balls that should be going through to home and that the catcher has a clear view of the throw coming home.

COACHING POINTS FOR THE CUTOFF

- The cutoff player takes a position directly in line with the throw about 30 feet (10 m) from home. The catcher calls "Left" or "Right" to help with alignment.

- The cutoff player waves both arms. The thrower's target is home plate.

- The catcher calls "Cut" if the ball is off line or if the throw is too late to get the runner going home. She then calls the base to throw to.

- The cutoff player turns the front shoulder to the target as the catch is made.

- A throw that is on line should *not* be cut even if it will bounce several times.

- When there is no cut, the cutoff player pivots away from the ball.

TEAM DEFENSE DRILLS

Practice as a team so you can execute in the game. Use runners so you can judge the timing and speed of the game. To practice with more than a couple of runners, work half the defense at a time in the field so that the other defensive players are available to run. For example, work the left side of the defense first and then switch to the right side. This allows both sides of the defense to face a lot of base runners and allows the starters to get baserunning practice.

Create pressure situations so players are prepared to handle them in the game. Emphasize individual fundamentals while doing team drills. Corners should practice fielding bunts with both hands and with their feet in position to make the anticipated throw. Practice communication: Players call "Bunt" loudly on the attempt and "Mine" when fielding the bunt. Start defensive players in their regular positions so timing and coverage are realistic.

Timing is critical when executing a pickoff. For pickoff drills, the pitcher should throw pitches at normal speed. Fielders should start from their regular defensive positions so they can learn when they need to break on the pitch. Rundowns require players to run full speed at the runner to make her commit, so fielders should practice the dart throw at this speed.

As players' skills increase and throws become accurate, use base runners so the defense can work on positioning, timing, and decision making. Working on specific plays with runners going full speed provides conditioning benefits as well as baserunning practice. Fungo hit all kinds of balls so everything is practiced.

ROLL BUNTS

Purpose: To practice fielding bunts.

Procedure: Players assume defensive positions for fielding bunts. A coach stands behind the catcher and rolls balls onto the infield to be fielded as bunts. Players practice throwing to different bases and play out all bunts even if they are foul.

CATCHER—THIRD BASE EXCHANGE

Purpose: To have the catcher practice covering third when the third-base player fields the bunt.

Procedure: This drill requires two catchers, two third-base players, and one or two second-base players. The catchers, each with a ball, are behind home plate. A catcher rolls a bunt to one of the third-base players, who throws to the second-base player covering first. The catcher calls "I have third" and runs to cover the base. She receives the return throw from first base and applies a tag at third base. The catcher then runs home in foul territory while the second catcher and second third-base player are executing the drill.

BUNT AROUND

Purpose: To practice bunting and bunt defense with two defensive teams on one infield.

Procedure: **Set up two bunt defenses, each using half the field. Use second base as a second home plate, and use third base as another first base (see figure 9.17). The pitchers are back to back with one pitching to home and one to second. Bunters are in a line at each home plate. They bunt and run to their first base with the defense making the play to the first base on their half of the field. Runners then continue running to the other bunting line. To keep the drill moving rapidly, use only one bat at each plate.**

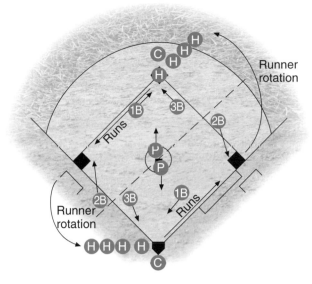

Figure 9.17 Bunt around drill.

PITCHER AND CATCHER THROW-DOWNS

Purpose: **To have the catcher practice throw-downs to the shortstop covering second and to have the pitcher practice fielding bunts and throwing to first.**

Procedure: **The drill requires a catcher, pitcher, shortstop, second-base player, and first-base player. Place empty buckets behind second and first base. The pitcher and a coach each have a bucket of balls. The pitcher pitches a ball to the catcher, who is wearing full gear (to make the drill gamelike) and is in proper receiving position. On the first pitch, the catcher throws down to the shortstop covering second. The coach, who is standing near the catcher, then rolls out a bunt, and the pitcher makes the play to first with the second-base player covering. The shortstop and second-base player both begin in their regular defensive positions so that base coverage is realistic. When players catch balls at the bases, they immediately drop them in the nearest bucket so that the drill can proceed rapidly.**

SHORT THROW TO FIRST

Purpose: **To practice pivot footwork while saving the pivot player's arm.**

Procedure: **A feeder has a bucket of balls from which to feed the pivot player. One pivot player or a single-file line of several players can perform the drill. The feeder throws to the pivot player from a distance of about 15 feet (4.5 m), from either the shortstop or second-base side of the infield. (You can also include feeds from the pitcher's position to the shortstop, who makes the pivot.) The receiver is several steps from the base, facing the feeder. She catches the ball, turns on the pivot, and makes a short throw to the first-base player, who is set up on the baseline midway between first and second. The emphasis is on making the pivot, so the pivot player can save her arm by throwing to the first-base player at half the normal distance. The pivot player returns to repeat the drill or goes to the end of the line.**

Variation: **Setting up obstacles in the basepath directly in front of second base makes the pivot more difficult and realistic. A football dummy or stuffed equipment bag can be used to simulate a sliding runner.**

TURNING THE DOUBLE PLAY

Purpose: To turn double plays as in a game.

Procedure: Infielders assume normal double-play defensive positions. The shortstop and second-base player shade several steps toward second. The hitter at home hits ground balls to all infielders so that they can practice proper angles, feeds, and pivots. The pitcher and the catcher field and throw to second base. The hitter sends all types of hits—slow grounders, high bouncers, and hard shots—to all parts of the infield.

Variations:

- Practice the pivot with a runner coming to second, first standing and then sliding.
- Use two runners (home to first and first to second) so that players can gauge the time element.

PICKOFF AT FIRST

Purpose: To have the catcher work on pickoff throws to first off pitched balls. The second-base player (need at least two players) works on timing as she takes the pickoff at first.

Procedure: A pitcher pitches to the catcher; the second-base player is in the normal starting position for a pickoff (several steps deeper while shading toward first). The second-base player breaks on the pitch in time to be at first base to receive the catcher's throw.

Variations:

- Add runners (wearing helmets) who work on leadoffs while the second-base player works on positioning and blocking runners off first.
- Add a shortstop. Runners alternate diving back, executing delayed steals, and performing straight steals to keep the defense honest. An extra second-base player calls the cues for the defense—for example, "Going."

THROW THROUGH AND SECOND-BASE PLAYER'S CUT

Purpose: To have the catcher practice throwing through to the shortstop covering second; to have the second-base player practice cutting and throwing home.

Procedure: The drill requires a pitcher, catcher, shortstop, and second-base player. On the first pitch, the catcher throws through to the shortstop covering second. The ball is returned to the pitcher. On the second pitch, the second-base player moves to the cutoff position behind the pitcher's rubber, cuts the throw, and throws home. Players continue to alternate between the two plays. Both throws from the catcher should be at the same height so that, if it were a game, the second-base player could cut the ball if the runner broke and the defense called "Home." Players begin in regular positions to work on timing and to make the drill gamelike.

Variations:

- Add runners to work on timing.
- Have the second-base player cut and throw to third.

RUNDOWN DART THROW

Purpose: To practice the rotation and the dart throw for rundowns.

Procedure: The drill involves three players. Two players in a line are facing one player who is the first receiver. The player at the head of the two-person line has a ball and runs toward her teammate, ready to use a dart throw. The receiver calls "Now" and closes the gap when receiving the ball. The thrower rotates to the end of the opposite line behind the receiver. Players run at medium speed. This is a good warm-up drill at the beginning of practice.

FULL-SPEED DART THROWS

Purpose: To improve accuracy of dart throws when running at full speed as needed during a rundown in a game.

Procedure: A player faces a partner about 20 feet (6 m) away. The thrower runs hard for three or four steps and then makes an accurate dart throw to her partner, the receiver, who closes the gap and makes an imaginary tag. Players retreat to starting positions, and the partner with the ball begins the drill again, going hard in the opposite direction. The focus is on running hard and making accurate throws.

RUNDOWNS WITH RUNNER

Purpose: To practice defensive aspects of rundowns with a runner.

Procedure: Two lines of fielders take defensive positions for a rundown with a runner between bases. Several runners stand by, ready to rotate in, or one runner can rotate to a defensive position after running. If the drill is not done on the diamond, number the bases so that the defense will know which is the lesser base. A coach throws the ball to the player at the front of one line. The defense may have to immediately make a throw to get the ball to the player who can chase the runner back to the lesser base. The players then work on proper execution of the rundown, using only three throws to get the runner. On the fourth throw, the runner wins and gets to rotate out.

THREE-PLAYER LINE RELAY

Purpose: To practice relay techniques and making accurate throws.

Procedure: Three players line up about 30 feet (10 m) apart in a straight line. The middle player acts as the relay. While facing the relay, a player at one end drops the ball over her own head. She turns and picks it up, locates the relay player, and makes the throw. The relay player waves and hollers until the ball is in the air. The relay player throws to the third player, who repeats the drill in the opposite direction. The relay player can move slightly off line to make it more challenging for the thrower to find the target.

OUTFIELD RELAY THROWS

Purpose: To practice relay throws from the outfield.

Procedure: With the defense on the field and a runner at first or second, the coach drops a ball behind an outfielder. The defense executes the relay. The catcher calls for the play at third or home.

Variations:

- Add the cutoff.
- Practice gamelike situations with runners running from home, second, and first on fungoed balls. Practice execution of the cut.

CUTOFFS AND TEAM DEFENSE

Purpose: To develop better decision making on the cutoff by executing the play with runners.

Procedure: A defensive team takes their positions. Alternate between starting a runner at first and then at second. A hitter or coach hits ground balls to the outfielders, who field the balls and throw to the first-base player in the cutoff position. If a pitcher is part of the drill, she works on backing up third or home. The team practices cuts and throws to second and third. Emphasize making good decisions about the cut and making good throws all around. If the outfielder catches the ball in the air, the defense plays it out as a ground ball to avoid wasting time.

Variation: To practice relays as well as the cutoff, players can let the ball go through the outfield, or the hitter can hit it over their heads.

PERFECT INNINGS

Purpose: To work on defensive execution by having a team competition with defense and base runners.

Procedure: Two teams compete against each other: one on defense and one running the bases. The coach hits the ball, and the goal is for the defensive team to make nine consecutive outs. Any mistake pulls the team off the field, and the other team goes on defense. Keep track of how many outs each team makes on defense to determine the winning defense. Try to simulate all routine situations that come up in a game.

COUNTY FAIR

Purpose: To practice all aspects of team defense with each player playing all positions.

Procedure: The drill starts with six players. These players are positioned at catcher, third base, shortstop, second base, first base, and center field. The remaining players feed into the center-field position from left field. A coach in left field keeps the nonparticipants busy working on ground balls or fly balls. The drill begins with a coach at home plate hitting a ground ball to the shortstop, who throws to first. The first-base player throws to the third-base player (on the bag), who then fires to second base to start a 5-4-3 double play. After throwing to first, the second-base player becomes a base runner at second. The first-base player then throws to the catcher in her stance at home plate. The catcher comes up and fires to second base as if a runner is stealing from first to second. (No one is covering second.) As the catcher fields the throw, the second-base player takes off as if trying to score from second on a single to center (as she rounds third, she flips her glove toward the dugout).

Because no one is covering second, the ball bounds into the outfield. The center fielder makes a "do-or-die" scoop and then fires the ball to home on a long hop to the catcher, who blocks the plate and tries to tag the second-base player sliding into home.

The coach then blows a whistle, and the players rotate as follows:

- The second-base player (runner) goes to left field to the end of the feeder line.
- The catcher moves to third base.
- The third-base player moves to shortstop.
- The shortstop becomes the second-base player and base runner.
- The first-base player moves to catcher.
- The first player in the line in left field moves to center field.
- The center fielder moves to first base.

As the center fielder arrives at first base, the coach hits another ground ball to the shortstop, and the sequence begins again. Initially, the coach may have to shout out the destination of each throw, but after two or three reps, players should be able to go through the sequence without any cues. This is a very snappy drill that really livens up practice. After about 15 minutes, each player will have gone through each position two or three times.

PITCHING FUNDAMENTALS

A special thank-you to Dee Dee Weiman-Kingsbury (associate head coach and pitching coach at Cal State University at Fullerton) for all her help in writing the pitching chapters. The remarks regarding working with pitchers are drawn from her experiences.

The game of softball has evolved so much in the past few years, and pitching has changed right along with it. The knowledge of the biomechanics of the game has improved, and as a result, softball instruction has also improved. Given current bat and ball technology, pitchers have to understand their craft better than ever before in order to be successful. Pitchers can't just blow the ball by the hitter anymore (or at least not very often). So where do we go from here?

In softball, it has been said that pitching is 90 percent of the game, and that is still the case. A good pitcher will still win many games for her team. But the definition of a good pitcher has changed a bit. The key requirements now are proper mechanics and accuracy. Of course, speed is important and will be discussed here. However, for a pitcher in today's game, knowing how to maximize her ability and being able to maintain good control of her mechanics and pitches are even more important.

Whether she is a beginner hoping to throw strikes or an overpowering ace confounding experienced batters, the pitcher controls the game. Certain fundamental concepts and elements are the foundations for success for all pitchers, regardless of age, size, or individual quirks. But every pitcher is different. Therefore, pitchers must experiment with grips, mechanics, and style to find what works for them. They have to learn to take an active role in honing their craft, and as Cindy Bristow puts it so eloquently, they need to "own" their skill.

Successful pitchers share several physical characteristics. Typically, tall pitchers have longer arms, and those long levers can produce greater speed. Heavier pitchers can throw harder if they use their greater mass to advantage. Larger hands make it easier to apply different grips. Although these attributes related to overall size are advantageous, some extremely successful pitchers are small in stature. Other desired attributes that players of any size can work to develop include arm strength, leg strength, endurance, flexibility, and coordination.

Although these physical attributes have an impact on a pitcher's success, certain psychological traits and skills play an even greater role. There is a difference between being a thrower and being a pitcher. What takes place above the shoulders ultimately determines the label that a player earns. Pitchers quickly learn that they are almost always the focal point. They need poise, confidence, and discipline (focus) to handle the attention and the various situations that occur. Over the course of a game, season, or career, all pitchers face adversity, and they must learn to handle it or they will not last. They must deal with umpires who don't give them the call they earned, pitches that miss their target, and balls that are hit hard despite their best efforts. Handling these challenges requires emotional control, discipline, and patience. Good recovery skills are necessary because pitchers must be ready to give their best on every pitch, sometimes immediately after a home run or a bad call.

Because they have the opportunity to control so much of the game, pitchers benefit from having an aggressive personality and a strong, competitive spirit. But along with that, they must have a good work ethic. Pitchers succeed in games because of the work they do in practice. If they don't want to work hard, to create and follow a plan to improve, and to be challenged during practice, they will struggle to perform well at game time. All pitchers need plenty of regular practice (no matter the level) to improve, stay sharp, and excel. Maintaining a rigorous schedule requires a desire to be the best, along with determination and dedication. And, as the center of attention, pitchers who possess these traits along with leadership skills can do much to bring their teammates together as a team and lead them to victory.

PITCHING STYLES

The two major pitching styles in softball are the windmill and the slingshot. Not many pitchers use the slingshot, but that doesn't mean that it doesn't work. Have you heard of Joan Joyce? You should know the name: Joan was a slingshot pitcher who achieved legendary status in the game of softball—and who by all accounts could throw the ball as hard as or harder than any of the young "studs" pitching today.

Please note that the following descriptions are for a right-handed pitcher.

Windmill

With the windmill technique, the arm makes a full circle from hip to hip before the ball is released. As the pitcher takes the ball from the glove, she straightens the pitching arm and swings the ball forward toward the batter, then straight up to the sky (the inside of the upper arm brushes the ear), and then down to the hip for release. The full revolution permits the arm to gather speed and act as a whip to deliver the ball at great velocity. Using the windmill, top pitchers can throw the ball in excess of 65 to 68 miles per hour. This delivery is glamorous because the full arm revolution is unique to softball pitchers. Because most pitchers use this delivery, the techniques described in the rest of the chapter assume a windmill delivery.

Slingshot

The slingshot is simply half of a windmill. The pitcher takes the ball back underhand from the glove and swings to a spot above the head before reversing the arm motion and pitching the ball. After the ball reaches the top of the backswing, all elements of the delivery and the mechanics for throwing different pitches are the same as those of the windmill. An advantage for the slingshot pitcher is that the hips open almost automatically toward third on the backswing of the arm. To increase the size of the backswing (the lever) for maximum arm and ball speed, the pitcher rotates the thumb upward and the palm away from the body as the arm extends back. Leading with the thumb and with a slight bend in the elbow, the pitcher can then get the ball to a position well above the head on the backswing.

FASTBALL MECHANICS

To learn or fine-tune the basic mechanics of throwing (whether slingshot or windmill), the pitcher must concentrate on throwing a simple fastball, which is the foundation for all other pitches. Pitching coaches today often choose not to work on the fastball, focusing solely on off-speed and movement pitches; however, it is crucial that pitchers start their workouts with drills that reinforce the fundamentals. In addition to doing basic drills with the fastball, pitchers should start with this pitch when they move to the mound and begin throwing full out. The fastball is also the best way to work on locating pitches.

Achieving sound mechanics through work on the fastball reduces the risk of injury. It prepares the pitcher for work on increasing speed, and it gives her a good solid base from which she can move on to other pitches without wreaking havoc on her mechanics. We often see, for example, a young pitcher with mechanical problems who says that she has six or eight pitches—and none of them do what they are supposed to do.

CRITICAL CUE:
Pitchers should develop mechanics, speed, and accuracy with the fastball before they throw other pitches.

She has no idea what's wrong with her biomechanics or how to fix them. She is equally clueless about the proper spin to put on the ball for her fastball or her other pitches. She has simply been told to do something, so she has done it. In this situation, coaches need to start over, present the basics of throwing, and teach the pitcher more about the craft of pitching.

Some pitchers' fastballs naturally have some movement, which is a bonus. This movement is usually an indication of great wrist snap, and it leads to very good movement when the pitcher starts throwing other pitches. When a pitch doesn't move, it doesn't fool the batter, and it can be hit very hard. For this reason, some coaches of advanced pitchers ask their pitchers never to throw a straight fastball. However, for many pitchers, the fastball is an important pitch. Not only does it improve mechanics, but when thrown with good location, it can be an effective pitch on its own. Many pitchers rely on the fastball when they need a strike.

Grip and Spin

For the fastball, the pitcher grips the ball across the seams with three fingers over the "C" on the ball. This should be the same grip as used for the overhand throw. The thumb is on one seam, and the fingers are on the opposite seam. Players with larger hands can use three fingers to grip the ball (see figure 10.1); pitchers with smaller hands will use a four-finger grip. The grip must be easy for the pitcher to find.

To learn to easily and automatically position the ball in the hand properly, the pitcher can hold the ball behind her back and practice finding the grip on her own just by feel. The ability to find the grip without looking at the ball will be a very useful tool in the future when she starts throwing other pitches.

When released with the "C" grip, the ball has a four-seam rotation, which is preferred for the fastball. The ball should rotate from 12 to 6 o'clock—or top to bottom. Make sure the ball is in the fingertips and not touching the palm of the hand. The ball is held by the fingers at the first knuckle; it should be held strongly and securely in the fingertips, not squeezed in a death grip. A grip that is too tight will lock the wrist and cut down on the speed of the ball. The pitcher can release the ball more quickly when using fewer fingers, resulting in greater speed. The more skin that touches the ball, the slower the speed of the pitch.

Holding the ball out in the hand creates the longest possible lever. The thumb and the middle finger are the power-producing digits. The thumb should be placed on a seam directly across the ball from the middle finger. This arrangement balances the line of force on the ball. The pinkie finger can be curled on the side of the ball. The index finger is curled slightly and placed closer to the middle finger than to the thumb. If the pitcher has to use a fourth finger, it too should be comfortably spread when placed on the ball. The position of the fingers must not tighten or lock the wrist. The grip must permit the wrist to snap easily. The following drills encourage proper wrist snap and finger release. More drills are provided at the end of the chapter.

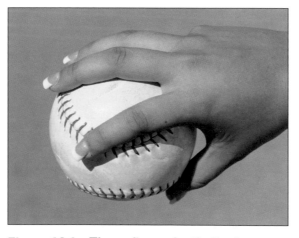

Figure 10.1 **Three-finger fastball grip.**

SELF-PITCH

Purpose: To practice the wrist snap and proper finger release.

Procedure: Using the pitching arm, the pitcher holds a ball out in front at shoulder height. She keeps the elbow straight and tosses the ball to herself using only a wrist snap and a fingertip pull against the seams to toss the ball up.

PARTNER PITCH

Purpose: To practice correct wrist snap and finger release.

Procedure: Partners stand 10 feet (3 m) apart and toss the ball to each other underhand, letting it roll off the ends of the fingers.

POWER LINE PITCH

Purpose: To practice the wrist snap and spin before pitching.

Procedure: This drill should be done as part of a pitcher's warm-up routine (see chapter 12). A power line is drawn in the dirt from the pitcher to the catcher, who is standing just a few feet away. The pitcher stands sideways with her toes on the power line and with her hips open. She rocks her hand back slightly (wrist bends back), then lightly brushes her hip while releasing the ball (see figure 10.2). She snaps the hand all the way through and watches the spin of the ball. To better see the spin, players can use a ball with a line drawn around the middle or a weighted ball such as the two-toned Cannonball.

Figure 10.2 Power line pitch drill.

Arm Swing and Arm Circle

The most important thing about the arms is to make sure they are tight to the body and always long and extended to create optimum arm swing (whip), which generates speed. Arm action must also be a natural motion in order to prevent injury and allow the pitcher to throw many innings. Many young pitchers have stiffness when they try to throw hard because there is too much tension in their motion. Also, a pitcher's arm circle may not be natural if the arm is too far from the body, rotated away from the body, or tucked behind the body. Arm swing should always be quick, long, and relaxed in drills as well as in the full pitching motion.

MIRROR PITCH

Purpose: To correct poor motion in the arm circle.

Procedure: The coach can slow the pitcher's motion down and lead her all the way through the motion using the proper mechanics. The player repeats the motion at home standing in front of a mirror. She throws a sock into the mirror while watching her mechanics and trying to feel it all. This encourages muscle memory of the proper motion. The player needs *many* reps to reteach herself the proper mechanics of the arm circle.

Glove Arm

Too many young pitchers do not focus on what their glove arm is doing. The glove arm is used for balance and should work together with the pitching arm to create momentum and speed. At the beginning of the motion, the glove is pointed at the catcher. Then, as the arms drop down into the end of the pitch, they mirror each other. It doesn't matter whether the pitcher slaps her hip (with the glove arm) for timing. What is important is that she feels both arms pulling down at the same time *and* feels the upper arm (biceps) driving into her side. The arms work together simultaneously for a balanced arm swing.

T DRILL

Purpose: To practice arm swing, wrist snap, and balance.

Procedure: After reinforcing her grip by doing wrist snap drills, the pitcher takes a step back (her feet are still on the power line) and begins this drill with her arms creating a T. From here, she lets the arms swing down equally and then snaps and releases the ball.

To make this drill more complicated, the pitcher starts with her arms down at her sides and with her weight mainly on her back leg. She lifts her arms into the T and lifts the left or front leg as well (see figure 10.3) so she can take a small step forward as the arms swing down and she releases. She is now working on arm swing, wrist snap, and balance (between upper and lower body), which translates into timing.

Figure 10.3   T drill.

Follow-Through

The follow-through may be referred to as "shaking the catcher's hand." Keep in mind, this is *after* the ball is snapped and released—an afterthought, so to speak. As the hand continues toward the catcher, it will naturally continue upward after release. To make sure that the hand and elbow don't bend upward prematurely, the pitcher focuses on using a long arm that pushes down through the snap and then reaches toward the catcher. The real advantage to the hand finishing up is that the pitcher feels that the fingers have finished the snap all the way. The arm should always stay on the power line through the finish of the pitch (see figure 10.4). If it doesn't, pitch location will suffer. The hips can hinder the path of the arm, so they must be in the correct position.

Stride and Hips

When coaches speak of improving mechanics and increasing speed, the area of the stride and hips is where the biggest corrections can be made. Many of

Figure 10.4   Follow-through position.

today's pitchers *do not* use their legs and *do not* understand what their hips and core should be doing. A power line drawn in the dirt helps pitchers stay in a direct line to their catcher and shows them what the feet are doing.

At the beginning of the pitch, as the pitcher starts to push off the mound toward the catcher, the front leg should first lift in an upward direction and then out toward the catcher. At this time, the arms are pushing out (long) toward the catcher and getting set to "catch the whip" at the front top of the circle. After the arms brush the

pitcher's ears, the arms are in prime position to start to increase speed, and this is where the hips will start to open. The best way to get the hips open is to ensure that the toe on the rubber pivots hard all the way open so the toe is pointing almost to third base. Now the pitcher is in the middle of her motion, and the hips are wide open for the arm to come through. The front foot, or stride foot, should land on the power line at more than a 45-degree angle to the catcher. (The toes point between one o'clock and three o'clock—see figure 10.5.) If the pitcher's timing is correct, the front foot will land as the arms are slightly above a T position. The arms and legs form an X (some call it a K—see figure 10.6 on page 228). The stride and foot placement should be consistent for each pitcher; before pitching, the pitcher can mark off the proper placement by walking heel to toe from the front of the mound toward the catcher six to six and a half steps. The pitcher then marks a cross line so that she has a visual of where to land (see figure 10.7 on page 228).

Figure 10.5   Stride landing position.

Figure 10.6 X position.

Figure 10.7 Landing on the mark.

Note that the arms are now starting to swing down at the same time. This is why it was so important to start with the glove arm well above the front shoulder. The arms work together, and both elbows can pinch tightly into each side. The pitcher can feel the power as both arms come down equally. At this point, some pitchers slap their glove down on the side of their leg for timing, and some come down much more quietly, but with just as much force. This is an individual preference, but the slap is *not* needed to create power.

WALK-THROUGH

Purpose: To incorporate striding while ensuring proper form.

Procedure: The pitcher starts slightly behind the rubber, standing with both arms up toward the sky. She then steps (walks) forward with her left leg (for righties), and her arms fall forward and down past her hips. Then, while her arms are still at the back of her swing (facing toward second base), she plants her right foot and starts her motion. She continues through her motion (holding on to the ball—not releasing it) and stops at the end of the pitch, facing the plate.

Variation: The pitcher slowly walks through the motion, but she stops in the middle of the pitch (in the X position) to check the leg, stride, and balance.

SIDEWAYS DRIVE WITH CONE

Purpose: To develop timing of the upper and lower body.

Procedure: One cone is placed about 6 to 6.5 heel-to-toe steps from the mound to mark the landing spot. Starting sideways on the mound with both arms out in front of her body, the pitcher swings her arms back behind her hips as she slides

Figure 10.8 Sideways drive drill with two cones to work on drive and drag.

her front leg back and up with the knee bent. From this position she drives forward into her motion and over the cone. She focuses on her leg kick and stride, along with upper- and lower-body timing.

The back knee must drive into the front and drag. If the pitcher needs to improve her drag, a second cone can be placed about halfway between the mound and the landing spot and the pitcher can work on dragging into it (figure 10.8), and if the pitcher needs to increase the length of her stride, the cone that marks the landing spot can be placed farther away (but not so far that the pitcher could fall over it; err on the side of caution). If the pitcher needs to work on keeping herself on her power line, she can put cones to the left and right of her power line to make sure that she is stepping toward the catcher in a straight line.

LEG-UP WITH CONES

Purpose: To practice pushing hard off the back leg while working on stride and balance.

Procedure: One cone is placed 6 to 6.5 heel-to-toe steps from the mound and another is on its side about half the distance to the landing spot. On the mound, the pitcher faces the catcher and assumes a stork position, standing on the back leg and bending the front leg up toward the chest. The pitcher pushes forward from the mound and reaches with the glove-side toe over the sideways cone and toward the landing spot.

CROUCH PITCH

Purpose: To increase arm speed and leg drive; to feel the whip in the arms.

Procedure: With the top of the shoulders facing the catcher and with the front knee bent, the pitcher pushes off the mound from a crouched position toward the catcher. For the pitcher, it will feel as if the arms are trying to catch up with the legs.

FULL PITCHING MOTION

After understanding and mastering the basic mechanics of the fastball delivery, the pitcher is ready to put it all together in a complete pitching motion. This section presents a more detailed breakdown of the full pitching motion. The pitch begins when the pitcher steps on the rubber, and that is where we begin.

Stance

College rules require the pitcher to start with both feet on the rubber. Some other levels require only one foot to be on the rubber. Pitchers must know which rules apply. Starting with both feet on the rubber is more difficult, but it is the position that will be required as the pitcher advances.

The goal is to generate as much power as possible while maintaining balance. When using two feet on the rubber, the pitcher spreads the feet out from front to back by placing the heel of the front foot (pivot foot) on the front of the rubber and placing the toe of the back foot (stride foot) on the back edge (see figure 10.9, top). The pivot foot is always on the pitching-arm side. The feet are placed no wider than shoulder width.

When the rules require only one foot on the rubber, the throwing-side foot is again the one placed on the front of the rubber (see figure 10.9, bottom). The back foot is placed one step behind the rubber in a spot that provides good balance. From that stance, the pitcher should be able to shift her weight forward easily and push off comfortably for the stride forward. Again, the feet are placed no wider than shoulder width.

At the beginning of the pitch (before striding forward), some pitchers slide the toe of the front foot across the rubber as a timing mechanism. The toe turns slightly open, which promotes the opening of the hips. Other pitchers pick up the front toe (maintaining contact with the rubber with the heel of the front foot) and then replant it back down before beginning to drive off of the mound.

Pitchers can alter the angle of their stance on the rubber in the same way that we change the setup on a pitching machine. To hit the outside corner, we angle the pitching machine slightly outside. For the inside corner, we angle the machine in that direction. The angle and placement of the front foot will allow the pitcher to hit the corners in the same way. To throw to the corners, the pitcher turns the front toe about a half inch in or out from the straight position she would use to throw down the middle of the plate. The batter will never notice the slight change that will allow the pitcher to hit the corners.

Two feet on rubber

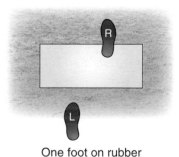

One foot on rubber

Figure 10.9 **Foot position on the pitching rubber.**

Presenting the Ball

The rules use a fancy term—presenting the ball—to describe how the pitcher must stand on the rubber to start the pitching motion. The body is upright and relaxed, and the pitcher should feel comfortable and balanced. The shoulders are level and square with the rubber. The ball can be in the glove or the hand, and the hands are separated. The arms should hang long and relaxed at the pitcher's side, with the shoulders down.

(If the shoulders are up, this means the pitcher is tense.) The pitcher takes a breath to relax the shoulders further, to let go of the past, and to focus on the next pitch. The rules require the signal to be taken with the hands apart. Weight is kept over the back foot to allow a proper weight shift and a momentum shift at the beginning of the motion. The pitcher then brings the hands together. She does not hold this position too long because her body will tend to tighten up, which will affect speed and control. She reaches into the glove and grips the ball, making sure to keep the grip well hidden from the third-base coach.

The First Move

When the pitcher is presenting the ball, the weight is on the back foot. The pitcher begins the motion by rocking forward from heel to toe with both feet, or sliding into position. The focus is on keeping the weight on the balls of the feet. The upper body leans forward, and the weight shifts from the back foot to the front foot (see figure 10.10). As the motion begins, body lean puts the pitcher's head and chest beyond her front foot. From here, the pitcher can go into various types of motions. Some pitchers swing back behind the hips with both hands, some swing back with only one hand, and some may simply come straight down and have the hands separate in front of the body. Whatever the preferred method, the hand and glove are together at the navel, and they push down and out as far as possible to create maximum arc and arm swing. The path of the hands is down (as if moving down the zipper of a jacket) and centered with the body. When the arms are extended, the pitching hand comes out of the glove, and the arm comes directly up to the ear. The body begins to straighten, and the glove is pointed at the catcher. The pitcher lifts the ball out of the glove with the palm of the throwing hand down and with the arm relaxed. The arm movement, or takeaway, is slower at the beginning and builds up speed at the top of the circle to create the whipping action. The pitcher thinks about being relaxed on the way up and accelerating on the way down. She must be careful not to rush. The knee of the stride leg is flexed and moving forward (see figure 10.11). The sequence is arm up, head up, and foot out.

Figure 10.10 **The pitcher rocks forward from heel to toe to start the pitching motion.**

Figure 10.11 **The knee of the stride leg is flexed and moving forward on the takeaway.**

The pivot leg bears the weight with the knee slightly flexed and the foot turned slightly outward (at a one to three o'clock position).

In a variation of the first arm movement, the pitching hand swings back outside of the glove. The glove stays over the ball as long as possible to hide the ball on the arm swing. From that point on, everything else is the same. Swinging the arm back creates a larger arm circle, which can increase speed. Bringing the arm straight back can also help keep the arm and shoulders in proper alignment. A disadvantage is that the ball is visible and an alert coach or batter may pick up the grip and the pitch.

Top of the Backswing

At the top of the backswing, the hips and shoulders are open, with the belly button facing third base. As the ball reaches for the sky, the back foot pivots. The simplest way to ensure that the hips open is to turn the pivot foot on the rubber about 45 degrees away from the body. This outward turn of the pivot foot—accompanied by a strong pivot and a solid push off the rubber with that same foot—help open the hips. The stride foot should land on a straight line running from the pitcher's nose directly to the catcher. The striding toes should point between one o'clock and three o'clock. The pitcher must be aggressive with the stride foot. She reaches out with the stride foot and feels the power from kicking the stride foot forward toward the plate (see figure 10.12). She thinks about moving the stride foot out, not just up. The force of the stride carries the body away from the rubber and creates power by helping to transfer body weight toward the batter. One major difference between elite pitchers and average pitchers is the length and force of that forward stride and kick.

The critical elements during the stride are being balanced when releasing the ball and having consistent foot placement. A pitcher may have her own style and may deviate from the line toward home plate. Even so, placement must be consistent. If the stride is not on the target line, make sure that the step is not across the body, a movement that would force the pitcher to throw across her body. The aggressive reach of

Figure 10.12   An aggressive stride.

the forward leg and the ability of the pitcher to maintain balance on her stride will determine the length of the stride. The upper body must stay upright, or tall, during the stride; the need to keep the body upright will also affect the length of the stride.

On the backswing, the biceps muscle of the pitching arm is close to or brushes the right ear. The pitching arm is extended (long), but not hyperextended. The pitcher must be careful not to lock the elbow. Not extending the arm is called short-arming, and it decreases the arc, greatly limiting speed. The pitcher must keep the arm loose with the wrist in a cocked position ready to whip the ball. At the top of the backswing, the palm has rotated outward to face third base (see figure 10.13). The arms form a 90-degree angle with the pitching arm straight up and the glove pointing at the catcher.

Middle of the Downswing

As the pitching arm reaches the middle of the downswing, the hips and shoulders are just beginning to close. The pitching-side shoulder is lower than the other, and the shoulders are back (see figure 10.14). The pitching arm is slightly bent with the elbow coming into the pitcher's right side. The wrist is cocked and the palm pointing away from the body. The body is upright. The stride leg is flexed to absorb the shock of the forward movement. The back foot drags off the rubber on the side of the toe at about a 45-degree angle, and the pitcher ends on one leg. This is called the flamingo position. (Dragging the toe keeps the feet legal; this is not replanting.) The arms work in opposition as the glove arm and pitching arm move down together. At this point, the pitcher has done a lot of work to get her power going toward the catcher. If she doesn't finish with power through the end of the pitch (via the leg drag) and toward the catcher, then a lot of speed can be lost.

Release

On the release, the striding foot is firmly planted with the knee still flexed. The upper body remains upright; the head is even or slightly ahead of the right knee and between

Figure 10.13 **Top of the backswing.**

Figure 10.14 **Middle of the downswing.**

Figure 10.15 Release point.

the feet. The hips and shoulders are starting to close, and the forearm of the pitching arm is close to or brushing the right side. The wrist is snapping fast, and the fingers apply resistance on the ball at release. The wrist goes from hyperextension to flexion. The pitcher thinks about dragging the fingers through. She should have the feeling that the ball is being pulled throughout the delivery, with the ball trailing the forearm and wrist up to the time of the wrist snap. This motion builds centrifugal force. The glove arm pulls down hard to the side of the front hip as the pitching hand comes forward.

The ball will go where the pitching hand is pointing at the time of release. The pitcher can imagine a dot in the middle of her palm; where the dot is pointing when she releases the ball is where the ball is going to end up. She releases the ball when the wrist snaps at the hip (see figure 10.15). The wrist goes from full extension to full flexion as it passes the hip. Beginning pitchers often snap at the elbow instead of the wrist, greatly sacrificing speed and control. When the elbow bends early, it also causes the ball to go up.

COACHING POINTS FOR FASTBALL PITCHING MECHANICS

- Make sure the grip is comfortable and firm yet doesn't lock the wrist. You need a relaxed wrist for a good, quick snap. Work on gripping the ball firmly while not tightening the wrist.

- Don't stop or pause during the arm circle. Don't stop the momentum you are building. Use one continuous motion.

- Don't guide the ball. Release the ball at your hip with a strong wrist snap.

- Use two checkpoints to keep the arm properly aligned. Your biceps brushes your ear at the top of the backswing, and your pitching hand brushes your hip at release.

- Don't step with the stride foot pointed toward home plate. Your hips will then not be able to open, and your belly button will not point to third base. You must land with the foot somewhere between the one o'clock and three o'clock positions.

- Don't short-arm the ball. The longer the lever, the greater the potential for producing force, just as a rock swinging on the end of a long string moves faster than one swinging on a short string. Keep your arm straight throughout the arm swing with a slightly flexed and relaxed elbow.

- Don't crow hop off the rubber, because doing so results in an illegal pitch. To try to get more impetus on the ball, some pitchers replant the pivot foot by pushing hard off the rubber and actually jump to a second push-off spot. Others simply step forward with the pivot foot and walk off the pitcher's rubber before they pivot. Keep your pivot toe on the rubber as you push off it, and drag the toe of your pivot leg on the follow-through so that you will not be called for being off the rubber.

- Don't hurry to assume a fielding position. Turning too early pulls your shoulders off line. You must keep your hips open until you release the ball and it is well on its way.

BROOM HANDLE PITCH

Purpose: To help new pitchers learn the wrist flip and release point.

Procedure: The coach holds a broom handle horizontally with the end touching the center of the pitcher's hip where the release point is. The pitcher takes her pitching arm behind and slowly pitches. The arm (just above the wrist) will hit the broom, making the wrist flick the ball. The pitcher does not throw the ball hard; the ball should not go far or fast, but the pitcher will feel how, where, and when to release the ball.

Leg Drive

Two theories exist on the use of the legs to drive off the rubber and follow through. Because the ball has already left the hand, the legs at this point have no effect on the pitch. The pitcher uses the legs to generate power by increasing the speed of the arm before releasing the ball. Therefore, the pitcher should choose the style that allows her to maintain her balance and develop maximum arm speed on the downswing.

- **Drag the back foot**—The toe of the nonstriding foot simply drags forward so that the knees of the pitcher come together. Using this technique makes it easier to keep the shoulders in line with the target.
- **Push off the rubber**—Once the arm passes the hip and the ball is released, the back leg comes through hard, propelling the right side through. As the back leg comes through, the front (stride) leg pushes up like a spring uncoiling. This helps drive the back hip through. The pitcher may actually jump up off the front leg. As the right side drives through, the back will arch, the hips will thrust forward, and the shoulders will come back. The pitcher then finishes tall. A disadvantage of this method is the tendency to close the shoulders and hips too early (before the ball is released), which shifts the body off the target line and reduces accuracy.

Follow-Through

To create maximum speed when releasing the ball, the hand must go even faster during the follow-through than it did at release. This is the only way the hand can attain maximum speed. The hand moves well out in front of the body. The pitcher can think of shaking hands with the catcher. The hand also finishes high. That can mean that the hand finishes at face level (see figure 10.16). For some pitchers, the elbow is up near the forehead with the biceps finishing near the cheek. If the arm is truly relaxed and acting like a whip, it will fly up to the end of its range of motion and then fall back down. Movement should be natural and comfortable. The pitching hand must be on line to the target, staying within the line of force and striving to complete the perfect circle. The glove arm stays close to the body so that the shoulders are not pulled off line. The glove pulls down hard and hits the outside of the front hip.

Figure 10.16 Follow-through position. The hand finishes high.

The pitcher's first responsibility is to pitch the ball. After the release, as she pushes off the rubber, she uses her forward momentum to bring the pivot foot forward and almost parallel with the stride foot. This enables her to achieve a well-balanced fielding position. The glove is waist high with the fingers pointing up and the pocket open toward the hitter. The pitcher should not hurry to reach this position; she must complete her follow-through. She waits until the pitch is well on its way before assuming the fielding position.

SPEED VERSUS ACCURACY

Pitchers need both speed and control. Pitchers must learn the speed at which they can control their pitching motion. If the delivery is not consistent, the pitches will not be accurate. True, the goal is to throw the ball hard. By concentrating first on developing maximum speed, beginning pitchers will develop the feeling, mechanics, tempo, and timing required to throw the ball hard. Control is specific to the velocity of the ball. The correct release point is speed specific and is determined by the velocity of each thrown ball. Therefore, decreasing speed will not necessarily improve accuracy. The idea that slowing down or lobbing the ball to home during the game will result in strikes is just not true! Only a consistent delivery and hours of practice will produce accuracy. Because the goal is to throw as fast as possible, pitchers should develop a consistent motion while throwing as fast as they can. Otherwise, they will have a tendency to try to guide the ball. Pitchers should throw hard against a wall or fence without worrying about where the ball goes. Eventually, they will develop accuracy at that speed and can start to throw to a catcher.

Cindy Bristow's Five Tips for Increasing a Pitcher's Speed

1. Legs start and hand finishes: A pitcher should start her pitch with her legs driving her body forward "hard and aggressively." This stride starts her momentum forward, and once the arm catches the whip (which accounts for a fast arm circle), the hand takes over, finishing the pitch with increased velocity, if the wrist is strong and powerful.
2. Don't get stuck in the middle: Once the power is driven toward the catcher, the next step is the middle of the pitch. Keep the momentum going forward and watch for weight either tilting backward or to the side. Tilting will greatly impede the speed. The middle is where you may need to take time to slow down the mechanics and make some mechanical fixes that will help in the long run.
3. The end matters most: Be sure to increase arm and hand speed at the right time— the end.
4. Move where it matters: The pitch can be broken into three parts: before release, release, and after release. Pitchers can lose speed after the release by slowing their leg drive or their arm speed. Make sure pitchers are finishing with their legs and allowing their arms to follow through to the catcher first before continuing upward.
5. Keep the parts in order: The worst thing a pitcher can do is to not have sequential movement. It is very easy to let the hips go ahead of time before the arm can clear them.

Adapted with permission from Cindy Bristow (www.softballexcellence.com).

All pitchers want to increase their speed. Speed comes from a smooth, relaxed delivery and from the centrifugal force created by a long, whiplike action of the arm. The pitcher swings and whips the arm; she doesn't just move it. Speed can be increased by the push off the mound and the snap of the wrist. A pitcher's strength also contributes. Changing grips and finger pressure can sometimes increase speed. Cindy Bristow offers several suggestions for pitchers and their coaches (see page 236).

Pitchers should throw only the fastball as they work on developing consistent mechanics. Use the following drills to develop speed first. When a pitcher can throw hard with consistent mechanics, she is ready to focus on accuracy. Until a pitcher is consistent in both areas, she shouldn't begin to throw other pitches.

SPEED DRILLS

Core strengthening is a must for any athlete and will certainly give pitchers more power and speed. Weight room work that focuses on the legs can be very beneficial. Pitchers can also run sets of stadium steps to improve their drive off the mound; a trainer can help them develop an appropriate program. But the best way for a pitcher to develop speed is to work on drills that emphasize proper mechanics every day. Using a weighted ball can help improve hand strength, arm speed, and speed of the wrist snap.

RICE BUCKET

Purpose: To increase hand strength.

Procedure: Players squeeze and twist their hands in a circular motion in a bucket of rice until fatigued. Players perform three to five repetitions.

LEG POWER TRIO

Purpose: To develop leg strength and speed.

Procedure: Players perform the drills described in the Stride and Hips section (see page 27) in the following sequence:

1. **Starting at the mound, the pitcher performs the sideways drive drill, sending 20 pitches over the cone. She moves four or five steps back, draws a power line, and does 20 more pitches. Then she steps back another four or five steps and does 20 more.**

2. **Starting at the mound, the pitcher performs the leg-up drill. She uses the power line and throws 20 pitches. She moves four or five steps back and does 20 more pitches. Then she steps back another four or five steps and does 20 more.**

ON-OFF

Purpose: To increase speed and stamina.

Procedure: The pitcher starts on the mound with a bucket of balls. She throws to the catcher as hard as she can for one minute, then takes one minute off. She repeats the pattern—one minute on, one minute off—two or more times.

DISTANCE

Purpose: To increase speed or flush soreness after throwing.

Procedure: The pitcher starts at the mound and throws two pitches, then takes two steps back. She walks into the pitch (takes a step onto the pivot foot before releasing the ball) and continues moving backward in this pattern as long as she can still reach the catcher on the fly (getting under the ball and giving it an arc). When finished, she comes back to the mound and walks forward through the mound while throwing 10 to 20 pitches as hard as she can.

PLUS THREE

Purpose: To increase the effort used to throw hard (to work harder at throwing harder).

Procedure: The pitcher throws fastballs from a distance that is 3 feet (1 m) longer than normal.

FASTBALL DRILLS

Pitchers must first develop a consistent delivery; then they can work on speed and accuracy. These drills isolate and emphasize the basic mechanics that are the foundation for developing speed and accuracy.

WALL CIRCLES

Purpose: To correct poor mechanics related to the arm circle.

Procedure: The pitcher stands as if planning to throw a pitch. She begins with the throwing shoulder almost against a wall. As she goes through the pitch, her body will open up and face the wall. She continues her motion, keeping her shoulder and hand close to the wall. The wall keeps the arm tight to the body and in the proper release position. The same drill can be done with the glove-hand side against the wall. This corrects the problem of opening up too soon and pulling the throwing side off of the pitching plane.

ARM-SPEED DEVELOPMENT

Purpose: To learn the feeling of arm speed and to develop acceleration through the arm circle.

Procedure: The pitcher works alone on her arm circle. The drill has two parts:

1. The pitcher stands in a sideways pitching position with the stride leg forward and the pitching arm above the head at the top of the circle. She moves the arm around in a perfect circle as fast as she can to get the feel of high arm speed. She keeps the arm totally relaxed (as loose as a noodle).

2. The pitcher then focuses on building acceleration through the circle. Still sideways, she begins with the pitching arm at waist level. The pitcher focuses on lifting the arm in a relaxed manner and increasing the speed of the arm by

accelerating on the downswing with a whiplike action. The arm is extended (elbow relaxed) to create the biggest arc and lever position. The longer the lever, the more force it can produce.

WALL PITCHING

Purpose: To develop speed and then accuracy.

Procedure: The pitcher stands 10 to 15 feet (3 to 4.5 m) from a wall (a handball court is perfect) and throws hard at the wall, focusing on mechanics and the feeling of throwing the ball hard. Standing close means the pitcher does not have to worry about accuracy. She works on throwing as hard as possible without sacrificing mechanics. When the pitcher has consistent mechanics, a target strike zone should be added. Use a piece of chalk or tape and draw a strike zone (a box) on the wall. Make the strike zone appropriate for the pitcher's height, and have her pitch from the proper pitching distance for her age group. An accurate throw will return the ball straight back. The repeated impact will quickly soften a ball, so keep using the same ball. Don't use a rubber ball that lacks seams because the pitcher must be able to grip the ball properly. An advantage of this kind of practice is that pitchers can do it on their own at any time.

X DRILL

Purpose: To add power to the release and consistency to the pitch.

Procedure: The pitcher assumes the X (or K) position. She has taken her stride, the glove hand is pointing toward the target, and the ball hand is at the highest point. From the third-base side, the pitcher's body position resembles the letter K. She brings the ball hand around toward the release point and pushes off the pitching rubber violently with the trail foot to square her body to the target.

WRIST SNAP UNDER KNEE

Purpose: To develop the wrist snap by isolating the wrist.

Procedure: Partners stand about 10 feet (3 m) apart. Pitchers can throw to pitchers. If the pitcher is right-handed, she kneels on the left knee with the right leg bent and the right foot flat on the ground. The pitching arm is placed against the leg, with the ball and hand under the knee. The pitcher flips the ball in the air to her partner by snapping the wrist.

NO STRIDE

Purpose: To promote proper ball release and speed.

Procedure: The pitcher delivers a ball to a partner without using a forward stride. The partner can be another pitcher, so this is a good warm-up drill. The stride foot is even with the pivot foot. The pitcher pitches the ball using good hip rotation, a strong snap of the wrist, and a good follow-through, focusing on proper hip and arm mechanics. Pitchers should be aware of the danger of not rotating the hips and therefore throwing only with the arm.

BASEBALL MOUND PITCHING

Purpose: To develop proper body lean and weight transfer.

Procedure: The pitcher pitches to a catcher off a baseball mound. The pitcher uses the baseball rubber, and the catcher is positioned at the regular softball distance. The angle of the mound forces a longer stride and helps the pitcher feel the importance of body lean and weight transfer.

10 STRIKES

Purpose: To develop accuracy under pressure (while also having fun).

Procedure: This is a good drill for young pitchers. It can be played with two or three pitchers and a catcher. The object of the game is to throw 10 strikes. The first pitcher throws as many balls as it takes to get to 10 called strikes. The next pitcher has to try to beat that number by throwing fewer pitches to get to 10 strikes. The catcher is the judge in this drill.

ACCURACY

Purpose: To improve accuracy by improving focus.

Procedure: As Cindy Bristow says, "A pitcher's accuracy is usually as good, or as bad, as her focus." In short, improving accuracy has more to do with focus than it does with mechanics. In this drill, a coach sits behind the pitcher or serves as the catcher. The pitcher gets fully warm and ready to throw fastballs. She gets 20 pitches and has to hit the inside target and then the outside target. If she misses on the inside target once, she then gets one other chance to hit it, but the pitch still counts. Count how many balls and strikes she gets as she attempts to throw to the required locations (in and out). After 20 pitches, tally up her score. A good score should be 75 percent or better; the pitcher can repeat the drill if she needs or wants to. We use this drill when our pitchers have trouble throwing strikes. We do not allow our pitchers to throw pitches with movement until they can get to this level of accuracy.

MOVEMENT AND OFF-SPEED PITCHES

As explained in chapter 10, a pitcher must develop the proper mechanics for the fastball and must be able to consistently execute that pitch before attempting to learn another pitch. She must know her release point, be able to make corrections, and understand how to alter the spin of the ball.

Pitchers should concentrate on developing one pitch at a time—and they should learn that pitch well. Many young pitchers want to learn several pitches right away, and they end up having mastery over none. Developing the muscle memory that leads to mastery of a pitch takes time, and there is only so much time available for practice.

Most pitchers will have a tendency to pick up on one or two pitches more easily than others. That is the place to begin. Once young pitchers have developed the ability to spot pitches well, they should begin with the changeup. The changeup can be a tough pitch to learn, but it is a useful tool to use until the pitcher is ready to develop movement pitches. Plus, the changeup contributes to a solid overall foundation for a pitcher.

Top pitchers seek to have about four good pitches, including an off-speed pitch. Some of the more elite pitchers will admit that they have the "one pitch" that really gets it done for them. If a pitcher has a pitch that is really effective (a reliable strikeout pitch), then the other pitches should complement that pitch. If a pitcher doesn't yet have one dominating pitch, then the best plan is to select pitches that cover the various areas of the plate and to set out to master each one. A good strategy would be to have a fastball, a drop, a rise, and a changeup. The easiest pitch for most pitchers to learn is the drop. The curve, the screwball, and the rise have many similarities; the rise is the most difficult to learn.

BALL MOVEMENT AND PACE

To be effective, any movement pitch must look like a fastball at first. For the break to occur at the right time (in relation to the plate and the hitter), the pitcher must think *fastball* first. This is another reason why pitchers should continually return to and try to perfect the fastball. The more expert a pitcher becomes with the fastball, the more effective she will be in throwing a movement pitch or an off-speed pitch.

Pitchers who struggle with movement pitches are thinking—and showing—*movement pitch* from the very beginning. Pitchers should not look or stand any differently on the mound when they are pitching different pitches. That is a dead giveaway. Why spend time hiding a pitch at your side if you are going to give it away in your setup? "Selling" or hiding the pitch helps it succeed. The less likely a batter is to predict the pace and path of the ball, the less likely she is to hit it. With the changeup, the element of deception is even more important than location.

A pitch that moves as it approaches the plate—up, down, in, or out—is more difficult to hit than a straight ball. Spin and speed make the ball move. The faster the spin, the greater the movement. The faster the wrist snap, the greater the spin and the faster the speed. For example, some changeups are thrown with no wrist snap, and as a result, they have no speed. Other changeups have a lot of spin and require a wrist snap, but they spin in the opposite direction of the plate and therefore lose their speed.

Seam Rotation

As a softball moves through the air, it moves in the direction of the least pressure. Four seams rotating against the wind and biting the air create more movement than two seams (see figure 11.1). For a four-seam rotation, the pitcher grips the ball across the seams with the thumb on one seam and the fingers on the opposite seam. When the pitcher looks at the ball to assume the grip, she should see a *C*. She should try to get the four seams turning at right angles to the direction of the break. The four-seam grip is very effective for throwing changeups because it helps reduce the speed of the ball.

A two-seam grip also works well for changeups and many pitchers prefer it. For a two-seam rotation, the pitcher grips the ball with the fingers going with the seams. The thumb is still under the ball on a seam for ball control. Altitude and weather affect ball movement. Humid or heavy air slows the movement and speed of the ball, and lighter air does the opposite.

Spin

The spin of the ball determines the direction it will move. The ball will break in the direction it is rotating (see figure 11.2). The spin on a rise ball is under the ball, up and back toward the pitcher. The spin on a drop ball is over the top, down and away from the pitcher. A curveball and screwball spin is sideways. From a right-handed pitcher, the curve moves away from a right-handed batter. A left-hander's curveball breaks in on a right-handed batter's hands and is a tough pitch to hit. The screwball moves in on a right-hander and away from a left-handed batter.

Grip

The pitcher uses the grip to impart spin to the ball in order to make it rotate a particular way. Hand size, finger length, and arm strength vary widely among pitchers, so each must experiment to find the grip and pressure points that produce the desired spin. The grip must be comfortable so that it does not produce tension in the wrist that could limit the wrist snap. The grip, wrist action, and follow-through are the keys to throwing "junk," or movement pitches. Good pitches break sharply just before they reach the plate.

Learning a New Pitch

Pitchers should use the following progression when learning a pitch:

1. Find a comfortable grip and then experiment to find a grip and finger pressure that create the greatest combination of spin, speed, and control. The coach can show the pitcher several grip options, but the pitcher must choose the one that works best for her. Don't be afraid to change grips throughout your pitching career. Remember, you are never at a point in your pitching where you know everything there is to know. Become a student of the game and constantly work to improve your techniques. Tiger Woods revamped his swing after many years of success at the top level of his game!

2. Assume the stride and pitching position, and spin the ball into your glove using only the wrist. Get comfortable with the snap, release, and finish of the pitch. You

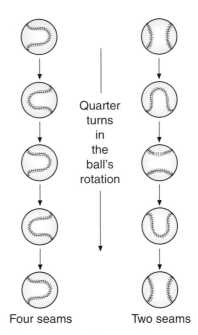

Figure 11.1 Four-seam versus two-seam rotation.

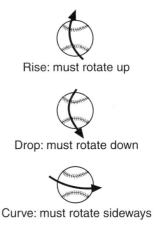

Figure 11.2 Rise, drop, curveball, and screwball spins.

can also do this with the catcher at a distance of about half the normal pitching distance. Alternatively, you can throw to the catcher from your knees.

3. Throw easily to a catcher 15 to 20 feet (4.5 to 6 m) away using a weighted ball, preferably the two-toned Cannonball (see figure 11.3) so you can see the spin. This helps develop proper spin as well as finger strength and wrist strength in each pitch.

4. Transition to a regular ball and throw easily to a catcher 15 to 20 feet away, concentrating on proper spin and release. Start without a full windup and stride. When successful, add a complete motion. To make it easier to see the spin, put a stripe on the ball or color the seams. The catcher can also provide feedback about the spin.

5. Use the Spin Right Spinner (see figure 11.4) to work on proper spin for each individual pitch. This training aid was developed by Cheri Kempf and is available through Club K Softball (www.clubkstore.com). The spinner is a disc-like replica of a regular ball designed to teach the spins and rotation directions of the softball.

6. Pitch at normal distance. Mix in your fastball from time to time to help with speed and movement.

Figure 11.3   The Cannonball.

Figure 11.4   The Spin Right Spinner.

DROP BALL

The drop is the most reliable pitch and the easiest pitch for most pitchers to learn. It is often the most effective pitch because it is the most difficult to hit solidly. A good drop pitch produces a lot of ground balls. The drop should never be thrown more than 4 inches (10 cm) above the knee. The best location is between the knee and the shoe tops. The drop ball breaks best when thrown low, and it becomes difficult to hit as it breaks out of the batter's line of vision. The batter sees only the top of the ball and is likely to hit it on the ground. If the pitcher misses with this pitch, she should be sure to miss down. With runners on, of course, the catcher must be able to block balls in the dirt.

The two common types of drop balls are the peel drop and the turnover drop. Pitchers who struggle with this pitch can throw a combination of the two.

Peel Drop

Most pitchers find the peel drop easier to learn than the turnover drop. The basic mechanics are similar to the mechanics for the fastball, so learning the peel drop is a natural progression. The difference is the emphasis on the spin and the lower follow-through. The spin is a true vertical spin that can produce a sharp or heavy drop.

- **Grip**—The pads of the fingers are across the seams for a four-seam rotation and the "C" grip. The preferred method is to have three fingers on the back of the ball and the pinkie curled on the side (see figure 11.5). The thumb should be across the seams on the opposite side of the ball. The ball is held more loosely in the hand than it is for a rise (see figure 11.11 on page 249).

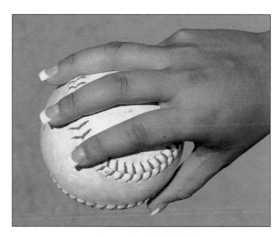

Figure 11.5 Peel drop grip.

- **Spin**—The spin is down and away from the pitcher and toward the catcher in a 6 o'clock to 12 o'clock rotation.

- **Mechanics**—The thumb is the first digit released from the ball. The ball rolls straight off the ends of the fingers with the palm facing the plate. The pitcher should feel the heel of the hand driving downward toward the ground with the wrist bent and fingers "dragging" on the back of the ball (toward second base). At release, the wrist should snap straight forward and up (see figure 11.6). The pitcher pulls up on the seams and feels the friction of the seams leaving the finger pads while imparting a downward rotation. If the spin is not vertical, the pitcher has not maintained a direct line of force to the target and has not kept her hand directly behind the ball. The stride is usually shorter so the pitcher's weight can get up and over the front leg. This also enables the pitcher to get the right body angle on the ball. She should make herself as tall as possible so the ball has more room to drop.

- **Follow-through**—The fingers should snap straight up and come to rest on the shoulder about armpit high. All four fingers should be touching the shoulder, indicating that the wrist did not rotate off line. A common error is to allow the elbow to drive backward up and away from the body after the snap.

Figure 11.6 Peel drop release.

This follow-through is slightly lower than the follow-through for other pitches. If the ball is too low, the pitcher should increase the follow-through to bring the ball up slightly.

- **Troubleshooting**—One of the biggest problems with this pitch is that if it is not thrown correctly the ball will stay flat and be very hittable. It takes some time and patience to get the feel of the correct release point and mechanics; therefore, pitchers need to be patient. This is a great pitch for a pitcher to mix with the fastball so she can differentiate between the two as she throws them.

Turnover Drop

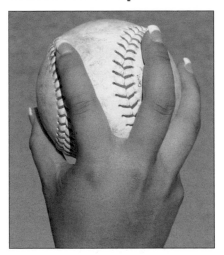

Figure 11.7 Turnover drop grip.

The turnover drop is probably the more popular of the two ways to throw the drop ball. Some pitchers can throw this pitch very hard with a lot of movement, and some can also take some speed off and throw it like an off-speed pitch. The turnover drop is the more difficult pitch to learn because it involves snapping the wrist over the ball and because timing becomes a factor. But if the pitcher's hand naturally turns over at release, this is the pitch for her. Good curveball pitchers often prefer this drop because the wrist snap is similar to what they use for the curveball. Some combine the two pitches and throw the drop-curve, which is also a very effective pitch.

- **Grip**—The index finger is pushing against a seam. A common method is to grip the "backward C" of the ball with the thumb on one seam and the index and middle fingers on the outside edge of the opposite seam where they can push against it (see figure 11.7).

  Variations include a split-finger grip with the first finger against the pushing side of one seam (the edge of the seam that the pitcher uses to create spin) and the middle finger against the pushing side of another seam. For this grip, the pitcher places the two pushing fingers against the two seams where they are closest together, at the most narrow point of the seam pattern. She must find a position that creates a four-seam rotation.

- **Spin**—The spin is down and away from the pitcher and toward the catcher. The turnover drop may not have a true vertical rotation like the peel drop. The spin may be down with both a counterclockwise and sideways rotation, producing a drop curve (see page 248 for more information about the drop-curve).

- **Mechanics**—As the ball approaches the bottom of the downswing, the pitcher must first make sure that she begins to tuck her elbow slightly behind her torso or hip. This gets her hand in the right position for release. The heel of the hand should approach the hip first with the fingers almost underneath the ball. The arm must stay tight to the body. When the forearm begins to brush the top of the hip, this initiates the wrist snap, and there should be a simultaneous lifting or shrugging of the pitching shoulder, trying to touch the right ear. At the top of the shrug, the fingers, wrist, elbow, and shoulder come over the ball and help push it down into the ground. With the shrug, the wrist begins to turn in automatically, similar to what happens in turning a doorknob to the left. The wrist snaps on top of the ball, and the fingers pull up and over the ball. The action resembles dribbling a basketball.

TURNOVER SNAP

Purpose: To help the pitcher see and feel the correct wrist snap for the turnover drop.

Procedure: The pitcher holds the ball with the palm up in front of the body. With the elbow in close to her side, she snaps the wrist over and throws the ball to the ground. The elbow must not fly out from the pitcher's side.

At release, the fingers holding the ball should be on top, and the thumb should be underneath and pointing at the ground. The thumb comes off first, and the pitcher should then feel the ball coming off the inside of the fingers.

The forearm should be close to or brushing the side at release. A common problem is for the elbow to extend away from the side. Be sure the elbow gets tucked behind the torso (just above the hip bone)—no chicken wings! The arm is slightly bent all the way through to the side as the pitcher leads with the wrist. Then she quickly snaps the wrist and gets over the ball (see figure 11.8). Pitchers normally think about keeping the arm long (extended) all the way through their side. However, a long arm at the snap would make it difficult to get the best snap possible and to keep the arm tight to the side. Using a little bit of arm bend and shoulder shrug coming into this pitch means that the elbow has nowhere else to go comfortably, so it ends up tucking slightly behind the hip.

The stride may be a bit shorter when throwing this pitch, but a common misconception is that the stride needs to be a lot shorter. A much shorter stride can result in the loss of velocity. The pitcher still needs a good leg drive throughout this pitch. Many pitchers say they feel a slight rocking motion, especially forward, when throwing this pitch well. Note that although the hips need to be open when throwing the fastball, the same cannot be said for the turnover drop. In this pitch, the hip may start the turn to close a little earlier than on the fastball. The arm and the hand are much faster than the hip turn, and the hand will tuck in front of the hip before it fully closes. If a pitcher tries to throw this pitch with the hips wide open, she will have a difficult time keeping the arm and hand close to her side, and the release point will likely get out in front of her body. This difference illustrates why each pitch should be mastered separately. If a pitcher tried to throw a rise ball with these mechanics, you'd want to duck!

Figure 11.8 Turnover drop release.

Figure 11.9   Turnover drop follow-through.

- **Follow-through**—The pitcher finishes the wrist snap with the hand and thumb pointed down. For many good drop-ball pitchers, their hand actually rotates all the way through to where the palm of the hand is facing toward third base. The hand finishes lower than the release point, between the legs at midthigh or lower (see figure 11.9). The pitcher focuses on keeping the follow-through close to the body. Some pitchers follow through with the back hip and leg coming over the ball and with the back foot landing close to the striding foot.

Peel-Turnover Combo

This pitch starts with the pitcher attempting to throw the peel drop. She uses the same grip and mechanics (figure 11.10a), but instead of pulling up on the finish, she executes a half turn over the ball (figure 11.10b) and finishes down as she would when throwing a turnover drop. Many young pitchers respond well to this pitch, because it is a much less aggressive way to attempt to throw the turnover.

Figure 11.10   The peel-turnover drop (a) begins like a peel drop but (b) finishes low with a half turn like the turnover drop.

Drop-Curve

This is a combination of the drop and the curve. It is meant to be thrown more like a drop than a curve. Here are the differences from the drop:

1. The stride is long and slightly across the power line.
2. The spin is down with both a counterclockwise and sideways rotation.

3. At release, the pitcher focuses on coming over the top of the ball at the hip, but once she is by the hip, she goes directly to finishing across the body and driving the hand into the inside of the left leg.

The drop-curve breaks down first, and the bend (curve) on the ball comes at the end, which keeps hitters chasing it. This pitch is very effective because it is difficult to hit solidly. And because the curve is at the end, many hitters will chase this pitch off the plate. A pitcher may not even have to throw the drop-curve for a strike once the hitter has seen it and the pitcher has established that she is able to throw it.

RISE BALL

The rise ball is the most difficult pitch to throw correctly because it requires complex wrist action at release and involves working against gravity. A good rise ball jumps as it approaches the batter. The pitcher should make the ball break to the hitter's armpits or above, (The exception is a low rise ball, which may be thrown by a pitcher who has mastered throwing the rise ball.) She cannot afford to have the pitch flatten out and miss low. She should use this pitch when she wants a fly ball or when facing a batter who goes after high pitches. Because the ball is up and in the power zone for most big hitters, it is a dangerous pitch that can lead to home runs. Slappers can also do damage because the ball is on the same plane as the eyes and bat. The rise ball should only be used as a strikeout pitch if it is a pitcher's best pitch. Some pitchers have been able to dominate using only this pitch.

- **Grip**—Four basic grips are used for the rise ball:

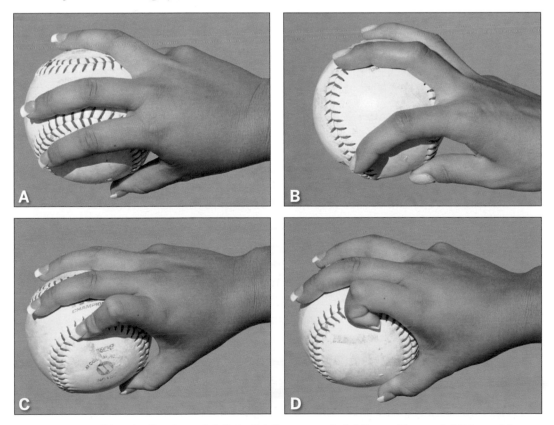

Figure 11.11 Rise-ball grips: *(a)* flat, *(b)* finger curl, *(c)* fingertip, and *(d)* knuckle.

Flat: The index and middle fingers are flat on the ball. The fingers can be together or split. If they are together, they should be on the inside of the same seam. A pitcher with large hands can use a two-seam grip with the fingers split on each seam (see figure 11.11*a*).

Finger curl: The index finger is curled with the inside of the index finger on the ball (see figure 11.11*b*). The middle finger and the ring finger are on or slightly in front of the two seams so the pitcher can push off of these seams at release. The thumb is on the bottom of the ball. The thumb can play a crucial part in throwing this pitch because it triggers or starts the snap.

Fingertip: The fingertip of the index finger is on the ball (see figure 11.11*c*). The pitcher must keep her fingernails short! The middle and ring fingers are on or slightly in front of the two seams.

Knuckle: The knuckle of the index finger is on the ball (see figure 11.11*d*). The middle and ring fingers are on or slightly in front of the two seams.

In all grips, the outside of the middle finger should be placed where it can push against a seam. The thumb is always placed on an opposite seam. The ability to use a bent index finger or knuckle depends on the size of the hand and fingers. Note that the ball rolls off the sides or bottom surface of the fingers for the rise and the curve.

- Spin—The spin is up and toward the pitcher, and the ball spins either completely backward or in a bullet spin that twists from left over the top to the right (see figure 11.12). The true backward spin is more difficult to master, and not many pitchers can actually achieve it. The backward spin is a four-seam rotation with complete backspin. The over and up spin is a two-seam rotation and seems to be the easiest and most effective because pitchers can actually execute it. Mastering the over and up spin leads a pitcher closer to being able to use true backspin!

Figure 11.12   Rise-ball over and up spin.

RISE-BALL SPIN

Purpose: To help the pitcher feel and practice the rise-ball spin.

Procedure:

1. **With a comfortable rise-ball grip, the pitcher holds the ball out in front of the body. She twists her wrist backward (a doorknob turn to the right) and makes the ball spin as she tosses it to herself. Pitchers can use a weighted ball to do this drill.**

2. **The pitcher stands sideways with her glove side to a catcher who is three to five steps away. The pitcher holds the ball on the palm of her pitching hand. She swings her arm backward and forward in a scooping motion, and while still focusing on a good wrist snap, she releases the ball from underneath with the palm up. Using a weighted ball helps the pitcher feel the ball ripping off the fingertips.**

3. **If a pitcher is really struggling with getting the hand under and inside the ball, she can work with a junior-sized football. She should scoop under the ball and snap it underhand, attempting to throw the football with a bullet spin on the ball in an upward fashion to a catcher.**

4. **The pitcher throws easy long tosses (70 to 80 feet [20 to 24 m]) to a catcher.**

The ball should go high (as if throwing over a telephone pole) to ensure that the pitcher is under the ball at release.

RISE-BALL ARM MOTION

Purpose: To help the pitcher get the feel of the arm motion for the rise ball.

Procedure: The pitcher stands against a wall with her pitching hand raised overhead and her palm flat on the wall. She makes a complete arm circle, keeping the palm flat against the wall and duplicating the arm motion for a rise. She rotates the hips through right after release to feel the arm and hips working together.

Figure 11.13 Rise-ball downswing.

- **Mechanics**—The pitcher lengthens the stride and keeps a stiff front leg. Body lean is slightly back (with a slight knee bend), and the right shoulder is lower, angled toward the ground (see figure 11.13). This posture helps the pitcher lower the release point and get under the ball. On the downswing, the wrist and arm turn so that when the arm reaches the back leg, the back of the hand and forearm are against the leg. Once again, the pitcher should think of slightly tucking her elbow so that her forearm and hand get in very tight (tight enough to brush her upper thigh at release). The knuckles of the pitching hand should be no higher than the back knee. Note that the pitcher's arm is between her body and the ball.

  The elbow is in and the arm is turned back as the heel of the hand leads to the release point. The wrist is cocked coming into the release area. At release, the hand is cupped under the ball with the little finger pointing toward home and with the palm of the hand pointing toward third base (see figure 11.14). The pitching hand is facing away from the side of the body. The pitcher snaps the wrist forward with the hand cutting underneath the ball to impart the backspin. The action is similar to turning a doorknob to the right. If it helps, the pitcher can focus on her thumb as the starter for the snap. She starts to pull the ball into a twist and then feels the rest of the fingers follow.

  The pitcher must get under the ball with a long arm. The body leans back at the point of release. The pitching shoulder should stay back so that the body faces third base throughout the pitch. However, the shoulder will begin to come forward through the release. The pitcher imagines she is pinching her arms into her chest. This keeps the ball down and does not allow the pitcher to fall out of the back of her motion and pull the ball up too soon. If the pitcher is getting full rotation on the ball, she should feel the thumb pointing down at release. The back knee bends more at release, enabling the pitcher to get under the ball.

Figure 11.14 Rise-ball release.

Also, at release, the pitcher bends into the pitch, which lowers the shoulder and helps her get under the ball. The body weight shifts forward *into* the front leg, which is now starting to provide resistance. The pitcher should feel as if she is slamming into a wall. The elbow is relatively straight at release, and any bend occurs only on the follow-through.

- **Follow-through**—The elbow stays tightly tucked into the side. The arm reaches out and continues up but short, moving into the chest or under the chin and into the right shoulder. The elbow should be in closer to the body than the wrist with the hand turned completely over. For the bullet spin, the palm is out and up with the thumb pointed upward. For the backward spin, the palm is still out and up, but the hand turns completely over, and the thumb is pointing down. The back leg needs to drive under and through the front leg that is providing resistance. Once the leg has kicked through, the pitcher may have the feeling that she is bouncing or falling back. This should happen after release; otherwise, the path of the ball will be high.

Rise-Curve

The rise-curve is a great chase pitch for good rise-ball pitchers. This pitch is thrown exactly like a rise ball until the finish. Instead of following through up and tight under the chin and to the right shoulder, the pitcher comes up and across the body into the left shoulder. This pitch rises first and *then* starts to curve away from the hitter.

CURVEBALL

As the name implies, the curveball curves sideways, moving in the direction of its spin. From a right-handed pitcher, the curve will move right to left, breaking away from a right-handed batter and breaking in to a left-handed hitter.

The curve can be used effectively in all parts of the strike zone. It can be thrown inside to a right-handed batter so that it breaks over the plate or over the outside corner. This pitch can also be thrown over the plate so that it breaks outside beyond the reach of a right-handed batter. The safest location is low and outside. The pitcher must be careful with a target low and inside; if she misses inside, the pitch will hit the batter. Most hitters are weakest at hitting outside pitches because they try to pull every pitch. When a pitcher has good control of both her inside pitches and her curve, she can move the batter on and off the plate. Pitchers should be able to throw the curve to both right-handed and left-handed batters. Throwing the curve at different speeds increases its effectiveness.

- **Grip**—The grip for the curve is the same as the grip used for the rise. Some pitchers will spread their fingers a little more. Holding the ball deeper in the hand and cocking the wrist more at release will result in a slower curve. The curve is easier to master than the rise because the motion is more basic. The curve is sometimes referred to as an underdeveloped rise ball.
- **Spin**—The spin is directly sideways. The ball rolls off the sides of the fingers to create proper sideways rotation. The ball does not come off the fingertips! The action is similar to turning a doorknob to the right. This spin may occur naturally for some pitchers. Some coaches don't like the curve because it stays on one plane as it moves sideways, making it relatively easy to see and hit. Pitchers can add an up or down spin to the curve to change the plane. A pitcher who understands spins and rotation can make the ball do many things.

CURVEBALL SPIN

Purpose: To help the pitcher develop and improve the spin on the curveball.

Procedure:

1. **The pitcher holds her hand out in front of her body with the palm up and the hand flat; the elbow is tucked behind her torso. She brings her fingers in toward the center of the body by moving her hand sideways. The snap should be so quick and tight that the pitcher feels as if it has wrapped about her hip. The finish is to the inside of the right hip. The pitching coach watches the wrist bone on top of the pitcher's pitching hand; the wrist bone should be pointing toward the catcher. The pitcher should flex her wrist to the point where this bone is prominent. Now add a ball and a comfortable curve grip. The pitcher spins the ball to herself or to a catcher using a strong sideways snap of the wrist and a twisting action with the fingers. Use a weighted ball to work on the spin.**

2. **To develop the spin, the pitcher can pitch a hockey puck (or the Spin Right Spinner) into a wall. She grips the puck around the edges with one flat side down. The focus is on keeping the elbow to the side, keeping the palm up, and developing the proper wrist snap.**

- **Mechanics**—The shoulders are level, and the body is upright. The stride is slightly shorter than that used for the rise ball and is slightly over the power line to create proper torque. The pitcher does not want to get completely under the ball; therefore, she must be careful not to drop the shoulder as she would for a rise ball. The arm is turned back as for the rise, and the hand position is the same—the hand is under the ball, and the little finger is toward the catcher. The key difference is in the wrist snap. The wrist snaps around the hip (toward first base), and the snap occurs a little sooner. The pitcher must be careful to snap the ball, not carry it! The middle finger really pulls the ball. The action is like a karate chop in front of the waist with the palm up, and the spin is created in the same way as when throwing a Frisbee.

The pitcher must set up for this pitch properly. She must reach a little longer and feel her hand under the ball at the back of the pitch. If she tries to short-arm the pitch (instead of keeping length), she will reduce the break and velocity. The elbow gets tucked into the side, and then the hand accelerates through and around the hip. For a tighter spin, the pitcher snaps the thumb to the target. The palm must stay up throughout the pitch. The elbow bends before the release (see figure 11.15). The forearm brushes against the side as the right hip is driven forward. The right hip closes more on this pitch, and the toe of the right foot drags to provide body resistance.

Figure 11.15 Curveball release.

Figure 11.16 Curveball follow-through.

The pitching shoulder also closes to the catcher and is higher than it is for the rise ball. The pitcher brings the right shoulder to the left. The knees should drive together, and the pitcher should feel the tight twist as her wrist, hand, and torso twist through the pitch. The back toe should have a very heavy drag and then release on the follow-through.

- **Follow-through**—The arm comes across the body at the waist, going from one hip to the other. The pitching elbow moves slightly away from the body just after release (see figure 11.16).

Backdoor Curve

The backdoor curve is a curveball thrown at the right-handed hitter's hip that breaks in to the inside portion of the plate. For a left-handed batter, the pitch is thrown at the plate, and it breaks in on the batter. The batter is often fooled into thinking that the pitch is off the plate and a ball. A left-handed pitcher would throw the backdoor curve at the hip of a left-handed batter so it would break onto the plate; for a right-handed hitter, she would throw it off the plate and have it curve onto the plate or throw it on the inside of the plate to break in toward the batter's shins.

SCREWBALL

The screwball has gained much popularity in the last few years. It is a very effective pitch that can be thrown for a strike to lead off a hitter or to get that second strike. The screwball can also be used to jam a hitter, forcing her to foul off the pitch and setting her up to chase a third-strike pitch on the outside of the plate or in the dirt low and outside. Left-handed hitters seem to have trouble with this pitch, especially if they are trying to slap the ball and are running up the line too quickly. Against slappers, this pitch should be kept low; otherwise, it will get up into the hitter's eye plane, giving her a chance to be successful.

- **Grip**—The grip for the screwball is the same as the grip for the rise and the curve, although some pitchers spread their fingers a little more for the screwball. The screwball is easier to master than the rise because the motion is more basic. Like the curveball, the screwball is sometimes referred to as an underdeveloped rise ball.
- **Spin**—The goal is to produce spin that moves in toward the hitter. Depending on how the spin is imparted it can move up or down while spinning right to left (when thrown by a right-handed pitcher).

- **Mechanics**—The pitcher needs to come into this pitch as if it is a fastball. The stride should be a normal one but slightly to the left of the power line. As the pitching arm begins to come down, the elbow should be tucked slightly behind the torso with the thumb leading the hand into the hip. The hips are wide open and in the "skinny" (completely sideways) position. The butt should bend slightly out of the way, and the arm should be tucked tightly into the inside of the hip at release (see figure 11.17). When the ball is released, the pitcher should simulate turning the doorknob to the right (as in the rise ball), but the pinkie finger directs the hand more toward the hitter and inside the ball. After the release at the hip, the hand stays very tight into the belly, and the forearm is parallel with the waist.
- **Follow-through**—As the arm is releasing the ball and coming through the body, the back leg should be kicking very hard to a figure four position with the knees nearly touching. The pitcher will be releasing the ball fully in the open position, and the

Figure 11.17 Screwball release.

kick comes through simultaneously with the wrist snap. After the release and kick, the legs finish with the foot landing parallel to the front plant leg. Once the arm has continued through the belly, it should make a quick turn to the right. This leaves the right arm in the form of an *L* at the right side of the body and facing the catcher. The pinkie finger faces upward, and the knuckles of the ring and middle finger face the catcher. The shoulders drive toward the plate to keep the torso momentum going forward. Watch for a tendency of the front left shoulder to pull to the left and open; this shoulder should continue to drive toward the catcher.

CHANGEUP

The purpose of the changeup is to deceive the batter. Hitting requires timing, and good pitching disrupts that timing. The changeup throws off the batter's timing and increases the effectiveness of other pitches. The changeup doesn't have to be fancy to be effective; it only has to fool the batter. Therefore, the pitching motion for the changeup must look like that of any other pitch. A changeup should be 15 to 20 miles per hour slower than the pitcher's fastest pitch.

The ideal location for the changeup is knee high on the outside corner. Because the batter has misjudged the speed, her hands should have already passed the ideal contact spot for the outside pitch. On the other hand, a hitter can commit early and still have a chance of hitting an inside changeup. The pitcher's ability to throw the changeup for a strike will also determine when she can throw it. A good changeup can be used in many situations, but a bad changeup should be used sparingly. Generally, the changeup is not used on a batter with two strikes who is protecting the plate or against a weak hitter who cannot get around on faster pitches. The changeup should not be used in a sacrifice or squeeze situation or when a steal is expected.

The changeup is a relatively simple pitch to learn. Unfortunately, because of the emphasis on speed, many pitchers do not work to develop a good change-of-speed pitch. The two types of changeups are the stiff-wrist changeup and the back-of-the-hand changeup.

Stiff-Wrist Changeup

The easiest release to use for the changeup is usually the stiff wrist, but the choice should depend on which release is easier and more comfortable for the pitcher. A problem with the stiff-wrist release is a tendency to stop the hand completely with no follow-through or to slow the arm way down at the back of the motion and give the pitch away. Also, it can be difficult to avoid snapping the wrist because doing so is so important for all other pitches. This technique is just the opposite of what the pitcher has worked so hard to develop. Now she palms the ball, locks the wrist, and pushes the ball.

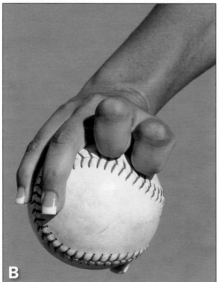

Figure 11.18 Two grips for the stiff-wrist changeup: (a) fingertips and (b) knuckles.

- **Grip**—The more skin on the ball, the slower the speed. Putting the ball deep in the hand against the palm locks or stiffens the wrist, greatly reducing the speed. Palming the ball with the fingers going with the seams causes any rotation to be a two-seam rotation. When gripping across the seams, pitchers tend to snap the ball and pull on the seams, thus increasing the speed. Going with the seams helps break this habit. Placing the thumb on a seam helps with control.

  The pitcher can try using one, two, or four knuckles on the ball; or she can use the fingertips on the ball. When using the fingertips on the ball, the fingers should be bent, and the nails should be digging into the seams or just in front of the seams (see figure 11.18a). If the knuckle grip is being used, the pitcher should grip the ball firmly with the thumb and little finger while placing the first bend (flat fingernail portion) against the ball's surface (see figure 11.18b). The grip must be secure enough that the pitcher can use her regular fastball motion without fear of losing her grip on the ball. The size of a pitcher's hands will eliminate the use of some grips. One problem with the knuckleball is that it is very easy for the hitters and opposing coaches to pick up because the pitcher cannot easily hide the knuckles coming off the ball. For this reason, the knuckleball is less popular at higher levels of play.

- **Spin**—The ball may or may not spin. The lack of speed, not ball movement, is what makes the pitch effective, so spin is not a concern.

- **Mechanics**—Differences in mechanics between the changeup and other pitches should be few and never visible to the batter. The pitcher locks or stiffens her wrist at the release point by spreading her fingers as wide as possible and pushing the ball with her palm. She does not use the fingers to push the ball because this would result in speed. Normal hand speed must be maintained into the release point. If the hand slows, the pitcher will tip the pitch and lose needed distance. The release is in front of the back hip. The pitcher must focus on staying under the ball and reaching out to hand the ball to the catcher (see figure 11.19). For some pitchers, stopping the wrist at the side by bumping the hip is effective.

- **Follow-through**—The pitcher should keep the follow-through low so that the pitch stays down in the strike zone. She turns her hand down at release as if shaking the catcher's hand. She may want to experiment with bumping the hip to stop the arm and limit the follow-through, or she may even try pulling back after releasing the ball.

Back-of-the-Hand Changeup

The back-of-the-hand changeup is the more difficult change to throw. Few pitchers use it successfully, but some of the best changeups you will ever see are thrown this way. It takes a lot of practice to learn the right release point and to be consistent. A difficulty with this pitch is that the pitcher may drop the ball when trying to keep the arm moving at full speed.

Figure 11.19 **Stiff-wrist changeup release.**

- **Grip**—The grip is not a factor in this pitch, so the pitcher should use one that is comfortable. Most pitchers use the fastball grip or an across-the-seams grip.

- **Spin**—The ball may spin excessively or simply float with little spin. The tighter the spin, the more the hitter may be fooled by this pitch, and the more drop the pitch can have at the end of its path. The back-of-the-hand changeup is most effective when it comes out of the pitcher's hand with nearly the same velocity as the fastball; the pitch then dies at the plate or loses a lot of speed just in front of it. The spin is either a direct backspin (12 to 6 o'clock) or a slight backspin with some sidespin, which is produced when the pitcher pulls to the left of the ball and around it during release and into the follow-through.

- **Mechanics**—As the pitcher begins her downswing (and well before the release point), she turns her hand over so the thumb comes down at the back of the motion; the back of the hand now faces the catcher (see figure 11.20a). The back of the hand leads into the release point, and the wrist snaps to release the ball (see figure 11.20b).

Figure 11.20 Back-of-the-hand changeup release: *(a)* Well before reaching the release point, the pitcher turns the ball over; *(b)* the pitcher snaps the ball at release.

COACHING POINTS FOR THROWING OTHER PITCHES

Drop Ball

- Take a slightly shorter stride to raise your release point. Doing this makes you taller and gives the ball a greater distance to drop.

- Lean slightly forward at release with your head and shoulders over your front foot. Emphasize landing on the ball of your foot.

- Throw the ball at about 90 percent of maximum speed. This allows the ball to drop more.

Rise Ball

- To increase the "hop" of the rise, experiment with spreading your fingers more on the ball and squeezing the ball out of the fingers at release. Doing this increases the resistance on the ball, thus creating more spin.

- Remember that a sideways spin will flatten out this pitch.

- Don't try to make the ball go up. Allow the spin to take it up.

- If the ball is curving instead of rising, make one or more of these adjustments:
  - Make sure your elbow is not flying away from your body at release.
  - Make sure your right shoulder is not too high coming into the release area.
  - Make sure your wrist snap is not sideways. Have your wrist and fingers rotate back toward your body after release.
  - Increase the spin by changing grip and finger pressure. Relax your fingers and wrist more.
  - If the ball is rising too much, make one or more of these adjustments:
  - Shorten your stride.
  - Make sure your release point is not too far in front of your body. Don't hang on so long.
  - Reduce the amount of follow-through.
  - Relax your grip, particularly the thumb pressure.
  - Lower your shoulder to get under the ball instead of bending at the back and getting behind the ball.

Curveball

- Be careful not to exaggerate your lean to the glove side. Too much lean will lead to a loss of control and will often result in a drop ball as you come over the ball. Let your wrist and shoulder create the spin.

- If the ball is sailing, make sure you are not throwing too fast. Think *spin* instead of *speed*. Also, check that you are not stepping forward with the right foot at release, which would carry your shoulder forward. Instead, drag your back foot to create body resistance.

- If the ball is rising instead of curving, make sure your right shoulder is not folding against your right side at release. Allow your elbow to move away from your body, and use a higher right shoulder.

- To maximize the curve, visualize a series of dots from the mound to the outside corner of the plate. Pitch along those dots.
- Experiment with striding across the body to see if you can improve your wrist snap and your ability to keep the ball in the strike zone. With the catcher in receiving position behind the plate, aim your stride foot at the catcher's left foot instead of her right foot to evaluate the effect of the stride on your curve.

Screwball

- Remember that using the legs is crucially important to the success of this pitch.
- Make sure you have open hips.
- Create a good body angle with a slight tilt forward, and get on top of the leg.
- Think of the pitch in two parts: (1) Drive as if throwing a fastball and get the legs and hips ready (with a lean); (2) slam hard into the front leg and finish to the right with the right foot planted almost even with the left foot.
- Finish with the arm in a hitchhiker position.
- Make sure the arm stays bent and higher (belly button height) through the snap.
- Keep in mind that if the arm extends too long through the snap, this will make the pitch drop at the end.

Changeup

- Remember that deception is the key to success. Have teammates and coaches look for any changes in your delivery that telegraph the changeup. Use a videotape to compare deliveries.
- Keep the ball low in the strike zone. Turn your thumb down at release, and keep the follow through low.
- Don't always throw a changeup in a given situation. Vary your pitch selection.
- Use the changeup to set up other pitches. For example, after throwing a changeup that is low and outside, you could throw a fast drop ball that is low and in.
- Do not throw a changeup to a batter who doesn't stride. The premature stride is what pulls batters off balance.
- Remember this: Great changeup pitchers don't throw the change near the strike zone where it can be hit. They get the strike by fooling the batter and getting her to swing at the motion, not the pitch. The ball may bounce in front of the plate, but the batter has already started to swing.

In General

- Remember that you are practicing and learning all of these pitches so you can use them as tools or weapons. Realize that you may be a different pitcher on a different day—and get comfortable with that. Be comfortable being uncomfortable.
- When a pitch isn't working, try to have success without it. Reestablish the pitch later if you can. The pitch can still be effective even if you're not having your best day with it.
- Don't overuse any one pitch during a game unless you are completely dominating a team. By using even a little bit of a mix, you will keep your best pitch sharper.

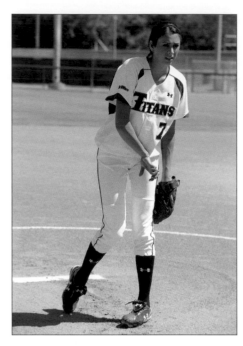

Figure 11.21 Back-of-the-hand changeup follow-through.

If the pitcher wants to put more sidespin on the ball, the back of the hand will brush the hip, and the pinkie will face the catcher (instead of having the back of the hand facing the catcher). After the ball is released, the hand continues around the front of the body and across the waist. The elbow is bent, and the pitcher focuses on driving the elbow directly toward the catcher.

- **Follow-through**—At release, the thumb is angled down slightly, and the follow-through is across the waist (see figure 11.21). The hand should finish below the hip to keep the ball angled down. If the thumb is pointing at the hip on release, the ball has a tendency to arc up before it goes down. Hanging a change can be costly.

SPECIFIC PITCH DRILLS

Use these drills to develop and feel the finer points of specific pitches. Emphasizing and seeing the visual patterns for each pitch will also help develop the proper release point and follow-through. Pitching under pressure is much more difficult than throwing in the bullpen, so coaches should also use competitive drills to create gamelike pressure during pitching practice.

Drop-Ball Drills

These drills can be used to work on the specific mechanics of this pitch. They teach proper mechanics and develop muscle memory.

LOW NET THROWS

Purpose: To focus on proper release and keeping the drop ball low.

Procedure: From a distance of about 10 feet (3 m), the pitcher throws into the bottom of a catch net, exaggerating her release of the drop.

BASKET THROWS

Purpose: To focus on making the ball drop by using a visual target.

Procedure: The pitcher throws from the regular distance and attempts to pitch the ball into a laundry basket at home plate. This drill helps imprint the image that the pitcher should see before every drop pitch. The pitch can be thrown to a bucket, but the ball will not ricochet as much off the softer basket.

BOUNCE BALL

Purpose: To develop the drop-ball release and a hard snap.

Procedure: The pitcher stands across from the catcher, who is also standing, at a distance that is about half the distance from the mound to the plate. A power line is drawn. Using a two-toned weighted ball, the pitcher takes a proper grip on the ball. Starting in the open position, she simulates her motion at about 50 percent speed. The pitcher attempts to snap the ball directly into the ground and out toward the catcher. Ideally, the ball will bounce on the ground about halfway between the two and then right up to the catcher's chest. A simpler version of this drill is for the pitcher to snap the ball directly down into the ground and back up to herself. Of course, this method is not as realistic as throwing to the catcher.

ROPES

Purpose: To learn to throw drops with proper break and movement.

Procedure: Set up two tees in front of both batter's boxes. Tie a bungee cord or rope to each tee at about the height of a hitter's knee. The rope should run across the entire strike zone from one batter's box to the other. The pitcher throws the drop pitch in a walk-through motion at 75 to 80 percent speed while trying to make the ball break over the rope and into the catcher's glove. This drill simulates where the ball should break, and it forces the pitcher to make the ball move and not just throw a low pitch.

The pitcher then throws drop balls while walking through at the mound. She starts at about 75 percent speed. Every three to five pitches, she adds a little more speed until she gets to 100 percent. (This helps the player ease into the pitch, but the drop is really the only pitch that you can do this with.) Once the pitcher has gotten the hang of the drill, she throws full out from the mound.

Rise-Ball Drills

These drills can be used to work on specific rise-ball mechanics and particularly the correct spin and release.

FOOTBALL TOSS

Purpose: To develop the correct rise-ball release.

Procedure: The pitcher throws a junior-size football underhand to a partner. She grips the ball with all the fingers along the seam, and the thumb is on the opposite side. When thrown, the ball should spiral. If it wobbles in flight, the pitcher's palm has turned toward the catcher at release.

LONG TOSS

Purpose: To practice getting under the ball for the rise-ball release. This also develops body and arm strength.

Procedure: The pitcher pitches to a catcher from second base or farther away, lobbing the ball up as if she is throwing it over a telephone pole. This action forces the pitcher to get under the ball. To develop strength, the pitcher keeps backing up from second base (moving back to center field and then to the fence) to see how far she can throw it.

Changeup Drills

These drills help pitchers work on location and on keeping the delivery consistent.

BUCKET TOSS

Purpose: To practice keeping the changeup pitch low.

Procedure: The pitcher pitches the ball into a bucket 2 to 3 feet (.6 to 1 m) in front of home plate. She avoids having a big loop in the pitch.

FAST AND SLOW

Purpose: To practice changing speeds.

Procedure: Working with a catcher, the pitcher alternates throwing fast and off-speed pitches. The goal is to keep the delivery the same.

Gamelike Drills

These drills prepare pitchers for the challenges that can come during the game. The more realistic the practice, the more comfortable and confident they will feel.

DUMMY OR LIVE STAND-INS

Purpose: To practice a pitch in a realistic setting.

Procedure: Various types of pseudohitters are on the market that can stand in and simulate a hitter. Or a teammate can stand there as a hitter (not swinging) so that the pitcher can perfect a new pitch. If the stand-in is holding a bat, the catcher must be in full gear. (We have seen balls hit the bat and ricochet into the catcher's face.) Once the pitcher feels ready, move to the field and have hitters try to hit the specific pitch that the pitcher is working on.

PLAY A GAME

Purpose: To experience gamelike pressure during pitching practice.

Procedure: The pitcher pitches a specific number of innings with the catcher calling balls and strikes. If there is a batter standing at the plate, she should assume different positions in the box and should stand in as both a left-handed batter and a right-handed batter.

THREE POINTS

Purpose: To create competition and pressure for the pitcher when pitching to a catcher's targets.

Procedure: The catcher gives a target; for advanced players, the catcher may also call a pitch. If the pitcher hits the target, she gets one point. If she misses, she loses a point. When the pitcher reaches three points, the game is over. Increase the difficulty by requiring every fourth pitch to be a changeup.

ON THE BLACK

Purpose: To attempt to place pitches on the black edges of the plate

Procedure: The pitcher tries to strike out live batters without throwing a strike by placing pitches on the very edges of the plate. (Only the white of the plate is a strike.) The catcher or coach charts the location of the pitches.

CHAPTER 12

PITCHING PRACTICE AND GAME MANAGEMENT

The amount of time that pitchers devote to practice depends on their age, goals, and commitment. College pitchers usually throw at least five days a week. The length of practice is usually based on time (typically one hour per day) or a certain number of pitches. Each pitcher should find the system that works best for her. A pitcher should not quit before she is tired nor go too far beyond the onset of fatigue. She must push herself, but realize that when fatigue sets in, fundamentals start to break down. Only perfect practice makes perfect.

To make the most of practice, the pitcher should have a plan and purpose for each day. Each pitcher should have a routine and should follow that routine every day in practice. Pitchers should also set goals every day in practice. To prepare her to do her best in the game, the pitcher's practice must be gamelike. She should know the drills that she needs to work on during practice in order to target her specific needs, and she should use a shortened version of that routine to get ready for game day.

The pitcher should throw to a real catcher and use a home plate whenever possible. She should vary the number of pitches of the same type that she throws consecutively and should alternate speeds. Practice should include game situations and throwing to live batters. This allows the pitcher to fight through adversity in practice, which helps prepare her for the game. For practice to carry over to the game, the pitcher must pitch in practice just as she would pitch in a game.

Pitchers should make conditioning a priority. Pitchers can never run enough. They should strengthen their legs because the legs can give out in a game. A weight training program will increase overall body strength and improve power. At the end of every pitching practice, pitchers should put ice on their arm to prevent swelling and soreness.

WARMING UP AND PRACTICING

A total-body warm-up is as important for a pitcher as it is for any other player. Pitchers should start with jogging to increase their body temperature. Then they should perform a good stretching program to stretch all the major muscle groups and to loosen up their joints. To begin warming up the arm, pitchers can throw easily overhand, then pitch slowly at a short distance (see figure 12.1), working on tempo and timing. Pitchers

Figure 12.1 Pitching from a short distance to set tempo, timing, and mechanics.

should start with three or four drills that help them check their mechanics every day. These core drills should become part of their prepractice and pregame routine.

Next, the pitchers can start working on the mound by throwing fastballs and hitting spots. After warming up with fastballs, the pitchers can move on to the changeup, getting it loose and mixing the change and the fastball together. Then they should concentrate on ball spin and work on one pitch at a time until each is working to their satisfaction. Pitchers should start in a short position, throwing at about 50 percent speed while working on the spins for *every* pitch (including the changeup). They move back gradually, increasing speed and distance until they are throwing full speed from the mound. The pitchers should throw at full intensity, with plenty of spin, but the arm swing should be loose. Each pitcher should begin with her primary pitch and work down the middle of the plate before moving to the corners. As she does so, she visualizes the path of a successful pitch, warming up mentally as well as physically.

A pitcher should not struggle with a pitch that is not working. She should go back to the basics, beginning with the spin and release, and make the necessary adjustments.

COACHING POINTS FOR COACHING PITCHERS

- Pitchers need to practice positive thoughts in their workouts. Coaches can help by pointing out the positives.

- Pitchers need to take the emotion out of pitching.

- Coaches always have a lot of information to give pitchers. Make sure the pitchers get the information a little at a time so they can work on one or two things at a time. Also make sure they know the order of importance. Be careful on game day not to give too much info. Practice is the place to get into details.

- Pitchers need to know why things are happening and how they can affect the outcome. Have the pitchers give you feedback and play an active role in finding what works best for them.

- Sometimes slowing things down or going back to square one is the best approach. Never let a pitcher bang her head against the wall too long. Move on to something that is productive. Pictures and video can be helpful especially for those who are visual learners.

- Certain traits will help a player become a successful pitcher. Coaches should look for these traits in their pitchers:
  - Athletic
  - Flexible
  - Strong wrist snap
  - Powerful
  - Quick reactions
  - Strong work ethic
  - Coachable
  - Mentally tough
  - Competitive
  - Confident, determined, highly motivated, and driven

Then she can throw all of her pitches hard, pinpointing targets and working with the catcher. This is the time to discuss the game plan—which pitches are working well, which do not feel as comfortable, and so forth.

Pitchers must tailor their workouts to where they are in the season and what they need to work on. For example, early in the year, workouts should be focused on improving mechanics and accuracy. These workouts will likely last longer because players' skills need sharpening and the players can push a little harder without it affecting a competitive performance. As they progress, they move from their best pitch to their worst, and they work on mastery of each. By the end of these "getting back in shape" sessions, the pitchers should be game ready.

For in-season practice, a pitcher should plan her week with the goal of being prepared for game day. For example, if the pitcher is going to throw on Saturday, she should start the week by "checking back in" with mechanics and the changeup. She can progress the next day to working on two pitches at a time (her better ones) along with the changeup. The third day, she can add two or three more pitches. On the fourth day, she should throw a full mix of all her pitches and maybe work with a stand-in or live hitter. The day before game day can be a shorter day. In practice, the pitcher should time her warm-up so that she knows how much time is needed to get warm and to be fully prepared by game time.

THE MENTAL GAME

Much of our philosophy about the mental game comes from the work of sport psychologist Ken Ravizza and is covered in his book *Heads-Up Baseball: Playing the Game One Pitch at a Time*. Several of his basic ideas can be applied to a pitcher's performance in practice, which directly relates to games (Ravizza and Hanson, New York: McGraw Hill, 1995, pages 79-85).

Ravizza identifies three common approaches to pitching:

1. **Prayer**—I hope I can do it.

2. **Primal**—I will pitch harder the next time.

3. **Perfect**—No mistakes.

None of these mind-sets is helpful, and all have to do with a lack of trust. Pitchers need to understand that they don't have to be perfect or have their A game all the time to be successful. They must keep it simple, and they must compensate and adjust. All players have strengths and weaknesses. Having a good performance does not mean being perfect; it means adjusting more easily to adversity—staying positive and being able to get rid of any negative thoughts.

The most important point to reiterate is that athletes play like they practice. What a player does in practice and the way she approaches her work in practice will be directly reflected in her performance in a game. A player's reaction to pressure situations and her level of confidence are not determined in the moment; they are determined by her mental preparation in practice.

Playing with confidence means that a player can successfully handle fear simply by trusting her ability and the work that she has put in. Think of it as "putting the hay in the barn"; that is, the practice and preparation—mental and physical—are stored away to be drawn from later. A big step toward attaining confidence is for a player to take responsibility for her thoughts and actions. Being in control of her thoughts and emotions allows her to control her performance.

But control is not absolute. Every pitcher needs to know what she can and cannot control. She cannot control everything that happens around her, but she can control how she chooses to respond to what happens. She *can* do whatever it takes to be in control of herself. A pitcher should learn what techniques (breathing, visualization, focal points, or following a particular routine) work best to help her let go of anxiety and negativity, allowing her to move on from a stressful situation. Then she can use those tools to handle the adversity.

Deep, relaxing breaths help loosen the shoulders and release any tension. They also help shut out distractions and focus the mind. The timing of the pitcher's breath is especially important. Most pitchers should take a release breath at the back of the mound and a refocusing breath before they step on the mound or as they take the signal. Each pitcher should find what works best for her.

Here are two simple exercises that can be used to clear the mind:

1. **Trace an object**—At the back of the circle, the pitcher stands with her back to home plate. She uses her eyes to trace (in fine detail) an image on the scoreboard or something beyond the outfield. She concentrates deeply while tracing a letter on the scoreboard or a distant image (e.g., tree, building). When her mind is totally clear, she turns and begins her normal routine as she approaches the rubber to deliver the next pitch.

2. **Perform an eye shift**—The pitcher shifts her eyes to follow an imaginary pattern on the ground: right, left, up, down. She mentally calls out a command (right, left, up, or down) and then shifts her eyes to that one spot; she then randomly calls another command and shifts her eyes to that spot. She continues this drill until her mind is clear. She must not choose a command in a logical order or pattern because that eye shift can be done automatically. The process of concentrating on following the commands clears the mind.

The pitcher should look forward to practice. She should eat well and be hydrated. She should write down some attainable daily goals and visualize working successfully on an aspect of her game that she would like to improve. Having a clearly defined mission or purpose provides direction and adds intensity to pitching workouts. After practice, the pitcher can evaluate how well she did in achieving her goals and then adjust her plan as needed.

Once practice starts, the pitcher must let go of outside stressors (these stressors will be there when practice is over). This is the time for the pitcher to focus on herself. The pitcher should develop a prepractice and pregame routine that she does every time. Having a routine will help her relax and build confidence to get to the task at hand. The routine conveys the sense that she is in her element and ready to go.

The pitcher should remember that the goal of pregame work is not perfection; the goal is to get her body ready to throw and to become comfortable with her pitches. She must flush bad thoughts before setting foot on the mound. No negative thoughts are allowed there. Once on the mound, she should keep it simple—letting go of all but the most essential information and remembering to breathe.

It is also helpful for a player to have a present-moment focus of "one pitch at a time." The idea of facing an entire game's or outing's worth of challenges and pressures can be overwhelming. Rather than strive to be "on" and in control for the entire time she is

CRITICAL CUE:
A person cannot be totally focused for two hours straight. This means that a player has to determine when to be fully focused and when she can let go a little. That itself takes practice.

on the mound, the pitcher can give each pitch her full focus and take time to release tension between pitches. There should be no thinking about the pitch before and the next pitch, no thinking of the final strikeout pitch or ending the inning. Her focus must be only on the task at hand—delivering the pitch she is about to throw as well as she can.

COACHING POINTS FOR MANAGING THE MENTAL GAME

- Trust your "hay in the barn," and trust what you have.
- Focus on the glove.
- Bring your best B game.
- Be in control—use your tools to get there.
- Use your routine to get into rhythm.
- Keep it simple, don't overwhelm yourself with too much information.
- Remember that no game is bigger than another; they are all the same.

GAME MANAGEMENT

The coach or catcher may call the pitch. When someone else makes the call, pressure on the pitcher is lessened; however, the pitcher may be given the right to overrule the calls. If the pitcher does not make the final decision, she should have confidence in any call that is made.

Pitchers should be committed to each pitch they are throwing. They must believe in the success of each one. If a pitcher doubts her ability to throw a called pitch effectively, she should not throw it! The pitcher may shake off a signal with a shake of her head to indicate "no." The reason for shaking off a signal could be that the pitcher does not feel confident with that pitch in that situation, she sees the batter doing something and believes another pitch would be more effective, or she remembers what happened the last time she threw that pitch.

Shaking off a pitch can cause several problems. The catcher may believe that she knows the best pitch to throw the batter and may think that the pitcher is not trusting her judgment; in this case, a "control game" may result. A timeout may be needed to discuss the situation and reach a solution the pitcher feels comfortable with. If necessary the coach can step in. Ideally the pitcher and catcher work to develop an understanding in practice so that disagreements during the game are infrequent and easily resolved. Too many timeouts disrupt the flow of the game for the pitcher and her teammates.

If the coach is calling the game and the pitcher shakes the pitch off, everyone is in a difficult position. Because it is so important for a pitcher to have confidence in every pitch she throws, some coaches believe that the pitcher (not the catcher or coach) must call the pitch to be thrown or at least have the final say. If the coach calls the game, the coach can make it clear, well ahead of game time, that the pitcher has the power to change the call. Or the coach and pitcher can work during practice to ensure that they are on the same page so that the coach is unlikely to call pitches the pitcher is not comfortable with.

Pitchers can better understand the decision-making process by reading the relevant section in chapter 14 and studying the pitch selection charts for the batter and the situation. Chapter 14 (which covers the catcher position) includes a section on calling pitches and covers many factors that go into choosing a certain pitch (see pages 292-295).

Once the pitcher has decided on the pitch, she visualizes the pitch hitting its target. She makes a mental picture of the path of the ball, using a series of dots to mark the path to the target. This exercise increases control, ball movement, and confidence.

Pitchers must approach every pitch the same way. The steps they take to the mound, the way they put the foot on the rubber, the place they hold the ball, the focus of the eyes—every physical movement should be the same regardless of the count, the score, or the situation. Having a familiar routine relieves pressure and allows the pitcher to focus on the task (see figure 12.2). The routine creates confidence and improves consistency. A consistent routine also sends a message to teammates and to the batter that the pitcher is in complete control!

Figure 12.2 Maintaining a consistent, controlled approach improves focus, conveys confidence, and prevents the opponent from picking up the type of pitch.

Many pitchers tip off their pitches by showing too much of the ball or by using different movements for different pitches. By practicing in front of a mirror or studying video of the deliveries, pitchers can make sure that they give nothing away.

Pitchers may telegraph pitches by

- not hiding the ball or grip from the base coach or batter;
- showing more yellow or white on the ball, particularly overhead or on the backswing;
- turning the glove or wrist differently;
- presenting the ball higher or changing the arm angle on certain pitches;
- making a different sound, especially on changeups or rises; or
- standing in different spots on the mound

For more ways that pitchers tip pitches, see page 21 in chapter 1.

Getting ahead on the first pitch is an important goal. Many batters take the first pitch. If this pitch is a strike, the chance that the batter will walk is greatly diminished. Pitches should be thrown to the corners of the plate, never through the center.

Pitchers should evaluate their pitches honestly. They should know their best pitch for each location, their poorest pitches, their strikeout pitch, and the pitch they'll throw when they need a strike. When pitchers are away from the practice and playing field, they should take time to think about their pitching performance. They need to analyze where things went wrong, how they handled it, and how to correct things in practice. By learning to "own" their skill, pitchers will be better able to make good corrections in practice and in games.

Pitchers know they will give up some hits, but they should remember that the outs they get will far outnumber the hits they allow. A great hitter will succeed only 4 times in 10.

The defense will get her out 60 percent of the time. Keeping in mind that the batter will fail most of the time—and that eight players are behind her to help when the batter does hit the ball—encourages the pitcher to adopt a confident attitude: *What is the big worry?*

Much of the game is out of the pitcher's control. The pitcher's only job is to throw the ball to the target. Pitchers have no power over what happens after that. When they realize this, the job of throwing each pitch becomes much easier. What pitchers can control is how they respond to what is going on around them!

Pitchers should avoid showing emotion on the mound. By letting the batter know that they've lost control, pitchers give the batter the advantage. Umpires are people too and don't like to be shown up in a game. Seldom will pitchers get a call if they have reacted negatively to the previous one. Instead, pitchers should use that energy to focus on a plan of attack for the next pitch. They should evaluate their performance and adjust as needed; then they should go into their routine and step up to give their best.

To be a team player, the pitcher must support her teammates the way she would want to be supported. In other words, the pitcher acknowledges great plays made behind her. If she pitches a no-hitter, she gives credit to the catcher. When a teammate makes an error, the pitcher exhibits no more displeasure than what she wants to receive when she unintentionally gives up a walk. When a fielder has a bad day and really needs support, the pitcher should be the first to offer encouragement. The pitcher is the center of attention and should use her position to be a leader.

CHAPTER 13

PITCHER AS A DEFENSIVE PLAYER

Once the pitch is delivered, the pitcher must prepare to function as another infielder. She quickly assumes a well-balanced position with the glove out in front of the body, the fingers up, and the pocket open toward the batter. A pitcher's defensive ability (fielding and throwing) will determine her defensive assignments. If the pitcher is an excellent fielder, the coach may want her to play every ball that she can easily reach. If she is less skilled than the first- and third-base players, she may be limited to backing them up and fielding only balls hit directly to her. The pitcher should know where the infielders are playing and should be careful not to deflect balls that are clearly another fielder's responsibility. Making an out on a deflected ball is extremely difficult.

Pitchers must often field slow rollers and push bunts that are going toward second base. Because the pitcher is running toward first, an underhand throw is the safest, the easiest to see, and the most accurate. The pitcher should field the ball with two hands when possible to make sure she catches it. For maximum reach, she may need to reach with only the glove and then quickly bring the hands together to get a grip for throwing. For the underhand throw, she locks the elbow and wrist and straight-arms the ball to the first-base player (see figure 13.1). The pitcher uses the same technique for the throw home on suicide bunts, concentrating on keeping the toss low for the tag. For all other plays, a good overhand throw is needed.

Figure 13.1 Straight-arm underhand throw.

POP-UPS

The general rule is that the pitcher catches any ball within the pitcher's circle or any popped-up bunts that aren't airborne long enough for the corners to reach them (see figure 13.2). On pop-ups to the other players, the pitcher can provide valuable assistance about the direction of the ball (up, back, first, third) and can warn of obstacles and fences. The pitcher may need to cover the base of the fielder catching the ball.

BACKING UP

The pitcher must back up all throws to the catcher from the outfield. When the play will be on the lead runner going to third, the pitcher should back up third base. If it is not clear where the play will be, the pitcher first runs across the foul line midway between third and home and then looks for the play before deciding where to go. The normal backup position is 15 feet (4.5 m) behind the receiver.

Figure 13.2 The pitcher is responsible for pop-ups in or near the pitching circle.

Occasionally, a base is left uncovered. This can happen when two players are going after a fly ball. The pitcher must look for any vacated base and quickly move to cover it. She should also be prepared to back up or participate in rundowns.

On a wild pitch or passed ball with a runner on third, the pitcher must cover home. As the catcher chases the ball, the pitcher continuously calls the catcher's name and waves her arms until the ball is released. The pitcher assumes a foot position at home that protects her legs from being taken out on a slide and gives the runner a corner to go to (see figure 13.3). She bends the knees, lowers the hips, and establishes a balanced position to apply the tag.

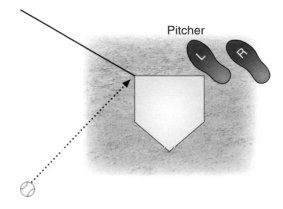

Figure 13.3 **Pitcher's foot position when covering home.**

CHECKING RUNNERS

The pitcher must be aware of all runners on base and must always consider them a threat to advance. As soon as she receives the ball in the circle, the pitcher checks the position of the runners; she checks the lead runner first. The pitcher must understand the look-back rule and use it to her advantage. When the pitcher has the ball in the circle and has caused the runner to stop after rounding a base, the runner must immediately advance or return to the base. The runner cannot delay, fake, or reverse direction. Once the runner returns to the base, she cannot leave again as long as the pitcher holds the ball. By understanding and effectively using this rule, the pitcher stops runners from advancing and takes the pressure off the defense.

Rules Pitchers Must Know:

Pitchers should know all rules pertaining to pitching so that their team is never penalized as a result of a pitcher breaking a rule. The rules that pitchers need to know include the following:

- Number of warm-up pitches the league allows at the start of the inning, when returning to pitch after having previously been removed, and when a pitcher is being replaced
- Ball rotation—when and how to get a new ball
- Time allowed between pitches
- Foreign substances on the ball, the use of resin, and the use of tape on fingers
- Illegal pitch, quick pitch, and no pitch
- Look-back rule
- Pitching within the width of the mound—staying within the pitching lane
- Feet on the rubber, front foot and drag foot

DRILLS FOR THE PITCHER AS A DEFENSIVE PLAYER

Pitchers must work on their fielding techniques to strengthen the infield. Including conditioning will give pitchers the strong legs they'll need to go the distance in a game.

PITCHERS FIELD AND COVER FIRST

Purpose: **To practice fielding all types of balls after delivering a pitch. This is an excellent conditioning drill as well.**

Procedure: **The drill works best with at least three pitchers, a catcher, and a hitter. If you don't have three pitchers, another player may play first, and pitchers rotate only on the mound. Pitchers form a single-file line at the mound, and one pitcher is at first to catch the throw. The pitcher pitches the ball to the catcher, and the hitter hits a ground ball back to the pitcher for fielding practice. The pitcher fields, throws to first, and then rotates to first to receive the throw from the next pitcher. After catching at first, the receiver rotates to the end of the fielding line. Vary the types of balls hit, hitting to each side of the pitcher and bunting and slapping as well. Include a sequence in which pitchers look imaginary runners back before making the throw.**

COVERING HOME

Purpose: **To practice footwork for covering home on wild pitches with a runner at third.**

Procedure: **Pitchers rotate on the mound, and catchers rotate at home. The pitcher throws a wild pitch (left or right, over her head, in the dirt) to the catcher in receiving position and then runs home to cover the plate for the return throw. The pitcher's feet must be well out of the way of the sliding runner. The pitcher should call the catcher's name and wave her arms until the throw is on its way. The pitcher receives the ball and makes a tag. Once it is clear that the pitcher knows how to assume a safe position, add actual runners to work on timing and tags.**

KNOCKDOWNS

Purpose: **To simulate a ball hit hard back to the pitcher off her shins or somewhere else on her body.**

Procedure: **The pitchers line up at the mound, and the first pitcher starts about 2 feet (.6 m) in front of the mound, facing home plate. A receiver (with a bucket to place caught balls into) is at first base, ready for the pitcher's throw. A coach with a ball stands close to the pitcher. The pitcher closes her eyes, and the coach gently tosses a ball off the pitcher's body. The pitcher has to find the ball, scoop it up with two hands, and throw to first. As an alternative, the coach can hit the ball to the pitcher, who catches it, drops it, and then has to quickly recover and throw. (As a variation, the pitcher can also kick the ball after dropping it.)**

RUN THE BALL TO FIRST

Purpose: To recognize when to run the ball and underhand toss it to first base instead of throwing overhand. This method is used when no one is on base, the ball is hit between first base and the pitcher, and the batter is not a slapper. It is also used if the pitcher has a poor overhand throw.

Procedure: Pitchers line up single file at the mound; a fungo hitter is at home (with a bucket of balls), and a receiver is at first. The pitcher begins with a windup without a ball, and the fungo hitter hits a ball directly at the pitcher or to the first-base side of the mound. The pitcher fields the ball first, then turns and runs toward first base. At the same time, she takes the ball out of her glove (hanging her throwing arm down to her side and out in front of her) with the palm of her hand behind the ball. When the pitcher gets a few feet from first base, she locks her elbow and pushes the ball underhand to the first-base receiver. The receiver puts the ball in a bucket. The pitcher returns to the end of the pitching line or replaces the receiver at first.

BACKING UP

Purpose: To incorporate the pitcher into defensive situational practice by having her back up third base or home.

Procedure: When a ball is hit to the outfield, the pitcher runs to foul territory on the third-base side in between home and third base, looking to see which base to back up. Depending on where the ball is hit and which base the runner is going to, the pitcher either backs up third or home.

DEFENSIVE REPS

Purpose: To have the pitcher practice fielding all types of balls and throwing to all bases.

Procedure: The pitcher goes through her pitching motion before she fields each ball. The pitcher must finish her complete motion before fielding so that bad habits do not form. Place buckets at each base to put balls in after they are caught. One receiver can rotate to different bases.

- *Grounders*—The pitcher goes through her motion, and ground balls are hit to every side so she can work on forehand, backhand, and straight-on fielding and throwing the ball. Work reps to every base, ensuring proper footwork and fielding mechanics.

- *Line drives*—Line drives (high and low) are hit to every side. Start off with slower hit balls and progress to harder shots. This drill helps pitchers build better confidence in fielding line drives. It teaches them to perform the proper fielding mechanics instead of shying away and then reacting. Eventually, pitchers react automatically because the fielding mechanics become muscle memory.

- *Pop-ups*—Pop-ups of all kinds are hit: short, low, high, foul, in between the catcher and pitcher. Also practice short but deep pop-ups that are over the pitcher's head so she learns to eliminate the chance of a blooper falling behind the mound for a base hit.

(continued)

Defensive Reps **(continued)**

- *Bunts*—The coach stands in the batter's box and tosses a bunt down either the first-base line or the third-base line. The pitcher practices going to every base (including home for the squeeze). Make sure the pitcher's feet line up properly for throws to the corresponding base. The force of the bunt dictates which footwork should be used.

THE CATCHER

As the only player who faces the entire field of play, the catcher has a unique opportunity to direct the defensive play of the team. A catcher can also help the pitching staff immeasurably by knowing the pitcher's abilities that day, by studying the batters, and by using that knowledge to exploit the batters' weaknesses. A good catcher also works with each pitcher's personality to bring out her best while helping her stay in control. The catcher and the pitcher (the battery) must work as a team if they are to be successful.

Successful catchers will demonstrate the following skills and characteristics:

- Agility and quick feet
- Strong arm and soft hands
- Quick reaction time and hustle
- Exceptionally strong knees and legs
- Size (bigger and taller) for blocking the plate and catching high and wide pitches
- Leadership of both the defense and the pitching staff
- Student of the game

Tradition says that a catcher should be a right-handed thrower so that a right-handed batter will not interfere with throws to second. Of course, left-handed batters will interfere in the same way on their side of the plate. Today we see an increasing number of good left-handed catchers. A left-handed catcher has a couple of advantages: Her body is in perfect position to field bunts and throw to first, and a runner at first cannot see her throwing arm during pickoff attempts. A good catcher is a good catcher no matter which arm she throws with.

EQUIPMENT

Catchers use a softball catcher's glove or a first-base player's glove with a web. To reduce the risk of common injuries—including bruising of the index finger and "fastpitch thumb" (in which the ligaments become jammed)—catchers must use a large pocket that provides some protection. The mask must fit snugly, be lightweight, and include some kind of throat protection. Full helmets are required at most levels, and the most common are the hockey-style masks, which don't require an additional throat protector attachment. These helmets are made to fit so that catchers can keep them on during all activities but can be easily removed if the catcher chooses. All protective gear must fit snugly. The chest protector should not sag or slide around and should protect the shoulders and collarbone as well as the chest. It should allow enough freedom to throw comfortably. Shin guards should include flaps to cover the top of the foot, and they should fit tightly so that they do not turn. These *must* fit to size. Many companies make shin guards, and all shin guards fit a little differently. Make sure they don't move at all when the catcher runs.

BASIC RECEIVING STANCE

Catchers squat about 150 times in a game. They can save their knees by going down with both heels on the ground as far as they can and then going to the toes.

The basic receiving position must be comfortable and well balanced, and it should allow the catcher to rise and move quickly. The feet are a little wider than the shoulders; the weight is on the inside of the feet and on the balls of the feet (see figure 14.1). The feet are in a half-step stagger with the glove-arm leg in front and the back foot even with the instep of the front foot. This position promotes a faster body turn as the catcher opens to throw. The knees are slightly angled in, and the heels lightly touch the ground. The butt is low as if sitting on a small stool.

With runners on, the catcher must raise the hips and butt, pressing the heels flat on the ground. Keeping the heels down has them in a position to push off immediately. The elbow(s) are in front of and outside the knees. The catcher takes a position in the box as close to the batter's back leg as possible without interfering with the swing. This position is usually within 2 to 3 feet (.6 to 1 m) of the batter's back leg. To protect her bare hand, the catcher places it on the side of her body, touching down close to her shoe. The best position from which to make a quick throw is to have the hand behind the thumb of the glove, but that position leaves the hand more exposed to injury. Most catchers can keep the hand positioned at the side without sacrificing too much speed. The fingers should always be closed in a loose fist with the thumb inside.

Figure 14.1 **Basic receiving position.**

GIVING THE TARGET

The catcher can help the pitcher be more accurate by showing her where to throw the ball. The glove should be as large as possible and held stationary until the ball has been released. By moving her body behind the glove, the catcher offers a bigger target. When moving her body, the catcher must be careful not to move too early and tip off the batter.

The catcher must know how much the ball breaks for each pitcher. If a pitcher is missing consistently, the receiver adjusts the target in the direction opposite the error. The catcher should know what the pitcher looks at when throwing. If the pitcher aims at the glove and the ball breaks from there, the catcher places the target on the corners. If the pitcher throws so that the ball breaks and lands in the glove, the catcher places the target just outside the strike zone.

CATCHING THE BALL

When receiving pitches, the catcher has her glove arm slightly bent at the elbow with the glove extended in front of the body. The shoulders are relaxed, and the elbows are down. The catcher does not reach for the ball. She lets the ball come to her and then gives with the catch. The catcher should attempt to catch all pitches with the fingers pointed up or toward the pitcher. Only on extremely low balls should the glove turn down. A pitch caught in that way rarely earns a strike call from the umpire.

More advanced catchers can point the fingers (the top of the glove) at the pitcher with the palm down after giving the target. This downward flip puts a break in the wrist and keeps it relaxed. As the ball is caught, the wrist gives with the pitch, and the glove backs up. This saves the hand and arm while helping to secure the ball.

The catcher focuses on the flight of the ball from the moment it is released until the batter hits it or the catcher secures it in the glove. The catcher must not shut her eyes. She can force a blink just before the pitcher releases the ball so that the eyes can stay open during the flight of the pitch.

The catcher must stay low until the umpire makes the call, being sure not to move and obstruct the umpire's view. For balls that are just out of the strike zone, the catcher shifts her body, but not her feet, to catch the ball. When the ball is farther out, she steps in the direction of the ball and shuffles her feet to make the catch.

Framing

Framing the ball is the technique of catching the outside of the ball as if the glove were a frame around a picture. By showing the umpire this view, the catcher can better sell the pitch as a strike. She catches the sides of the ball for inside and outside pitches, and she catches the top of the ball for high and low pitches (see figure 14.2, *a-d*). When possible, she catches low pitches with the palm down. When she catches a low pitch with the palm facing up, the catcher has effectively widened the picture, causing the ball to look lower than it is. On the catch, she rotates the wrist slightly toward the plate and holds the position until the umpire makes the call. The catcher should not use this technique when the pitch is obviously a ball because the umpire will think she is begging or test-

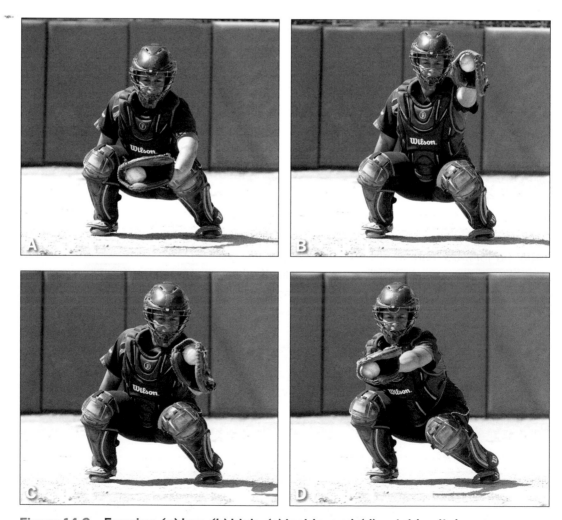

Figure 14.2 Framing *(a)* low, *(b)* high, *(c)* inside, and *(d)* outside pitches.

ing the umpire's intelligence. To practice framing, have a partner stand in front of the squatting catcher and move a ball on a stick to simulate low, high, inside, and outside pitches. The catcher moves the glove to frame each pitch.

Blocking Balls

Low balls that can't be caught should always be blocked. Even with the bases empty, the catcher should be in the habit of blocking all balls in the dirt. This effort gives the pitcher confidence in throwing drops, and it keeps the catcher sharp.

The catcher must try to keep her body in front of the ball and keep the ball in front of her body, using the chest protector to block the ball. On low balls directly to her, she replaces her feet with her knees (see figure 14.3). She kicks out as quickly as possible, as if ropes were tied to her ankles and pulled out from under her. The receiver gets low to the ground, falling on the shin guards. The body should be in the shape of a *C* over the ball and angled to the plate. The arms are relaxed with both hands on the ground. The catcher shrugs the shoulders forward, and with the chin down, she looks the ball into the chest protector. The glove is used to protect the trap door (i.e., the gap between the legs) as well as the lower body. The glove is open, but the goal is to block and stop the ball, not to catch it. The bare hand is close by, ready to grip the ball for any throw or tag. With a runner at third, the catcher must think of blocking and smothering the ball. With a runner at first, she should try to block it, catch, and throw.

Figure 14.3 Blocking the ball low in front.

On a ball to the side, the catcher must make every effort to get behind the ball. The hands initiate movement to the ball. The catcher follows the hands by jumping in the direction of the ball and landing on the knees (see figure 14.4). The emphasis is on driving the outside knee out and down. The body must be angled with the belly button toward the plate so that balls will rebound forward instead of bouncing away sideways. The glove goes down to block any gap under the legs. Every catcher has a weak side and can compensate by turning the body a little more toward the plate on the weak side.

The catcher can also step in the direction of the ball with the nearer foot and drop down on the back knee. She pushes off with the back foot, supporting her weight with the stepping leg. The glove is pointed down, and the body is over the ball and angled to the plate.

Figure 14.4 Blocking the ball to the side on both knees.

Passed Balls and Wild Pitches

To prepare for the possibility of a passed ball or wild pitch, the catcher should throw balls at the backstop before each game to see how and if they rebound. If a ball gets by in the game, the catcher can then go straight to the ball. The catcher runs hard after every ball and grabs it with both hands, positioning her body so that she is sideways to her target. She needs to keep her body low as she listens for the player covering home. This throw does not require a step, but staying low helps keep power in the legs for shifting weight from back to front. Depending on the distance of the throw, a sharp underhand throw may get the job done. An accurate sidearm throw is a good option for those who have not mastered the hard (line-drive) underhand toss. Either way, this throw needs to be practiced. It should not be overhand. The shouts of the player covering home often indicate how quickly the catcher needs to throw. When she does not have time to look, she simply throws at her teammate's voice.

Foul Tips and Foul Balls

The key to catching foul tips is to be close to the batter. The catcher reaches for the ball and doesn't pull the glove back when catching it. She must remember that on caught foul tips the ball is live and in play. With inside pitches to a right-handed batter, the ball will usually be fouled off to the catcher's left. Outside pitches will be fouled to the catcher's right.

As soon as the catcher realizes that the ball has been fouled off in the air, she should pivot with her legs, stay in a low position, and explode in the direction of the ball. She should not stand straight up because this will hinder her ability to dive for the shorter foul balls. The pitcher or the corners should help by calling the direction of the ball, saying something such as "Up three" or "Up one." If the ball is over the catcher's right shoulder, she turns to the right. A ball over the left shoulder calls for a pivot to the left. Foul balls behind the plate have a tendency to drift toward the infield. Therefore, whenever possible, infielders should make the play.

If the mask does not hinder the catcher's vision, then leaving the mask on is the safer and easier option. (Wearing a helmet makes the mask more difficult to remove.) If the mask obstructs the catcher's vision or she feels more comfortable catching with the mask off, she can remove it after determining the direction of the ball. The catcher must not drop the mask until the ball is located. Then, as she goes after the ball, she tosses the mask in the opposite direction, far enough away that she will not step on it.

Catching the ball with the glove above the shoulders provides some time to recover should the ball be bobbled. Basket catches are more difficult to master, but they are sometimes the best choice when the ball is spinning and descending in an unpredictable path. Balls that the catcher plays with her back to the infield usually drift back to her.

Intentional Walks

When the pitcher throws far outside to walk the batter intentionally, the catcher stands upright facing the pitcher; the catcher's feet are at the extreme edge of the catcher's box on the opposite side from the batter. For a right-handed batter, the catcher reaches out with the right arm parallel to the ground and uses a fist or glove as a target. For a left-handed batter, this is reversed. After the pitcher releases the ball, the catcher quickly moves behind the ball to be certain of making the catch.

Pitchers who have difficulty throwing accurately to the extended glove can instead throw to the outside shoulder of the catcher as she stands at the edge of the box. The catcher's body provides a bigger target, and the catcher is in a better position (behind the ball) to catch the pitch (see figure 14.5).

The defense must protect against a pitch thrown so close to the batter that it could be hit. Because the ball will be pitched outside, the corner player on the same side of

Figure 14.5 Position for an intentional walk when the pitcher aims at the catcher's outside shoulder.

the diamond as the outside pitch must stay back in case the batter reaches out and goes with the pitch. For a right-handed batter, the first-base player plays back in regular position. The third-base player moves way in to cover home in case of a wild pitch.

THROWING TO BASES

To throw out runners, a catcher needs a strong arm, a quick release, and quick feet. Having a strong arm is great, but having an accurate arm is even more important. A catcher with a strong arm is no good to anybody if she keeps throwing the ball hard to center field. Each of these aspects can be improved with practice and by using proper techniques. Good catchers stop runners who try to advance. They also give the defense more time to make outs by preventing runners from getting big leadoffs.

Footwork

To get the feet into throwing position, the catcher uses either the pivot or the two-step method. A real advantage of the two-step method is that the added momentum from taking two steps puts more speed on the ball, which is beneficial for players with weaker arms. This method also works well on outside pitches and pickoff plays with a right-handed batter. The catcher can step and catch the ball in front of the throwing shoulder at the same time, a movement that provides a quick release and a stronger throw. The two-step method is more difficult and slower when used on inside pitches because the catch is in front of the left shoulder and the ball must be brought to the throwing shoulder as the step is made. With a left-handed batter, this step brings the catcher close to the batter, who may interfere with the throw. (For a left-handed catcher, of course, the foregoing situation works the opposite way.) Use of the pivot in these instances helps the catcher keep away from the batter and opens up the throwing lane. The pivot requires a strong arm, quickness, and strong legs to spin or jump into position. A good catcher is able to use either style, depending on where the ball is caught.

- **Pivot**—As the catcher starts to stand and pulls the ball back in preparation for the throw, the weight shifts to the back foot, and the body turns in that direction. The player spins on the ball of the foot until the front shoulder points at the target. When the ball and the weight are over the back pivot foot, the glove arm extends forward, and the striding foot steps in the direction of the target. Another option is a jump shift, which is simply a quarter turn and throw.
- **Two-step method**—As the catcher receives the ball, she simultaneously rises and takes a short step forward with the throwing-side foot to the ball. The stepping foot should be angled outward at about a 45-degree angle, with the inside anklebone pointing at the target. All the weight is on that foot. The catcher then takes another step directly to the target. The added momentum from taking two steps can help increase the speed of the ball. The catcher turns comfortably sideways with the feet outside the shoulders. She should check the length of the stride. On a long stride, the throw goes up. On a short step, the throw goes down. If the shoulders are not turned sideways (and the front foot is turned less than 45 degrees), the throw will drift to the shortstop side of second.

The Throw

Throwing mechanics for the catcher are similar to those for outfielders. The catcher receives the ball with both hands and quickly separates the ball from the glove. She does not bring the throwing hand across the body to get the ball. Instead, the catcher turns the body and brings the glove to the throwing hand. She then brings the ball back past the ear, making sure the ball does not drop below the shoulder. The action is similar to shooting an arrow with a bow. Keeping the hands and arms in tight will increase quickness. On the backswing, the fingers and palm rotate away from the thrower. This hand rotation is critical because it puts extra snap on the ball.

The catcher's throw differs from the outfielder's throw primarily in its more compact windup. (For information on throwing mechanics, refer to chapter 5.) In the forward motion, the elbow is above the shoulder throughout the entire throw. The catcher should think about getting both the elbows and the hands up high. The higher the throwing arm, the easier it is to pull down on the seams to produce the desired vertical spin. The catcher pulls the glove arm down inside the body to stay on the target line. Although the arms work in opposition, the action is unlike swimming, in which the arms are outside the body. That motion will pull the catcher's shoulders off line. The catcher uses the abdominal (core) muscles to pull down on the torso and increase power.

A shoulder-high pitch to the throwing shoulder promotes a quick release because it brings the catcher up to throwing position. A pitchout (waist-high outside fastball) allows the catcher to move away from the batter and concentrate entirely on the throw. For a quicker release to third, a left-handed catcher should exaggerate the stagger in the stance. The same is true for a right-handed catcher throwing to first. The exaggerated stagger turns the shoulders closer to throwing position for quick throws to the corner bases.

A batter's position in the box may appear to put her in the catcher's throwing path. The catcher should not waste precious time moving around the batter; instead, the catcher maintains her position and throws by or over the batter's head. She will not need to think about this because her hand and release point will automatically adjust to create a throwing lane and avoid hitting the batter. If there is no way the throw will get by the batter, then, depending on the batter's position in the box, the catcher either steps in front of the batter to make the throw or uses a drop step and throws behind her. Time is critical, so the catcher should always try to move directly to the target.

Pickoff throws to first or third should go to the far side of the base. Throws to second base go slightly to the inside of the base. The catcher should not aim for a perfect throw at the sliding runner's foot; a knee-high throw gives the fielder a chance to make the catch and then the tag. On a passed ball, the first-base player takes a position on the outside of the base and gives a target with her outside hand. On a bunt, the catcher throws from inside the diamond to an inside target. With a runner going to first, the throw must never go across the basepath. See chapter 7 for more details on how infielders should position themselves to cover each base.

On a low pitch, a strong catcher may choose to throw from the knees or with one knee down. She must get the hands and ball up high and concentrate on pulling down with the abdominal muscles. Strength and confidence can be developed by starting at a short distance and building up to regulation distance. The knee throwing drill on page 298 is a good way to master this skill.

Fielding Bunts

On all bunts, the catcher must get out of her squat position in a low, explosive manner. Most catchers have a tendency to stand up and then run after the bunted ball. In bunt situations, the catcher raises the hips in the receiving position as she does in a steal situation. On a bunt to the right, the catcher hustles to get in front of the ball. She does not follow (chase) and reach for the ball as it rolls. She explodes low and beats the ball; she gets in front of the ball to field it. To make an accurate throw, her body should be positioned, as she gathers the ball, in the direction of the base she is throwing to.

She picks up the ball with both hands in the middle of the body and between the legs to ensure balance. The feet are already in position to make the throw to first. Taking an extra step before throwing is fine. On a bunt to the left side and near the foul line, the catcher uses a reverse step (turning toward the glove) and then makes the throw to first or second. She throws overhand when time permits. When the catcher needs to make a quicker throw, she throws partially sidearm from a semicrouch position. Additional details on bunt coverage are provided in the section on bunt defense in chapter 9 (see page 188). If the catcher can see well with the mask on, she does not need to get rid of it on bunt plays.

OTHER DEFENSIVE RESPONSIBILITIES

Catchers do much more than catch the pitch. In addition to playing bunts in front of home plate, the catcher is responsible for holding runners tight or picking off any base runners trying to advance. A catcher needs to take charge of base runners and do everything she can to keep them from reaching home, whether this means making a force play at home or blocking the plate. Other defensive situations involving the catcher include relays, cutoffs, pickoffs, and rundowns. These are discussed in detail in chapter 9. If there are no runners on base and the batter hits an infield grounder, the catcher's responsibility is to hustle and back up first base in case of a bad throw.

Holding Runners

With runners on base, the catcher must always be expecting a steal; therefore, she cannot be in a full, deep squat. As soon as she catches the ball, the catcher must check the location of the runners from a position in front of the plate. By taking that position, the catcher shortens the throw and eliminates the possibility of slipping on the plate. The best way to stop a runner or chase her back is with the eyes. By looking and being prepared to throw, the catcher may discourage thoughts of stealing. If no throw is necessary, the catcher returns the ball sharply to the pitcher. The catcher uses the same motion for every throw, whether to the pitcher or to a base. The throw to the pitcher goes to her left shoulder, thus serving as a practice throw to second base.

Covering Home Plate

When covering home plate on a play with the bases loaded, the catcher should focus on catching the ball, tagging the base, and turning the double play to first. This is a relatively easy play because the approaching runner is not a big factor. The most difficult play for a catcher is when the runner is coming home and the catcher must catch the ball, block the plate, and make the tag. Fear of a collision can cause the catcher to take her eyes off the ball to see where the runner is. Hard contact can make it difficult to hold on to the ball. Even all the equipment is not a real comfort. Proper positioning and lots of practice under gamelike conditions can help the catcher prepare for this critical play in which a mistake means a run.

Force Plays   When there is a chance for a double play, the catcher waits to receive the ball with her throwing-side foot on the plate and her chest facing the thrower to provide a good target. Like a good first-base player, the catcher does not overcommit on the stretch; the ball must be caught first, so the catcher maintains a well-balanced receiving position. The catcher stretches to catch the ball with two hands in order to make a quicker transition to throw; then she does a quick hop-step-pivot (crow hop) toward first base to make the next play. She must not pull her foot, and she must make sure the umpire can see the foot on the base. The most important out is the one at home. Therefore, some coaches have the catcher wait behind the plate, catch the ball there, and then step on the plate with the right foot or step across with the left and drag the right foot across the plate. (This is the same action as turning a double play at second.) This position allows the catcher to adjust for errant throws and also ensures that the umpire can see the tag of the base. However, on a close play at home, the catcher must use the first method and stretch to get the ball as soon as possible. A throw to third does not require a full pivot, but the catcher must be sure to get the shoulders properly aligned as she steps toward third on the throw. When practicing the force play at home, use a runner from home so the catcher has a realistic measure of the time and quickness she needs to complete a double play.

Blocking the Plate   As the catcher waits to receive the ball, she should take a position up the third-base line 2 to 3 feet (.6 to 1 m) from home and in fair territory. The left foot is in line with the left corner of the plate, and the left leg and knee directly face the runner. If the runner slides into the leg, the knee will flex with a normal range of movement, reducing the risk of a knee injury. The feet are comfortably spread with the knees bent, and the catcher is ready to move if the ball is thrown off line. Although the lower body is square to the runner, the upper body is turned to catch the ball. Body position is relatively low, putting the catcher in a better position to catch a bounced ball or to drop down to block the ball if necessary. While making this play, the catcher is also in position to block the runner from the plate.

The catcher must focus on the ball and catch it before a play can be made. Doing this is difficult because players have a tendency to look for the incoming runner and worry about a collision. The catcher should not reach for the ball but should let it come to her. When the throw is off line, she must go get the ball and then dive back to apply the tag.

The catcher catches with both hands to secure the ball and then turns to face the runner. The body and glove are lowered to block the runner's path to the plate (see figure 14.6). The left leg remains facing the runner, and the right knee is bent and on the ground. The catcher holds the ball in the throwing hand inside the glove and places the glove on the ground in front of the left foot. The body is in a low C position facing the runner. Body weight is transferred forward as the tag is applied. The tag is made with the back of the mitt at the lowest part of the incoming runner's leg or, if she is diving, on the hand. The catcher doesn't reach to make the tag; she lets the runner tag herself. As the tag is made, the glove and arms give with the impact to keep the ball from being jarred loose. Immediately after the tag, the catcher takes both hands high in the air to prevent the runner from attempting to knock the ball loose and to be ready for any further play.

If the runner attempts to go back door (to run beyond the plate and return from behind), the catcher does not chase her. The catcher waits for the runner to come back to the plate—as the runner must—and applies the tag there.

On plays in which the runner is hung out to dry and obviously going to be out, the catcher makes the tag and tries to avoid a collision. She should remain on her feet, move up the line, and make the tag. If a runner attempts to collide with her, the catcher should use a drop step to avoid the collision and pivot away while making the tag.

Figure 14.6 Blocking the plate.

Backing Up

With no runners on or when the infield may be attempting to complete a second-to-first double play, the catcher should back up first base on ground balls to the infield or to right field. As soon as the ball is hit, the catcher runs parallel to the foul line in foul territory.

She establishes a position in a straight line with the throw and stays 10 to 15 feet (3 to 4.5 m) behind the player receiving the ball at first. The catcher does not back up first when a runner is at second or third. She never leaves the plate when there are runners who may advance to home.

WORKING WITH THE UMPIRE

The attitude of the battery and their action toward the umpire can affect the umpire's performance. The pitcher and catcher should never become emotional because no umpire likes to be embarrassed. Although intimidation may have an impact on some umpires, consistent calls do not result. Catchers, not pitchers, should ask the questions. Catchers should be calm, tactful, polite, and rational and should ask while looking straight ahead. If the catcher turns around, the crowd will notice, and an umpire may think he is being shown up. If the umpire is repeatedly not calling a certain pitch, catchers can ask if they are blocking the view and how the pitcher is missing the plate. Catchers should rarely complain and only when they know that questioning a call will keep the umpire sharp and will not be perceived as threatening. Catchers should know the umpire's strike zone; if that zone is consistent, the catchers should adjust their target appropriately. They must not be stubborn and lose strikes because they refuse to adjust. We know a hall of fame catcher who applied perfume throughout the game—it can't hurt!

The catcher should know the rules that relate to her position, including the following:

- Dropped third strike
- Batter's interference
- Checked swing appeal
- Obstruction
- Foul tip; runner stealing
- Hit by pitch
- Foul balls on bunts
- Calling time-out with runners on

GIVING SIGNALS

When giving signals, the catcher assumes a squat position with the weight on the balls of the feet, the heels up, and the knees narrow. Right-handed catchers have the glove on the left knee with the pocket facing the other knee to hide the signals from the third-base coach or runner. The bare hand is against the crotch, and the fingers are spread. Left-handed catchers must turn slightly away from third base in order to use the left knee to hide the signals (see figure 14.7). Signals should be deep, concise, consistent, and definite. Pitchers gain confidence from signals that are given quickly and firmly. Catchers must be sure that their movement does not give away the signals. The muscles in the forearm may tip off the batter. On a changeup, the catcher often jumps forward;

Figure 14.7 **Giving the signal.**

on a rise ball, the head often moves up. Each finger represents a pitch. Additionally, signals may be given with a closed fist, a wiggle of the fingers, or a combination of signals. The catcher may also pat the left or right leg to indicate an inside or outside location. A pitcher may shake off a signal if she does not agree with the pitch called. When the pitcher shakes off the catcher too often, it usually means that there are problems that need to be worked out. Other teams may see this and take advantage. It may fire them up and add momentum to their game. In between innings, the pitcher and catcher need to get on the same page.

With a runner on second, the catcher may need to use a series of signals. She should use at least three signals and predesignate which set will be live. If visibility is a problem, she can tape the ends of the fingers with athletic tape to help the pitcher see them better.

The catcher will also give signals to the defense for pickoffs and pitchouts. Because these plays require teamwork, the defensive players involved need to know that the play is on. They should give a return signal to confirm that they are ready. With this advance knowledge, they can make the necessary defensive adjustments. They can break on the pitch if they know that a pitchout is on and the batter will not be hitting the ball. The signals may be oral (using a player's last name or the team name when calling out encouragement) or physical signs, usually given when the catcher is standing before going to the squat. Sometimes the signal will indicate that the play will occur on the second pitch.

Don't assume that young catchers can quickly and precisely flash a signal. Many are not comfortable or proficient at sign giving and need to practice the skill.

MIRROR SIGNALS

Purpose: To teach the catcher to give signals that are easy to see.

Procedure: In full squat, the catcher gives signs in front of a mirror. She will be able to see what the pitcher sees. This gives the catcher an idea of how easy or difficult her signals are to read.

SIGNAL RUN-THROUGH

Purpose: To let the catcher receive constructive feedback on her signal giving.

Procedure: During practice, the catcher goes through the entire sequence of events, including sign giving. This gives the coach or pitcher an opportunity to critique any problems.

When catchers are practicing giving signals, the coach can walk around to identify the angles from which the signals can be read. Catchers must know where their teammates can see the signals and where the offense might pick them up.

CALLING PITCHES

Good catchers have the ability to observe the batter, interpret those observations, and understand how to use different pitches. They effectively use the pitcher's strengths to limit the batter's success. Although pitchers control the game, the smart and educated catcher controls the pitcher and gives her the chance to succeed.

Coaches and catchers should approach every game with a plan. Before the game, coaches should do research on the batters, team tendencies, and conditions that may affect the outcome. In warm-ups, coaches and catchers should find out what the pitcher is capable of that day. Between innings, they should study the next three batters—having the scorer or chart keeper review what those batters did last time—and develop a plan for the next inning.

Many factors must be considered in deciding what pitch to call. These include the pitcher's capabilities, what pitches are working that day, the batter's capabilities, and the game situation. Field conditions are important as well. Does a fence make the rise ball vulnerable to home runs? Is the infield soft or hard? Will ground balls get through quickly or will they die? Is the ground wet, making ground balls difficult to field? Must the team adjust for the wind?

A good plan begins by recognizing and identifying three strike zones: the hitter's zone, the pitcher's zone, and the umpire's zone (see figure 14.8). The hitter's zone is where she can make the best contact and where she likes to swing. It is smaller than the pitcher's zone and is located more in the middle of the plate and midway between the knees and armpits. The

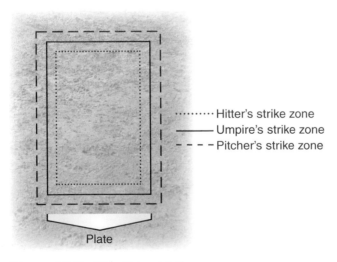

.... Hitter's strike zone
——— Umpire's strike zone
– – – – Pitcher's strike zone

Plate

Figure 14.8 The three strike zones.

pitcher's zone is the largest, because she hopes to get strike calls and swinging misses with balls slightly outside the official strike zone. The umpire's zone should be what is defined by the rule book, but it will depend on the umpire's judgment and what she or he really calls. Catchers should understand the best location for each pitch within the three zones, and they should use and adjust to the zones as necessary.

- When ahead in the count, the catcher calls for pitches to the pitcher's strike zone, just outside the batter's zone. The goal is to make the batter swing at the pitch.
- When behind in the count, the catcher calls for pitches to the umpire's strike zone while trying to avoid the batter's strength.

The catcher can apply several general rules when calling pitches:

- In tight situations, the catcher should rely on the pitcher's best pitch, not the batter's weakness. If the pitcher gets beat, let it be with her best pitch. The pitcher should challenge the hitter.
- The catcher should keep the pitcher ahead in the count. On a 2-2 count, she doesn't ask the pitcher to throw a pitch that she couldn't call for on a 3-2 count. They need the strike now!
- If the first two batters were out on their first pitch, the catcher should know that the next batter is probably taking and should go right after her with a sure strike.
- The catcher can use one pitch to set up another and increase its effectiveness. She can move the batter off the plate with an inside pitch and then use the outside corner.
- The catcher should be careful not to get into a pattern that the opponents can recognize and thus anticipate.
- After two strikes or with two out, the catcher must not let up. She must stay focused and keep the pitcher focused on throwing one pitch at a time.
- The catcher should understand the probable outcome of each pitch if it is hit. Drops tend to produce ground balls, and rises generally result in balls in the air. Outside pitches to a right-handed hitter usually go to the right side, and inside pitches are usually pulled to the left. The probable outcomes are the opposite for lefties.
- Every batter, regardless of her place in the order, deserves respect.
- As hitters develop and add power, catchers must urge their pitchers to keep the ball low, use the corners, and mix speeds.

In calling for a certain pitch, catchers and coaches can only use their best judgment based on the information available. They must believe in the call, knowing it is the best choice they can make. If the result is unfavorable, they should not second-guess the decision. Doing so will drive them crazy and cause them to doubt the next decision. Instead, they should simply take whatever can be learned from the result and save it for future reference.

What pitches should the catcher call? Table 14.1 summarizes what can be learned from the batter and how to use that information to advantage in selecting the pitch and location. Table 14.2 summarizes the game situations that must always be considered. Both coaches and catchers can use these charts to develop a plan that works for the pitcher and the team.

Table 14.1 Pitching Chart Based on the Batter

Batter	Characteristics	Weakness	Pitch and location
Psychological	Anxious approach to plate	Lacks confidence	Changeup, rise ball—high
	Swings at first pitch	Overaggressive	Waste pitch off the plate
	Made fielding error	Pressing	Waste pitch, changeup
Position in box	Up in box	High fastballs	Fastest pitch on corners Rise ball—high Changeup—low and outside
	Back in box	Balls with stuff, drop balls	Drop ball, breaking ball
	Crowds plate	Inside pitches	Fastball, curve—inside
	Off plate	Outside pitches	Fastball, changeup, curve, drop ball—outside
Size	Stands tall, is tall	Low pitches	Drop ball—inside
	Crouches	High pitches	Rise ball, high fastball—inside or outside
Hands	Chokes up	Outside pitches	Drop ball—outside
	Held high	Low pitches	Drop ball, low fastball—inside or outside
	Held low	High inside pitches	Rise ball, high fastball—inside
	Held away from body	Inside pitches	Drop ball, rise ball—inside
Stance	Closed	Inside pitches	Drop ball—inside
	Open	Outside pitches	Low pitches—outside
Stride	Away from plate	Outside pitches	Same as open stance
	Toward plate	Inside pitches	Same as closed stance
	Overstrides	High pitches	Rise ball—inside or outside Curve or changeup—low and outside
	No stride		No changeups
Weight shift	Lunges, front-foot hitter	Off-speed, high pitches	Rise ball—inside or outside Changeup or curve—outside
Swing	Late	Lacks bat speed	Fastball—inside; no changeups
	Hitch, uppercut	High pitches	Rise ball—inside or outside
	Chop	Low pitches	Drop ball—inside or outside
	Big	Off-speed pitches, outside pitches	Changeups, low outside pitches
Hitting style	Slapper	Low outside, high inside, and low inside pitches	High fastball, rise ball—inside (at head) Drop ball, low changeup—outside
	Bunter	Low pitches if batter is tall	Low inside or high inside or outside pitches
	Pull hitter	Outside pitches	Outside pitches, changeup
	Opposite-field hitter	Inside pitches	Any inside pitch
	Weak hitter	Fast pitches	No changeups or off-speed pitches

Table 14.2 Pitch Chart Based on the Game Situation

Situation	Desired result	Pitch and location (right-handed batter)
Bunt	Pop-up or poor bunt	Rise ball—inside or outside
		Drop ball—low and inside
Steal	Ball up and outside for catcher	Fastball—outside or pitchout
Runner on second	Ground ball to left side	Best low pitch—inside
Runner on third, less than two outs	Strikeout or ground ball to left side	Best low pitch—inside
	No fly balls	Strikeout pitch—low
Double-play possibility	Ground ball	Low pitch
Bases loaded, none or one out	Ground ball to left side	Low inside
Intentional walk	Called ball easy for catcher to handle	Medium fastball—well outside, chest high
Pitchout	Pitch that batter cannot hit	Fastball—outside, waist high

COACHING POINTS FOR THE CATCHER

- Remember that the catcher is like the quarterback of a football team. You must lead the defense and keep the pitcher under control at all times.

- Hustle on every ball, including passed balls, all foul balls, when covering at first, and between innings. Your alert, aggressive play can set the tone.

- Return the ball sharply to the pitcher. Don't lob it, but be sure she is ready.

- Learn to work with your pitcher. It is your job to bring out her best. You must learn how best to work together. You and the pitcher control most of the game.

- Block every ball even when the bases are empty. Doing so is good practice, increases your confidence, and lets the pitcher know she can throw the same pitch when runners are on.

- Work with the umpire. Keep your emotions under control. Never let others see you arguing or questioning a call. Ask questions to get the results you want.

- Be a team leader. All your teammates are looking to you. Use this to your team's advantage.

- Study your opponents at every available opportunity. Figure out how you can beat the batter and the team. One observation and one piece of information may make the difference.

- Be vocal. Use a commanding voice when communicating.

CATCHER DRILLS

Catchers need regular practice to develop their skills. They should practice in full gear so they learn to use their body appropriately. This also makes the drills as gamelike as possible. Catchers must regularly practice blocking balls, catching foul balls, and making throws to all bases, as well as working with the infield on turning double plays and fielding bunts. The skills that a catcher is weakest in should be practiced daily until she can confidently execute that skill.

There is never enough time to practice everything. Be careful that you do not waste the catcher's practice time by using her during infield practice to simply catch the throw from the infielders and hand the ball to the coach. Use the catcher for the portion of infield practice that does require the catcher's involvement in a true game situation. For the other parts of infield practice, have another player do the catching, or rotate infielders to act as catcher. During that time, the catchers can work on blocking, throwing, and other catcher-specific skills off to the side. Do team plays involving the catchers all at once so they can use their time well.

When catchers are practicing blocking low balls, be sure the balls are thrown like a pitched ball. Use soft safety balls or tennis balls when first beginning blocking drills, and make sure the catchers are in full gear. Catchers should practice both removing the mask and catching balls with the mask on. They should dive when necessary and be willing to get dirty! But they should dive *only* when necessary; many aggressive catchers dive for everything and miss balls they could have caught if they hadn't dived too soon or at all.

Drills for throwing out actual base runners are included in chapter 3.

NO HANDS

Purpose: To learn how to use the body to block the ball.

Procedure: Balls are thrown from about 30 feet (9 m) away. The catcher places her hands behind her back. With shoulders rounded and head down, she drops directly to her knees to block balls. The goal is to keep the ball in front of the body and near the plate. The catcher should also work on blocking balls that are a foot or two off the plate.

Variation: The catcher wears boxing gloves or special flat fielding gloves so that she doesn't try to catch the ball but blocks it instead. She keeps her hands by her knees.

WALL BLOCKS

Purpose: To learn how to block and to practice being quick off the feet.

Procedure: The catcher sets up against a cement wall, or inside a racquetball court. In full gear, she faces the wall in a squat position about 4 to 5 feet (1.5 m) away. The thrower is behind the catcher and throws a ball off the wall so it will bounce in front of the catcher, simulating a pitch in the dirt. To make it more difficult, the catcher can move closer to the wall and block a bouncier ball such as a tennis ball or racquetball. These balls move much quicker and will train the catcher to round her shoulders to keep the ball from rebounding off to the side.

COVERING HOME ON WILD PITCHES

Purpose: To practice making throws to a player covering home after recovering passed balls or wild pitches.

Procedure: The catcher assumes a squat position. Another catcher or a pitcher faces home plate and throws wild pitches that the catcher lets go by. The thrower then covers home to receive the return throw from the catcher. Alternatively, balls can be spread out around the backstop for the catcher to throw.

BLOCKING WILD PITCHES

Purpose: To practice blocking wild pitches and making subsequent throws to home.

Procedure: Taking balls from a full bucket on the pitcher's mound, the pitcher throws every ball in the dirt in front of the catcher. She should vary the pitches—some to the glove side, some right at the catcher, and some to the backhand side. After all the balls in the bucket have been thrown into the dirt, the balls will be scattered around the catcher. Before throwing the last ball, the pitcher must warn the catcher. Once this ball is blocked or gets by the catcher, the catcher must get all the balls as fast as she can. The pitcher (usually the coach) grabs the empty bucket and runs to home plate. The catcher must make accurate throws to home so the pitcher (with proper foot position for covering home) can refill the bucket. Any wild throws (throws past the pitcher covering home) must still be retrieved by the catcher and thrown to home to complete the play.

CATCHER AGILITY

Purpose: To improve agility and the ability to catch foul balls.

Procedure: The catcher lies flat on her belly. A partner tosses simulated foul balls behind the catcher, calling "Ball!" as the ball is tossed. The catcher scrambles to make the catch.

FOUL-BALL TOSS

Purpose: To practice catching foul balls.

Procedure: From the normal receiving position behind the plate, the catcher fields foul balls thrown to all areas. The tosser faces the catcher and makes an underhand toss. A pitching machine can also toss the ball. The ATEC Rookie pitching machine has a foul-ball setting that can even impart backspin.

FOUL-TIP TOSS

Purpose: To practice quick, one-step diving catches and to learn when not to dive.

Procedure: With the catcher in a normal receiving position, a coach stands in the batter's box, practicing from both the right and left sides of the plate. The coach pretends to swing through and tosses up a ball in either foul or fair territory. This drill will help the catcher develop quickness out of the catching stance. The catcher must make the decision to dive or not, but exploding low will become a must in order to be successful for this drill.

FOUL-BALL COMMUNICATION

Purpose: To practice communicating and working together to catch foul balls.

Procedure: A catcher, pitcher, third-base player, and first-base player set up in their regular defensive positions. Foul balls are tossed in all directions in foul territory. Players assist each other in calling the direction of the ball, calling for the ball, and making the catch.

TWO-STEP CATCH

Purpose: To learn to catch with the throwing foot forward as the foundation for the two-step release.

Procedure: The catcher plays catch with a partner. She receives each throw with the right foot forward (if right-handed) and then steps with the opposite foot to make a two-step throw. This drill can be done during warm-ups.

QUICK PIVOT

Purpose: To help the catcher develop a quick pivot.

Procedure: From the squat position, the catcher pivots to the throwing position as quickly as possible on the command "Throw." She uses the jump pivot as well.

Variation: **A coach holds the ball in front of the catcher and then drops it. The catcher tries to pivot before the ball touches the ground. Create a contest by progressively lowering the height from which the ball is dropped.**

QUICK FEET

Purpose: To improve the catcher's quickness.

Procedure: A pitcher throws from a distance of about 20 feet (6 m), pitching the ball inside or outside to a catcher in receiving position. The catcher's hips are up in order to improve quickness for throwing out a runner. After catching the ball, the catcher quickly moves her feet and assumes the throwing position with both arms up; then she freezes in that position to check for proper alignment.

KNEE THROWING

Purpose: To practice throwing from the knees and to improve arm strength, abdominal (core) strength, and the vertical overhand throw.

Procedure: Two catchers kneel about 30 feet (9 m) apart on one or both knees. They throw back and forth, using an overhand throw and pulling with the abdominal muscles. They gradually increase the distance until the throws are about 6 feet (2 m) farther than the distance to the bases.

FOOTBALL QUICK RELEASE

Purpose: To develop a quick release with a small arm circle.

Procedure: From the catching position, the catcher throws footballs to second base. Throwing a football means the catcher cannot make a large arm circle or she will lose her grip and drop the ball. She must make a small circle right around the ear with both hands. Without the large arm circle, the drill emphasizes complete rotation of the shoulders and a strong forearm snap. The catcher must not throw a curveball. Because of the size of their hands, females have a tendency to use an overhand curveball motion when throwing a football, leading with their elbow. The coach must emphasize a complete downward wrist snap off an over-the-top throw. This is a great drill to help catchers develop body awareness. The better the catcher understands why she is doing something and the way the correct motion feels, the more easily she can adjust her throwing motion.

TIMED THROWS

Purpose: To evaluate quickness of release and speed of the throw.

Procedure: The catcher is in full gear so the drill is gamelike. The catcher catches a pitched ball. The coach starts a stopwatch when the ball enters the glove and stops it when the ball is released or when the ball reaches the shortstop's glove at second base. Time from pop to pop. For college catchers, a good time (from glove to glove) is between 1.65 and 1.75 seconds. High school catchers should make the throw in less than 2 seconds.

CATCHER TO BASES

Purpose: To practice throwing to bases.

Procedure: An infielder covers each base. The pitcher delivers the ball, and the catcher throws to the player covering the base. A batter stands in the box, and the coach adjusts the batter's position so that the catcher learns to create a throwing lane. Using runners allows the catcher to judge the quickness of her throw. (If you do not want players to slide, have them swing wide—away from the infield—as they approach the base.)

RANDOM-BALL CONDITIONING

Purpose: To practice throws to bases and to improve conditioning.

Procedure: Randomly place six to eight balls in front of home. From the squat position, the catcher explodes to a ball and throws to a receiver at the base, hustles back into the catching position, and continues until all of the balls have been thrown. Repeat the drill with the catcher throwing to a different base.

CATCHER FIELDING BUNTS

Purpose: To practice fielding bunts and throwing to a base.

Procedure: The catcher is in a squat position. A thrower behind her rolls out bunts for the catcher to field and throw to a receiver at the base. The catcher should explode low from the box and get ahead of the ball.

RECEIVING LINE DRIVES

Purpose: To improve the catcher's ability to receive throws from the outfield (while saving outfielders' arms).

Procedure: A hitter stands with a bat and a bucket of balls near the grass line just behind the shortstop position. The hitter hits line shots at the catcher so that the ball takes one or two hops to the catcher. The hitter moves around the field so that the ball is coming from all areas of the field. The catcher makes the catch and also practices making a tag. Later, the coach can add a "Safe!" call and yell out a base to have the catcher come up throwing to the designated base.

Drill	Hitting	Bunting & Slap Hitting	Baserunning	Team Offense	Throwing	Catching	Infield	Outfield	Team Defense	Pitching	Pitcher as Defender	Catcher	Page #
Chapter 1: Hitting													
Batting Tee													
No stride	X												23
Two stride	X												23
Long tee hitting	X												24
Soccer ball	X												24
Back knee down	X												24
Tomahawk hitting	X												24
Bingo	X												24
In-out tee swing	X												25
Bat control	X												25
Two or three tees	X												25
Horse	X												25
Toss													
Back-hand Wiffle toss	X												27
Location toss	X												27
High toss	X												27
Back toss	X												27
Two-ball toss	X												27
Front bounce	X												28
Self-toss up the middle	X												28
Front screen toss	X												28
Angle screen toss	X												28
Quick hands	X												29
Snapbacks	X												29
Dotted balls	X												29

(continued)

Drill	Hitting	Bunting & Slap Hitting	Baserunning	Team Offense	Throwing	Catching	Infield	Outfield	Team Defense	Pitching	Pitcher as Defender	Catcher	Page #
Chapter 1: Hitting *(continued)*													

Machine

Drill	Hitting	Bunting & Slap Hitting	Baserunning	Team Offense	Throwing	Catching	Infield	Outfield	Team Defense	Pitching	Pitcher as Defender	Catcher	Page #
In close	X												29
Execution	X												30
Going for the contact record	X												30
No pull	X												30
Hitting game	X												30

Hitting Mechanics

Drill	Hitting	Bunting & Slap Hitting	Baserunning	Team Offense	Throwing	Catching	Infield	Outfield	Team Defense	Pitching	Pitcher as Defender	Catcher	Page #
Wall stride	X												30
Shadow	X												31
Stride to launch	X												31
Front elbow	X												31
Glove in armpit	X												31
Resistance swing	X												31
Bat on neck	X												32
Fence swing	X												32
Mirror swing	X												32
Rope hitting	X												32
Line-drive cord	X												33
Power	X												33
Tracking	X												33
Underload swings	X												33
Five at a time	X												34
All but the kitchen sink	X												34
Strength series	X												34

Drill	Hitting	Bunting & Slap Hitting	Baserunning	Team Offense	Throwing	Catching	Infield	Outfield	Team Defense	Pitching	Pitcher as Defender	Catcher	Page #
Chapter 2: Bunting and Slap Hitting													
Air bunt		X											46
Partner front soft toss		X											46
Pepper		X											46
Target bunting		X	X										46
Four-corner bunting		X											46
Suicide squeeze		X											47
Indoor suicide squeeze		X											47
Bunting and baserunning		X	X				X						47
Slapper's fence swing		X											47
Slap and run around cone		X											48
Alternate bunts and slaps		X											48
Two tees		X											48
Chapter 3: Baserunning, Stealing, and Sliding													
Pawing action			X										51
Baserunning													
Catch the tennis ball			X										68
Home to first			X										68
Foul-line leadoffs			X										68
Timing the jump			X										69
How far from first?			X										69
Leadoffs with multiple runners			X										69
Pickoffs			X				X		X		X	X	69
Watch and take advantage			X										70
Football up and down			X										70
First to third			X		X	X	X	X					70
Sacrifice fly with runners			X		X	X		X				X	70

(continued)

Drill	Hitting	Bunting & Slap Hitting	Baserunning	Team Offense	Throwing	Catching	Infield	Outfield	Team Defense	Pitching	Pitcher as Defender	Catcher	Page #
Chapter 3: Baserunning, Stealing, and Sliding *(continued)*													
Read the ball in the dirt			X							X		X	71
Scoring from second			X		X	X		X				X	71
Team racing			X										71
Stretching a single to a double			X		X	X	X	X				X	72
Beat the ball home			X		X	X	X					X	72
Let her rip	X		X										72
Bang the bats			X										73

Sliding

Drill	Hitting	Bunting & Slap Hitting	Baserunning	Team Offense	Throwing	Catching	Infield	Outfield	Team Defense	Pitching	Pitcher as Defender	Catcher	Page #
Coach assist			X										73
Cushioned headfirst slides			X										73
Every base sliding			X										74
React to the ball and play in left field			X										74
Timed run			X										74
Chapter 4: Team Offense													
Pitching machine execution	X			X									91
Hit-and-run	X		X	X	X	X	X	X	X			X	91
The bunting game		X	X	X	X	X	X		X	X	X	X	91
Execution out of the hat	X	X	X	X	X	X	X	X	X	X	X	X	91
Move her over and score that runner!	X	X	X	X	X	X	X	X	X	X	X	X	92
Offense versus defense challenge	X	X	X	X	X	X	X	X	X	X	X	X	92
Situational hitting practice	X	X	X	X	X	X	X	X	X	X	X	X	92

Drill	Hitting	Bunting & Slap Hitting	Baserunning	Team Offense	Throwing	Catching	Infield	Outfield	Team Defense	Pitching	Pitcher as Defender	Catcher	Page #
Chapter 5: Throwing													
Finding the grip					X								95
Two-hand pickup					X								95
Scarecrow					X	X							109
Release and spin					X								109
Sequence throwing					X								109
Self-toss and throw					X	X							110
Sidearm correction					X								110
Triangle catch and throw					X	X							110
Square catch					X	X							111
Quick release					X	X							111
Throwing to a target					X		X	X					111
Throws for release times					X	X							112
Thrower in the box					X	X							112
Wet ball					X								112
Stay low throws					X								112
Throwing on the run					X								113
Show the ball					X	X	X						113
Circle backhand flips					X		X						113
Hit-ball line flips					X		X						113
Target throw					X								114
Golf softball					X								114
Three-second infield					X	X	X						114
Throwing 3-2-1 game			X		X	X	X	X					114
Get the runner			X		X	X	X		X				115

(continued)

Drill	Hitting	Bunting & Slap Hitting	Baserunning	Team Offense	Throwing	Catching	Infield	Outfield	Team Defense	Pitching	Pitcher as Defender	Catcher	Page #
Chapter 6: Catching													
Positioning the glove						X							119
Ground Balls													
Hit, field, and toss to bucket						X	X	X					132
Soft hands						X	X	X					132
Ready, set, go						X	X	X					132
Partner scoops						X	X	X					132
Line scoops						X	X	X					133
Explode through the ball						X	X	X					133
Cone rolls						X	X	X					133
Champ or chump						X	X						133
Fence range						X	X	X					134
Everydays						X	X						134
Two-hitter infield					X	X	X						135
Infield range						X	X						135
Softball soccer					X	X	X	X					135
Diving													
Knee dives						X	X	X					136
All out					X	X	X	X					136
Fly Balls													
Drop-step reaction						X	X	X					137
Zigzag						X	X	X					137
Ball toss for inside and outside rolls						X	X	X					137
Football						X		X					137

Drill	Hitting	Bunting & Slap Hitting	Baserunning	Team Offense	Throwing	Catching	Infield	Outfield	Team Defense	Pitching	Pitcher as Defender	Catcher	Page #
Chapter 7: Infield													
Moving to the base							X						146
Bad hops at first						X	X						146
Three throws from the catcher					X	X	X					X	146
Chase and fake					X		X						155
Rotating infield					X	X	X						160
Merry-go-round						X	X						161
4 × 4 gut					X	X	X						161
Four corners					X	X	X					X	162
Infield loop					X	X	X				X	X	162
Chapter 8: Outfield													
Around the ball					X	X		X					177
Fielding at the fence					X			X					178
Tennis racket fly balls						X	X	X					178
Communicate and cover						X		X					178
Bloopers						X	X	X					178
Down the line, up the alley					X	X	X	X					179
Decisions			X		X	X	X	X	X				179
Outfield around					X	X	X	X					179
Second to home and home to second			X		X	X		X	X				181
Holding the runner to a single			X		X	X	X	X	X				181
Weave					X	X		X					182
Four in one					X	X	X	X	X				182

(continued)

Drill	Hitting	Bunting & Slap Hitting	Baserunning	Team Offense	Throwing	Catching	Infield	Outfield	Team Defense	Pitching	Pitcher as Defender	Catcher	Page #
Chapter 9: Team Defense													
Timed DP					X	X	X		X				205
Roll bunts					X	X	X		X			X	214
Catcher–third base exchange					X	X	X		X			X	214
Bunt around		X	X		X	X	X		X	X	X	X	214
Pitcher and catcher throw-downs					X	X	X		X		X	X	215
Short throw to first					X	X	X		X				215
Turning the double play			X		X	X	X		X		X	X	216
Pickoff at first			X		X	X	X		X	X		X	216
Throw through and second-base player's cut			X		X	X	X		X	X		X	216
Rundown dart throw					X	X	X	X	X		X	X	217
Full-speed dart throws					X	X	X	X	X		X		217
Rundowns with runner			X		X	X	X	X	X		X	X	217
Three-player line relay					X	X	X	X	X				217
Outfield relay throws			X		X	X	X	X	X		X	X	218
Cutoffs and team defense			X		X	X	X	X	X		X	X	218
Perfect innings			X		X	X	X	X	X		X	X	218
County fair			X		X	X	X	X	X			X	218
Chapter 10: Pitching Fundamentals													

Fundamentals

Drill	Hitting	Bunting & Slap Hitting	Baserunning	Team Offense	Throwing	Catching	Infield	Outfield	Team Defense	Pitching	Pitcher as Defender	Catcher	Page #
Self-pitch										X			225
Partner pitch										X			225
Power line pitch										X			225
Mirror pitch										X			226

Drill	Hitting	Bunting & Slap Hitting	Baserunning	Team Offense	Throwing	Catching	Infield	Outfield	Team Defense	Pitching	Pitcher as Defender	Catcher	Page #
Chapter 10: Pitching Fundamentals													
T drill										X			226
Walk-through										X			228
Sideways drive with cone										X			228
Leg-up with cones										X			229
Crouch pitch										X			229
Broom handle pitch										X			235

Speed

Rice bucket										X			237
Leg power trio										X			237
On-off										X			237
Distance										X			238
Plus three										X			238

Fastball

Wall circles										X			238
Arm-speed development										X			238
Wall pitching										X			239
X drill										X			239
Wrist snap under knee										X			239
No stride										X			239
Baseball mound pitching										X			240
10 strikes										X			240
Accuracy										X			240

(continued)

Drill	Hitting	Bunting & Slap Hitting	Baserunning	Team Offense	Throwing	Catching	Infield	Outfield	Team Defense	Pitching	Pitcher as Defender	Catcher	Page #
Chapter 11: Movement and Off-Speed Pitches													
Drop													
Turnover snap										X			247
Low net throws										X			260
Basket throws										X			260
Bounce ball										X			261
Ropes										X			261
Rise													
Rise-ball spin										X			250
Rise-ball arm motion										X			251
Football toss										X			261
Long toss										X			262
Curveball													
Curveball spin										X			253
Changeup													
Bucket toss										X			262
Fast and slow										X			262
Gamelike													
Dummy or live stand-ins										X			262
Play a game										X			262
Three points										X		X	263
On the black	X									X		X	263
Chapter 13: Pitcher as a Defensive Player													
Pitchers field and cover first					X						X		276
Covering home			X								X		276
Knockdowns					X	X					X		276

Drill	Hitting	Bunting & Slap Hitting	Baserunning	Team Offense	Throwing	Catching	Infield	Outfield	Team Defense	Pitching	Pitcher as Defender	Catcher	Page #
Chapter 13: Pitcher as a Defensive Player													
Run the ball to first					X	X	X				X		277
Backing up									X		X		277
Defensive reps					X	X					X		277
Chapter 14: The Catcher													
Mirror signals												X	292
Signal run-through											X	X	292
No hands												X	296
Wall blocks												X	296
Covering home on wild pitches					X						X	X	297
Blocking wild pitches					X							X	297
Catcher agility						X						X	297
Foul-ball toss						X						X	297
Foul-tip toss						X						X	297
Foul-ball communication						X	X		X		X	X	298
Two-step catch						X						X	298
Quick pivot												X	298
Quick feet					X							X	298
Knee throwing					X							X	298
Football quick release					X							X	299
Timed throws					X							X	299
Catcher to bases			X		X	X	X					X	299
Random-ball conditioning					X		X					X	299
Catcher fielding bunts					X	X	X					X	300
Receiving line drives					X	X						X	300

Judi Garman is one of the most successful coaches in college softball history, having retired as the nation's winningest coach in 2000 after coaching for 28 seasons and earning a career record of 1,124-416-4 (.727) and 7 national championships as a player and coach.

Garman was a Canadian all-star outfielder and member of two Canadian national championship teams. Garman began her coaching career at Golden West College in Huntington Beach, California, and won four consecutive national junior college championships from 1975 to 1978. She then established the softball program at California State University at Fullerton in 1980. She built it into one of the most successful softball programs in the United States, winning the Women's College World Series Championship in 1986 following two runner-up and three third place finishes. From 2000 to 2002 Garman coached the Italian National Team to a European Championship and a fifth-place finish at the 2002 World Championship.

Garman served as president of the National Fastpitch Coaches Association (NFCA) from 1990 to 1991 and was inducted into their Hall of Fame in 1993. She resides in Redstone (Aspen), Colorado, and Palm Desert, California.

Michelle Gromacki is the head coach of Cal State Fullerton softball, one of the most prestigious programs in the nation. Under Gromacki's guidance, the Titans have staked their claim to five Big West Conference championships, including four consecutive conference titles from 2000 to 2003. In 2006, Gromacki was named Regional Coach of the year.

Gromacki served as an assistant coach for the U.S. national team from 2001 to 2004. More recently, she served as assistant coach of the U.S. women's national team at the 2010 ISF World Championship in Venezuela.

Gromacki played for Cal State Fullerton and was the catcher on the 1996 national championship team. She continued her playing career with the Redding Rebels and took home three national championship titles in women's major fastpitch. She was also on the U.S. national team for 10 years. She competed in many international tournaments and won gold medals in all of them.

Gromacki is one of the NFCA college coaches instructors and also conducts speaking engagements all over the world. She resides in Huntington Beach, California.